THE UNITED STATES AND THE
MIDDLE EAST

THE UNITED STATES AND THE MIDDLE EAST

A Search for New Perspectives

edited by

HOOSHANG AMIRAHMADI

State University
of New York
Press

Published by
State University of New York Press, Albany

For information, address State University of New York
Press, State University Plaza, Albany, N.Y., 12246

Amirahmadi, Hooshang, 1947–
    The United States and the Middle East : a search for new
perspectives / Hooshang Amirahmadi.
        p.   cm.
    Includes bibliographical references and index.
    ISBN 0-7914-1225-3 (alk. paper) : $59.50. – ISBN 0-7914-1226-1
(pbk. : alk. paper) : $19.95.
    1. Middle East—Foreign relations—United States. 2. United
States—Foreign relations—United States. 3. United States—Foreign
relations–1945– I. Title.
DS63.2.U5A824   1992
327.73056—dc20   91-38541
                                                          CIP

10   9   8   7   6   5   4   3   2   1

CONTENTS

PREFACE AND ACKNOWLEDGMENTS

The Middle East has been the scene of several cataclysmic events in recent years, including three wars since 1980: the eight-year Iran-Iraq war (1980–1988), the Israeli invasion of Lebanon (1982), and the United States–led war against Iraq (1991). These three wars not only inflicted heavy damage on the economic infrastructures of Iran, Iraq, Kuwait, and Lebanon, they also led to a significant increase in the U.S. involvement in the region. In recognition of this later development, this book focuses on U.S policy in the Middle East.

In particular, the book advances a critical analysis of U.S. Middle East policy and offers alternative perspectives. A major objective of the book is to indicate areas of shortcomings in this policy in the wake of the ongoing global and domestic changes and draw attention to the need for new and more plausible policy. The book also conveys the idea that for such perspectives to emerge, Middle East studies and education in U.S. universities and foreign policy institutions should be restructured to reflect recent global and regional realities.

Although historical development of the policy is given, the book focuses on the post-World War II diplomatic and military initiatives, including the post-Cold War changes, and evaluates their roots and consequences. Included are such watersheds as the Arab-Israeli conflict, the Palestinian question and Lebanon, U.S.-Iran relations following the Iranian Revolution, the Irangate fiasco, the Central Command and the reflagging of Kuwait's tankers, and the U.S.-led war against Iraq. The important role of U.S. media and Middle East studies and education in U.S. foreign policy is also emphasized. A concluding chapter focuses on the ongoing global restructuring and the U.S quest for world leadership in the wake of the Persian Gulf War.

For a more comprehensive picture to emerge, the authors have covered a wide range of issues that have an impact on U.S. policy in the region: religion and Islamic movements, Arab nationalism, political economy and oil, social and cultural factors, overt and covert foreign policy initiatives, war and military strategy, the role of media and education, and global changes. The interdisciplinary approach is complemented by a methodology that emphasizes historical-critical analysis and case studies. However, no attempt was made to impose any methodological uniformity or ideological orthodoxy. The contributors also present diverse analyses and come from a variety of nations including the United States, Iran, Arab countries, and Europe.

The contributors were asked to follow the system of transliteration recommended by the *International Journal of Middle East Studies*. Persian and Arabic words are spelled in accordance with the *Webster's Third International Dictionary, Webster's New Geographical Dictionary,* or as they commonly appear in ordinary English usage. Whereas attention was given to consistency across chapters, the main concern has been with consistent transliteration within each chapter. However, the keen-eyed readers will note random inconsistencies, but such is the nature of transliteration format and language.

A number of people and institutions have contributed towards the publication of this book. I would like to thank the New Jersey Department of Higher Education, the New Jersey Committee for the Humanities, and Rutgers, The State University of New Jersey, for their generous financial support for an international conference on the Middle East that became the main impetus for production of this volume. My gratitude also goes to Professor James Bill who read the introduction and made significant editorial and stylistic changes. I remain particularly indebted to my students Edward Ramsamy, Elaine Gonzales, and Kavitha Ramachandran, who helped in every aspect of the editorial process and assisted me in writing the concluding chapter. I would also like to thank Susan Geraghty at SUNY Press for her help. Finally, I thank my students in the summer session 1991 course on the United States and the

Middle East for their critical comments and other technical and intellectual support.

Needless to say, none of the individuals or institutions just named above bear any responsibility for the ideas and opinions expressed in this book, or for its errors and shortcomings. For these the individual authors remain accountable.

Hooshang Amirahmadi

NOTES ON CONTRIBUTORS

Hooshang Amirahmadi holds a Ph.D. in City and Regional Planning from Cornell University. He is an associate professor in the Department of Urban Planning and Policy Development and director of the Middle Eastern Studies Program at Rutgers University. He helped found the Center for Iranian Research and Analysis (CIRA) and was its executive director 1985–1990. Professor Amirahmadi's publications include five books: *Revolution and Economic Transition: The Iranian Experience* (State University of New York Press, 1990); *Post-Revolutionary Iran,* coeditor (Westview Press, 1988); *Iran and the Arab World,* coeditor (St. Martin's Press, 1992); *Reconstruction and Regional Diplomacy in the Persian Gulf* (Routledge, 1992); and *Urban Development in the Muslim World,* coeditor (CUPR Press, Rutgers University, 1992). He has also written numerous journal articles, book chapters, and reviews. He has been a frequent contributor to many national and international conferences and is published in conference proceedings. Translations of his writings and his original contributions have been published in Persian. Dr. Amirahmadi is a consultant to UNDP, the World Bank, the Agh Khan Development Network and several developing nations on matters of postwar reconstruction, disaster planning, and national spatial development. He is also a frequent contributor to the media on Iran, the Middle East, and U.S. foreign policy.

    Naseer H. Aruri received his Ph.D. from the University of Massachusetts in Amherst. He has been on the faculty of University of Massachusetts-Dartmouth, since 1965, where he chaired the department of Political Science from 1969–1977. He is author of *Jordan: A Study in Political Development* (The Hague: Martinus Nijhoff, 1972); *Enemy of the Sun: The Poems of Palestinian Resistance* (Washington, D.C.: Drum and Spear Press, 1970). He is also editor of *Middle East Crucible: Studies on the Arab-Israeli Confrontation of 1973* (Wilmette, Ill.: Medina University Press

International, 1975). He has also contributed many chapters to books on the Middle East and has translated other works into Arabic. His latest book is *Occupation: Israel over Palestine*. This book was selected by *CHOICE* magazine as one of the "Outstanding Books for 1984–1985." He has also been published extensively in scholarly journals, including *Middle East Journal, Journal of Palestinian Studies,* and the *Muslim World*. He is a frequent contributor to weekly magazines in Europe and dailies in the Arab world. He is a three-term member of the Board of Directors of Amnesty International-U.S.A. since 1984.

Eliane C. Condon holds a Ph.D. from Columbia University. She is currently associate professor at the Graduate School of Education, Rutgers University. She is the author of four books: *Cultural Orientation Manual for Health Care Providers* (Cultural Awareness Project, New Jersey, 1977), *Special Education and the Hispanic Child* (with C. Cuerio-Ross and J. Yates Peters, Teachers Corp MAN Network, 1979), *Understanding the Cultural Context of ESL Instruction* (Department of State Education, Albany, New York, 1973). *Understanding American Culture* (Department of State Education, Albany, New York, 1973). She has also written numerous journal articles, book chapters, and reviews.

Richard W. Cottam holds a Ph.D. from Harvard University. He is emeritus university professor of Political Science, University of Pittsburgh. He is the author of four books; *Nationalism in Iran, Competitive Interference and Twentieth Century Diplomacy, Foreign Policy Motivation,* and *Iran and the United States: A Cold War Case Study*. He has also written numerous journal articles, book chapters and reviews.

Eric Davis received his Ph.D. from the University of Chicago. Currently, he is associate professor in the Department of Political Science at Rutgers University. Between 1980 and 1985, he was a member of the Social Science Research Council's Joint Committee on the Near and Middle East, where he directed a project on state formation in the Arab oil-producing countries. He is author of *Challenging Colonialism: Bank Misr and Egyptian Industrialization, 1920–1941,* coeditor of *Statecraft in the Middle East: Oil, Historical Memory and Popular Culture,* and articles in journals such as *Studies in Comparative International Development, Review of Middle East Studies,* and *Middle East Report*. He has been the recipient of grants from the National Endowment for the Humanities, the Wissenschaftskolleg ZU Berlin, the Shelby Cullom Davis Center for Historical Studies, the Hoover Institution, and the New Jersey Department of Higher Education.

William A. Dorman holds a M.J. degree from the University of California at Berkeley and teaches at California State University, Sacramento, where he is professor of Journalism and Peace and Conflict Studies. He is an associate of the Center for War, Peace and the News Media at New York University. He is coauthor with Mansour Farhang of *U.S. Press and Iran: Foreign Policy and the Journalism of Deference,* and has written extensively for publications and journals ranging from *Columbia Journalism Review,* and *World Policy Journal* to the *Bulletin of Atomic Scientists* and *Race and Class.*

Richard A. Falk is currently Visiting Olof Palme Professor in Sweden while on leave from his normal appointment as Albert G. Milbank Professor of International Law and Practice at Princeton University. His educational background includes a B.S. of Econ., University of Pennsylvania, 1952; LL.B., Yale Law School, 1955; J.S.D., Harvard Law School, 1962. His concerns with the Middle East include serving as Vice Chair of the MacBride Commission that issued a report on the Israeli invasion of Lebanon in 1982. His more recent books include *The Promise of the World Order* (1987), *Revolutionaries and Functionaries: The Dual Face of Terrorism* (1988), and *The Revitalization of International Law* (1989).

Mansour Farhang received his Ph.D. in Political Science from Claremont Graduate School. In 1982–83 he was a research fellow and lecturer at Princeton University's Center for International Studies. Since then he has been professor of Politics at Bennington College. Professor Farhang served as revolutionary Iran's first ambassador to the United Nations, resigning in protest when the Ayatollah Khomeini broke his promise to accept the UN Commission of Inquiry's recommendation to release the American hostages in Tehran. In the early period of the Iran-Iraq War, he also served as then-President Bani-Sadr's envoy in negotiations with international peace missions attempting to settle the conflict. He has written extensively on Iran, international relations, and U.S. foreign policy for a variety of publications including *SAIS Review, Inquiry,*

World Policy Journal, Harvard International Review, The Nation,
the *Progressive,* the *New York Times, Los Angeles Times, Washington Post,* and the *Christian Science Monitor.* He is author of
*U.S. Imperialism: From the Spanish-American War to the Iranian
Revolution* (South End Press) and *U.S. Press and Iran: Foreign
Policy and the Journalism of Deference,* coauthored with William
A. Dorman, (University of California Press).

Elizabeth J. Gamlen holds a Ph.D. in peace studies from University of Bradford, England. She has written several journal articles and research reports on various issues pertaining to the Persian
Gulf. She has also been a frequent contributor to many international conferences.

Richard B. Parker holds an M.S. from Kansas State University.
He is currently president of the Association for Diplomatic Studies
in Arlington, Virginia, a private, nonprofit organization associated
with the Foreign Service Institute of the Department of State. He
served as ambassador to Algeria, Lebanon, and Morocco in the
period 1974–1979 and was subsequently editor of the *Middle East
Journal* between 1981–1987. He is author of three books: *North
Africa, Regional Tensions and Strategic Concerns; A Practical
Guide to Islamic Monuments in Cairo;* and *A Practical Guide to
Islamic Monuments in Morocco.* He has written articles in *Foreign
Affairs,* the *Air University Review,* and *International Insight.* He
has also written articles for the *New York Times,* the *Wall Street
Journal,* and the *Los Angeles Times.*

Abraham Resnick holds an Ed.D. from Rutgers University. He
is currently professor of Social Studies Education at Jersey City
State College. He was the former president of the New Jersey
Council of Geographic Association. He has authored numerous
student texts including *The Holocaust* (Greenhaven Press, San Diego Press, forthcoming), *Bulgaria* (Childrens Press, Chicago,
1991), and *Siberia: Unmasking the Myths* (GEM Publications,
1985). He has written numerous journal articles, trade books,
teachers' manuals, and other pedagogic tolls.

Stuart Schaar holds a Ph.D. in Oriental Studies and European
History from Princeton University. He is currently professor of
Twentieth-Century, Middle East and North African History at
Brooklyn College. He has written for the *New York Times,* the
Christian Science Monitor, the *Nation,* and is a regular contributor

to the British journal *Race and Class*. His works have also appeared in edited volumes. He is the current cocoordinator of the Emergency Committee on Lebanon.

   Joe Stork holds a Ph.D. from Columbia University. He was the cofounder of *MERIP* and is the current editor of *Middle East Report*. Dr. Stork's publications include *Middle East Oil and the Energy Crisis* (Monthly Press Review, 1975). He has also written numerous journal articles and is a frequent visitor to the Middle East. He worked with the Peace Corp in Turkey.

PART 1

Introduction

CHAPTER 1

The United States and the Middle East: A Search For New Perspectives

Hooshang Amirahmadi

The Middle East remains the most turbulent of all world regions, a fact reflected in Iraq's recent annexation of Kuwait and the subsequent United States–led war against Iraq. Other potentially explosive conditions include the fragile cease-fire between Iran and Iraq, the unrest caused by the revival of political Islam, the dormant civil war in Lebanon, the Palestinian uprising in the West Bank and Gaza, the Arab-Israeli conflict, and the continued foreign interference in the internal affairs of the region. The far-reaching implications of a Middle East in crisis become clearer when one recalls that the region is the most important source of the world's energy supply and is strategically critical for world peace and economic prosperity. It contains such important waterways as the Persian Gulf and the Suez Canal, is adjacent to a disintegrating Soviet Union, and occupies a central position between the three continents of Europe, Africa, and Asia.

For a variety of historical, ideological, economic, and diplomatic reasons, Americans have been particularly influenced by the regional and international consequences of the crises and events in the Middle East. In recent years, the critical nature of the U.S.-Middle East relations have been highlighted by such events as the United States–led war in the Persian Gulf, the hostage drama, highjackings, the Iran-Contra affair, the explosion of the U.S. Marines' headquarters in Lebanon, the "Tanker War" in the Persian Gulf, Iraq's attack on the USS *Stark* (during which thirty-seven

3

American marines were killed), and the United States bombing of Libya. Yet, the American people remain disturbingly ignorant of the Middle East, which they often view in terms of such stereotypes as fanaticism, barbarism, and terrorism; these stereotypes are propagated by the mass media and a few political "experts" in and out of the government. Moreover, formal education about Middle Eastern affairs remains the monopoly of a select few in higher education, whereas students in elementary and high schools learn very little about the geography, history or cultures of the region. Equally disturbing is the fact that most Middle East centers, institutes, departments, or programs in U.S. universities and a few "think tanks" function as isolated enclaves divorced from both the real policy process and the internal dynamism of the Middle East.

In the meantime, the changing social, economic, ideological, and political conditions in the region and the world are producing new realities that hardly correspond to the old myths which constitute the basis for existing U.S. policy toward the Middle East. The Cold War ideology, which saw the region in terms of the East-West dichotomy and the "Soviet threat," has outlived its purpose and needs to be replaced by a new perspective. Yet, instead of adjusting to the new situation, American policy makers tend to reinforce the old myths in new forms as many chapters indicate in this volume. The result is a relatively unfavorable U.S. economic and political influence in the Middle East despite its vastly increased military presence and success in the region.

The situation must be also viewed in relation to two critical developments in the world since the 1970s: (1) the growing integration of the largely interdependent nation-states into an increasingly globalized world; and (2) the emergence of a multipolar world system where the use of offensive force has become the least plausible way of achieving foreign policy objectives, whereas negotiation and diplomacy are receiving added attention. In particular, the United States, which enjoyed economic and military hegemony into the early 1970s and was able to unilaterally use force to impose its demands on other nations, is no longer able to do so in many significant cases, the victory in the Persian Gulf War notwithstanding. The prevailing anglocentric and chauvinistic orientations in international diplomacy are also incapable of adapting to a world in which competing world-views and cultural forces are reasserting themselves as never before.[1] The Americans must, therefore, learn about other histories and cultures, respect their divergent viewpoints and expectations, interact with them on the basis of such universal values as national sovereignty, equality, mutual respect, and shared benefits. The American administration must also work in the direction of promoting negotiations, international education, and cross-cultural dialogue across the globe and must help resolve conflicts wherever possible.

This book provides a critical and historical analysis of U.S. Middle East policy in terms of its objectives, assumptions, means, and consequences. It attempts to present the major pros and cons of this policy and draw attention to alternative perspectives in line with the emerging new realities in the region and in the world. The book is organized into seven parts and thirteen chapters. In the introductory chapter in Part 1, the editor pulls together, *thematically,* the arguments of the contributors to the book by focusing on their specific conclusions and policy recommendations. The themes are organized into the following five general and interrelated headings: from attentive detachment to oblivious engagement; an amalgam of contradictory objectives; inappropriate means and disastrous results; old myths and new realities; and need for a new perspective.

Part 2 gives the historical development of U.S. policy in the Middle East by concentrating on the post-World War II watersheds and diplomatic-military initiatives. In Part 3, U.S. policy toward the Arab-Israeli conflict and the Palestinian question is detailed. Part 4 discusses U.S.-Iran relations following the Iranian Revolution and the Irangate fiasco. In Part 5, the U.S. Central Command, the reflagging of Kuwaiti oil tankers, and the United States–led war against Iraq in the Persian Gulf is analyzed. Part 6 focuses on connections between U.S. Middle East policy, media and Middle East studies, and education. Finally, in the concluding chapter in Part 7, the editor extends the arguments of the book by bringing into a single framework the many disparate facts and ideas about the pros and cons of U.S. Middle East policy, the ongoing global restructuring and the nature of the emerging world system, and the U.S. quest for world leadership in the wake of the victory in the Persian Gulf War. I shall place my arguments into a larger global perspective to indicate their relevance for a more plausible American foreign policy in the 1990s.

A relatively comprehensive picture of the U.S.-Middle East relations emerges from the analysis in this book as contributors develop different perspectives, approach their subjects from various disciplines, provide rich and up-to-date information in a historical context, and address a wide range of issues and topics. They include religion and Islamic movements, Arab nationalism, war and military strategy, geopolitical considerations, political economy and oil, social and cultural factors, overt and covert foreign policy initiatives, the role of media and education, and global changes. These and other subjects are considered in relation to each other and in terms of their relevance to U.S.-Middle East relations. The interdisciplinary approach is complemented by a methodology that emphasizes historical-critical analysis and case studies. However, no attempt is made to impose any methodological uniformity or ideological orthodoxy.

Generally convinced that the policy is defective and in a state of turbulence, the contributors argue for a complete overhaul of the policy and search for new perspectives more in tune with emerging regional and global realities. In particular, they view a foreign policy based on the use of offensive force, covert or overt, military or otherwise, as that least plausible in the current multipolar and balance-seeking international environment, where human relations have become globalized and nation-states are more interdependent than ever before. They also call for a reassessment of the assumptions and methods of current policy and for minimization of the prevailing misconceptions and stereotypes about the Middle East.

The book also conveys the idea that for such perspectives to emerge, the existing gap between Middle East studies and foreign policy processes must be bridged by increased interaction between the two, and that the curriculum in Middle East education should be restructured to reflect cultural diversities and commonalities as well as recent changes in the global and regional political economy. The contributors call for a new kind of international education, one which promotes negotiation and cross-cultural communication as the most important tools for fostering improved international understanding. For an effective and lasting change, however,

Middle East education should begin at the secondary schools and colleges and seek necessary channels to disseminate such education to the general populace.

FROM ATTENTIVE DETACHMENT TO
OBLIVIOUS ENGAGEMENT

The United States should be considered an old player in Middle East politics rather than a new player in an old colonial quarry, as most Americans and Middle Easterners often tend to perceive the situation. Indeed, American diplomacy has evolved over a long period of time and has gone through several distinct stages, beginning with attentive detachment in the middle of the nineteenth century to oblivious engagement since World War II.[2] By *attentive detachment* I refer to the isolationist, largely muted, but more or less thoughtful policy that the United States pursued in the Middle East until World War II. *Oblivious engagement,* on the other hand, alludes to the post-World War II interventionist and largely misconceived U.S. diplomacy in the region. The Truman Doctrine in 1947 initiated this approach, which has survived for approximately forty years. At present, however, the United States remains in the same invidious position that Britain was at the end of the World War II, indicating that U.S. policy in the region still awaits a major change.

In Chapter 2 on United States policy in the Middle East, Richard Cottam correctly emphasizes the suddenness with which the United States had to engage in Middle East diplomacy. Specifically, he argues that the United States was "catapulted" into a position of preeminence in the region in the beginning days of the Cold War era after the "abdication" of the British and French involvement in the Middle East. This followed the inability, in the post-World War II period, of these two preeminent Western powers to play a major diplomatic role in the area after decades of active engagement there. Therefore, the American government unexpectedly had to deal with a region in which it had limited interest and little expertise or experience. In Cottam's opinion, this hasty introduction to the Middle East became a source of difficulty from which U.S. policy never recovered. This also partly explains the subsequent U.S. reliance on Israel as a strategic ally.

In Chapter 3 on United States policy in the Middle East and its tragedy of persistence, Richard Falk periodizes U.S. active involvement in the Middle East into three stages: from 1945 to the end of the Cold War; after the Cold War; and the challenge of the Persian Gulf Crisis. Notwithstanding these changes, asserts Falk, U.S. Middle East policy has remained "remarkably consistent." The first stage began with World War II: "One of the great shifts brought about by the war against fascism," writes Falk, "was to move, by stages, Western influence from its British and French locus to that of the United States . . ." That war also became the starting point for the Cold War and the new "bipolar geopolitics" that superseded colonialism. In this containment period, the Middle East was viewed, from the prism of the Cold War, second only to Europe in importance for the Western interests and security defined, in Falk's words, in terms of "access to cheap and abundant oil supplies, the very basis of post-World War II economic prosperity." It was also during this period, after the 1967 Israeli victory over the Arabs in particular, that the U.S.-Israeli strategic alliance was formed.

In the post-Cold War era, writes Falk, the United States became "the predominant extra-regional influence in the Middle East" as the Soviet Union withdrew from the Third World following Gorbachev's "new thinking" and *perestroika*. U.S. policy in this short time, however, in Falk's words, became "singularly unimaginative" and "geographically complacent." With the Soviet threat all but vanished, policy makers in Washington began to wonder if any serious threat challenged oil and Israel. The Iraqi invasion of Kuwait ended all speculation and gave the Bush administration a new focus. The lack of preparedness, however, explains Falk, became the source of several "blunders," which resulted in the bloodiest U.S. intervention ever in that part of the world.

In Chapter 4 on United States policy toward the Arab-Israeli conflict, Naseer Aruri provides a very useful periodization of U.S Middle East policy based on its strategy for containment of the Soviet Union. He identifies "two general phases" of "containment through military alliances," followed with an "interlude of attempted containment through nationalism" and "containment through regional influentials." Aruri dates the first phase from the Truman Doctrine to the Nixon Doctrine, which became the starting point for the second phase that ended with the collapse of the Cold War order in 1990. He also underscores the fact that the United States had to hurriedly fill a vacuum left by Britain in 1971. This is an interesting observation, given that Americans were already well engaged in the Middle East politics.

Aruri's observation indicates a lack of long-term planning and an inattentiveness to changing circumstances in the region. The observation also speaks to the de facto nature of U.S. policy in the Middle East especially from an implementation perspective. This latter characteristic of the policy is demonstrated particularly by the U.S. decision to reflag the Kuwaiti tankers. According to Elizabeth Gamlen in Chapter 8, on United States strategic policy toward the Middle East, the Central Command, and the reflagging of Kuwait's tankers, the decision was taken "hastily" and with little assessment of its military and political consequences. Gamlen also shows that, although the policy intentions were more or less clear, there was confusion regarding how best to achieve them. She also questions the American administration's claim that the policy was successful; indeed, the very limited success had to do more with problems in the Iranian side than with the policy's appropriateness.

The fact that U.S. policy makers often remain oblivious to the cultures, histories, and internal dynamics of the Middle East or to the consequences of their actions is well illustrated in Chapter 6, where Mansour Farhang focuses on the misperceptions and reactive behavior of U.S. policy toward the Islamic Republic of Iran. Several other chapters in this volume also point to such oblivious and reactive behavior, including Chapter 7 by Stuart Schaar on the Irangate and the Middle Eastern connection and Chapter 9 by Eric Davis on the myths and realities surrounding the Persian Gulf War. American reactive behavior during the Persian Gulf War is also underscored in Chapter 13 by Hooshang Amirahmadi on global restructuring, the Persian Gulf War, and the United States quest for world leadership.

The fact that important aspects of Middle Eastern life often remain irrelevant to the U.S. policy makers is also reflected in this country's minimal concern for Middle Eastern education, as indicated in Chapter 11 by Richard Parker on Middle Eastern studies and United States foreign policy and Chapter 12 by Hooshang

Amirahmadi, Eliane Condon, and Abraham Resnick, where they give a retrospective and prospective view of Middle East studies and education in American universities, colleges, and secondary schools. Indeed, the present American policy leaders are largely from the generations that came of age in the 1950s and 1960s, when the world outside the U.S. was hardly recognized by most American students and educators except in terms of the Cold War ideology.

AN AMALGAM OF CONTRADICTORY OBJECTIVES AND INTERESTS

The foreign policy of any nation is based on some real and changing national interests rather than any immutable abstract principles. There is often a large gap between propaganda and actual policy. The United States is no exception here, and therefore understanding its real policy in the Middle East requires more than just taking a particular administration's word for it. Yet, the most important fact about U.S. policy in the Middle East is that it tends to simultaneously pursue a multiple of overlapping, conflicting, or inconsistent economic, political, and strategic interests. The "paradoxical" nature of the U.S. policy toward the Arab-Israeli conflict is well demonstrated in Chapter 5 by Joe Stork's examination of the U.S. policy toward the Palestinian question. He argues that "U.S. interests in the Middle East, as elsewhere, are determined on the basis of strategic considerations and access to resources and markets. On all these grounds . . . Israel appears to be a relatively insignificant factor, and one would expect a policy more solicitous of Arab, and Palestinian, interests." He then continues: "It is precisely this paradox which underlies a debate in U.S. policy-making circles that is as old as the Palestine-Israel-Arab conflict itself."

Moreover, the mix of U.S. interests, public or private, has changed over time and with administrations and individual players. However, as most chapters in this volume indicate, dominance in the region remains the core purpose of the present Western diplomacy in the Middle East. Carl Brown in his book on *International Politics and the Middle East* has also shown this by comparing the present-day Western diplomacy in the region with that of the "Eastern Question" and finds significant resemblance between the two. In both cases, he argues, the pattern of the regional politics would have to be explained primarily in terms of external domination of the Middle East, which was once largely self-contained and independent. The way to understand this, he insists, is to focus on the "patterns of behavior" of the "players" or "rules of the game" rather than on individual policy initiatives, crisis, or confrontation.[3] In Chapter 4, Aruri also indicates that, since the Truman Doctrine, U.S. Middle East policy has sought to "keep the balance overwhelmingly in the U.S. favor."

At a more specific level, however, U.S. policy objectives in the Middle East over the past several decades, until the collapse of the Cold War order in 1990, may be identified as follows: (1) containing alleged "Soviet expansionism" in the Middle East and whenever possible excluding that country from the region's diplomatic games; (2) assuring uninterrupted flow of Middle Eastern oil to the West at cheap, stable prices and recycling the petro-dollars in the interest of the American economic system; (3) protecting the security of Israel and preserving its military superiority in the region; and (4) preserving the status-quo politics in the Middle East as represented by the "moderate" and pro-American conservative governments such as Saudi Arabia and the Persian Gulf sheikhdoms. Additionally, some of the chapters in this book (for example, those by Aruri and Stork) indicate that the U.S. policy has had the effect, if not the intention, of preventing unity or coordination among Muslim and Arab states and at times has led to regional conflicts among ethnic and religious groups and states. For example, in Kissinger's words, as reported in Chapter 5 by Stork, among his post-1973 goals was to "break up the Arab united front."

Note that the order of this list does not imply a hierarchy of significance, as various administrations have ranked U.S. interests in the Middle East differently, depending on the policy makers' preference and the circumstances of the time. Nor is the academic community unanimous on the issue. Cottam in Chapter 2 argues that, ever since World War II and for a surprisingly long time afterwards, three major interests have underpinned the U.S. policy in the Middle East. The "primary" concern was to contain Soviet expansionism and influence in the region. The other two "secondary" interests included ensuring a steady flow of Middle Eastern oil and petro-dollars to the West and defending the security of

Israel. A fourth tactical goal was to maintain the status quo and the conservative regimes. As Cottam notes, reconciliation of these multiple objectives and their safeguard from the three threatening forces of the Soviet Union, nationalism, and resurgent Islam has been the most perplexing issue of U.S. Middle East policy, at times leading to serious inconsistency in practice.

Falk also maintains that these same concerns were indeed responsible for the change in the U.S. policy from isolationism to interventionism following the 1956 Suez Campaign. In particular, he gives the following "lines of foreign policy priority": "ensure that control over the major oil fields remained in friendly hands," "oppose any extension of direct Soviet influence," "resist revolutionary nationalist tendencies," and treat "Israel as an indispensable strategic ally." In Falk's view, "The core tension for policy makers was to reconcile closeness with Israel . . . while sustaining a positive relationship with the moderate Arab regimes . . ." In the post-Cold War period, argues Falk, the policy has been "characterized by a dual preoccupation: ensuring favorable access to Gulf oil and upholding Israeli security as specified by the Israeli government."

Gamlen in Chapter 8 also insists that the U.S. decision to reflag Kuwaiti oil tankers was primarily motivated by its desire both to sustain the flow of the Middle East oil to the West at a stable price and to exclude the Soviet Union from the strategically located Persian Gulf. These were considered overlapping goals as the Soviet threat was assumed to be directed primarily toward the Middle East oil fields. In reality, however, and as Gamlin indicates, reflagging "endangered" the oil supply and flow, especially in the short run. Other concerns included the need to regain credibility with the Arab states in the aftermath of the Iran-Contra affair and U.S. concern that Iraq might be defeated. Gamlen indicates that, to the U.S., the 1973 Arab Oil Embargo underscored the strategic nature of Middle Eastern oil for the West, and the Soviet invasion of Afghanistan reinforced the perceived Soviet threat to the region. By 1980, Carter declared the Middle East a region of "vital interest" to the United States. Stuart Schaar in Chapter 7 also argues that U.S. policy in the Middle East has pursued a military goal ever since World War II, a goal largely influenced by the Persian Gulf's strategic position and the superpower rivalry in the region.

Eric Davis in Chapter 9 on the United States—led war in the Persian Gulf also underscores the oil and the Israeli factors. In his words, "This then was a war about oil and its economic and political consequences." But he insists that the U.S.'s "real motive" has to be sought elsewhere, in "a choice between Israel and Iraq"; after the latter began challenging the former's military dominance and security in 1990, the U.S. apparently chose Israel over Iraq. Aruri in Chapter 4 adds the concern for the Saudi security ("the Reagan codicil"), but like Davis, Stork and Falk, he underscores the U.S.-Israeli special and strategic relations. The strategic alliance with Israel, Aruri argues, was "rationalized as a necessary part of the post-World War II containment of communism." This occurred after Israel was transformed from a "liability" to an "asset" following the 1967 Arab-Israeli War. In Chapter 10 on media, public discourse, and United States Middle East policy, William Dorman discusses in some detail the role of a "pro-Israeli media" in shaping and protecting the "special relationship" between the United States and Israel.

The fact that U.S. interests in the Middle East at times are intermingled with those of Israel was well demonstrated during the Persian Gulf War as indicated by Amirahmadi in Chapter 13 and Davis in Chapter 9. A case study of such entanglement is provided by Schaar in Chapter 7, where he presents a comprehensive analysis of the Irangate or Iran-Contra affair. In explicating the fiasco, he indicates the intricacies of U.S. entanglements in the Middle East, including the important Israeli factor. Using primary Israeli sources not available outside that country, Schaar explains the various American and Israeli motives for the covert operations including the sale of arms to Iran and the divergence of a part of the proceeds to the Nicaraguan Contra. He argues that a major aim was to overthrow the Ayatollah Khomeini regime by the "moderates" in the military. This was an Israeli plan that was in fact adopted by part of the U.S. administration. Other motives included anti-Arabism (the Israelis "peripheral policy"), continuation of the Iran-Iraq War, and opportunity for making exorbitant profits through sale of arms to Iran. This last motive, according to Schaar, was very important and was backed by Israeli military-industrial interests. In particular, Israel initiated the covert operation largely for selfish motives, while the United States was pursuing ill-defined and contradictory strategic interests. The Reagan administration, he maintains, also became interested in the adventure of Israel's sales of arms to Iran partly because of its failure to overthrow the Sandinistas. For the Islamic Republic, however, at the time embroiled in a war of survival with neighboring Iraq, all that mattered was to replenish its military arsenal, an important pragmatic consideration.

Finally, I wish to extend the discussion on the policy interests by reporting here the useful classification of American "interests" offered by James Bill in *The Eagle and the Lion*.[4] Although his analysis focuses on Iran, it is equally applicable to the Middle East more generally. According to Bill, "organizational interests" are at the root of bureaucratic conflict and rivalry within the administration, between various high-ranking officials and agencies. Elections and other domestic politics tend to reinforce these types of interests, which in turn are inimical to rational foreign policy making. Powerful politicians, businesspersons, bankers, industrialists, lawyers, and even academicians work hard to promote their selfish "private personal interests." "General public economic interests," on the other hand, have centered on Middle Eastern oil; the areas of contest here have changed from control in the 1950s, to production in the 1960s, to pricing in the 1970s. Lastly, there are "international political interests," which are divided into an "offensive protective interest" concerned with security of Israel and a "defensive containment interest" directed against Soviet "expansionism." To rationalize these interests, James Bill argues, an "ideology" of anticommunism had to be propagated. The dialectics between the two sets of interests then led to what he calls "ignorance" of objective political realities, ultimately resulting in a "distorted" foreign policy.

INAPPROPRIATE MEANS AND DISASTROUS RESULTS

Like any other superpower, the United States has used a variety of malignant and benign means to achieve its interests in the Middle East. These have included both peaceful and violent methods carried out by means of covert and overt operations. Generally speaking, malignant means have been used against "unfriendly" forces; that is, forces that have called for change in the domestic status quo and demanded autonomy from outside dominant powers. Such forces have usually included revolutionary movements, communists, nationalists, religious populists, and radical reformists. On the other hand, benign means have been used with respect to "friendly" forces including Israel, reform resisters, "moderate" and conservative Arab states, and anticommunist—anti-Soviet dictators.

Overt actions have included a variety of violent or peaceful diplomatic, military, and economic measures. Diplomatic means have consisted of persuasion or pressure applied directly or through the medium of the United Nations, friendly states, or influential individuals in and out of the region. Military force has been used in direct confrontation with nationalist or radical forces or indirectly as support for strategic or tactical friends, often anticommunist dictators or conservative governments in control of strategic assets. Economic means have consisted of trade embargoes, economic sabotage and sanctions, and financial blockades through the leverage of the IMF, the World Bank, multinational banks, the GATT, and the OECD, among other international organizations. As Middle Eastern economies remain largely dependent on the West for their export (oil) markets, industrial inputs including technology, and food supplies, such measures tend to cripple the local economies and consequently to delegitimize governments.

Covert operations have also been applied in a variety of forms: fomenting coups against radical leaders, financing pro-Western opposition groups, and reinforcing interstate conflicts have been standard CIA tactics in the Middle East. Power rivalries among certain leaders, ideological differences, border conflicts, religious disputes, and ethnic quarrels have all been exploited at one time or another. Interstate conflicts have been among major sources of the arms race and wars that, in turn, have been the most profitable business for the West (and the East) and a major method for recycling petro-dollars. The huge investment in the defense sector and destruction that have resulted from wars have also tended to perpetuate the underdevelopment and dependency of the Middle East. Iraq, Iran, Kuwait and Lebanon are notable examples. As a United Nations report put it, the United States—led war against Iraq wrought "near-apocalyptic" results on the economic infrastructure of that country, virtually relegating it to a "preindustrial age."[5] These outcomes have, in turn, helped reproduce subordination of the Middle East to external powers.

Aruri in Chapter 4 indicates two distinct periods in U.S. Middle East policy with respect to the means it used to achieve its objectives: the containment through surrogates and direct intervention. During a short interval, the United States even tried to use nationalism against its rivals in the region. According to Cottam in Chapter 2, intervening in domestic politics of the states in the region in opposition to nationalist and revolutionary forces and establishing close relations with the anticommunist and authoritarian governments of such "traditional elites" as found in Turkey, Iran (the Shah), and the "moderate" Arab regimes have been among the major means of accomplishing the policy of containment through surrogates. These regimes were also willing to limit opposition to Israel, to expand economic ties with the United States, and to suppress any demand for nationalization of the oil sector. The United States also sought to maintain these regimes' political stability by preserving the regional status quo. As Gamlen points out in Chapter 8, the United States sought to protect its interests in the region by propagating friendly regimes through lavish military assistance. Similar views are also expressed by Falk in Chapter 3, Aruri in Chapter 4, and Stork in Chapter 4. They argue that various U.S. administrations came to view nationalists (e.g., Musaddiq, Nasser, and Palestinian leaders) as cat's paws of the Soviets whereas unpopular dictators (e.g., the Shah of Iran, the Greek Royalists, and Iraq's Nuri al-Said) were propagated as Jeffersonian democrats.

Finally, most authors in the volume indicate that the United States continues to utilize covert actions, offensive force, economic means, military strategy, and diplomatic means to achieve its objectives in the Middle East. They demonstrate this by focusing on the Iran-Contra fiasco, the tanker war, the building of a rapid military intervention force for use in the Persian Gulf, and a variety of economic and extraeconomic measures the United States used to influence the hostage drama in Tehran and Lebanon. The most recent example of an overt military action is of course the war against Iraq. The United States has also used what Stork in Chapter 5 calls the *peace process,* which has not always been undertaken with good intents; in the Arab-Israeli conflict, for example, Stork tells us that the peace process was used to create an "illusion of purposeful activity." These measures were ostensibly used to protect U.S. interests in the Middle East. But as the authors indicate, they point to profound confusion and indirection in U.S. policy toward the region.

Specifically, American policy in the Middle East, argues Cottam, was on the verge of total disintegration in the late 1980s, indicated by the Reagan and Bush administrations' inability to deal with a number of seemingly unexpected developments in the Middle East. Examples included the emergence of political Islam as the primary focus of populist appeal, the increasing passivity of the Soviet Union in the region's affairs, the U.S. failure in Iran, and the near total expulsion of Americans from Lebanon. The United States also found itself unable to deal with the Iraqi annexation of Kuwait except in the language of force and destruction. Although Falk argues that, overall, the result for the United States in the Middle East has been "mixed," others in the book point to the collapse of U.S. policy in Iran, Lebanon, and the Persian Gulf; they consider this as indicative of the failure of U.S. postwar diplomacy in the Middle East except for the language of force. The response to these developments also indicate confusion, bewilderment, and lack of coherence. This is not to say that U.S. Middle East policy is senseless; rather the emphasis is hoped to underscore the extent of the problem. Such random, erratic measures as the war against Iraq, the bombing of Libya, and the fixation with terrorism simply underline this conclusion.

OLD MYTHS AND NEW REALITIES

The chapters in this book point toward a number of factors that have been responsible for the deficiency of U.S. Middle East policy. They include obsolete assumptions, conflicting or inconsistent policy interests, belief in the use of force, obliviousness to the history and dynamics of the region, stereotyping and cross-cultural misunderstandings, persisting misjudgments and factional politics within the policy-making process, insensitivity to the changing nature of the world politics, and the lack of informed, high-quality education on the Middle East. These essentially interrelated factors are largely indigenous to the policy-making process and tend to reinforce the exacerbating effect of one another. Because they "interlock in a system that highly resists reform," to use the words of James Bill, their resolution cannot be considered but within a holistic framework and in terms of truly systemic change.[6]

In Chapter 4, Aruri correctly emphasizes that: "The [U.S.] policy was built on the proposition that there existed a legitimate world order, for which the United States assumes the major responsibility and that the Soviet Union, together with disaffected Third World nations, including Arab nationalist forces, were intent on challenging that order." He questions the accuracy of this superpower confrontation thesis and considers the U.S. assessment of Soviet intentions "distorted." In Chapter 2, Cottam also questions some of the basic tenets of American Middle East policy particularly the one concerning the "aggressive expansionism" of the Soviet policy, an assumption that remained the cornerstone of the U.S. Cold War diplomacy. He indicates that Soviet policy over the past several decades has been characterized by a growing "defensive passivity"; this has resulted from "an altered Soviet purpose" rather than because of any containment strategy of the United States, as American policy makers like to argue. This fact, according to Cottam has been long known to the U.S. administrations who have indeed cooperated with the Soviets on many occasions. Nevertheless, the United States needed to continue in the path of Cold War diplomacy because it did not want to appear allied with the Soviets against its closest friends in the region. The Israeli lobby in Washington was also responsible for the tenacity of the Cold War ideology, as was the need to legitimize the massive peacetime defense budget of some $300 billion a year.

Cottam indicates that the U.S. policy makers have long been divided over how to deal with the Soviet Union. Advocates of the Cold War ideology continued to insist on excluding the Soviet Union from Middle East diplomatic initiatives (e.g., Kissinger's shuttle diplomacy and the Camp David Accord). In sharp contrast, more moderate members of various U.S. administrations have argued for cooperation with the Soviet Union in Middle East affairs (e.g., the Rogers plan of 1969 and Carter's Declaration of October 1977). This division persists even after the historic changes in the Soviet Union and Eastern Europe. For example, in March 1990,

Defense Secretary Richard Cheney argued against CIA Director William Webster's thesis that the Soviet Union was no longer a serious threat to the U.S. national security. However, the Persian Gulf crisis and the Soviet cooperation with the United States against Iraq did change American perceptions toward Soviets but still not completely; the United States continues to remain cautious about developments in the disintegrating USSR and many old Cold Warriors have not changed their attitude toward the old myths even though the Warsaw Pact and Comecon have both been dismantled and *perestroika* has become synonymous with capitalist development in a moribund Soviet Union, where the Communist Party has lost its monopoly and grip over the society and socialism is about to become a legacy of the past.

Gamlen and Davis also question the assumption that the Middle East oil remains threatened by forces unfriendly to the West and that to ensure a steady flow of "reasonably priced" oil supplies from the region to the West, intervention was needed. As Gamlen indicates, the disruption in oil supplies has in the past resulted from faulty U.S. diplomacy rather than the Soviet intervention. For example, whereas the Iran-Iraq War did not disrupt the oil supplies in any significant way, the reflagging policy led to an increased disruption of the Persian Gulf shipping and oil commerce. Ironically, the declared aim of the policy was the reverse effect.

Davis in Chapter 9 also documents the fact that the Persian Gulf crisis did not produce any significant and lasting disturbance in the oil markets although both Iraq and Kuwait stopped producing oil. If any, the U.S. intervention in the crisis led to an increase in oil prices. Various chapters in this collection also point to the faulty nature of U.S. foreign policy assumptions concerning the communist threat to political stability in the Middle East. In the post-Cold War period, no one in the administration seems to take the so-called communist threat seriously, although many remain seriously concerned with Islamic movements in the area. The U.S. fear of nationalism also seems unfounded, as indicated by Falk, Cottam, and Aruri among others in the collection.

As most chapters in this volume indicate, postwar U.S. foreign policy has operated largely on the assumption that force, military or otherwise, may be used to achieve foreign policy objectives. Amirahmadi in Chapter 13 attempts to dislodge this assumption and argue that the use of force, which may have been effective for the pre-1970s world, is neither necessary nor plausible under the current condition in the world. Force may still be used to destroy the "enemy" but it can hardly be used to achieve meaningful objectives. American policy makers have been disappointingly slow in grasping the epoch-making significance of this extremely important development in international politics. In particular, he argues that the *offensive* force is *diminishing* in its ability to gain intersocietal hegemony, defined as the ability to control foreign and domestic policies of other states within the world system in accordance with the hegemon's needs and purposes. *Offensive force* refers to any violent capacity used to introduce change in or impose domination over something in spite of its will. This is distinguished from *defensive force,* which most often is successfully used to resist such a change or domination and control.

With these definitions, the United States—led war against Iraq was an offensive war; a war that destroyed Iraq, but achieved only a few of its many objectives while creating many more new problems. Amirahmadi also underscores the irrelevancy of an international diplomacy today that is based on the assumption of a *unipolar* world; that is, a world in which the United States remains the only superpower, with the Soviet Union, Japan, and the Europe as its junior partners. As is increasingly recognized, the world is moving away from the Cold War *bipolar* world system (two-superpower model) toward an essentially integrated but *multipolar* world system. Amirahmadi argues that implications of this change will be far reaching for a harmonious management of international relations and for the U.S. quest for world leadership in the wake of the victory in the war against Iraq.

OTHER FALLACIES

U.S. Middle East policy has also suffered from a number of other fallacies, including ignorance of the regions's history and internal dynamism, cultural misunderstandings and the resulting stereotypes, and misconceptions or miscalculations. Obliviousness to the culture, history, and internal dynamics of Iran, according to Farhang in Chapter 6, has plagued U.S. policy toward postrevolutionary Iran with illusions, incoherence, and indecisiveness. He illustrates this thesis by drawing from two examples: the Shah's admission to the United States by President Jimmy Carter in 1979, and the secret U.S.-Iran arms for hostage deal (the Irangate scandal) during the Reagan administration in 1985–1986. In both of these episodes, according to Farhang, U.S. policy makers remained "totally oblivious" to the consequences of their decisions. In the Shah's case, he indicates that Americans failed to anticipate that the religious leaders in Tehran would soon find anti-Americanism a potent instrument of mobilization and legitimization in Iranian politics and would use the occasion to take hostage the embassy personnel and consolidate their power. America's hasty reactions (e.g., Carter's Tabas failed rescue mission and Reagan's authorization of the CIA to help overthrow the Islamic Republic) had Ayatollah Khomeini believing that "bold and intransigent" action was the only way to deal with the United States, an attitude that led to Iran's support for hostage taking in Lebanon.

In the Iran-Contra episode, Farhang also finds that the Iranian government made a pragmatic decision whereas the U.S. administration had been fooled by the Israelis, whose declared purpose was to promote "moderates" in the Islamic leadership; in fact they were pursuing an anti-Arab profit-making operation. A similar conclusion is also reached by Schaar in Chapter 7, who finds the Israeli interests even more pervasive in the episode. In other words, Iran and Israel both "outsmarted" the United States by drawing it into the game to achieve their own particular motives. Davis in Chapter 9 and Dorman in Chapter 10 suggest similar U.S.-Israeli relations. In sum, according to Farhang, the United States failed to understand that postrevolutionary Iran had been radically transformed and could not be returned to Pahlavi days, that Israel could not play the mediating role it claimed to play, and that the domestic contexts of the hostage crisis and the Iran-Contra scandal were no less important than their international contexts.

Obliviousness to the domestic context and stereotyping are also illustrated by other examples of U.S. Middle East involvement. One such case is entanglement with the Shi'a Muslims of Lebanon, perhaps the most misunderstood community in that forlorn country. This is a highly relevant subject for U.S.-Middle East relations, as it was in Lebanon that U.S. policy almost totally collapsed. As Augustus Richard Norton has argued, the prevailing Western stereotypes of the Lebanese Shi'a, including the religious nature of the Shi'ite activism, is unfounded.[7] For example, Amal, he maintains, is decisively not a religious movement, and Hizbullah is best understood in terms of a radical political organization. Instead, he emphasizes the "milieu of Lebanon" and the political diversity and competition that marks the politics of the Shi'ites. Rather than stressing sensational acts of political violence, Norton demonstrates that any coherent picture of the Shi'ites of Lebanon must also take into account the social and cultural marginality of the community, which has been, in turn, steadily undermined by decades of profoundly significant socioeconomic change.

Obliviousness to domestic Middle East politics is promoted by a variety of institutions in the United States but most notably by the media and the government. In their book-length study of the U.S. press and Iran, Dorman and Farhang argue that "The major shortcoming of American press coverage of Iran for twenty-five years was to ignore the *politics* of the country. This failure was rooted in the assumption that the political aspirations of Iranians did not really matter."[8] Stereotyping is indeed well ingrained in the minds of many American policy makers, organizations, and individual citizens. As Dorman in Chapter 10 and Amirahmadi *et al.* in Chapter 12 have argued, Middle Easterners are often automatically identified with terrorism, religious fanaticism, fundamentalism, radicalism, violence, nihilism, antimodernism, and barbarism among other similar labels. Americans also commonly confuse ethnic and religious affiliations of the Middle East peoples and have a distorted picture of their ways of life: all Middle Easterners are Arab, all Arabs are Muslim, and all Muslims are terrorists; the Middle East is also considered the land of oil, camel riders, belly dancers, and rulers out of the Thousand and One Nights; oil is to be found in everybody's backyard.[9]

Some of these and other stereotypes have resulted from the lack of an adequate, formal education on the Middle East as discussed in Chapter 12 by Amirahmadi *et al.* and in a recent report titled "One Nation, Many People: A Declaration of Cultural Independence," submitted to the New York State Education Commissioner in June 1991.[10] Others are indeed the products of informal education. Laurence Michalack has demonstrated this and writes that the American popular culture often associates Arabs with "theft, adduction, rape, knives, fighting, murder," and Dorman adds, "unrepressed sexuality, and anti-Western attitudes."[11] As Edward Said has shown, Orientalist scholarship has been equally liable for the distorted picture of the Middle East in the West.[12] The most important influences, however, come from Western governments and media as demonstrated by Davis in Chapter 9. He argues that these forces together produced what he calls a new "mythology" that surrounded the Persian Gulf War, resulting in "the desensitization of American and Western youth to the horrors of war." In his view this "provides a model of thought and behavior for the Western public that can be trotted out in future crises."

The Western governments' attempt to dominate the region is thus a powerful source of distortion in images of Middle Easterners in the West. Ironically, and as indicated by Brown, Middle Eastern leaders are so conditioned by this historical experience with external interference that they usually tend to automatically seek it at times of conflict. The crisis over Kuwait represented the latest demonstration of this fact. This is so because most such leaders lack legitimacy and therefore rule by force and dependency on outside powers. At the same time, however, a powerful countertendency for regaining the lost regional political autonomy and order is set in motion. The result, according to Brown, is a kind of politics that the "unsympathetic outsider sees as xenophobia or nihilistic radicalism."[13]

The role of the media in facilitating such outside dominance of the region is well explained in Chapter 10 by Dorman. This is done in a variety of ways. The "non-Israeli Middle Eastern peoples" are often portrayed as "Indo-Europe's slow learners, people who can survive only in the custodial care of a Westernized power, or a Westernized dictator." Dorman also insists that the U.S. media tends to marginalize and dehumanize Middle Easterners, reducing them essentially to peoples with "inherently violent and unstable cultures" and that the media "dehumanization" project helps pave the way for American intervention in the region. He argues that media affects U.S. Middle East policy by a process he calls *framing* with which "by using a certain phrase or image," the media "construct a particular kind of social reality for the reader or viewer." In other words, framing results from "what you put in, what you leave out, the words and images you choose, and what you emphasize."

Lastly, Parker points to the "essential irrationality" of the U.S. foreign policy process and identifies "miscalculations," rooted in "misconceptions" about others, as a role of politics in the Middle East. American Middle Eastern policy, he indicates, is made by "default" rather than long-term thinking and is based on public opinion shaped by the president, the media, and the "pundits," some of whom have had no Middle Eastern experience or education. Parker divides these pundits into three categories: those who can "comment on any subject they choose," and who will be "listened to by the administration"; those who are free to "comment on all subjects" but have "little impact"; and a large group who are invariably referred to as "experts." They include academics, consultants, and ex-military officers, some of whom have in the past served in the army intelligence operations. This group is not listened to but "they collectively provide most of what often become the accepted wisdom."

Unfortunately, the public is ready to accept almost anything from these pundits, many of whom, along with the mass media, follow the administration's lead and thus contribute to the false understanding that all Middle Easterners, excepting for Israelis, are anti-American and that the United States is always right. Parker stresses the "abysmal" level of understanding in the United States of the Middle Eastern affairs even among the policy makers. They have little time to learn or listen to specialists and need only "practical recommendations in two short paragraphs." For example, there is little knowledge of the region's geography, history, cultures, and languages. He points out that the public, is "instinctively antiintellectual" and that the American people find "complexity fatiguing." This should not be unexpected as stereotyping encourages simplistic understanding at the expense of complex analysis. Indeed, the first victim of stereotyping is complexity. He also indicates that despite progress in studies and education on the Middle East, the immediate impact on policy has been little.

THE NEED FOR A NEW PERSPECTIVE

The need for a candid review of the U.S. policy toward the Middle East and for a new perspective is stressed in all chapters in this volume. Carl Brown has called on the policy makers to "abandon efforts to organize the Middle East and foreswear unilateral doctrines," because "no single outside power has been able unilaterally to address [Middle East] problems and bring the region into its orbit."[14] Gamlen insists that the old "gunboat diplomacy" is inappropriate in the context of the present changing world and that the United States is better off revising its policy reliance on military solutions. She indicates the main direction of such a revision by exploring a number of options that the United States could have pursued as advisable alternatives to reflagging the Kuwaiti tankers. In particular, she asserts that the United States would have been better off if it had cooperated with the Soviet Union or had made the naval escorts multilateral in nature. The United States could also have involved the United Nations and pursued an even-handed approach to ending the Iran-Iraq War.

Cottam argues that revisions have to be made particularly in the U.S. view of resurgent Islam in the Middle East, the Arab-Israeli Conflict, and U.S.-Soviet relations, which until recently remained an example of "the asymmetry of activism of the competing superpowers in the region." Such revisions, he insists, must account for the new realities in the region and the world. In particular, he argues that, although the Cold War between the United States and the USSR was over by the mid-1980s, "the Cold War–generated patterns persisted." This was demonstrated by the U.S. "reflexive" reaction to the Kuwaiti crisis. The conservative regime there and in the Arabian Peninsula had to be protected. He also points to the United States's continued concern for the security of Israel, a concern that will shape the form and content of U.S. Middle East policy in the 1990s.

Falk calls for exerting pressure on Israel to accept the establishment of a PLO-led state in the West Bank and Gaza, combined with internationalization of Jerusalem. He also argues that the United States should rethink its arms sale policy in the region because "as the experience with Israel suggests, militarism may lead to expansionism rather than to a sense of serenity and diplomatic flexibility." Stork also recommends that the United States needs to take "decisive steps" and develop real interest in bringing about a two-state solution to the question. Aruri stresses the power of the "Israeli lobby" in Washington in blocking any such solutions but remains hopeful: "Now that the Cold War has ended, strategic assets will no longer be measured by traditional and outmoded criteria; the United States cannot forever make Israel its only unexamined commitment of post-World War II." He then asks a pertinent question: "having restructured its relation with the Soviet Union, Eastern Europe, Central America and the African National Congress, is it not time for a similar reevaluation of its posture toward Israel and Palestine?"

Farhang's specific recommendations for eliminating the impasse in relations between Iran and the United States may be generalized for the Middle East as a whole. He indicates that a candid discussion of the impasse in Washington is the most significant first step toward ending it. In particular, the United States should remove its blinders with regard to Iranian history and reality: Musaddiq was not a procommunist and the Shah was not a modernizer or the Ayatollah Khomeini an irrational fanatic. Moreover, the United States must understand that Iran can and does have a purposeful and endogenously inspired foreign policy and that the Islamic Republic is seeking independence and respect for its autonomy. The United States must also pay more attention to the impact of domestic politics on foreign policy and broaden its perspective beyond liberal democratic contexts. Furthermore, U.S. behavior must not lead to prejudice and stereotyping of Iranians as "religious fanatics," among other labels. Finally, U.S.-Iranian policy must be rescued from the short-term benefits of opportunistic politicians on both sides.

Schaar's analysis, however, indicates that various constraints face Americans in initiating such a candid discussion of their ill-conceived policies in the Middle East and a blunt search for a new perspective. The Israeli lobby, for example, influenced various U.S. administrations into diverting attention to the so-called funds divergence issue, away from implicating Israel, in the Iran-Contra scandal. He also points to the complicity of Congress and the mainstream press in this. Moreover, hearings, reports, and news accounts all lacked analysis connecting U.S. and Israeli policies to actual events in the Middle East. In particular, the Tower Commission Report did not put its dense description of events in any historical and policy context. Several authors in this volume have also pointed to these obstacles as well as to others, including the vested interests in the military-industrial establishments and in the administration.

The lack of an appropriate Middle Eastern educational agenda may be also considered among the factors that prevent the United States from revising its policy in the region. The role of education is emphasized by Amirahmadi *et al.* in Chapter 12, by Parker in Chapter 11, and by Dorman in Chapter 10. The importance of an appropriate education on the Middle East is also underscored in a number of other publications.[15] Specifically, Parker advances the thesis that if educators are to help promote peace and positive international relations, the teaching about countries of the world "must start in primary and secondary schools, in Sunday schools, in popular literature, not with a graduate thesis on Abbasid court etiquette and things like that." Dorman also calls for a restructuring of journalism programs in the universities to account for the biases against Orientals; otherwise little will change regardless of how much international education is given to the students. Dorman also predicts that, with the Cold War over, the U.S. media may gradually shift attention from the Soviet Union to the North-South issues. It is also possible that the national security requirement may again impose itself on news reporting and analysis. A well-designed program for the future journalists should take account of this possible trend.

Educators must focus on teaching geography, history, current events, and international relations in the early grades. If this were to occur, there would be a natural flow of interest and command of international issues upward in the vertical articulation of the social studies curriculum. Then, at the high school level, sophisticated topics about international issues could be better addressed. In the final analysis, the real beneficiaries of this approach will be the college student who, in Parker's view, has become increasingly ignorant of rudimentary geography and history. As a more-educated college student means a more-sophisticated future policy leader, the approach could lead to an improved U.S. Middle East policy. Parker also calls for an increased role for Middle East studies in shaping foreign policy initiatives and indicates the difficulties of bridging the present gap between the two.

These and other general and interdisciplinary strands are also detailed in Chapter 12 by Amirahmadi *et al.* They are concerned particularly with the undoing of the cultural bias portrayed in the media and reflected by many U.S. citizens against those of Middle Eastern heritage and the stereotypic information about the peoples and cultures of the Middle East. They stress the importance of a high-quality educational program on the Middle East in secondary schools and institutions of higher education for the formation of a more-appropriate foreign policy. At a more specific level, a high-quality education on the Middle East should include understanding of the geography and history of the region and their impact on the regional geopolitics and life-styles of the people; a comprehension of ethnic, family, and social norms and how changes are altering traditional relations is also important; knowledge of the three principal religions of the Middle East and their importance in shaping regional events must be stressed; and the negative impact of the mass media and their profit-political motives must be fully exposed and critically assessed. Such an education should also promote historical perspectives on colonialism, nationalism, religious factionalism, and territorial disputes that have resulted in years of conflict and strife. Other issues of major significance for a deeper understanding of the Middle East include problems relating to foreign intervention, security, autonomy, and sovereignty and an appreciation of how the Middle East has played an important role in world civilization and its contemporary significance for world peace.

As Amirahmadi has argued in the concluding chapter and elsewhere, such a program should also advocate internationalization of the curriculum as well as incorporation of national-specific perceptions and experiences. This approach is particularly relevant in the present global village, which is caught between the two diametrically opposing and at the same time reinforcing tendencies of integration and disintegration. The primary aim of such an education should be to promote cross-cultural communication to foster better global relations. As a first step in this direction, the distinction between "West" and "Others," made by the Anglo-American anthropology, must be rejected. But it should also promote the understanding that use of offensive force will be increasingly unacceptable in the emerging world community of largely interdependent nation-states and that international dialogue is becoming increasingly indispensable. A major condition for such a learning process involves a pedagogy that combines into a common format what is shared between the Middle East and the outside world, the West in particular, and what divides these cultures. This system of education promotes the exchange of knowledge and experiences as well as perceptual differences and shared views among nations by combining them into a common format and facilitates learning through contrasts and comparisons.[16]

In sum, notwithstanding a long history of involvement in the Middle East, American policy in the region seems to suffer from the lack of adequate experience, an absence of a well-defined long-term perspective, and heedlessness to the history and internal dynamics of the Middle East. The one obvious objective of the present U.S. Middle East policy is essentially directed toward external domination to keep the region subordinate via military strength. However, emerging global realities, including growing globalization and multipolar power centers, are rendering this policy ineffective. A new policy, based on mutual understanding, respect, and cooperation rather than confrontation, is required. But the combination of ignorance, prejudice, stereotyping, and piecemeal, militaristic, chauvinistic, and confused attempts to deal with the events in the Middle East is only making the United States more vulnerable in the region.

The United States would do well to revise not only its Middle Eastern policy but also its understanding and education on the Middle East. In particular, it needs to abandon the old myths and modes of operation in favor of new realities and alternative perspectives. The revisions are mandated not only because the U.S. policy in the Middle East has failed to promote a more friendly relationship between Americans and the peoples of the Middle East, but also because the region is critically important for world peace, development, and cooperation. The United States has a great opportunity to participate in the ongoing global reordering with intelligence and grace, and emerge as a satisfied partner in power sharing. As indicated by historical experience, declining empires tend to give rise to restorationist ideology. Can the United

States prove an exception to the rule? If the Persian Gulf War was of any indication, the answer is, unfortunately, negative and thus disappointing for all who wish to see a more prudent U.S. policy for the Middle East.

NOTES

1. Ali Mazrui, *Cultural Forces in World Politics* (London: James Currey, 1990).

2. For the evolution of U.S. Middle East Diplomacy, see L. Carl Brown, *International Politics and the Middle East: Old Rules, Dangerous Game* (Princeton, N.J.: Princeton University Press, 1984); James Bill, *The Eagle and the Lion: The Tragedy of American-Iranian Relations* (New Haven, Conn.: Yale University Press, 1988); John S. Badeau, *The American Approach to the Arab World* (New York: Harper and Row, 1968); Malcolm H. Kerr, *Elusive Peace in the Middle East* (Albany: State University of New York Press, 1975); George C. Lenczowski, *The Middle East in World Affairs,* 4th ed. (Ithaca, N.Y.: Cornell University Press, 1980); Bernard Lewis, *The Middle East and the West* (New York: Harper Torchbooks, 1960); William R. Polk, *The United States and the Arab World,* 3d ed. (Cambridge, Mass.: Harvard University Press, 1975); William B. Quandt, *Decade of Decisions: American Policy Toward the Arab-Israeli Conflict, 1967–1976* (Berkeley: University of California Press, 1977); John A. DeNovo, *American Interests and Policies in the Middle East, 1900–1939* (Minneapolis: University of Minnesota Press, 1963); and Lawrence Evance, *United States Policy and the Partition of Turkey, 1914–1924,* (Baltimore: Johns Hopkins University Press, 1965).

3. See L. Carl Brown, "The United States and the Middle East: What's the Game? Who Are the Players?" paper presented at the International Conference on Recent Developments in the Middle East and Their Implications for Curriculum in International Studies, Rutgers University, New Brunswick, N.J., April 25–26, 1987. See also his *International Politics and the Middle East.*

4. See Bill, *The Eagle and the Lion,* pp. 425–432.

5. "Report by the Secretary-General on Humanitarian Needs in Kuwait and Iraq in the Immediate Postcrisis Environment by a Mission to the Area Led by Mr. Martti Ahtisaari, Under-Secretary-General for Administration and Management," dated March, 20 1991; S/22366. (New York: United Nations Security Council, 1991).

6. Bill, *The Eagle and the Lion,* p. 446.

7. See Augustus Richard Norton, "A Countersensational Perspective on the Shi'a of Lebanon," in Hooshang Amirahmadi and Nader

Entessar, eds., *Reconstruction and Regional Diplomacy in the Persian Gulf* (London: Routledge, 1992).

8.   William A. Dorman and Mansour Farhang, *The U.S. Press and Iran: Foreign Policy and the Journalism of Deference* (Berkeley: University of California Press, 1987), p. 13.

9.   See Jack G. Shaheen, *The TV Arab* (Bowling Green, KY: Bowling Green State University Popular Press, 1984).

10.   For a summary of the report and debate on its pros and cons, see *New York Times* (June 21, 1991), pp. A1 and B4.

11.   Laurence Michalack, *Cruel and Unusual: Negative Images of Arabs in Popular American Culture,* ADC Issues 19, January 1984.

12.   Edward Said, *Orientalism* (New York: Vintage Book, 1979).

13.   See Brown, "The United States and the Middle East."

14.   See ibid.

15.   See, for example, Bill, *The Eagle and the Lion;* and Dorman and Farhang, *The U.S. Press and Iran.*

16.   Hooshang Amirahmadi, "Universalism in Planning Education: Toward an Interactive Pedagogy," *Ekistics 55,* nos. 328, 329, 330 (1988).

PART 2

U.S. Middle East Policy in Historical Perspective

CHAPTER 2

U.S. Policy in the Middle East

Richard Cottam

America's role as the preeminent Western power in the Middle East took shape suddenly following World War II. The British and French, with long Middle Eastern experience, abdicated leadership to the Americans. They did so with great reluctance and with little confidence in their successor's competence, but with an awareness that this was their only real option. World War II had inflicted terrible wounds on both countries, and neither would soon again be able seriously to aspire to first-class power status. The American acceptance of the primacy of its role in the area was gradual. American policy makers entered the world of Middle East politics without any real sense of the history of the area and with few ideas of what role America should play. But an American policy soon began to take coherent form.[1] In 1947 the Truman administration accepted responsibility for guiding the United Nations into an endorsement of the majority plan for the settlement of the Palestinian issue and hence for the emergence of Israel as an independent state in the area. Then in 1948 the Truman Doctrine was proclaimed and in so doing the U.S. government accepted responsibility for preserving the independence of Greece, Turkey, and Iran. But it would be another decade before a fully integrated American policy toward the region would take shape. The responsibilities of American policy makers were enormous, and their understanding was at best shallow. But for the next generation and a half the United States would be the dominant external power in the region and would exercise an influence far greater than that, not only of the old Western imperial powers, but also than that of the Soviet

Union, which was soon to be classified as a superpower and was very much part of the Middle East.

American policy makers concerned with the Middle East came to understand early that three interests must be taken into account in the formulation of an integrated American policy toward the area. These interests were central to the American foreign policy process, and American policy as it took form would have to reconcile the three. The first of these interests was that emanating from a broad public consensus that emerged in the United States shortly after World War II: that the Soviet Union was an expansionary power and, if not contained, would expand deeply into the Middle East and such an expansion would be highly deleterious to American security interests. There was, in other words, an intensely perceived threat from the Soviet Union within the American public and within the Truman administration. Isolationism had been a historic policy preference of the American people but one that had been seriously discredited during World War II. After the war, containing Soviet expansionism became the most important objective of American policy toward the Middle East, and the once isolationist United States now was prepared to accept Western leadership in dealing with this strategically critical area deep in the Eastern hemisphere.

The second interest related closely to the first. The dependence of Western industry on Middle Eastern oil was a matter of early and serious concern. The defense aspects of that concern were more important in defining this interest than were pressures on policy makers from the oil and related industries. But this was an area of major economic interest group activity; and the two concerns, satisfying the demand of an important domestic interest group and securing the economic health of the United States and its western European friends, were in close harmony.

The third interest reflected the terrible history of the Jewish people in World War II and indeed throughout their diaspora in Europe. A strong yearning among Jews for a homeland of their own followed the appearance of nationalism in Europe and was deepened by the experience of the holocaust. The American government and people were sympathetic with this feeling, and American policy makers responded positively to requests that the American government make a concerted effort to gain approval in the

United Nations and in the community of nations generally for the independence of Israel. Then, following Israel's gaining independence in 1948, a strong interest developed for helping Israel defend that independence.

There were, of course, other interests, but these three largely determined American policy in the region. As it evolved, American Middle East policy indeed would reflect a reconciliation of the three interests. But this reconciliation process would occur over a decade and involve two American administrations and countless policy debates over specific issues. A formula developed by which the competing interests could be reconciled, but it was not a consciously developed formula. Instead the formula emerged gradually over time as a consequence of assessing the costs and benefits of a myriad of smaller policy decisions. But the formula that finally emerged would prove to be, in its general outline, one of surprising durability.

A critical early question was how American policy would deal with the forces of rapid change in the region. In particular, how would American policy deal with the emergence of nationalism in the Middle East, especially in Turkey, Iran, and the Arab world? With regard to dealing with the first American policy interest, that of containing a perceived Soviet expansionism in the region, the force of nationalism could be a major asset. Regional nationalists would certainly have as a primary objective the creation of fully independent and sovereign nation states. They would be opposed to any perpetuation of imperial control in the region by the old and declining imperial powers. But they should be even more opposed to any imposition of external control by the Soviet successors of Tsarist Russia, a long-term imperial power in the region.[2] As such, many American policy makers assumed, regional nationalists should be the natural allies of the American foreign policy purpose in the area: that is, to halt any Soviet expansionary efforts.

Whatever the logic of this position, in practice American policy had difficulty maintaining any long-term alliance with the force of local nationalisms. However, the response was very different with regard to the nationalism of the three major peoples of the region, the Turks, the Iranians, and the Arabs. It was most favorable to Turkish nationalism. Political development in Turkey had progressed a good deal faster than in Iran and the Arabic-speaking areas. Under the leadership of Kemal Atatürk, Turkey had incorporated secular nationalism as a fundamental tenet of a resurgent Turkey. After World War II and in the period of American preeminence in the region, Turkish political leadership was both assertively nationalistic and pro-American. The struggle between the forces of tradition and of modernization had been won by the latter, and therefore in Turkey there was never the option for the United States, as there was in Iran and the Arab states, of working with traditional elites. However, Turkey was to a considerable degree polarized and in more than one dimension. America's allies in Turkey tended to be the more conservative elements. Leftists, and in particular leftist intellectuals in Turkey, not unnaturally, came to see the conservative Turkish political elite much as nationalists in Iran and the Arab lands saw their traditional leaders: that is, as lackeys or even agents of Western capitalist imperialism.

American policy toward nationalism in Iran crystallized in the early 1950s. Americans concerned with Iran, like those concerned with Turkey and the Arab world, included a good number who did view the nationalistic element as a natural ally in the struggle against perceived Soviet expansionism in the area. But when the forces of Iranian nationalism, strongly allied with religious leaders, came to power in Iran in 1951, they did so on a platform of establishing full Iranian sovereignty in matters relating to oil. As the Iranians saw it, British control of Iran's oil was objectionable, not only because an enormously valuable resource was being exploited by and in the interests of Great Britain and a British company but also because the Anglo-Iranian Oil Company was believed to be a host company for British political officers who indirectly had been controlling the political destiny of Iran. In their view the British had a well-developed working relationship with traditional forces in Iran—landowners, tribal leaders, conservative religious leaders, and the Iranian court. It was a useful alliance for both. Traditional leaders were willing to defend the political and economic interests of the British, and the British, in turn, would intervene on their behalf against the forces calling for rapid change, forces that were challenging the prerogatives of the traditional elite. Confrontation with America's vital ally, Britain, thus was unavoidable for the Iranian nationalist government of Dr. Mohammad Musaddiq. Iranian nationalists had hoped for American sympathy if not support for their cause. But within two years the Americans would be involved in the overthrow of Musaddiq. The American government decided to do so far less, however, because of the oil dispute than because of the chaotic conditions that had developed inside Iran. A strong "Yankee Go Home" campaign was conducted by communist and other leftist elements in Iran, and Musaddiq, in the era of Senator Joseph McCarthy, appeared to be at best "soft on communism." The Truman administration, although annoyed with the emotionalism of Mussadiq's anti-British policy, was not open to the proposal of participating in a coup. The view that Iranian nationalism with its popular base of support would be useful in containing the Soviets persisted. But not long after Eisenhower became president and the Dulles brothers became, respectively, Secretary of State and Director of Central Intelligence the United States government entered into an alliance with the British and conservative Iranians to overturn Musaddiq. As the Dulles brothers saw it, the Musaddiq regime was neither popular nor a bulwark against communist subversion. To the contrary, they believed it constituted an invitation to Soviet subversion. On August 19, 1953, the coup was successful and an era of intense American involvement in support of the dictatorship of the Shah of Iran began.[3]

This decision was indicative of an emerging pattern that would soon dominate as well in the Arab world. Where the forces of rapid change, led largely by secular nationalist leaders, were confronted with strong resistance from traditional elements, American policy increasingly sided with the latter. The nationalists tended to be suspicious of the West and to prefer a policy of nonalignment. Having spent their lives struggling against Western imperialism, as they saw it, nationalist leaders were much too distrustful to contemplate any kind of an alliance with the West. Traditional leaders in contrast saw a close relationship with the Americans as the best and possibly the only means for maintaining their position and their prerogatives. They had for some time had such a relationship with the British or the French, and they were comfortable working closely with representatives of a Western power.

Policy toward the force of nationalism in the Arab world was favorable for a longer period of time than in Iran, however. The leader of Iranian nationalism, Dr. Musaddiq, was a proponent of enlightenment values. In contrast, the emerging leader of nationalism in the Arab world was Gamal Abdul Nasser, who believed that the kind of change he advocated was possible only in an authoritarian system. Paradoxically, Nasser's authoritarianism made him more rather than less attractive to American policy makers. Unlike Musaddiq, Nasser was willing to deal forcefully with communists, religious fundamentalists, and any other group that constituted a potential threat to the regime. He had a sufficiently strong support base to provide stability and was fierce in his determination to preserve Egypt's sovereign independence. Nasser resembled Atatürk, a model for American policy makers, a tough nationalist who could be counted on to stand up to Soviet aggression without equivocation. Within the American bureaucracy Nasser was viewed as a natural ally, sometimes by individuals who participated actively in Musaddiq's overthrow.[4]

Still, other Arab leaders, more traditional and less willing to make strong nationalist appeals to attract popular support, were also viewed as anti-Soviet. One in particular, Nuri as Said of Iraq, was a tough, highly competent leader who saw a long-term alliance with the West as very much in the interests of the traditional elite as well as the Arab world. Nasser and Nuri as Said were bitter rivals within the Arab world, the one representing the forces of rapid change, the other preferring change that was far more directed, controlled, and slower in pace. Nuri as Said was a British protege and prototype of the preferred leader for the British in the Middle East, the kind of man they described as a "Westernized oriental gentleman" or "WOG." American policy in Iraq was entirely comfortable with Nuri as Said, and there was no real ideological split among American bureaucrats concerned with the Middle East. Nasser in Egypt and Nuri as Said in Iraq were both natural allies in the endeavor to contain perceived Soviet expansionism. There is no real indication they were seen as representing, respectively, the forces of rapid change and traditional elements who favored a tightly controlled change process and hence natural enemies.[5]

However, it soon became apparent that with regard to the other two major objectives, the free flow of oil to Western industry and the security of Israel, support for Nasser would present serious complications whereas support for Nuri as Said would not. Nasser, though an Egyptian nationalist, thought of himself as an Arab as well and was accepted in much of the Arab world as the greatest of Arab nationalists. Because, just as in Iran, control of oil by imperial power oil companies was viewed by nationalists as undesirable, Nasser had to assume a pro-nationalization stance or risk losing his credibility with nationalistic elements. Nuri as Said, in contrast, had little interest in appealing to popular support and was more than willing to resist nationalistic demands.

But the decisive factor that would lead the Americans away from Nasser was the sense of threat he generated in Israel. He was seen in Israel as the most dangerous of Arab nationalist leaders and the comparison with Mussolini occurred easily. Serious confrontation developed in February 1955 when the Israelis attacked an Egyptian garrison in the Gaza Strip. This led to a request by Nasser for arms sales from the United States. When the United States, concerned at the prospect of arming Israel's primary enemy, procrastinated, Nasser turned to the Soviet bloc for his arms purchase. This plus Nasser's policy of nonalignment annoyed Dulles and resulted in the Dulles's cancellation of American financial assistance for the construction of the Aswan Dam. Nasser, who saw the Aswan Dam as the centerpiece of his economic policy, in outraged response nationalized the Suez Canal company. Dulles then attempted to back away from confrontation with the forces of Arab nationalism. But the British and French were determined to stand up to so serious a challenge to old imperial prerogatives, and Israel suddenly had some important allies in its purpose to eliminate the threat from Nasser. The Israelis in October 1956 attacked Egypt; and the British and French, in poorly disguised collusion with Israel, began moving into the Suez area with the objective of removing Nasser from power. Dulles and Eisenhower responded by placing heavy economic pressure on the British and French to compel them to withdraw their forces.[6] The confusion of the situation was compounded when the Soviet Union, itself embarrassed by the Hungarian revolution, threatened a nuclear attack on London and Paris. Not for the first or the last time in the Middle East, the United States and the Soviet Union appeared as de facto allies in a major engagement.

In the aftermath of the confusion of the Suez diplomacy, American policy in the Middle East shifted sharply. The so-called

Eisenhower Doctrine was proclaimed, by which the United States offered aid to any Middle Eastern state asking for support against Soviet aggression or that of a regional surrogate of the Soviet Union. In programmatic translation the Eisenhower Doctrine, it soon became apparent, was an effort to isolate and destroy the influence of Gamal Abdul Nasser. Dulles had a few months earlier wooed Nasser's tentative ally, Saudi Arabia, out of the pro-Nasser camp. In April 1957, the United States gave full support to a royalist coup in Jordan that overturned a democratic and pro-Nasser Arab nationalist regime. In August 1957 an abortive American orchestrated coup against Nasser's Syrian ally would be attempted. American policy in the Middle East had crystallized. The pattern established in Iran now would be applied to the Arab world with reasonable consistency. For the next generation there would be an implicit alliance with the British, Israel, Turkey, the Shah's Iran, and a group of Arab regimes referred to by the code terms of "moderate" and "responsible." The latter served the short-term American purpose very well indeed. They were anti-communist, more than willing to enter into close and friendly economic relations with the United States and its allies, and for the most part willing to limit their opposition to Israel to the realm of rhetoric. As they included many of the most important oil producers, their friendship was highly valued.[7]

American policy in this era came to be identified with the maintenance of stability. So characteristic a feature of American diplomacy did this pursuit of stability become that it came to be thought of as a highly desirable end in itself. In fact, of course, the pursuit of stability was tactically instrumental for an American foreign policy, which had a strategic goal of preserving a status quo perceived as favorable for all three of the primary American objectives in the area. American policy did indeed suffer many serious setbacks. The coup in Syria failed and in doing so led directly to the temporary unification of Egypt and Syria in the United Arab Republic under the leadership of Gamal Abdul Nasser. Nuri as Said of Iraq was overthrown, and in response, the United States felt compelled to intervene in the 1958 Lebanon civil war. But until the Iranian revolution occurred, American policy continued to follow the the main lines of the model that had crystallized in 1957.

Soviet policy in the Middle East was assumed by all post-World War II American administrations to be an important aspect of an overall expansionist effort. Specific Soviet policies, however, did not always conform to expectations based on an assumption of a highly aggressive purpose. Some did. Even before World War II had come to an end, the Soviet Union was putting extraordinary pressure on two important Middle Eastern states, Iran and Turkey. In fact, Soviet assertiveness in these two cases along with Soviet policy in Eastern Europe, essentially inaugurated the Cold War. Soviet troops occupied northern Iran in 1941 in conjunction with British forces, which occupied central and southern Iran. Both powers agreed to leave Iran within six months of the termination of the war. But in 1945 two autonomous republics were set up in Iran under Soviet protection, in Iranian Kurdistan and Iranian Azerbaijan. The United States government protested these actions vigorously in the United Nations, and in 1946 the Soviet Union did in fact withdraw its forces from Iran and allow these two regimes to be overturned and their territory and people returned to Iranian control.[8] Why the Soviet Union allowed its two client regimes to be so easily disposed of remains an unanswered question. Certainly there was nothing to indicate an American response that went beyond protesting in the United Nations. But, although few official Americans thought so at the time,[9] the view came to prevail that the Soviet retreat was a response to a show of will and determination on the American part. Indeed, throughout the next generation and a half a Soviet policy that appeared to be cautious to the point of passivity was accepted as a manifestation of successful containment and not of an altered Soviet purpose.

A Soviet threat to Turkey at the close of World War II and a demand for two Turkish provinces, Kars and Ardahan, were rejected by Turkey with the backing of the United States. The Soviet response was one of bluster and some movement of armed forces but ultimate acceptance of the status quo.[10]

Following these two important episodes, Soviet policy in the Middle East for almost a decade was largely nonassertive. In fact in one important regard it paralleled American policy. The Soviet Union not only supported the creation of the state of Israel, it was amenable to the sale of Czechoslovakian arms to Israeli forces fighting their war of independence.

Most puzzling was the Soviet response to the overthrow of Mohammad Musaddiq in Iran. The American government in overturning the Musaddiq regime had taken the important step of direct and frontal opposition to the Iranian national movement. Furthermore it had replaced a government that was nonaligned with a regime that for some years was dependent for its very survival on American financial and diplomatic support and was fully committed to the American foreign policy objective of containing the Soviet Union. It did so in a country that had a 1200-mile border with the Soviet Union. Surely one could expect from an expansionist Soviet Union, at the very least, a rapid move to ally with the Iranian national movement and thereby take full advantage of the deep anger of Musaddiq supporters at his overthrow. It is difficult to imagine an American government confronted with a parallel Soviet action in Mexico not moving militarily against what would surely be perceived as a satellite regime. The Soviets would have had difficulty overcoming Iranian historical distrust in making an alliance with Iranian nationalism. But in fact they did not even make the effort. On the contrary good and close relations were established with the Shah that, except for a few fairly minor incidents, persisted until a few weeks before the Shah's overthrow.[11]

Two years later, however, the Soviets made a different choice with regard to Arab nationalism than they had with regard to Iranian nationalism. Not only did they agree to Nasser's 1955 request of a sale of arms but also, when the United States withdrew its offer to finance the Aswan Dam, willingly gave substitute assistance. The Soviet Union, however reluctantly, had chosen to side with the Arabs in the Arab-Israeli conflict and to become the great-power mentor of Arab nationalism.[12]

However, the rhythm of Soviet support for the Arabs in their successive wars with Israel was difficult to reconcile with the image of Soviet aggressiveness. Beginning with the 1956 Israeli invasion of the Sinai, Soviet policy followed a consistent pattern: they seemed to content themselves with selling arms to friendly Arab regimes, protesting when the Israelis defeated the Arabs, and then replenishing the Arab arms usually in the form of sales with long-term credit provisions. The pattern was last fully apparent in the 1982 Israeli invasion of Lebanon and its aftermath. However, there was one important exception. The Soviet response to the 1973 war was not initially seriously at variance with the established pattern. Soviet expectations seem to have been that this would be simply one more Arab defeat.[13] But when the Egyptians and Syrians performed unexpectedly well on the battlefield the Soviet response was one of uncharacteristic vigor. They initiated a substantial airlift of needed supplies to both Arab states and in addition pursued a vigorous diplomacy that appeared to be designed to minimize Arab losses.[14]

Possibly the most telling case of Soviet passivity occurred in 1974.[15] In that year a Kurdish rebellion against the government of Iraq was triggered by the Shah of Iran in collaboration with the governments of the United States and Israel. The plan to do so had been broached first by the Shah to President Nixon in 1971. Its purpose was to destabilize and possibly overturn the Iraqi government in which Saddam Hossein was then the behind-the-scenes strong man. The Iraqi government had a friendship agreement with the Soviet Union, and Iraqi arms were primarily of Soviet vintage. The conflict with the Shah was old and bitter. The two governments interfered in each other's internal affairs, and each made an effort to encourage dissident elements against the other. In addition the Iranians secreted Soviet arms captured from the Arabs by Israel across the Iraqi border with the purpose of leading the Iraqis to suspect that the operation was a Soviet one.

The case is truly extraordinary. The United States, Iran, and Israel were acting in collusion against a close friend of the Soviet Union, using a minority ethnic group, the Kurds, who are also to be found in the Soviet Union in substantial numbers, attempting to present the operation as a Soviet operation and doing so within 200 miles of the Soviet Union. The Soviet response to all of this was largely restricted to the rhetorical level. Iraq defeated the Kurdish rebels; and the Shah, rather than engage in combat with Iraq, agreed to a settlement that accepted border changes the Shah had unilaterally imposed but also included an acceptance of defeat for the Kurds and the termination of active subversion by each against the other.[16] An Iraqi policy drift away from the Soviet Union and a developing peaceful modus vivendi with the Shah's Iran followed this agreement.

In December 1979, the Soviet Union executed its most aggressive action in the Middle East since the Azerbaijan intervention in

1945. After apparently some weeks of debate and consideration, the Soviets sent troops into Afghanistan to carry out a dual mission: to remove the leadership of a Marxist and pro-Soviet regime that had by virtue of a policy of brutality and suppression alienated much of the Afghan population and to support the Marxist regime now under a new Soviet-imposed leadership. For the first time in a generation Soviet policy seemed to conform with American imagery. The Carter administration fearing additional Soviet aggression, possibly including a move into Iran, took a strong stand. In effect, by what was to be referred to as the Carter Doctrine, the Soviets were placed on notice that any attempt to move into the Persian Gulf arena would be resisted actively by the United States.[17] However, Soviet policy fairly quickly returned to a more familiar passive stance. The early scenarios of a Soviet use of Afghanistan as a first step toward the Persian Gulf, Arabian Sea, and Indian Ocean began losing their plausibility. The thesis that the Soviet move was made to preserve a friendly regime on the Soviet border and to deny Afghanistan to a hostile Islamic regime or a regime that might be close to the United States or PRC was surely defensible.

The case was made earlier that American policy crystallized in 1957 in the form of a de facto alliance with the British, Israel, Turkey, the Shah's Iran, and moderate Arab regimes. The primary American purpose was to contain a Soviet Union assumed to be strongly expansionist. But, with the exception of the move into Afghanistan, Soviet policy after 1957 had not conformed to these expansionist expectations. However, the unexpected passivity of Soviet behavior did not result in a significant alteration in the American view of Soviet intentions in the area. The conclusion was easily drawn that the Soviet Union, confronted with a tough American stand in support of its friends and allies, had simply accommodated to American assertiveness. The imagery of the Soviet held by American officials appears to have remained fairly constant. Certainly there was no official expression of a view of a more benign Soviet policy.

However, American policy toward the Soviet Union after 1957 was often at logical variance with a rhetoric that was based on a Cold War image. Even earlier, in fact in the immediate post-World War II era, American and Soviet policies on occasion appeared to be parallel to the point of a de facto working relationship. In 1948, for example, both great powers supported the formation of the Israeli state. Furthermore, Soviet policy from that point on was consistent in its support of the right of Israelis to sovereign independence. Then, as noted previously, both the United States and the Soviet Union opposed the Israeli, British, and French action against Egypt in 1956. The implicit collaboration was uncomfortable, however, and the sharp American policy shift in 1957 may have been in part the consequence of a reaction to the realization that policy had been allowed to drift into the anomalous position of appearing to be allied with the Soviet Union against America's closest friends in the region.

The crushing defeat the Arabs suffered in the 1967 conflict with Israel and the easy Soviet acquiescence in that defeat did lead to a subtle shift in American policy. It was difficult to imagine in the aftermath of that major event that either the United States or Israel was confronted with an immediate security threat in the region. However, when the efforts of Gamal Abdul Nasser in Egypt to conduct a war of attrition against Israel led to another major Egyptian defeat, Nasser turned to the Soviets for assistance. This came in the form of SAM ground-to-air missiles, which effectively halted the Israeli air raids on Egypt and led to a potential confrontation with the United States in 1970. The Rogers plans put forward in response by the Nixon administration in effect called for Soviet-American cooperation to stabilize the situation in the area. Because implicit in these plans was the assumption that the Soviet Union would cooperate in an effort to bring an end to the Arab-Israeli conflict, American policy appeared to be drifting away from the notion of an ineluctably expansionist Soviet purpose. It would be difficult to reconcile such a move with the Cold War imagery that continued to be advanced in official American rhetoric. Later in October 1977, Jimmy Carter's administration signed a declaration, referred to as the October Declaration, which followed exactly the same pattern. In both cases Israeli opposition was the critical factor in negating the American efforts. The conclusion can be drawn that, in spite of a persisting description of an aggressive Soviet Union, actual policy was beginning to adapt to the cautious and passive Soviet policy described earlier.

Another pattern began to appear in the formulation and execution of American policy. The initiatives, such as the Rogers plans and the October Declaration, which seemed to accommodate to a more benign view of Soviet intentions, emanated from the State Department. Opposition to those policies seemed generally to center in the National Security Council. This pattern was especially apparent as the government of the Shah of Iran began to lose control to a revolutionary situation. At that time Zbigniew Brzezinski, Carter's National Security Advisor, convinced Carter that the Iranian revolution owed much to Soviet support and could not be allowed to succeed. The Department of State, on the other hand, saw the revolution as essentially a product of internal forces and came to favor a policy of dealing with the contending elements of an emerging regime.[18]

The replacement of the regime of the Shah of Iran, who accepted enthusiastically a role as the primary American surrogate in the area, with the anti-American Khomeini was a serious blow to the formula that had emerged in 1957 for American policy. Iran under the Shah was a major factor in American efforts to contain the Soviet Union. Iran's location was of critical importance for a containment strategy, and the size of its population and its industrial and resource wealth made it potentially an exceedingly important ally. In the last fifteen years of the Shah's rule, Iran was emerging as a power of universal, not simply regional, importance. Thus even though it did not defect to the Soviet bloc, it did leave the American bloc and in so doing left a major void that could not easily be filled.

But, as serious as Iran's defection from the American bloc was for American policy, the Iranian revolution had even more serious implications for American policy. The political force of a resurgent Islam quickly developed into one of, if not the most, important disturbances in the region. American policy, it was suggested earlier, had encouraged stabilizing a generally favorable status quo in the region. Now there was a new and major challenge to that stability, and the new regime in Iran was, at the very least, its exemplar. How would American policy adjust to this new challenge to regional tranquillity? The initial American response to the revolution was to accept it and try to reach some accommodation or at least modus vivendi with it. However, the anger and resentment of the new Iranian leaders at an American policy that, as they saw it, had imposed a hated dictatorship on the country and then had done everything it could to maintain and strengthen the hold that regime had on the state was too great for an easy reconciliation. The taking hostage of American diplomats was carried out for the express purpose of demonstrating to Americans and other external powers as well that Iran would no longer countenance such behavior. When the Soviet Union occupied Afghanistan, the Iranian foreign minister took the diplomatic lead of Islamic states in condemning the action and demanding its reversal. Thus Iran, long regarded as the strategic prize for which the Soviets and Americans were in hot contention, was taking on both superpowers at once, including the one with which it had a 1,200-mile border. It was bewildering behavior, and neither the Americans nor the Soviets developed a response of any consistency.[19]

In Khomeini's world-view, there were two blocs of state actors, the oppressors and the oppressed. The Soviets and the Americans were the leaders of the oppressor bloc and Iran was conducting the first really significant challenge to oppressor hegemony. In his view, Soviet and American differences were real but both great oppressors valued oppressor hegemony so highly that they would unite to put down any serious oppressed world challenge.[20] Khomeini expected a major oppressor response to the calculated humiliation of the hostage taking. The inability of the United States to release its diplomats should demonstrate to both the oppressors and to the oppressed peoples the weakness of the oppressors and the great moral strength of the oppressed. It was inevitable, Khomeini felt, that the oppressors would mount a major response. Thus when Iraq attacked Iran in September 1980, Khomeini viewed the attack as the expected oppressor response. The attack, he assumed, was initiated and orchestrated by the United States, supported by the other great superpower, and conducted by a joint American-Soviet puppet leader, Saddam Hossein of Iraq, and an assortment of American Arab lackeys representing the Arab regimes the Americans described always as "moderate."[21]

The fact that there was no empirical support for this Iranian view does not detract from the intensity with which it was felt. Furthermore, both American and Soviet policy responses to Iranian behavior were such as to appear to confirm the Iranian view.

Within a few years both the United States and the Soviet Union were in effect "tilting" toward Iraq in that long and destructive conflict. This was exactly the behavior Khomeini had predicted, and he and his lieutenants were fortified in their view that Iran was struggling against an oppressor world conspiracy. But how, in fact, is one to explain this most important case of de facto Soviet-American collaboration? If American policy was concerned primarily with the containment of perceived Soviet expansionism in the Middle East, how could support for a regime that had a friendship agreement with the Soviet Union, maintained close personal relations with the Soviet Union, and operated with a weapons system that was still largely composed of Soviet-produced weaponry be defended?

The answer to that question is fairly easily discovered. The so-called moderate Arab regimes had over a generation become an integral part of the operating, though not formalized, alliance system that American policy had generated after the Suez crisis. This meant that in American military planning for dealing with various contingencies of Soviet aggression a major role had been identified for the Arabian peninsula area. Then, even more important, a sense of responsibility to America's long-time allies had developed and there was a good deal of sensitivity, especially within the Department of State to the strongly expressed interests of these regimes.[22] Thus when the leaders of the moderate regimes began to perceive a terrible threat from resurgent Islam and to rationalize that threat in terms of the needs of the alliance, the American policy makers were sympathetic. The probably unplanned consequence of this was to push American policy inexorably in the direction of hostility toward Iran and toward elements of resurgent Islam that were perceived as internal threats to these regimes. It was a policy that could be described as one of incremental drift; that is, a major strategic line was developing as the result of a large number of day-by-day decisions designed to buoy up friendly Arab regimes.

There was, however, a fundamental fragility to what was developing into a major policy alteration. Initially a major reason for supporting the so-called moderate Arabs was because such support was instrumental in halting Soviet expansionism and maintaining the free flow of oil to Western industry. But when that policy was formulated, Iran under the Shah occupied the front line opposed to the Soviet Union. Now a new Iranian regime, although diplomatically isolated, showed even greater determination to resist any Soviet advance. Logic would seem to dictate that such an Iranian regime should be a primary American ally. In contrast the moderate Arab regimes tended to be militarily weak, unable to attract any popular enthusiasm and vulnerable to internal opposition. Among American policy makers who were particularly inclined to see the Soviet Union in the Cold War mold, again heavily represented in the National Security Council, the appeal of attempting to restore an allied relationship to Iran was strong. Apparently these people saw in President Reagan's concern for the release of American hostages held by Islamic organizations in Lebanon the possibility for not only enlisting Iran's help for their release but also the possibility of a significant move toward restoring good relations with this anticommunist Iranian regime.[23] The effort to do so was unprofessional, however. The Iranian view of the American role in the Iran-Iraq War was deeply held and included a belief in Soviet-American collaboration in that war. Therefore, the overture was going to be misinterpreted as an admission of defeat for the Soviet-American client, Iraq, and the effort to depict the United States as primarily interested in joining with Iran in opposing the Soviet Union was going to be seen as rank deception.[24] But the failure of that effort did not obviate the logic of the view that Iran was far more important to the achievement of the primary American interest in the area, that is, containing Soviet expansionism, than were the moderate Arabs. There was strong evidence here of a major policy disagreement. The Department of State, responding to years of Soviet passivity in the area, was far less concerned with containment than were other officials, particularly those in the National Security Council. Furthermore, the State Department had had long and friendly relations with moderate Arab regimes, and the notion that regional stability was an objective and that the moderate regimes were essential for that stability was deeply ingrained.

For over a generation and a half, containment of the Soviet Union dominated American policy concerns, only a few episodes of which could be described as potentially serious confrontations between the two superpowers and only one really was extremely dangerous. The United States confronted the Soviet Union loudly and effectively in Security Council debates concerning the Soviet reluctance to withdraw its troops from Iranian Azerbaijan in 1946. But American documents make clear there was no real possibility of a military confrontation simply because the United States lacked the capability to do so.[25] As indicated previously, the Soviet decision to withdraw is still today something of a mystery. Nevertheless the incident is clearly thought of after the fact as the first example of a successful American confrontation with the Soviets.

The next serious case occurred after the coup d'etat in Iraq in the summer of 1958 and the subsequent American military move into Lebanon. There is little question that the American action was viewed in Washington as standing up to Soviet aggression acting through its United Arab Republic surrogate.[26] But here again the course of events suggest there was little substance to support the image. When the Americans left Lebanon a new government had been established with full American support. It included as the prime minister Rashid Karami who had been one of the leaders of the side of the warring factions against which the Americans had intervened. The American intervention, happily, resulted in a reasonably stable coalition including a number of individuals who were Karami allies. Any thought of confrontation in this case clearly had been illusory.[27]

However in 1970 in the month called Black September a far more dangerous episode occurred. King Hussein, responding to advisors who felt the Palestine Liberation Organization was operating out of control in Jordan, launched an attack on the military arm of the PLO. Syrian President Jadid, a Baathist and strong proponent of Arab nationalism, sent some tanks across the border to assist the Palestinians. Responding to this move, President Nixon and his national security advisor, Henry Kissinger, worked out a contingency plan that included the use of the American Sixth Fleet to stop any Soviet military response. Kissinger's plan also called for an Israeli move across the border to assist King Hussein against what was perceived to be a military operation by the Syrian surrogate of the Soviet Union. There is nothing to indicate that the Soviet Union was seriously considering any counterresponse. But in any event the Israeli move proved unnecessary because of internal developments in Syria. Jadid was about to be ousted by the current Syrian president, Hafez al Assad, and the latter refused to provide air support for the tanks sent to assist the Palestinians. King Hussein's air force then easily disposed of the tanks and the crisis never really developed. It is an important case nevertheless in that it indicates a good deal about American imagery. Kissinger assumed that the lack of a Soviet response was due to the strong American action.[28] But there is little available supporting evidence for that view. As in the Lebanon case, the American expectations seemed to have been illusory.

The one really dangerous near confrontation occurred after a cease fire had been agreed to following the Arab-Israeli 1973 War. Soviet military and diplomatic activity in that war had not conformed to the cautious and passive pattern described previously. The Soviets apparently had advised strongly against the attack against Israel and had expected another major Arab defeat. But when after the first day it was apparent that the Arab military performance would be surprisingly effective the Soviets quickly inaugurated an airlift to both Syria and Egypt. They were equally energetic in promoting a diplomatic move to bring about a cease fire that would preserve some of the Arab military gains. Finally, after the Israelis had succeeded in crossing the Suez Canal and beginning the encirclement of an Egyptian army, they gained Kissinger's agreement to a cease fire and both sides accepted the proposal. However, the Israelis continued to encircle the Egyptian army and on October 24, 1973, the Soviets sent a note to the American government suggesting either a joint intervention to enforce the cease fire or, should the Americans decline, a unilateral Soviet move to do so. The American response was to place its forces on nuclear alert and the world faced some extremely uncomfortable hours of uncertainty. However on the morning of October 25 a European proposal for sending in a United Nations force was accepted by both superpowers and the crisis came to an end.[29] In this case, unlike the previous ones, the American view was not purely illusory. Soviet behavior had diverged sharply from a by now implicitly recognized pattern and resembled more closely a pattern to be expected given the expansionary image. However, Soviet behavior in sum could well be described as defensive. The case would be impossible to substantiate that the Soviets had encouraged the Arab attack. Furthermore from the very beginning the Soviets tried to persuade the Arab side to work for a cease fire—even when there was some reason to believe that Arab success could be a good deal more than modest. It is also reasonably clear that the Soviets believed the cease-fire violations were entirely the responsibility of the Israelis and that Soviet credibility with the Arabs rested on her ability to compel a compliance with the cease fire. However, the Soviet note to the Americans was a strong one and Soviet military activity such that the stark American interpretation of Soviet intentions was understandable.

In retrospect the alacrity with which the Soviets accepted the proposal for a UN military force to police the cease fire argues against any picture of intentional confrontation. Even more, the Soviet acquiescence in the almost immediate move of Sadat away from his Soviet protector and toward his recent American foe coincides with a defensive interpretation. Indeed the Soviet acceptance of the Egyptian shift in alliance conforms to the passive pattern. By the time of the Israeli invasion of Lebanon in 1982 there is nothing to indicate that either the Israelis or the Americans seriously considered even the possibility that Soviet assistance to her close Syrian and PLO friends would not follow the passive pattern.[30]

The Soviet move to occupy the cities and highways of Afghanistan in December 1979 was, as remarked, their second unambiguously aggressive move in the Middle East in the postwar era. But it was not seriously confrontational. Afghanistan was far too distant from the United States to be a likely locus of confrontation. It did become a Cold War battleground, however. Resistance to the Soviet occupation pervaded Afghan society. Traditional elements, tribal and religious, opposed the Soviets with the same tenacity the British had experienced in Afghanistan in the nineteenth century. They were joined in opposition by much of the modern community as well, especially including religious-led elements. Refugees by the hundreds of thousands poured into Pakistan and Iran, and virtually all of Afghanistan away from the major cities and trunk highways was under rebel control. This opposition presented the United States with an opportunity it could not ignore. American aid to the rebels, either direct or through the government of Pakistan, grew steadily and a strong association with the Afghan rebels developed, an association that soon became vested-interest connected with a substantial American bureaucratic community assigned the task of maintaining resistance to the Soviets. Thus when the Soviet Union began signalling its willingness to leave Afghanistan, the suggestion was not seriously explored by the American government. The Afghan situation remained, therefore, one of the primary sources of tension between the two superpowers in the Middle East. It also posed a problem for the United States in formulating a general policy toward resurgent Islam. Many of the closest American allies among the Afghan rebels fell into that category. American policy thus was confronted with the anomaly of giving enthusiastic support for a movement that increasingly American policy was opposing elsewhere in the Middle East.

The Arab-Israeli conflict has been a primary source of disturbance in the region throughout the postwar era. It remains, in the 1990s, along with the challenge from resurgent Islam and a reassertion of Arab nationalist demands, one of the major disturbances in the area. The Soviet-American conflict, in contrast, as it evolved in the region in the 1980s became less and less a major source of regional disturbance until, as the 1990s began, it was no longer a serious factor. For American policy makers the task of reconciling the objective of seeking long-term security for Israel and the objective of containing perceived Soviet expansionism, largely in the form of subversion in Arab states, had been the core problem in policy formulation. As described previously, the formula that crystallized in 1957 for American policy was one in which the strongest proponents of Arab nationalism and the most intransigent opponents of Israel were opposed and their more conservative Arab opponents supported. The price paid in adopting this policy was that the proponents of Arab nationalism turned to the embrace of the Soviet Union. However, this price proved not to be exorbitant because the support the Soviet Union granted these allies was at best lukewarm. Soviet policy appears to have included a strong determination to prevent the confrontational potential in the conflict from developing. A major consequence of what amounted to Soviet passivity was that the leverage American allies derived from a strong and persisting diplomatic and military support from their mentor was far greater than the leverage the Soviet alliance granted progressive Arab regimes.

An important manifestation of the assymetry of activism of the competing superpowers in the region was the primacy of the American role in seeking a formula for the solution of the Arab-Israeli conflict. At no time did Soviet diplomacy approach that of the United States in terms of the vigor of the search for a formula. But American efforts alternately explored two very different general formulas, one of which has been acceptable to leaders of Arab nationalist regimes but opposed by Israel, and the other of which has been acceptable to Israel and, to a lesser degree, the so-called moderate Arab regimes but unacceptable to Arab nationalists.

The first formula is associated with the Rogers plans of the early Nixon administration and the so-called October Declaration of the early Carter administration. It called for a joint Soviet-American–sponsored conference of all the major participants, including a large representation of Arab regimes and, in some form, the PLO. The hoped for outcome was a comprehensive settlement that would be generally acceptable to Israel and the entire range of Arab states. The exact form the settlement would take was, of course, left for the flow of diplomacy to determine. But in general outline it would include some acceptable form of self-determination for Palestinians in Gaza and most of the West Bank, recognition of Israel within established boundaries as a sovereign member of the regional community, and a mutually acceptable security guarantee for all of the participants. The assumptions that underlie this formula were (1) that the Soviet Union favored stability in the region and could be counted on to help guarantee that stability, (2) that Arab nationalism was a force that must be taken into account in constructing an acceptable formula, and (3) that there was a consensus for peace in Israel and in the Arab world generally that could be teased out by skillful diplomacy. This formula was identical in its general outline to the peace formula the Soviets have advocated essentially without change since 1968.[31]

The second formula is associated with Kissinger's step-by-step negotiations with Israel, Egypt, and Syria after the 1973 war, the Camp David formula, and the various Israeli proposals for a settlement. It called for direct negotiations by the participants with the United States playing a mediating role and the Soviet Union entirely excluded. The anticipated outcome would be bilateral peace treaties with successive Arab states and Israel that would provide for mutual recognition within recognized boundaries, some form of autonomy for Palestinians in Gaza and Judea and Samaria (this is the terminology used to refer to the West Bank—it is important because it is a symbolic reflection of the view that the West Bank is the core territory of ancient Isreal), and the establishment of normal diplomatic and economic relations. The assumptions that underlie this formula were strikingly different from those underlying the first formula. They were (1) that the Soviet Union could and should be excluded from these negotiations, (2) that Arab nationalism is a spent force that can be disregarded as a probable source of future difficulties, and (3) that there is no general consensus for peace in the Arab world that could be teased out but that such a consensus can be generated in the most moderate states and, after success in this bilateral endeavor, gradually in the entire Arab world as the reality of a permanent Israeli presence in the area comes to be comprehended.

The second formula was the basis for a negotiated settlement between Israel and Sadat's Egypt. But it was rejected by all other Arab states. The early Reagan administration returned to a modified version of the first formula, one in which Soviet participation was still excluded, as the Reagan Plan. It was summarily rejected by Israel and the Reagan administration made no serious effort to revive it. Virtually all of the proposals since that rejection have been close to the first formula. Even such "moderates" as King Hussein found it necessary to insist on a comprehensive approach and an international conference in which both the United States and the Soviet Union were intimately involved. Israel, however, is most unlikely to consider seriously such a plan as long as her perceptions of a substantial power advantage over the Arabs endure.[32]

American financial, military, and diplomatic support are critical ingredients in Israeli security concerns. Isolated as Israel is in world diplomacy, strong backing from the American superpower has to be a prime strategic objective of any Israeli government. Thus far Israel's success in achieving and maintaining that support has been close to optimal. But the problem of continuing to receive that support has a paradoxical dimension. The intensity of American concern for the Middle East was largely derivative from a perceived threat in the area from Soviet expansionism. In other words, the American willingness to expend scarce resources in the area was largely a product of perceived threat. The rapid diminution of that perception, a phenomenon that is accompanying the end of the Cold War, could lead to American disinterest and a sharp reduction in willingness to make major budgetary investments in the area. It enhances the case for returning to a formula that calls for a comprehensive settlement with international guarantees.

The third major American foreign policy interest in the region, to ensure the free flow of Middle Eastern oil to Western industry and to participate in the petro-dollar—based economic growth of the region, has been surprisingly unimportant in generating major foreign policy lines. The reason for this is not difficult to discover. The American policy formula that crystallized in the 1950s for the region had as a central feature an alliance with moderate Arab regimes. These regimes included most of those that were the major Arab oil producers and that of oil-rich Iran. The American relations with these regimes was hence symbiotic. They tended to see American support as necessary for their survival and thus were more than willing to engage in close economic cooperation with the United States. The fragility of this relationship was made apparent, however, in 1973. In that year Arab producers stood behind Syria and Egypt in their attacks on Israel and established an effective boycott of regimes, including the American, which were seen as overly solicitous of Israel. At the same time, a producers market developed and the Shah of Iran, America's close friend, took the lead in raising astronomically OPEC pricing of oil.[33] For a few months following these events the critical importance of the oil interest for American policy makers was very clear. On September 23, 1974, simultaneous speeches by President Ford and Secretary of State Kissinger[34] threatening retribution to those oil producers who were willing to play casually with the health of the world economy were good indicators of the seriousness with which this crisis was viewed by the oil-consuming world. For a brief moment it appeared that this crisis was sufficiently serious that it might replace the Soviet-American conflict as the prime source of world, or at least regional, conflict. Had this materialized, the American policy formula for the Middle East would have collapsed, and in all likelihood, some starkly different alliance patterns would have developed.

The oil crisis passed very quickly, however. Conservation, the expansion of supply and the early end to the Arab boycott combined to reduce the immediate danger. Within a few years oil scarcity was replaced with a glut of oil supplies. Even such cataclysmic events as the Iranian Revolution and the Iran-Iraq War were insufficient disturbances to restore a sense of crisis. However, projections of a return to scarcity were widely accepted and the appearance of the Khomeini regime in Iran marked the entry into oil politics of a regime committed to the use of the "oil weapon" as a means for punishing offending consuming nations and as a primary source of leverage for defeating what Khomeini saw as a Zionist-imperialist conspiracy to maintain imperial hegemony in the region.

Iranian oil policy since the Revolution, however, suggests that the threat perceived from a revisionist regime such as Iran's to the free flow of oil is largely illusory. The regimes of Iran, Iraq, Libya, and Algeria, which can be regarded as favoring a radical alteration of the relations of the Middle East with the United States and Europe, all have major economic development programs that call for an optimal oil income. These programs are essential in each case for long-term regime stability. Policies that risk a cut-off of that income are not likely to be followed on even a medium-term basis. Indeed, a strong case could be made for the proposition that fear on the part of consumers is more likely to result in shortages and price rises than is the effort of producer regimes to use the "oil weapon." In the medium and long run, oil supplies and pricing are likely to reflect the economic imperatives that emerge from the increasingly pervasive international economic system. Nevertheless, when Saddam Hossein sent his troops into Kuwait, the response was to view his actions as a threat to the supply of oil to world industry. Justifiable or not, the perception of threat to oil interests was real, and defense of that interest was the primary basis for justifying the quick transfer of United States forces into the Gulf region.

American policy in the Middle East has been a major factor in regional developments in the past generation and a half. Perhaps the most important consequence can be seen as following from the decision to oppose the forces of secular nationalism in Iran and in the Arab world. The decision was in tune with a general aim of attempting to preserve a regional status quo that was perceived as being favorable to the major objectives of American policy in the region. Nationalism in Iran and the Arab world was a driving force for change in the area and, as such, highly disruptive of that status quo. It was viewed as producing the kind of chaos and confusion that could add to the subversive potential for Soviet penetration of the area, as potentially capable of disrupting the flow of oil to Western industry and, especially Arab nationalism, a threat to the security of the recently born state of Israel. American opposition to nationalist leaders did succeed in defeating and discrediting them. But it could not and did not halt the force of rapid change. In this brief period of American policy preeminence in the region, the population of the region came alive politically. Whereas at the beginning of the period only a fraction of the population was politically participant, by the end of the period the great mass of the population was predisposed to play a major role in politics. The traditional willingness to acquiesce in the determination of policy by a tiny elite had disappeared. At the beginning of the period secular nationalist leaders such as Musaddiq and Nasser became the focus of populist appeal and the men to whom the newly awakened looked for leadership and guidance. By the end of the period sectarian leaders, particularly Islamic leaders, had replaced the secular nationalists as the primary focus of great populist movements. Had they not been defeated and discredited by external, and particularly American, actions, secular nationalists, it is reasonable to believe, might have prevailed. In any event, at the end of the Cold War period in the Middle East, American policy was confronted with a dynamic force, that of resurgent Islam, that was much more threatening to a status quo, viewed as highly favorable to American interests, than regional nationalisms had been.

The American strategic purpose in the Reagan years was clear enough: to contain in the Middle East as elsewhere the expansionary tendencies of Soviet policy. But the task of translating that purpose into a sensible tactical plan of action was daunting. The state actors whose policies were primarily responsible for the flow of events in the Middle Eastern region now were Israel and the Islamic Republic of Iran, not the Soviet Union. Israel by its invasion of Lebanon in 1982 had altered the situation in the eastern Mediterranean area. Iran in advancing its messianic purpose even if only by example was encouraging some and alarming others throughout the region. Just how these two developments related to the Soviet-American conflict was not at all self-evident. In fact neither great power had really developed a coherent policy for dealing with either crisis area. Both supported the forces of resurgent Islam in some areas and opposed them in others. In the Iran-Iraq conflict their policies were startlingly parallel, each tilting toward Iraq.

The retrospective case is easily made that, despite the colorful Cold War rhetoric of the Reagan administration, the Soviet-American conflict in the Middle East was essentially over by the mid-1980s. The parallelism of Soviet and American policy in the Persian Gulf was symptomatic of that fact. But Cold War–generated patterns persisted. The alliance with the oil-producing regimes of the Arabian peninsula proved to be especially important. It had been a central feature of the policy formula that had crystallized in 1957. The alliance served each of the major American objectives. The regimes were anticommunist, accommodating in their economic policies and willing to restrict opposition to Israel to the level of rhetoric. By 1990 the concern with containing communism was gone, the oil flow was following the dictates of larger economic imperatives, and Israeli military superiority appeared unassailable. Yet when Saddam Hossein invaded one of these long-time allies, Kuwait, the American reaction was reflexive. The remaining "moderate" and "responsible" Arabian peninsula regimes must be protected and the Kuwaiti regime restored. There was little indication that a careful analysis of the vital interests that were threatened had been made. Nor was there anything to suggest that a strategic decision had been made to oppose the revitalized forces of Arab nationalism or of politically resurgent Islam although leaders representing both tendencies denounced the American military move into Saudi Arabia. A new United States policy thrust was likely to emerge in the 1990s as it had in the 1950s that would reconcile the competing needs of primary American interests in the Middle Eastern region. But those interests in the 1990s appeared to be far less central than had been the overriding interest of containing perceived Soviet expansionism in the 1950s. Despite the vigor of the American reaction to Saddam Hossein's aggression, therefore, longer-term American policy in the Middle East appeared likely to be far less obtrusive than it had been a generation earlier. Of the three major interests that concerned United States policy in the Cold War era, the one that appears most likely to be seriously threatened in the 1990s is that of the security of the state of Israel. There are significant indications that a strong populist movement could develop in the Arab world with a force capable of producing a broader unity among Arabs. Should this occur, whether based on Arab nationalism, resurgent Islam, or some combination of the two, the isolation of and threat to Israel would certainly emerge as a serious concern for American decision makers. Their responses could well be the major factor giving definition to the new thrust of American policy in the region.

NOTES

1. For a good general analysis of American policy in the Middle East, see Seth P. Tillman, *The United States in the Middle East: Interests and Obstacles* (Bloomington: Indiana University Press, 1982).

2. See Selig Harrison, *The Widening Gulf: Asian Nationalism and American Policy* (New York: Free Press, 1978). Harrison makes a strong case for dealing with nationalism in Asia.

3. See Richard W. Cottam, *Iran and the United States: A Cold War Case Study* (Pittsburgh: University of Pittsburgh Press, 1988).

4. This is described from firsthand knowledge by Miles Copeland, *The Game of Nations* (London: Weidenfeld and Nicolson, 1969).

5. See Waldemar Gallman, *Iraq Under General Nuri: My Recollections of Nuri al-Said, 1954–1958* (Baltimore: Johns Hopkins University Press, 1964).

6. For the best treatment of this period, see Kennett Love, *Suez: The Twice Fought War* (New York: McGraw-Hill, 1969).

7. Neither the Jordanian nor the Syrian coups have been given the analytical treatment they deserve. For one of the few references, see Patrick Seale, *The Struggle for Syria: A Study of Post War Arab Politics, 1954–1958* (New York: Oxford University Press, 1965).

8. For a history of Soviet-American relations in the Azerbaijan and Turkish cases, see Bruce Kuniholm, *The Origins of the Cold War in the Middle East* (Princeton, N.J.: Princeton University Press, 1980).

9.   See *United States Foreign Relations, 1946*, Vol. 7, pp. 563–66.

10.   Robert Rossow, Jr., "The Battle of Azerbaijan," *Middle East Journal* (Winter 1956): 17–32.

11.   Shahram Chubin and Zabih Sepehr, *The Foreign Relations of Iran: A Developing State in a Zone of Great Power Conflict* (Berkeley: University of California Press, 1974). Also see Rouhollah Ramazani, *Iran's Foreign Policy: A Study of Foreign Policy of a Modernizing Nation* (Charlottesville: University of Virginia Press, 1973).

12.   See Alvin Z. Rubinstein, *Red Star on the Nile: The Soviet Egyptian Influence Relationship Since the June War* (Princeton, N.J.: Princeton University Press, 1977).

13.   Ibid., pp. 262–64.

14.   Ibid., pp. 275–76.

15.   *The Village Voice* (February 16, 1976).

16.   For an analysis of this event as a factor in the Iran-Iraq War, see Tariq Ismael, *Iraq and Iran: Roots of Conflict* (Syracuse, N.Y.: University of Syracuse Press, 1982).

17.   On Afghanistan, see Henry S. Bradsher, *Afghanistan and the Soviet Union* (Durham, N.C.: Duke University Press Policy Studies, 1983).

18.   For opposing interpretations of American policy by officials of the Carter administration, see Gary Sick, *All Fall Down: America's Tragic Encounter with Iran* (New York: Random House, 1985); and William H. Sullivan, *Mission to Iran* (New York: W. W. Norton, 1981).

19.   For a good view of official bewilderment, see Warren Christopher *et al.*, *American Hostages in Iran: The Conduct of a Crisis* (New Haven, Conn.: Yale University Press, 1984).

20.   Richard W. Cottam, "Iran's Perception of the Superpowers in Iran Since the Revolution," in Barry Rosen, ed., *Iran Since the Revolution* (Brooklyn: Brooklyn College, 1985).

21.   See this picture in a speech by Hojatolislam Hashemi Rafsenjani, FBIS, South Asia (February 9, 1983), p. I-1 and a speech by Ayatollah Khomeini, FBIS South Asia (February 14, 1983), p. I-1.

22.   For a description of policy in the area illustrating this point, see Thomas Naff, ed., *Gulf Security in the Iran-Iraq War* (Washington, D.C.: National Defense University Press, 1985).

23.   The point is developed in the Tower Commission report.

24.   For illustrations, see Tehran Domestic Service, FBIS South Asia (March 25, 1987), pp. I-1–2; and a speech by President Khamenei, FBIS South Asia (March 20, 1987), p. I-1.

25.   *United States Foreign Relations* 6 (1946): 460.

26.   For an illustration of the American viewpoint at the time, see

Thomas Schelling, *Arms and Influence* (New Haven, Conn.: Yale University Press, 1966), p. 49.

27.   On the Lebanon case, see Alexander George and Richard Smoke, *Deterrence in American Foreign Policy: Theory and Practice* (New York: Columbia University Press, 1974), pp. 309–62.

28.   For Kissinger's account, see Henry Kissinger, *White House Years* (Boston: Little, Brown and Company, 1979), pp. 594–631.

29.   For a critical view of Kissinger's role, see Roger Morris, *Uncertain Greatness* (New York: Harper and Row, 1977), pp. 246–49, 251.

30.   For a revealing picture of Israeli intentions, see Zeev Schiff and Ehud Ya'ari, *Israel's Lebanon War* (New York: Simon and Schuster, 1984).

31.   See William Quandt, *Camp David: Peacemaking and Politics* (Washington, D.C.: Brookings Institution, 1986).

32.   For a good analysis of Israeli thinking, see Mark Heller, *A Palestinian State: The Implications for Israel* (Cambridge, Mass.: Harvard University Press, 1983).

33.   For a good summary of oil policy, see Mohammad E. Ahrari, *OPEC: The Failing Giant* (Lexington: University of Kentucky Press, 1984).

34.   The Kissinger speech was made before the United Nations General Assembly, *New York Times* (September 24, 1984), p. 12:4. Ford's speech was in Detroit, *New York Times* (September 24, 1984), p. 12:3.

CHAPTER 3

U.S. Foreign Policy in the Middle East: The Tragedy of Persistence

Richard Falk

In underlying respects, the U.S. foreign policy toward the Middle East has been remarkably consistent since the end of World War II (after having been virtually nonexistent prior to 1945). One of the great shifts brought about by the war against fascism was to move, by stages, Western influence from its British and French locus to that of the United States and, for a period, but to a far lesser degree, to the Soviet Union. That is, a complex mixture of unipolar and bipolar geopolitics superceded the regional allocations of influence associated with the colonial period. With the ending of the Cold War, the Soviet influence has receded, leaving the United States the predominant extraregional influence in the Middle East, but also the object of acute enmity on the part of the peoples in the region.

This dynamic has climaxed in 1990 in reaction to Iraq's August 2 invasion of Kuwait, reinforced by a brutal occupation and accompanied by holding hostage thousands of Westerners. The United States responded immediately to the invasion, deploying major military forces in the region and by the demand for unconditional and total Iraqi withdrawal from Kuwait. The United States also mobilized wider regional and global participation in the course of shaping a collective response to the invasion and skillfully achieved a strong mandate for its approach from the UN Security Council. As the postinvasion developments unfolded over the course of the next several months, it became increasingly evident that the outcome of the Persian Gulf Crisis would have profound implications for the Middle East and for U.S. policy toward the region that would not become fully evident for several years, at the very least. While the crisis remained unresolved, the following assessment of the United States–led response seemed most persuasive: if Iraq could have been persuaded to withdraw without resort to direct and major warfare, then the U.S. approach would be widely applauded, including in the region, as substantially successful, whereas if Iraq were either to sustain its annexation claim without an effective challenge or if a devastating war ensued, then the United States would be widely blamed.

In fact, of course, the Gulf War ensued, with a devastating display of American military supremacy. Iraq accepted the UN terms, including not only withdrawal from Kuwait, but intrusive claims to ascertain whether all weaponry of and facilities associated with weaponry of mass destruction situated within its territory was destroyed. The United States emerged as the unchallenged arbiter of the region's future, with all sides acknowledging this outcome. The anticipated backlash did not materialize. The Arab world seemed reluctant to question politically the military outcome. So the military victory over Iraq opened political space for U.S. initiative in relation to regional restructuring, including with regard to the Arab-Israeli relationship. Whether American diplomacy will be as successful in "peace making" as it was in "war making" remains to be seen.

With these general considerations in mind, it is possible now to depict the main contours of U.S. foreign policy toward the Middle East, bearing in mind that the turbulence of the era makes any assessment lose relevancy with great rapidity. The contention of the chapter is that a consistency of U.S. policy toward the region is evident over the last several decades, but that a rupture for the worse could occur if the Gulf Crisis had ended unsuccessfully for the West. In any event, it is almost unavoidable to conceive of U.S. foreign policy toward the Middle East in three stages: from 1945 to the end of the Cold War; after the end of the Cold War; the challenge of the Gulf Crisis.

FROM 1945 TO THE END OF THE COLD WAR

The complexity of the Middle East resists easy generalization. The U.S. foreign policy was to varying degrees sensitive to variations from country to country and through time, but it was also driven by some underlying objectives that imparted an impression of consistency. It will not be possible here to consider the nuances of application, but rather to discuss what appear to be the driving forces.

It became evident after 1945 that the European colonial powers most active in the region lacked the will and capability to sustain their presence sufficiently to uphold Western economic and geopolitical interests in the region. This process of displacement involved the substitution of U.S. for British and French influence, and as well as a degree of Soviet patronage of anti-Western regional tendencies even in the face of hostile attitudes toward Marxism and domestic communist parties. Such an interaction between the two superpowers in the region set the stage for the central Cold War theme: U.S. support for conservative Arab governments that looked to Washington for arms and protection and opened their economies to international capital, and U.S. hostility to nationalist regimes that looked in some way to Moscow for support and challenged the privileged positions of Western economic interests, especially in connection with oil. In other words, even without the complicating presence of either the Cold War or Israel, U.S. policy in the region was guided by the basic conviction that radicalizing political tendencies of any sort would endanger the Western interest in favored access to cheap and abundant oil supplies, the very basis of post-World War II economic prosperity in the North. This conviction from the very outset included the view that Soviet expansion into the region directly was unacceptable and that any Soviet effort to project its influence through diplomacy and aid was threatening and warranted U.S. resistance by all feasible means. In this regard the geopolitical importance of the Middle East as the link between Europe, Asia, and Africa added to the stakes, making the region second only to Europe in importance during the course of the Cold War.

The earliest confirmations of this central commitment occurred in relation to Iran, with U.S. insistence that the Soviet military forces withdraw from Iran's northern provinces in 1946 or face an immediate showdown. Even more revealing was the U.S. response to the success of Musaddiq's movement oriented around secular constitutionalism and economic nationalism, leading to the fall of the Shah from power and to the nationalization of the Anglo-Iranian Oil Company, principally owned by British Petroleum. Despite Iran's willingness to negotiate some formula of compensation, the West responded with a boycott of Iranian oil and the portrayal of Musaddiq as an hysteric and fanatically xenophobic political leader. The Musaddiq government, although middle class and reformist in outlook, was attacked as dangerously radical, destabilizing the country in such a manner to ensure its later takeover by the Tudeh Party, a Moscow-oriented communist party influential among workers in the oil fields. Against this background, the United States relied on a public posture of hostility and a CIA-directed program of destabilization, culminating in the 1953 coup that brought the Shah back to power, solidified U.S. influence in Iran, and gave American oil companies almost 50 percent of the restructured Iranian oil industry.[1] This sequence of developments, perceptions, and immediate and longer-range effects express the wider regional policies of the United States during the Cold War years. After 1953 the United States helped the Shah solidify his domestic rule; sustained this support despite evidence of massive violations of human rights in subsequent years; and supplied the Iranian government with such abundant military hardware as to make Iran into a so-called regional superpower by the early 1970s that was so designated by Washington, avowedly as a kind of burden sharing for the sake of regional stability, and regarded, at the time, as an important component of the Nixon doctrine. The latter policy arose directly from the American experience of failure in the Vietnam War, a sense of U.S. overextension combined with the frantic search for innovative methods by which to sustain Western influence and interests throughout the Third World.

The response to Nasser's Egypt is confirmatory, and extends the pattern to encompass the Israeli factor. Nasser came to power through a military coup that overthrew a weak and quite traditional Egyptian government. Nasser, like Musaddiq, was an ardent nationalist and augmented these sentiments with a strong Arabist zeal that projected both a vision of a pan-Arab union and the destruction of the state of Israel, depicted as a humiliating projection of Western power into the region at the expense of the Arab world. Nasser's politics generated great enthusiasm among the Egyptian masses and, more widely, within the Arab world, although conservative Arab governments in the region felt threatened by what they insisted was a threat of Egyptian expansionism. Nasser was attracted to neutralist positions on East-West questions and was an ardent early champion of the nonaligned movement. Such a posture was viewed in Washington at the time as extremely threatening, especially when it led Nasser to accept economic assistance from Moscow in connection with the construction of the Aswan Dam project and to proceed with the nationalization of the Suez Canal Company.

In reaction to the latter development, and to Egypt's indulgence on its territory of Palestinian "freedom fighters" staging violent cross-border raids against Israel, the Suez invasion was carried out as a joint operation of Britain, France, and Israel in 1956. This Western military initiative was undertaken at a time when world public attention was fixed on the Soviet intervention in Hungary to suppress in bloody fashion a nationalist uprising under the leadership of Imre Nagy. The United States, perhaps in part because not adequately informed by the invading countries in advance, opposed its closest allies and sided with the basic demand of its adversary, Egypt, in calling within the United Nations for withdrawal. It was the Dulles era in U.S. foreign policy, and there may have been some lingering disposition to support a strict interpretation of the UN Charter prohibition on the use of force in situations other than self-defense. The Korean war was still a fresh memory, and the defense of South Korea had been justified by a strong U.S. insistence that the use of military force across an established international boundary was an instance of aggression that could not be tolerated. Also relevant, no doubt, was the unacknowledged U.S. effort to complete the process of displacing the European powers in the region. After the Suez Crisis Anglo-French influence diminished dramatically, and the region became a Cold War arena in which the two superpowers both sought to extend their influence, although not to an equal degree. The U.S. position was always more clearly ascendent and assertive, especially in relation to the critical core questions of Persian Gulf oil and the security of Israel.

In the period after Suez, the United States role and goals in the region became more explicit. It was clear that the United States would use direct and indirect military power to balance its containment objectives, which included acting against indigenous extensions of revolutionary nationalism as well as extensions of Soviet influence. The U.S. policy attempted to reconcile safeguarding Israel and lending support to the "moderate" Arab regimes in the region.[2] An important episode involved the landing of U.S. Marines in Lebanon in 1958 to protect the country against an alleged danger of "indirect aggression" in the form of Nasserite subversion. With the Arab defeat in the 1967 war with Israel, which quadrupled the size of Israel, put Israel in control of Jerusalem, and demonstrated its military prowess, the character of American policy began to make some subtle changes. Israel emerged as an independent force for "stability" in relation to Arab radicalism, "a strategic asset" rather than a liability. Nevertheless, U.S. support for Israel created tensions with even conservative Arab governments and began the process of alienating the peoples of the region. This posture of U.S. support for Israel hardened in this period as pro-Israeli domestic groups built a solid bipartisan political base in Congress that increasingly constrained the Executive Branch in its pursuit and definition of the national interest in the Middle East. The United Nations, especially the General Assembly, became an arena within which the Arab countries pressed their basic demand that Israel withdraw from the territory occupied in 1967, insisting that peace required steps toward realizing Palestinian self-determination. The Palestinian cause gained far greater public attention through airline hijacking and other varieties of political terrorism. The Palestinian Liberation Organization emerged in this post-1967 environment as the controversial representative of the Palestinian people, and Arafat became the dominant leader.

These various themes persisted throughout the 1970s. The Arab failure in the 1973 war created a wide agreement in the Arab camp that it was no longer realistic to seek the defeat of Israel on the battlefield and, to some degree, made it also evident that the Palestinian struggle would continue until some sort of genuine Palestinian homeland in the form of a PLO state was established. The U.S. government associated its policies mainly with the Israeli interpretation of these developments, but did its best to maintain positive relations with the moderate Arab governments. In the aftermath of the Arab defeat in 1973, the oil weapon was used for the first time against the West in the form of a partial embargo of exports and a dramatic increase in oil prices. At first, fear and panic swept through Western countries, given grass-roots vividness by memorably long lines of cars waiting near gas stations to fill their tanks. It was in this period that American leaders, including Kissinger, hinted broadly at a possible military intervention in the Gulf if the economic pressures became overwhelming. Throughout the 1970s oil prices continued to rise, but the effects were less harmful to the West than initially supposed. An atmosphere of normalcy was briefly reestablished, and American goals in the region seemed to do well—Kissinger's shuttle diplomacy broke the negotiating deadlocks to enable the establishment of some provisional security arrangements between Israel and her Arab neighbors; Sadat reversed course in the mid-1970s by repudiating Soviet help and, at the same time, opened Egypt to international market forces. The highlight of Sadat's policy reversal was his historic journey to Israel that built the political basis for the Camp David process. The United States welcomed these developments, and President Jimmy Carter provided the auspices for the negotiations that led Egypt to recover the Sinai while normalizing relations with Israel. Sadat's approach was treated by other Arab governments as a betrayal of the Palestinian cause and an abandonment of Arab unity in relation to Israel. Egypt became isolated in the Arab world, and the Arab League symbolically moved its headquarters for more than a decade from Cairo to Tunis. Sadat was regarded by Washington as second only to the Shah as friend in the region, and thus his assassination at fundamentalist hands was viewed as a great loss for the United States. The failure of the Egyptian people to mourn Sadat's death was widely noted and found puzzling in the West, where he had earned respect, even admiration, for his initiatives.

United States regional interests, however, came under serious attack in Iran during the late 1970s from the unexpected direction of Islamic fundamentalism. Over the years the U.S. government had viewed the religious right as a marginal presence in Iran and rather useful to the extent that Islamic militants tended to be intensely anti-Marxist. The Iranian Revolution challenged many of the fundamental tenets of U.S. foreign policy, revealing the hollowness of the Shah's hold on the Iranian people despite oil wealth, considerable modernization of the economy, a powerful military capability, and an efficient internal police apparatus. Ayatollah Khomeini's leadership style, with its anti-American, anti-Israeli, antimodern zeal, inflicted a real shock on the Washington foreign policy establishment. With Khomeini's victory came, after some clear indications that the new Iranian rulers were embarked on their own campaign of repression, the ordeal of the hostage crisis in 1979–1980 that helped destroy Carter's presidency and bring Ronald Reagan's neoconservative outlook to the White House.

During this period there also occurred the Soviet invasion of Afghanistan and a concern in Washington that the use of Soviet military power beyond its territory might be a prelude to a westward strike at the oil. Carter reacted as if the Cold War had intensified in a critical and dangerous fashion. The United States, in a mini-anticipation of its response to the Gulf Crisis, sent its leading officials to friendly capitals throughout the Arab world, promising increased supplies of arms and the creation of a U.S. rapid deployment force capable of projecting military power all over the region should any further threats to the status quo emerge. It was, also, assumed that Soviet capacities to project conventional military power in the region were much greater than anything the United States could hope to put together. To allay these concerns and to create a deterrent effect, the Carter administration issued publicly Presidential Directive 59 that threatened to meet any danger with a sufficiency of force, which, given the logistical situation, was generally understood as conveying a U.S. intention to use nuclear weapons, if necessary, to protect its interests in the Middle East.[3]

A further reaction to these adverse developments was to move the United States into an explicit strategic partnership with Israel, which meant giving Israel free hand in pursuing its own security and expansionist ambitions. The culmination of this relationship was the unprovoked attack by Israel on Lebanon in 1982, resulting in the siege of Beirut, the expulsion of the PLO presence, continuous civil violence in Lebanon, and the horrifying spectacle of the massacres at Sabra and Shatila, large Palestinian refugee camps. Israel's military victory in Lebanon led to serious political setbacks, as the Lebanese population resisted occupation by a variety of violent means, and Israel felt obliged to withdraw its military forces, although retaining by way of a compliant Christian military force, a security zone in southern Lebanon. More serious for Israel was the effect of the 1982 war on the Palestinian movement. Instead of producing the intended effect of demoralizing Palestinian nationalism in the Occupied Territories, Palestinian militancy was reborn in late 1987 in the form of the *intifada*.

The Cold War dimension remained an important element. Moscow lent its support for opportunistic reasons to the revolutionary nationalist regimes in the region, including those of Iraq, Syria, and Libya, and was supportive of PLO diplomacy and a consistent opponent of Israel. In effect, in the United Nations and elsewhere in international diplomacy, the Israeli-Palestinian conflict was perceived in standard East-West terms. In some settings, a variety of international efforts were made to disentangle the two sets of concerns, positing the Palestinian cause on its own merits. Much of the Third World looked upon the Palestinian struggle in this spirit and treated it as second only to the antiapartheid movement in order of significance. Such militancy, given the tight U.S.-Israeli relationship in this recent period contributed to the rising tide of anti-United Nations sentiments in the U.S. government and among the American people through the 1970s and into the 1980s.

Certain tendencies persisted during the Cold War era, giving U.S. foreign policy toward the Middle East its basic coherence. Shifts in approach are best understood as tactical adjustments to a situation of complexity and almost continuous crisis. Once the U.S. role as guardian of Western interests in the region emerged unmistakably in the years after the 1956 Suez Campaign, the lines of foreign policy priority were evident: a commitment to ensure that control over the major Gulf oil fields remained in friendly hands, the related effort to oppose any extension of direct Soviet influence, to resist revolutionary nationalist tendencies whether emanating from Left or Right, the resolve to oppose the spread of Islamic fundamentalism, and finally, the treatment of Israel as an indispensable strategic ally and as a state whose freedom of action would be protected against hostile Third World and Soviet bloc pressures. The core tension for policy makers was to reconcile closeness with Israel (and then with Sadat's Egypt) while sustaining a positive relationship with the moderate Arab regimes that were intensely anti-Israeli, at least in their official posture, and with respect to Arab mass attitudes. This task was simplified by the extent to which these Arab moderate regimes, including the Gulf dynasties, were more afraid of Arab nationalism, including that of the Palestinians, and Islamic fundamentalism, than of Israel, and indeed shared with Israel an antipathy to all forms of revolutionary politics in the region. Despite this underlying compatibility, the tension was real, surfacing during crises, when calls for Arab solidarity on behalf of the Palestinian cause became very insistent.

An assessment of U.S. foreign policy success during this period leads to a mixed picture. The overriding effort to intervene against national strivings, most of all those of the Palestinians, may have saved low oil prices for the West, but it did so at the cost of generating widespread anti-Americanism, which has surfaced in a number of distinct settings in the Middle East. The U.S. government definitely pursued a foreign policy in the region driven by its state interests, subordinating concerns about the well-being of the peoples and their aspirations. This attitude of normative complacency has also spilled over into the geopolitical agenda as well. The inability to pursue a balanced policy toward Israelis and Palestinians definitely hurt the credibility of the United States as evenhanded guarantor of stability in the region. Whether that inability was principally a consequence of Israeli support within U.S. society or represented an evolving decision to link up with Israel as a strategic partner in the region, remains an open question. Undoubtedly, both elements played a role.

The relationship to Iran exhibits also the pitfalls of shortsighted opportunism and cynicism. The disruption of constitutionalism in the 1950s led directly to the eruption of fundamentalism twenty-five years later and in a form that directly challenged U.S. strategic and economic interests. In 1980 the United States indirectly encouraged the Iraqi attack on Iran and allowed the Iran-Iraq War to unfold without ever taking steps to condemn Iraq's illegal recourse to force. From the perspective of 1990 such cynicism was neither a success at the time nor has it served the United States well over time. Of course, it is impossible to tell what the consequences might have been for Iran and for U.S.-Iran relations if the United States had respected Iranian self-determination during the Musaddiq years or had not, later on, encouraged Saddam Hussein to embark on his expansionist war against Khomeini's Iran. But surely it can be concluded that neglect of popular aspirations generates resentments that will under some conditions produce a vicious backlash, while in other situations appear to be without great cost.

AFTER THE COLD WAR

As Gorbachev's leadership took hold in Moscow after 1986 and the Soviet Union began to apply "new thinking" to its foreign policy, one could discern an overall reduction in Soviet involvement on a unilateral basis in relation to Middle East issues. East-West confrontations gave way to cooperative efforts under UN auspices to resolve violent conflict, most notably the arrangements for Soviet withdrawal from Afghanistan and the Iran-Iraq cease-fire. In effect, the Cold War ended with a Soviet withdrawal from the Third World in general, leaving the United States unchallenged at a regional level.

These changes were, of course, welcomed in Washington, at first guardedly, but by the end of the decade with enthusiasm. It seemed to make the protection of Western interests a less burdensome undertaking. Without Soviet backing, revolutionary nationalism seemed far less dangerous. The main Cold War danger, evident during the nuclear alert declared to discourage the dispatch of Soviet troops to rescue the beleaguered Egyptian Third Army in 1973, was as escalation of conflict beyond regional boundaries or the threat or use of weaponry of mass destruction to overcome a local imbalance in conventional military capabilities. Furthermore, aside from the smoldering ruins in Lebanon and drama generated by the *intifada,* there seemed no serious threat to the basic U.S. concerns in the region—oil and Israel; even the PLO had moderated its tone of militancy and agreed in 1988 to pursue Palestinian statehood by diplomatic means despite the implacable rejection of Palestinian claims by the Israeli government and its repeated reliance on excessive violence to quell resistance activity in occupied Palestine.[4]

Finally, Iraq seemed weakened and exhausted by the long and inconclusive, yet costly, war with Iran and had been widely discredited as a legitimate government in light of its use of chemical weapons on the battlefield against Iranian troops, and even more so, against Kurdish civilians living in northern Iraq. Even Qadaffi had backed away from a confrontational approach, conceivably chastened by the U.S. military attack in April of 1986, and Libya diminished its support for an array of armed struggle movements around the world.

In sum, then, U.S. foreign policy toward the Middle East

seemed less problematic than at any point since World War II. The way the Cold War ended seemed in the early months of 1990 an unmixed blessing to the architects of American policy in the Middle East. At the same time, American foreign policy in this short period was singularly unimaginative, so much so that it can be indicted as geopolitically complacent. Such an indictment gains force with the hindsight provided by the Gulf Crisis. The United States made no effort to use the end of the Cold War as a moment when it might have been quite feasible to have tipped the balance in favor of the establishment of a Palestinian state in the Occupied Territories and exerted influence to emancipate Lebanon from a variety of foreign intrusions. Especially on the Palestinian question, the United States had been victimized in both geopolitical and normative terms by weak presidential leadership. Public opinion in the United States would have almost certainly followed a change of official policy on the status of the PLO and the need for a Palestinian state, and it could have altered dramatically the Arab perception of the United States by most of the people in the region. At the very least, it seems like an initiative that should have been explored far more seriously than it seemed to have been. Instead the Bush administration was apparently persuaded that despite several decades of unresolved struggle and violence, the Israeli-Palestinian conflict was still not "ripe" for resolution, a monumentally silly approach given the circumstances.[5]

THE CHALLENGE OF THE PERSIAN GULF CRISIS

At its outset the Gulf Crisis startled both leaders and citizens in the United States and elsewhere. At the very time when there was a general sigh of relief because the end of the Cold War was supposed to have resulted in "the end of history" or, at the very least, a pause in confrontational and strategic war-threatening crises, a new danger erupted. In such a setting, Iraq made a move that more directly threatened the oil lifeline of world capitalism than anything the Soviet Union or its regional allies had ever attempted during several decades of Cold War tension and a series of Arab-Israeli wars. The Iraqi invasion of August 2, 1990, is replete with ironies of this sort. Another is that at the very time that the West celebrated its victory over socialism by declaring that only market-oriented constitutionalism is a legitimate basis for government, it rushed headlong to the defense of Kuwait, a victim of aggression to be sure, but certainly not a political order with many attributes of democracy.

It is also worth examining the Gulf Crisis as an exercise in post-Cold War foreign policy by the United States and as such to become aware of some rather gross deficiencies. By December 1990, the United States had committed five major blunders in reaction to Saddam Hussein's dangerous challenge. Such a course of conduct raised a real doubt about whether the United States would be able to fulfill the global role (a kind of pax Americana II) that it assumed in the Gulf Crisis. One expression of this doubt is the unexpected nostalgia for the supposed balancing and mutually restraining impact that bipolar tensions produced in regional settings, particularly in Europe and the Middle East where it was evident in any crisis that the catastrophe of world war must be avoided at all costs. It is obvious that such inhibitions were not operative in the Gulf Crisis.

The first blunder made by the United States concerned the onset of the crisis itself. From the diplomatic setting and satellite intelligence the U.S. government had ample warning in the days prior to August 2 that Saddam Hussein was contemplating an invasion as one option in his challenge directed at Kuwaiti oil pricing and pumping from Rumaila oil field. Whether such a prospect was discussed at the upper echelons of government we do not know, but it should have been. We do know that the American ambassador in Kuwait, April Glaspie, who met with Saddam shortly before the invasion and was apparently more preoccupied with establishing positive relations with the Iraqi leader than in communicating the serious consequences for Iraq and the region of any use of force against Kuwait conveyed a basically reassuring message in Baghdad, implying that the encounter with Kuwait was basically an inter-Arab affair.[6] In the new regional situation, without the rules of the Cold War rivalry in operation, the United States, as custodian of Western interests in the region, had a clear responsibility to signal the seriousness of an Iraqi invasion *prior* to its occurrence when it clearly should have apprehended the danger. Whether a more appropriate preinvasion diplomacy would have had the desired deterrent effect we cannot fully know, but we can criticize U.S. policy making for its failure to take reasonable preventive steps, thereby suggesting a deeper U.S. failure to adapt its global and regional roles to the requirements of peace and security in the new international situation.[7]

A second blunder involved the style and substance of the U.S. response as put forth from the earliest period after the invasion. President Bush articulated the demand of the gathering coalition in maximal terms—unconditional withdrawal plus reparations plus, at times, a seeming intention to remove Saddam Hussein from power and put him on trial as a war criminal plus a clear commitment to the elimination of Iraq's arsenal of chemical and biological weaponry, as well as its allegedly incipient nuclear weapons program. These demands were posited in this manner presumably to discourage all diplomatic approaches. This discouragement materialized explicitly during the crisis in the form of disparaging peace missions led by such former leaders as Willy Brandt and Ted Heath, dissuading the UN secretary-general from playing any kind of mediational role and projecting an image of disinterest in proposals that give Iraq some facesaving diplomatic space to cover the humiliation of retreat and withdrawal. The United States put forward this maximal program despite the realization, which sharpened in later weeks, that a desert war could be bloody on both sides and that high technology tactics were of uncertain military utility and their use might cause a major backlash in the Islamic world. At the outset of the crisis, Bush treated Saddam and Iraq almost as if a replay of Noriega and Panama was in the cards. To the extent such an impression is accurate, it suggests a dangerous ignorance about the fundamental difference between the two situations, especially the capability and resolve of Iraq to inflict serious harm in retaliation. The essence of the U.S. blunder is one of geopolitical overextension, promising too much in a setting where the effort to deliver could be expensive, and made it far more likely that the crisis would end in what at the time appeared to be failure; namely, warfare or a collapse of the coalition or both. If the United States had set more modest objectives, then "success" could be more easily claimed, and it would have been far more likely that the UN sanctions would be sufficient over time to induce Iraq's withdrawal. Also, Saddam would have a far greater incentive to seek a diplomatic escape route and avoid an outcome likely to be a disaster for Iraq and for himself. Again, if the United States played the sort of leadership role it had assumed for itself in the Gulf

Crisis, then the international community would have the right to expect diplomatic prudence and an approach that minimized the risk of unnecessary warfare.

The third blunder by the United States is closely related to the second blunder. Bush can be commended for his initial recourse to the United Nations, the mobilization of a broad coalition of states in favor of coercing Iraq's withdrawal from Kuwait, and the establishment of a comprehensive sanctions program centered around choking off Iraqi trade with the rest of the world. It seems reasonable and effective to use the framework of the United Nations for these purposes, but what the Bush administration had additionally done was to combine coercive diplomacy with what might be described as "a war of nerves"; that is, the threat to wage offensive war against Iraq if it failed to meet the demands set in UN resolutions (which incidentally do not go nearly as far as the U.S. maximal goals). Insinuating the war of nerves into the response process had a number of unfortunate consequences: by threatening war credibly, the odds on the actuality of war were greatly increased— tensions between the parties were heightened in a manner likely to cause alarmist misperceptions and even the temptation to strike first; a situation was created in which an incident, possibly deliberately caused by a third party interested in provoking war (for instance, a terrorist attack on the hostages being held in Iraq during the first several months) that neither side intended (a war by accident and drift of the sort associated with World War I). That is, by waging a war of nerves the UN coalition lost substantial control over the response process. Also, by seemingly threatening war as a policy option doubts were raised about the legitimacy of the UN response and whether the organization was truly acting as an independent agent of its membership rather than a rubber stamp for the U.S. approach. For the United States to insinuate the war of nerves into the formal decision process of the United Nations was to push a position that was both unsound and undermined to some degree the advantages gained by the earlier recourse to the organization.[8] It is also worth noting that to mobilize support for a response endorsing a war of nerves, the United States had to make demeaning side payments of various sorts that facilitated Syria's further domination of Lebanon and overlooked China's continuing campaign of repression toward its own forces of dissent.[9]

The fourth United States blunder related to the unfortunate logic of the response process that evolved prior to January 16, 1991. By failing to support a sanctions approach unambiguously, any outcome would have been tainted by its militarist character; that is, either warfare would have ensued or the UN "success" could have been attributed to mounting a credible threat of warfare. In either alternative, the precedent established conveys a basically unfortunate message to the future. A third possibility existed that almost materialized in the form of French defection from the coalition. The expectation of war would undermine the international coalition and erode the domestic consensus within the United States. Had these processes gained momentum as the January 15 deadline approached one could even have imagined a political collapse of the response process, allowing Iraq one of the few ways to resolve the crisis without withdrawal.

The final blunder could have turned out, under other circumstances, to have been a blessing in disguise—the Bush administration acted so unilaterally *within* the American political process that it failed to build a strong domestic consensus for its way of proceeding. As a result, it faced in January a rising crescendo of both citizen and congressional opposition and a deeply divided establishment. It is a premise of U.S. foreign policy that it is difficult to maintain a course of action under these conditions. The Vietnam experience illustrates the difficulty of maintaining a war policy once the elite goes public with its inner doubts about the wisdom of the policy. Thus, Bush's failure to proceed more "constitutionally" might have enabled, even at an advanced stage of the crisis, for the response process to be redirected in desirable ways.

Of course, the perception of these blunders has been superceded by the outcome of the Gulf War and even more by the longer-term effects of the Gulf War in the region and in relation to the United Nations. Any critical mid-term assessment of the approach followed by Washington had to be tempered all along by two major qualifications. First of all, the U.S. response in the early months could have been far worse and more destructive of post-Cold War world order values. The United States did, at first, seek the backing of countries in the region and leading states generally, and it made various sorts of moderating concessions to build as a wide a coalition as possible. As well, the United States pursued its geopolitical goals within the formal framework of the United Nations and thereby contributed greatly, at least temporarily, to raising the prestige of the organization to new heights. Also, up until the outbreak of the war, reliance on coercive diplomacy arguably minimized the prospect of an actual use of force, as well as temporarily exhibited a concerted and serious resistance by the entire organized international community under U.S. leadership to flagrant aggression against a small state that had been formalized by Iraq's annexation of Kuwait, the first occasion on which a member of the United Nations had been purportedly extinguished by such a *diktat*.

Also, it is always easier to criticize than to do. The United States took the initiative in responding to Iraq's aggression in a manner that at the very least stemmed Saddam's ambition to project power beyond Kuwait. Without such a U.S. role it is doubtful in the extreme that the will and capability to respond effectively could have been mobilized. As such, a dangerous and cruel dictator with a large military establishment would have been left "at large" in the Middle East. The United Nations would not under these circumstances have been able to respond in any kind of serious manner, fostering an impression of its impotence. It is arguable that the United States endeavored for some months to achieve an Iraqi withdrawal without provoking a major war. And although the United States clearly could have handled its role in a more responsible fashion, it is also the case that the new international situation was unfamiliar; the regional guidelines and balances characteristic of the Cold War had collapsed, but in a manner that eluded the perception of most experts. Under these conditions it is hardly surprising that ambitious or desperate leaders take unexpected risks and that global actors are taken by surprise. Furthermore, the criticism of the United States should not be construed as an exoneration of Saddam Hussein; he made colossal geopolitical blunders, failing to appreciate Western hypersensitivity to any threat to stable control over Gulf oil and aggravating the overall predicament by provocative acts of brutality in occupied Kuwait. Saddam embarked on adventurism in foreign policy that could easily have ended in his personal demise and produced the devastation of his country. Indeed, the magnitude of Iraq's blunders may help to explain to some degree the initial sense of surprise that greeted the invasion of Kuwait.[10]

Although this chapter was largely written before the onset of war on January 16, this pattern of blunders on both sides eventuated in a war detrimental to all of the actors engaged and productive of suffering for the peoples of the region, including the Israelis. The role of the United Nations in this process is bound to remain controversial for years to come. Its key decision, Security Council Resolution 678, delegated virtually unrestricted discretion to the United States to wage war after the deadline date in a manner of its own choosing. It has become even clearer after the outbreak of hostilities that the collective character of the coalition was largely a fiction. Except for Great Britain, other coalition partners were merely informed of decisions reached outside the UN framework by President Bush and his "war cabinet" of close advisors. Indeed, it is alleged that some coalition-member governments found out about the course of the war and US diplomatic positions only by watching CNN.

The repercussions of the Gulf War have been profound, but anticipating them is almost impossible at this stage. Much will depend on the longer-term reaction in the Arab world and the degree to which the war is followed by a serious regional peace process, engaging the United States and Israel.

CONCLUDING OBSERVATIONS

As stressed, the outcome of the Gulf War has cast a long, if still uncertain, shadow over the near future of U.S. foreign policy toward the Middle East. But, perhaps, even this banality should not be asserted too confidently. The complexity of the region and its underlying turbulence suggests that the future will continue to generate a series of surprises. Just as preoccupation with Left-oriented radicalism was replaced by anxiety about the spread of Islamic fundamentalism, and as the Cold War was followed by the Gulf Crisis, it is quite likely that the interplay of contending tendencies will produce unexpected alignments, challenges, and opportunities that will make the image of reality commonly held by policy makers in 1991 seem almost irrelevant in a matter of a few years, and conceivably within a few months, or possibly within the space of the next several days.

At the same time, the main contention being put forward is that United States foreign policy over the period considered has been characterized by a dual preoccupation: ensuring favorable access to Gulf oil and upholding Israeli security as specified by the Israeli government. Such a preoccupation has led U.S. foreign policy to reinforce stabilizing and conservative tendencies in the region and oppose radical movements, which tend to be anti-Western often and militantly pro-Palestinian. As these latter movements enjoy popular backing, the U.S. role in the region is resented, often bitterly, especially by those political and social forces stressing Arab, Islamic, and national identities. The echo of this resentment is a racist backlash in the West that is intertwined with a thinly disguised hostility to Islam, a dynamic revealed and aggravated by the interaction between the West and the Islamic world that unfolded out of the publication of Salmon Rushdie's *The Satanic Verses* several years ago.

Without passing moral judgment on the priorities of U.S. foreign policy during the period considered, the execution of this policy has been hampered by two factors: the successful orchestration of domestic political pressures in the United States to constrain substantial deviations by politicians in either political party from a rigidly pro-Israeli approach to the question of Palestinian self-determination; and an unfortunate absence of a clear definition of United States interests by a series of presidents so as to create more political space enabling foreign policy to close the gap between Israeli security and Palestinian self-determination. The Palestinian issue has been allowed to smoulder far too long. The United States possessed the leverage and the incentives to move closer to a settlement, but it has failed to do so, complicating its relationship to the Middle East and possibly endangering its role in the region. With the reemergence of Europe as a global actor, possibly in tacit concert with Japan, it would not be surprising if United States economic and political influence itself is not challenged in the course of the next decade, especially if the aftermath of the Gulf War is viewed as a failure.

There is a final element. The United States contributed greatly to the militarization of the region in the 1970s and 1980s through its arms sales policies. Such policies were motivated partly by the belief that providing friendly governments in the region with modern weaponry would help with the task of containing revolutionary nationalism and partly, in the last decade or so, increasingly, to help offset trade deficits through export earnings deriving from arms sales. During the Cold War years such an attitude toward arms in Washington led the Soviet bloc to adopt a similar approach in its relations with the more radical governments in the region. The cumulative effects of this approach has been damaging to the underlying goals of U.S. foreign policy in the region. The competitive dynamics of militarization produced an expensive arms race in the region that diverted resources from social and political undertakings. As Iran's experience demonstrated, mindless militarization can make a government more, not less, vulnerable to internal forces of opposition and more, not less, dependent on outside help and therefore less legitimate from a nationalist point of view. As the encounter with Iraq has shown, yesterday's recipient of arms may become today's enemy, and the higher the level of militarization the more complicated is the challenge of response. As the evident vulnerability of Saudi Arabia during the Gulf Crisis revealed, billions spent on modern weapons systems and virtually unlimited funds for arms acquisitions do not necessarily translate into security against external threats—after all its efforts over the years to buy the latest weaponry, Saudi Arabia still appeared defenseless at the time of the Iraqi move against Kuwait (and, as Israel has demonstrated, the capacity to achieve security is not contingent on the size of territory or population). And, finally, as the experience of Israel suggests, militarization may lead to expansionism rather than to a sense of serenity and diplomatic flexibility. Rethinking the future of arms sales to the Middle East in the new atmosphere of East-West amity is an obvious necessity, although even if attempted at this stage, it may come too late.

In the end, the major opportunity for Washington in the Middle East remains what it has been for more than two decades: to exert pressure on Israel to enable the establishment of Palestinian autonomy in occupied Palestine (and Gaza), combined with the internationalization of Jerusalem, possibly in the form of an experiment in multiple sovereignty reinforced by a structure of international guarantees. Given the outcome of the Gulf War, moving toward a genuine Palestinian solution as quickly as possible is not only the decent thing to do, but it also happens to be the most pragmatic way to mediate between safeguarding a reasonable conception of Israeli security and upholding the wider political and economic interests of the West and of the United States in the region. Of course, the dynamics of Palestinian support for the Iraqi cause in the war has been invoked by Israel as a new justification for blocking the path to eventual reconciliation. Without resolving the core Palestinian grievance, it is only a matter of time before a new conjuncture of regional forces seizes on this explosive issue to provoke yet another round of bloodshed and warfare.

It is true that a dismal realism has swept through the Arab world in response to the decisiveness of the Iraqi defeat. Even the Palestinians seem now inclined to accept what months earlier was unthinkable—negotiations leading to the sort of "autonomy" proposed in the Camp David Treaty for the occupied territories. Whether this involves temporary resignation, a tactic to improve the present living circumstances of the Palestinians, or a willingness by the Palestinians to take half a loaf as the best foreseeable bargain remains obscure.

For the time being, the region seems stunned by the spectacular battlefield results of Desert Storm, but it would be rash to assume that this apparent submission to the American version of "the new world order" is more than a temporary condition.

NOTES

1. Kermit Roosevelt, *Countercoup: The Struggle for the Control of Iran* (New York: McGraw-Hill, 1979); Richard W. Cottam, *Nationalism in Iran*, 2d rev. ed. (Pittsburgh: Pittsburgh University Press, 1979).

2. *Moderate* is used here in a special sense and refers mainly to relations of such states to the West and to radical nationalist challenges, especially that posed by the Palestinians, to the overall regional status quo. These governments over the years consistently have waffled on the Palestinian cause, supporting an anti-Israeli diplomatic position in global arenas and donating funds to the PLO, but withholding the sort of economic and political leverage in their possession. Such governments were not necessarily at all moderate toward their own societies, if moderation is understood either in relation to the observance of human rights or adherence to democratic practices. In this regard, the Gulf states were moderate, but only in this very special geopolitical sense.

3. P.D. 59, even if controversial in its thinly veiled reliance on nuclear weapons to uphold Western interests in the Middle East, did at the very least signal Washington's geopolitical intentions in a manner that

with the failure to signal Baghdad that Western global interests would be seriously challenged by an Iraqi invasion of Kuwait. In this latter instance, a public signal would not have been required, but a diplomatic communication that was delivered with an accompanying seriousness would have achieved the necessary result. Instead, the available evidence indicates that despite advanced warnings of a likely, or at the very least, a possible Iraqi move against Kuwait in August 1990, Washington was too preoccupied, inattentive, or conceivably complicit, to signal its sense of commitment to the integrity of Kuwaiti sovereignty. See also pp. 77–78.

4.   Public attitudes in the United States prior to the Gulf Crisis were shifting in support of a more positive response to Palestinian claims, and there was some indication that the U.S. government was growing impatient with the Shamir government's stubborn refusal to relinquish control over the territories occupied during the 1967 war. It was in these territories that an international consensus was forming during the late 1980s in support of the establishment of a Palestinian state under PLO leadership. Of course, this shift of attitude has been nullified, at least for now, by PLO support for Iraq in the Gulf War.

5.   See Richard N. Haass, *Conflicts Unending: The United States and Regional Disputes* (New Haven, Conn.: Yale University Press, 1990), especially pp. 30–56.

6.   See *New York Times* (September 23, 1990), p. 19.

7.   See note 3 and the text on p. 72. Of course, an alternative line of explanation here is that the United States welcomed the invasion as providing a pretext to shatter the Frankenstein it had helped construct during the prior decade. In that view, Glaspie's role was more calculating than complacent.

8.   The war of nerves was officially, if perhaps unwittingly, endorsed by Security Council Resolution 678 on November 29, 1990, authorizing member states to use "all necessary means" if Iraq failed to comply with UNSC resolutions by January 15, 1991; the vote was 12 in favor, 2 opposed (Yemen, Cuba), and one abstention (China).

9.   *International Herald Tribune* (November 30, 1990).

10.   In discussing the blunders associated with the US handling of the Gulf Crisis only geopolitical or realist dimensions are being considered; criticism along moral and legal lines would be far harsher, of both sides, but for differing reasons.

PART 3

U.S. Policy toward the Arab-Israeli Conflict and the Palestinian Question

CHAPTER 4

U.S. Policy Toward the Arab-Israeli Conflict

Naseer H. Aruri

INTRODUCTION

Since the end of World War II the Middle East was largely viewed by the U.S. establishment through the prism of the Cold War and East-West relations. The U.S. strategic doctrine underlying the entire course of the Cold War was based on a distorted assessment of Soviet intentions. The Carter Doctrine as well as the Reagan codicil remained consistent with the substantive assumptions of the Truman Doctrine, which had set a pattern of direct or indirect intervention in the Middle East to keep the balance overwhelmingly in the U.S. favor.

The policy was built on the proposition that a legitimate world order existed, for which the United States assumes the major responsibility, and that the Soviet Union, together with disaffected Third World nations including Arab nationalist forces, were intent on challenging that order. A succession of U.S. doctrines and strategies, which expressed a resolve to contain that challenge, included the Truman Doctrine (1948), the Eisenhower Doctrine (1957), Kennedy's flexible response, the corollaries of limited nuclear war, counterinsurgency, the Johnson Doctrine (1965), the Nixon-Kissinger Doctrine (1969), and finally the Carter Doctrine (1980) and Reagan's codicil (1981).

America's global posture had thus been characterized by an impressive consistency in terms of policy objectives, since Kennan's

Mr. X article.[1] The pursuit of these objectives in the Middle East region reveals two general phases that entailed a wavering between direct intervention and reliance on surrogates and regional influentials: (1) containment through military alliances, followed by an interlude of attempted containment through nationalism; (2) the politics of informal alliances and regional influentials. The first phase during the period 1948–1960 was dominated by vigorous and consistent attempts to build a network of military alliances that would link NATO with SEATO, thus forming a wall of encirclement around the Sino-Soviet periphery. The potential members of the alliance were Arab and Islamic states but not Israel. The interlude between 1960 and 1966 saw the United States seek a rapprochement with radical Arab nationalism in an attempt to "contain" the Soviet Union. The latter phase during 1967 to the present had its principal emphasis on the promotion of a conservative constellation of forces including Arab and Islamic states as well as Israel. The de facto alliance of regimes, which shared U.S. strategic perspectives, was counted on to hold the region within the U.S. sphere of influence. Crisis in the projected alliance, however, contributed to zigzags in U.S. policy between a direct U.S. presence in the aftermath of the downfall of the Shah's regime in Iran and reliance on surrogates. Actually the second phase of U.S. policy will be divided into subphases showing these policy swings.

Regardless of the means employed to accomplish America's policy objectives, however, these objectives remained constant: to ensure through the threat to use force, either directly or via certain regional influentials, that the status quo remained unalterably and irrevocably in the U.S. favor. And that implied a fairly high level of U.S. economic penetration through control of the area's strategic waterways and its most precious resource, petroleum products (comprising 40 percent of world reserves) and vast market, all of which were defined as a matter of national security. The status quo, which U.S. policy attempted to uphold during the past four decades, was a region free of Soviet intrusion and free of nationalist forces committed to social transformation, Arab unity, and liberation from foreign domination and occupation. Israel, which largely shares that perspective, was seen as an anchor for the existing order, serving to buttress conservative Arab regimes and to threaten the radical nationalists. The policy itself was rationalized as a necessary part of the post-World War II containment of communism.

PHASE I. CONTAINMENT THROUGH MILITARY ALLIANCES

The Truman Doctrine and Its Derivatives

During the 1950s the defense of the vast economic and strategic interests of the United States was predicated on a network of alliances pulling together conservative pro-Western regimes in the region and on the readiness of the U.S. to intervene directly. These interests developed during World War II with Middle East oil serving U.S. strategic supplies in the Far East. The lend-lease supply line to Russia had to be maintained with the aid of U.S. troops in Iran. A network of U.S. air bases in Saudi Arabia, Libya, and Egypt served as a link between North Africa and the Far East.

The growing weakness of the British empire convinced the United States that its wartime presence in the Middle East would have to be extended. Gradually, the United States perceived itself as the replacement for Britain and France and the sustainer of Western interests in a future bipolar world. The emerging view of the Middle East as a strategic prize, which must be denied to the Soviet Union, found an early expression in President Truman's Army Day address in 1946: "The Near and Middle East . . . contains vast natural resources . . . lies across the most convenient route of land, air and water communication . . . might become an arena of intense rivalry among outside powers . . ."[2]

The president underscored U.S. determination to prevail in such rivalry by committing military and economic aid to support Greece and Turkey on March 12, 1947, shortly after Britain declared discontinuation of its own aid program. The Truman Doctrine, which embodied that commitment, ushered an era of U.S. intervention to contain a presumed Soviet threat. The principal instrument of an interventionist policy was the military pact. In his message to Congress on May 24, 1951, President Truman urged the establishment of a Mutual Security Program: "In the free nations of the Middle East lie half of the oil reserve of the world. No part of the world is more directly exposed to Soviet pressure. There is no simple formula for increasing stability and security in the

Middle East. The program I am now proposing is a balanced program for strengthening the security of the Middle East."[3]

The "balanced program" included two stillborn regional military alliances—the Middle East Command, a British idea; and the Middle East Defense Organization—both of which were rejected by Egypt in 1951. Britain and the United States, however, continued to search for a formula that would fulfill the objectives of Western policy in the Middle East. They found it in the ill-fated Baghdad Pact when Iraq broke ranks with the Arab League and announced its decision to conclude an alliance with Turkey, a country that already had a treaty with Pakistan. Iran became the fourth regional member of the Baghdad Pact in 1955. Britain was a full-fledged member of the pact, but the United States refrained from formal membership, participated in some of its military committees, and provided military aid. The pact corresponded with the concept of the Northern Tier put forth by Secretary of State John Foster Dulles in 1953. At that time, he had correctly concluded that the Arab states were "more fearful of Zionism than of the communists."[4] And yet the Baghdad Pact did not bypass the Palestine problem. In fact it polarized the Arab world along the lines of neutralism versus pro-West. That polarization was exacerbated by the Israeli raid on Gaza on February 28, 1955, killing thirty-eight persons and exposing Egypt's military weakness. The arms that President Nasser of Egypt required to bolster his defenses were not to be found in the West, where the price was adherence to Western-sponsored military alliances. In fact, he found them in the communist bloc after his attendance at the conference of Afro-Asian states at Bandung in April 1955. It was reported that Chinese Premier Chou En-Lai had suggested to Nasser that the Soviets might be responsive to a request for arms.[5] The Egyptian-Czech arms deal, which ended Egypt's dependence on the West for weapons, was announced on September 27, 1955.

The Suez War

By the end of 1955 America's allies were visibly upset by the unfolding events in the Middle East. Britain's failure to replace its 1936 treaty with Egypt by a regionwide alliance such as the Middle East Command, which would permit the continuation of the British military presence in the Suez Canal area and other parts of the region, came as a great disappointment. Instead, the new Nasser government had successfully negotiated British evacuation in 1954, thus making the Egyptian Army, rather than British forces, the ultimate repository of power for the first time since the 1882 British occupation. Moreover, the Egyptian army was equipped with Soviet weapons, a fact that symbolized the entry of the Soviet Union as a major power to the area, hitherto considered a Western lake.

The United States' other ally, France, was extremely unhappy with Egypt's material and diplomatic support for the Algerian struggle for independence and held Nasser responsible for the escalation of the resistance in the mid-1950s. Also, Nasser was just the kind of leader that Israel did not want to see emerge on the scene, as the following comment by Prime Minister David Ben-Gurion testifies: "I always feared that a personality might rise such as arose among the Arab rulers in the seventh century or like him (Kemal Atatürk) who arose in Turkey after its defeat in the First World War. He raised their spirits, changed their character, and turned them into a fighting nation. There was and still is a danger that Nasser is this man."[6]

As the combined interests of Britain, France, and Israel converged on the need to deal Nasser a crushing blow, the United States was eager to avoid conflict. Given the eminent decline of Anglo-French influence in the region, the United States was ready to fill a power "vacuum." It did not matter that the Eisenhower administration was in the midst of an election campaign; U.S. national interests required a firm stand against aggression. Less than two weeks before the Suez invasion, Dulles articulated these interests at a high-level policy meeting in candid terms:

> We are in the present jam because the past administration had always dealt with the Middle East from a political standpoint and had tried to meet the wishes of the Zionists in this country. That had created a basic antagonism with the Arabs. That was what the Russians were capitalizing on. It is of the utmost importance for the welfare of the United States that we get away from a political basis and try to develop a national non-partisan policy. Otherwise, we may be apt to lose the whole area and possibly Africa. This would be a major disaster for Western Europe as well as the United States.[7]

President Eisenhower dispatched two letters on October 27 and 29, 1956, to Ben-Gurion, warning that a hostile initiative by Israel could endanger the emerging close relationship between the two countries.[8] And when the invasion took place on October 29, the United States issued an equivocal condemnation and worked through the United Nations to secure withdrawal of all foreign forces. President Eisenhower made it clear in a national address where the United States stood: "The actions taken can scarcely be reconciled with the principles and purposes of the United Nations to which we have all subscribed . . . there can be no peace without law. And there can be no law if we were to invoke one code of international conduct for those who oppose us and another for our friends."[9] Such pursuit of balance had also been seen earlier when the United States temporarily suspended aid to Israel on September 18, 1953, for refusing to comply with a U.N. request to suspend work on its hydroelectric project in the demilitarized zone near the Syrian border.[10] It also condemned the Israeli raid on the village of Qibya in the West Bank the following month and decreased aid in 1954.

The Suez war would have been a catalyst for the improvement of Arab relations with the United States, which in turn was conscious of Egypt's importance for the realization of its policy objectives. Egypt was pivotal for U.S. efforts to cultivate close relationships with Saudi Arabia in order to ensure steady oil supplies to Europe and to facilitate U.S. economic penetration in the Middle East. Hence, the United States was reluctant to accept Israeli overtures for a formal alliance and a guarantee of security, particularly as Israel deliberately refrained from defining its boundaries. Dulles was reported as telling Israel's ambassador Abba Eban that America could not "guarantee temporary armistice lines."[11] He and Eisenhower were extremely fearful of alienating the Arab world and driving it toward the Soviet Union. But the withdrawal of U.S. funds, promised earlier for the Aswan Dam project, as well as the enunciation of the Eisenhower Doctrine derailed the attempted rapprochement.

The Eisenhower Doctrine

The Eisenhower Doctrine was proclaimed by the president before a joint session of Congress on January 5, 1957, to which he appealed for discretionary power to spend up to $200 million in aid for the region. He sought and obtained authorization to employ U.S. military force against "overt armed aggression from any nation controlled by international communism."[12] It was made rather clear that Egypt, as the principal advocate of revolutionary Arab nationalism and Arab unity and the spoiler of America's alliance policy, was the principal target of the doctrine. Like the Baghdad Pact, the Eisenhower Doctrine served to polarize the region, drawing the lines sharply between conservative pro-Western regimes (Saudi Arabia, Jordan, Lebanon, Iraq) and nonaligned nationalists (Egypt, Syria, Yemen). Moreover, it ensured that the Middle East's regional and local conflicts were now integrally tied to the Cold War. And just as the Baghdad Pact had provoked Syria to sign a military alliance with Egypt and seek Soviet arms, the Eisenhower Doctrine paved the way for a civil war in Lebanon, a military coup in Iraq in 1958, and led to the first U.S. military intervention in the area. American pronouncements that Syria's commander-in-chief, Afif Bizri was a "card-carrying communist" encouraged Turkey to place troops along Syria's border and caused Egypt and the Soviet Union to pledge aid to Syria against imperialism. When, on August 13, 1957, the Syrian government accused three diplomats of the U.S. embassy in Damascus of conspiring to overthrow the government, Washington responded by expelling the Syrian ambassador. Loy Henderson, Undersecretary of State was then dispatched to a Baghdad Pact meeting in Ankara, where he later announced the applicability of the Eisenhower Doctrine to Syria: "We have analyzed the situation and it is our belief that the present state of affairs in Syria tends toward gradually handing Syria over to Russia in the name of Arab patriotism, progress and neutrality."[13] He expressed anxiety about Syria becoming "a victim of international communism and, as such, become a communist base to further threaten the independence and integrity of the region."[14]

The Eisenhower Doctrine was also applied in Jordan during the spring of 1957, when the country's first government to emerge from a free parliamentary election was abruptly dismissed by King Hussein. The ensuing street demonstrations protesting the dismissal were declared by the monarch as the work of international communism aimed to overthrow him. Secretary Dulles naturally agreed: "We have great confidence and regard for King Hussein because we really believe that he is striving to maintain the independence of his country in the face of very great difficulties. . . . It is our desire to hold up the hand of King Hussein in these matters to the extent that he thinks that we can be helpful."[15] A few days later the king was awarded $10 million, but he denied that it was part of the $200 million allotted to the Eisenhower Doctrine. Incidentally King Saud had also received $50 million three months earlier as payment for renewal of the lease of Dahran base for five years.

Lebanon was the third Arab country in which the Eisenhower Doctrine was involved. President Camille Chamoun, who was seeking an unprecedented second term in 1958 and thus facing internal opposition, claimed that his opponents were armed and financed by Syria, which was already labeled as communist-influenced, and called for U.S. intervention in accordance with the doctrine. The United States obliged by sending the marines in July 1958.

The Origins of the U.S.-Israeli Special Relationship

The Eisenhower Doctrine, which was introduced as House Joint Resolution 117, became law on March 9, 1957. It was described by Melvin Gurtov as having marked "a watershed in U.S. policy towards the Middle East because it specified the area as a vital national interest."[16] By contrast, "the Truman Administration had treated the area as though it were vital." From that point on, threats to the vital national interests would be construed so broadly that they would include actions by nationalist forces challenging conservative regimes, Israeli transgression, or U.S. hegemony. That was probably the beginning of the evolution of the U.S.-Israeli special relationship, which reached the stage of maturity in the aftermath of the June 1967 War and developed into a strategic alliance during Reagan's presidency.

America's attempts to cement closer relations with Nasser's government were also crippled by the formation of Israeli terrorist cells in Egypt, which bombed U.S. installations in Egypt to make them look like the work of Egyptian nationalists. These attempts also fell victim to the Eisenhower administration's chronic inability to come to terms with Arab nationalism and nonalignment. Accordingly, the Arab-Israeli conflict would be handled only in the context of the Cold War. An outright alliance with Israel would drive the entire Arab world toward the Soviet Union; on the other hand, evenhandedness invited domestic pressure from Zionists and their allies and yet failed to persuade Egypt and her allies to give up their independent foreign policy course, in accordance with Washington's wishes. Dulles's monumental failure was his inability to understand Nasser's zest for real independence after seventy years of foreign domination. Cheryl Rubenberg summed it up this way:

> In the end, Eisenhower's and Dulles's frustrations with Nasser and their desire to bring an end to his tenure became an integral aspect of American Middle East policy and contributed considerably to the decision to build up Israel—on the one hand as a means of unseating Nasser, and on the other, as an outpost of American power that would protect all the American interests in the Arab World that Washington had been unable to protect through direct relationships with the Arab States themselves.[17]

Noam Chomsky quotes a declassified National Security Council memorandum of 1958 noting that a "logical corollary" of opposition to radical Arab nationalism "would be to support Israel as the only strong pro-West power left in the Near East."[18] Frail attempts were made during the late 1950s and early 1960s by the Eisenhower and Kennedy administrations to effect a rapprochement with Arab nationalism. The erosion of conservative power in the region, in the aftermath of the Iraqi coup of 1958 and the U.S.-British interventions to shore up unpopular regimes in Lebanon and Jordan was the principal motivation for a new policy that would utilize the ascendant Arab nationalism in the containment of communism. To that end, President Eisenhower himself spoke of "bold constructive action" that he would be prepared to take and said that he has been "nagging our boys to get ourselves a long-range plan in the Middle East."[19] The late Malcolm Kerr wrote in a seminal article that realizing the pitfalls of the Eisenhower Doctrine and Nasser's popularity throughout the Arab world, the State Department decided that a strong Egypt was perhaps an important asset.[20] To that end, President Eisenhower put forward a proposal for respecting Arab neutrality in a major address to the UN General Assembly on August 13, 1958. The domestic environment, however, proved unreceptive to a major reorientation affecting traditional allies and friends (Britain, France, and Israel) and perceived enemies like Egypt and Syria. A major opportunity for an international settlement of the Middle East crisis was therefore missed, and the Israeli invasion of Arab land in 1956 was to be repeated by new generations in 1967, 1978, and 1982. But unlike 1956, the invasions of 1967 and 1982 were supported by the United States.

PHASE II. CONTAINMENT THROUGH REGIONAL INFLUENTIALS

Israel and the Nixon Doctrine

By the end of Eisenhower's presidency, American policy, which encouraged formal alliances to contain Soviet influence and Arab nationalism, had suffered a serious failure. The region was polarized between conservative pro-Western monarchies and "radical" nonaligned military republics. The decade of the 1950s was marked by an erosion of monarchical power and a corresponding ascendancy of nationalism. Western interventions in Egypt, Lebanon, and Jordan were not sufficient to stem the tide of revolutionary nationalism. That tide, which ushered successful uprisings in Iraq and Yemen in 1958 and 1962 and generated challenges to the political order in Jordan and Lebanon in 1957 and 1958, was seen as a viable threat to American strategic and economic interests. It was postulated that the defeat of the United Arab Republic (Egypt and Syria) would remove the potential threat to the stability of the conservative system and thus would assure the continued exploitation of the region's resources by American business. This conclusion was reached during Johnson's presidency by prominent members of Congress and the military. A tendency to identify U.S. security interests with a militarily strong Israel was beginning to take hold in Pentagon circles in the 1960s. A congressional subcommittee on Middle East peace concluded in April 1967 that the United Arab Republic constituted the principal obstacle to peace, thus legitimizing the future offensive that came to be known as the Six Day War. Israel, which prior to 1967 was receiving the highest per capita aid from the United States of any country—a fact that remains true until today, had indeed anticipated a proxy role for itself prior to the 1967 war and prior to the Nixon Doctrine. A spokesman for the Israeli Foreign Office expressed that readiness on June 11, 1966: "The United States has come to the conclusion that it can no longer respond to every incident around the world, that it must rely on a local power, the deterrent of a friendly power as a first line to stave off America's direct involvement. Israel feels that it fits this definition."[21]

Indeed, Israel had emerged as the principal U.S. surrogate, entrusted with keeping the status quo in the West's favor. The defeat of Egypt and Syria in June 1967 and the subsequent rise to prominence in inter-Arab affairs of such conservative Arab states as Saudi Arabia was cited as a vindication of this assumption. Although the offensive against Egypt and its brand of Arab socialism was not to involve the deployment of American troops, the 1967 War brought about consequences desirable not only to Israel, but to the United States as well; namely, the defeat of Nasserism as a potent force in Middle Eastern politics. This fact was emphasized by the former prime minister of Israel, Levi Eshkol, in 1968: "The value of Israel to the West in this part of the world will, I predict, be out of all proportion to its size. We will be a real bridge between the three continents and the free world will be very thankful not only if we survive, but if we continue to thrive in secure and guaranteed frontiers."[22] The June War, in which the American "hose and water" were placed in the hands of Israeli "fire fighters," anticipated the Nixon-Kissinger Doctrine. The Nixon-Kissinger Doctrine was premised on the ability and willingness of certain countries in key regions of the world to play the role of police under the direction of the United States. The doctrine was articulated in several presidential speeches and policy statements beginning with the Guam Speech of November 3, 1969, and the State of the Union Message of 1970.[23] The new guiding principle postulated that unilateral intervention was expensive at home and unpopular abroad. Thus, Israel, guaranteed a "margin of technical superiority"[24] over its Arab neighbors, was thrust into a position of dominance enabling it to bring about conditions suitable to United States as well as Israeli interests. Nixon's "State of the World Message" explicated this concept of partnership thus: "Others now have the ability and responsibility to deal with local disputes which once may have required our intervention." The *New York Times* reported that the Nixon administration remained "firmly committed to Israel's security and to her military superiority in the Middle East, for only *Israel's strength can deter attack and prevent a call for direct American intervention*"[25] (emphasis mine).

The first test of this partnership concept came in 1970, when during the confrontation between the Palestinian nationalist movement and the Jordanian army, the United States alerted airborne units from its Sixth Fleet, which began to steam toward the eastern Mediterranean, and Israel expressed readiness for intervention in the event of a Palestinian triumph over Hussein. Since the battle of al-Karameh (March 1968), which galvanized Palestinian and Arab masses into action, the guerilla movement was beginning to be viewed as a serious challenge not only to Israel but to America's ambitions in the area as well as to the conservative Arab states. The Rogers plan of December 1969, which was based on UN Resolution 242, was, in fact, intended to effect a Jordanian settlement that would bypass the Palestinian resistance. It was followed by a determined Jordanian attempt to suppress the Palestinians, who had already begun to rival Hussein for sovereignty in Jordan. The unfolding of events in Jordan in the autumn of 1970 suggested a close coordination of policies between Jordan, the United States, and Israel, whose interests converged on the need to contain the Palestinian national movement. For the next twenty years, succeeding U.S. governments attempted to reduce the Palestinian movement to manageable proportions and render it peripheral to any Middle East settlement.

The October 1973 Arab-Israeli War and the ensuing oil embargo enabled U.S. secretary of state Henry Kissinger to embark on a post-Vietnam war strategy in the Middle East. Gradually, the big four talks on the Middle East, which began shortly after the 1967 War, had dwindled to talks between the two superpowers. By the end of the October 1973 War, the United States was beginning to act as if there was only one superpower in the Middle East. Kissinger's shuttle diplomacy as well as the American decision to ensure the failure of the Geneva conference at the end of 1973 marked the start of a new era in Middle East diplomacy. The phrase *peace process* became synonymous with U.S. diplomatic efforts conducted in a solo fashion. One of the salient features of U.S. diplomacy was its consistent opposition to the internationalization of the Palestine question and the Arab-Israeli conflict. The United States was to emerge as chief arbiter despite a steadily growing special relationship with Israel, which compromised its credibility as mediator.

Kissinger's post-October 1973 mediation revealed three objectives. The first was to enhance an already eroding eclipse of Soviet influence in the region. The departure of some 20,000 Soviet personnel from Egypt, a standing U.S. objective, as well as Sadat's de-Nasserization program began the process of reorienting Egypt away from nonalignment toward the United States.

The second objective was to obtain a political settlement capable of creating a transformation of the very nature of the Arab-Israeli conflict; a settlement that would remove the conflict from its ideological context and transform it into an ordinary territorial conflict. Such approach was inherently detrimental to the Palestinians and Arab nationalists, who viewed the struggle as one against settler colonialism and imperialist penetration. Kissinger devised a settlement that would highlight the global concerns of American policy makers and address the economic and strategic imperatives of American foreign policy; that is, the steady flow of oil to the West, the security of American investments and trade with the Arab world, and the stability of the region.

The third objective was to provide Egypt with such a vested interest in stability (through economic aid and territorial adjustments) to ensure its neutralization and effective removal from the Arab front against Israel. The aim was to give the United States the necessary leverage needed to pressure Syria and the PLO into making significant concessions to Israel.

The Sinai accord negotiated by Egypt and Israel under U.S. auspices in 1975 was calculated to achieve that end. It granted Israel time to consolidate the occupation and build up its offensive capability vis-à-vis the Arab states on the eastern front. Moreover, it granted Israel, for the first time, what amounted to an American security guarantee. According to the September 1975 "U.S.-Israel Memorandum of Agreement," the United States was to hold "consultations" with Israel in case a third party (meaning the Soviet Union) intervened militarily. Furthermore, the United States agreed to be "fully responsive . . . on an on-going and long-term basis" to Israel's military requirements. Translated into figures, the *New York Times* (October 31, 1975) put that commitment at $2.24 billion annually, the bulk of which was used to acquire the latest equipment in the American arsenal, including the 450-mile Lance Pershing missile, the F-15 and F-16A fighters, and the laser-guided "smart bombs." The introduction of this massive equipment into the Middle East signified a special brand of Vietnamization. The United States began to restrict its role to supplying the military muscle that enabled surrogates or regional influentials to maintain the balance in her favor.

The United States furthermore committed itself in the "U.S.-Israel Memorandum of Agreement" to continue to refuse to recognize or negotiate with the PLO until the latter recognized Israel's right to exist and agreed to abide by UN Security Council Resolution 242. No such demands were made on Israel, which still refuses to recognize the PLO and the peoplehood of the Palestinians. Israel of course contests the operative paragraph of Resolution 242, which calls for Israeli withdrawal from occupied Arab territories. The practical implication of Kissinger's 1975 memorandum, which decreed a diplomatic blockade against the PLO, was thus twofold: first, the final settlement of the Palestine question would not be based on any form of Palestinian sovereignty in the West Bank and Gaza; second, Israel, as the principal surrogate and cornerstone of U.S. policy in the region, would be guaranteed access to military technology and the latest equipment in the U.S. arsenal. The implied marginalization of Palestinian national rights, inherent in the Sinai Accord, was to be confirmed and developed further in later American plans.

The Carter Doctrine and the Regional Influentials

By the end of the Ford administration, the list of regional influentials was headed by Israel and Iran. The former acquired a global mission in addition to the regional role already discussed. The global role included arming and training U.S. clients in Central and South America and maintaining a special relationship with South Africa.[26] The Shah's regime in Iran, which was making a serious bid for the role of police of the Gulf, suppressed a leftist insurgency in Dhofar against pro-Western Oman.

Carter's contribution to the unfolding strategy was the incorporation of Egypt into the constellation of regional powers that would relieve the burden of U.S. intervention. The Camp David formula, which created a separate peace with Israel, would free

Egypt to join the ranks of the regional influentials and make its contribution to regional stability.

That strategy, however, was dealt a severe blow when the new recruits were upset by internal unrest. The Shah's regime was over-thrown by an Islamic revolution in 1979, and two years later Sadat was assassinated by Islamic activists. Not only was Iran a principal anchor and linchpin of American interests in the Gulf; it was also a test case for the Nixon Doctrine. Iran was to determine whether U.S.-trained forces would be effective in arresting social revolution in a crucial region of the Third World. The Islamic Revolution created an irreparable breech in the informal security arrange-ments of Henry Kissinger. George Ball put it succinctly thus: "If the debacle of Iran proves anything, it is that we cannot assure—as the Nixon Doctrine assumed—the security of a strategic region by stuffing a backward state with massive quantities of arms."[27] In-stead of relying on surrogates, Ball continued: "We should sub-stantially beef up our presence in the Indian Ocean, assist the Saudis with surveillance [hence, the AWACS two years later] and give constant reminders of our improving ability to deliver quickly, even from American bases."[28] In the aftermath of the Iranian Rev-olution, a strategic adaptation combined direct intervention with reliance on partners. A rapid deployment force (RDF), conceived by presidential advisor Zbigniew Brzezinski in 1977, would enable the United States to become the principal guarantor of its enor-mous economic and strategic interests. Arrangements for access to strategic bases were made by the Carter administration with Egypt (Ras Banas and Cairo West), Somalia (Berbera), Kenya (Mom-basa), Oman (El-Messira and Seeb), and Israel. Joint U.S. military exercises were undertaken with Egypt, Oman, and Somalia. Oper-ation "Bright Star," conducted in November 1981, was a test of RDF ability to defend American interests in coordination with local forces.

Carter's "security framework" for Southwest Asia (as U.S. pol-icy makers began to refer to the region) was given concrete mean-ing by the enunciation of the Carter Doctrine on January 23, 1980: "Let our position be absolutely clear: Any attempt by any outside force to gain control of the Persian Gulf region will be regarded as an assault on the vital interests of the United States of America, and such an assault will be repelled by any means necessary, including *military force*"[29] (emphasis mine). This new commitment was to receive added impetus with Reagan's pledge to defend Saudi Arabia against *internal* threats as well: "We will not permit Saudi Arabia to be an Iran. . . . No way we will stand by and see it taken over."[30] That became known as the Reagan codicil, which together with the Carter Doctrine was to mark yet a new approach to the Arab-Israeli conflict.

President Carter and the Arab-Israeli Conflict

President Carter's approach to the Arab-Israeli conflict reflected his overall strategy for the Middle East. The region's "influentials" would have to be accommodated in consonance with the extent of their contribution to America's security arrangements. Three phases in the evolution of Carter's policy may be discerned: first, Carter the candidate; second, Carter, the statesman in pursuit of a Geneva settlement; and third, Carter, the broker of a separate peace, which neutralized Egypt, paved the way for the Israeli invasion of Lebanon, and marginalized the Palestinians.

Carter, the Candidate   Carter was explicit during the campaign on what he expected the Arabs and Israelis to do for the sake of peace. He called on the Arabs to take "tangible and concrete actions, including first of all the recognition of Israel; second, diplomatic relations with Israel; third, a peace treaty with Israel; fourth, open frontiers by Israel's neighbors; last, an end to embargo and official hostile propaganda against the State of Israel." His position on the Palestinians was consistent with those of the Nixon and Ford administrations: "I would not recognize the Palestinians as a political entity; nor their leaders until after those leaders had first recognized Israel's right to exist . . . ultimately, I believe that we will see the legitimate interests of the Palestinians met. My preference would be that, if they are granted territory by Israel, that it be on the West Bank of the Jordan, administered by the nation of Jordan."[31] But in reply to a question on the matter put to him by the *Jewish Telegraphic Agency,* Carter expressed a position that paralleled that of Israel: "The PLO is not the group to deal with in solving the Palestinian problem. The PLO is an alliance of guerilla organizations, not a government in exile. The PLO is unrepresentative of the Palestinian problem. The PLO should not participate as an equal partner in any resumed Geneva's peace conference because the PLO's stated aims are diametrically opposed to any peace which envisions the continued existence of Israel."[32]

As for Carter's expectations from Israel, he found it unnecessary to go beyond what the Israeli government was willing to concede: "Israel must withdraw from some of the territories occupied. I would not try to force the Israelis to relinquish control of the Golan Heights or Old Jerusalem." He called for a general settlement, perhaps in Geneva, to be reached by direct negotiations between the parties. He absolved Israel of any wrongdoing by saying that such settlement would not be based on the "faulty" premise that Israel caused the Palestine problem.[33] He told a group of Jewish leaders that his administration would give Israel "undeviating, unequivocal" support asserting that "this is not just a political statement. As a Christian myself, I think that the fulfillment of Israel, the coming of that nation, is a fulfillment of Biblical prophecy."[34]

Carter, the Statesman   The second phase in the evolution of Carter's foreign policy extends from the time Carter assumed office in January 1977, when emphasis was placed on a Geneva-style comprehensive settlement based on an Israeli withdrawal on all fronts and a recognition of the right of Palestinians to a homeland, until November 1977, when Anwar Sadat derailed that process with his unprecedented journey to Israel.

The premises of the Carter administration policy in the Middle East were discussed rather candidly in an annual review presented by Assistant Secretary of State for South Asian and Middle Eastern Affairs Harold Saunders to the Subcommittee on Europe and the Middle East of the House International Relations Committee on June 12, 1978. Working with so-called moderate Arab nations was considered essential for achieving a political settlement, assuring a secure and prosperous Israel and securing the economic well-being of the United States as well as the capitalist West. The new relationship was described euphemistically as one of interdependence, and it by no means implied a tilt toward the Arabs or a reduction of the U.S. commitment to Israel. The Saunders review states: "What kind of U.S. relationship with the Middle East can we see five or 10 years from now? On many occasions the real underlying question is: Are we not reducing our support for Israel in favor of the Arab nations? The answer to the latter question is unequivocally no."[35] Containment of social revolution via Arab surrogates was also made very clear:

> Radical forces could again take advantage of conditions that would follow failure of the peace negotiations—Moderate Arab leaders have turned to the United States for cooperation in achieving both peace and development. Their success will limit the role of radical forces. Their degree of success will, in turn, in large part determine whether Israel faces the future surrounded by radical and hostile states or by nations which are committed to peace and orderly progress.[36]

The unfolding strategy would, therefore, try to strike a balance between the Arabs' peace imperative and Israel's security imperative. Israel would have to be taught the virtues of enlightened self-interest; the Arabs would have to be assisted in shaping a consensus linking Jordan to a tamed PLO, which would have to effectively qualify its insistence on being the sole legitimate representative of the Palestinian people. President Carter said in his first news conference following the inauguration: "If the Palestinians should be invited to the meeting [at Geneva] as agreed by the other participating nations, along with us, it would probably be as part of one of the Arab delegations."[37] President Sadat, who had already expressed a desire for a formal link between a "Palestinian state" and Jordan, reiterated the same in the presence of Secretary of State Cyrus Vance in Cairo on February 17, 1977, adding that this should be an "official and declared link"; that is, a confederation to be announced *before* a Geneva conference was convened.[38] Most Arab leaders conveyed the view that the PLO ought to receive an invitation as a full participant in the Middle East conference, but they were willing, at the same time, to exercise pressure on the PLO to accept any "procedural rule—from becoming part of a single Arab delegation to staying from the conference altogether letting the other Arabs negotiate for them."[39] The implication of that stand was not lost on Israel's foreign minister Yigal Allon, who commented: "this is the first nail in the coffin of the Rabat Conference."[40]

During the spring of 1977, President Carter felt impelled to provide the Arab leaders with a facesaving device regarding the Palestine question. Yet he had to respond to internal and party pressures with regard to Israel and its own definition of peace. His Clinton, Massachusetts, speech on March 16, 1977, revealed this dilemma and hinted at the way out: he would accept Israel's framework of a settlement, providing Israel accepts his obligation to provide that facesaving device to Arab leaders.[41]

Carter's dilemma, however, was intensified when the Likud bloc assumed power in Israel, for the first time, in the summer of 1977. The Revisionist prime minister, Menachem Begin, was now publicly implying that the West Bank and Gaza were not occupied territories. *Judea and Samaria* became their new name and the *Arabs of Eretz Israel* his new designation of the Palestinians living there. Carter's plan was now in serious jeopardy. Initially, the president decided to rise up to the challenge. When asked if he would find some means of pressure or persuasion should the Israeli position at Geneva be quite different from his own, Carter replied: "I would try to marshal the support of the leader, first of all. Secondly, the opinion of his people back home, the constituencies that might exist in our own country that would have influence around the world, opinion that exists in the European community, and in the Arab nations as well."[42]

President Carter's "offensive" against Menachem Begin was climaxed in the Joint U.S.-USSR Statement on the Middle East on October 1, 1977, in which the United States agreed to associate the USSR with the settlement in Geneva and for the first time used the phrase Palestinian *legitimate rights*.[43] The joint declaration was met with intense opposition by Israel and her constituencies in Congress and the American Jewish community, and it was effectively abandoned by the Carter administration. The Dayan-Carter Working Paper of October 5 rendered it ineffectual: "Acceptance of the Joint U.S.-U.S.S.R. Statement of October 1, 1977 by the parties is not a prerequisite for the reconvening and the conduct of the Geneva conference."[44] Meanwhile Israeli Foreign Minister Moshe Dayan released a draft of the secret working paper to the Knesset, which reveals that Carter and Vance had not only retreated from their commitment to assure a form of PLO representation at Geneva, but in fact accepted Begin's definition of a settlement regarding the West Bank and Gaza.[45]

The impasse that ensued following Carter's ill-fated "offensive" was interrupted by Anwar Sadat's sudden visit to Israel on

November 19, 1977. His interest and that of Begin converged on the need to keep the Soviet Union out of Middle East diplomacy. Thus the focus of attention had shifted away from Geneva to the Middle East.

Carter and Camp David   The third phase of Carter's Middle East policy began with Sadat's Jerusalem visit and ended with the Camp David Accord on September 17, 1978. Zbigniew Brzezinski's famous "bye-bye PLO" underscored the administration's abandonment of behind the scenes efforts to make the PLO a "qualified" negotiating partner.

Sadat's trip ushered a new era in the diplomatic history of the modern Middle East, in which the guidelines of a settlement were being formulated mainly by Israel. Carter and Sadat lost whatever initiatives they may have entertained in the past. The Begin Plan, unveiled in December 1977, was advanced as Israel's "contribution to peace," in response to the Sadat trip. It envisaged the formation of an administrative council in the West Bank and Gaza with jurisdiction over local education, religious affairs, commerce, agriculture, tourism, health, and policing. Israeli authorities were to remain in charge of "security," foreign, and economic affairs. A committee of representatives of Jordan, Israel, and the Administrative Council was given authority to determine the legality of all acts by the administrative council, while Israeli settlements were to continue unabated. The plan itself constituted a reaffirmation of Begin's sovereign claims in the West Bank and Gaza. As such, it was at variance with the stated policies of both the United States and Egypt. Yet both Carter and Sadat finally accepted Begin's concept of autonomy as a framework for Camp David; they differed with him on the extent of self-government that it implied. Whereas Begin subscribed to limited autonomy, emphasizing that it was autonomy for the people but not the land, Carter and Sadat favored a "full autonomy." A deliberate ambiguity, however, saved the three leaders and facilitated the agreement, which was hailed in the United States as America's most impressive achievement in the Middle East. But Carter's retreat before Israel and her domestic constituencies, coupled with Palestinian resolve to guard their national rights, restricted that achievement to a separate and "cold peace" between Egypt and Israel.

From Special Relationship to Strategic Alliance: The Reagan Period

Strategic Consensus versus Special Relationship While the Reagan administration adhered to the Carter approach of combining direct intervention with the utilization of regional surrogates, its major efforts were directed toward building what former secretary of state Alexander Haig called a "consensus of strategic concerns."[46] The emphasis was not on formal alliances, but on strategic cooperation: with Israel, Egypt, Saudi Arabia and other conservative Arab and Islamic countries in the Middle East. According to General Haig, the security of Saudi Arabia was intertwined with that of Israel: "We are wholeheartedly and permanently committed to the security of Israel. Without a strong Israel, our hope to improve the prospects for peace and security in the region cannot be fulfilled. A secure Saudi Arabia and a strong U.S.-Saudi relationship are central to these same tasks."[47]

Accordingly, the central assumption of the strategic consensus was the need to subordinate the Arab-Israeli conflict and its requirement of comprehensive settlement to the Soviet "threat" and the requirement of "comprehensive security." The Palestine question, which came to be regarded by the Reagan administration as secondary, would cease to enjoy its usual priority as the region's principal concern. Its divisive effect on the regional powers would thus be contained, and the collective energies would be marshalled to meet the challenges to stability.

In practice, however, the project was hampered by the U.S. special relationship with Israel, which proved to be incompatible with strategic consensus. The United States had simply failed to offer the Arabs and Israel a viable formula for cooperation. The issues that divided them at the time included the U.S. proposed sale of AWACS to Saudi Arabia, the Israeli raid on Iraq's nuclear research facility, the Golan annexation, the proposed Jordanian strike force, the Israeli intervention in Lebanon, and the Palestine question.

The attempt to reconcile the two endeavors foundered when the Reagan administration failed to satisfy the minimalist position of the Arab component of the strategic consensus. Neither the Fahd Plan nor the Fez Plan[48] evoked even a slight measure of enthusiasm from Washington, despite strong implications of Arab willingness to recognize Israel as part of a peaceful settlement. Even the Reagan plan of September 1, 1982,[49] was allowed to drift into oblivion after it was promptly and categorically rejected by Israel. The administration had also failed to make a determination on whether the Israeli use of American-supplied aircraft in the bombing of the Iraqi nuclear facility had violated the amended Arms Control Act of 1976. That act restricts the use of American-supplied arms to acts of "self-defense" and requires the president to report any violations to Congress. More blatant was the Israeli invasion of Lebanon in the summer of 1982, and U.S. complicity in that invasion,[50] as well as its association with Israel's war aims: the quest for a new political map of Lebanon, and the attempt to obliterate Palestinian nationalism and reduce Syria to manageable proportions. President Reagan spoke of an "opportunity" that the war of 1982 had afforded. He placed the Israeli "achievements" within the context of America's broader goal of promoting stability in the region. But the prospects for building a strategic consensus, which required evenhandedness, were hardly improved by a virtual U.S. partnership in an Israeli war followed by the attempted imposition of humiliating terms as the price of Israeli withdrawal.

The strategic consensus had also suffered from the inability of the Reagan administration to obtain congressional approval of money and arms for Jordan and Israeli cooperation in the creation of a climate for negotiations. The endeavor to set up a Jordanian logistics force (JLF) as a rapid deployment force for the Gulf was seen by Reagan as an assured instrument for keeping the Straits of Hormuz "open." It was also intended to operationalize the Reagan codicil to the Carter Doctrine by facilitating intervention in internal crises in the Gulf states. But despite a clear intent to deny Jordan an autonomous decision over its use and despite the administration's conveyance of its "determination to see that Israel's qualitative technological edge is maintained,"[51] congressional opposition remained unabated. It was rather ironic that the Reagan administration had planned to ask Israeli defense minister Moshe Arens to intercede with congressional opponents of the Jordanian force.[52] But Israel remained publicly opposed to one of Reagan's principal ingredients of strategic consensus, and her opposition to the Jordan missile deal dealt that project a deadly blow. Reacting to all this, King Hussein made a rare suspension of his diplomatic poise. His *New York Times* interview of March 16, 1984, was the harshest public blast at U.S. policy by any Jordanian official. It seemed as though, Jordan had finally declared independence in foreign affairs. The king said that "Israel is on our land . . . by virtue of American military assistance and economic aid." He continued: "It is there by virtue of American moral and political support to the point where the United States is succumbing to Israeli dictates. . . . This being the case, there is no way by which anyone should imagine it would be possible for Arabs to sit and talk with Israel as long as things are as they are. . . . You obviously have made your choice, and your choice is Israel. Therefore there is no hope of achieving anything."[53] The stipulation that arms shipment be linked to Jordanian acceptance of Camp David, among other conditions, led the king to raise a concern about the "U.S. and its double standard everywhere," and to accuse the United States of having "succumbed to Israeli dictates," as well as to those of "AIPAC and Zionism." On January 5, 1985, the Jordanian Army commander Lt. General Zayd Ibn Shaker announced that Jordan had purchased a Soviet air defense system. The cancellation of the Stinger missile deal in March 1984 thus resulted in arms purchases by two pro-Western Arab countries (Jordan and Kuwait) from the Soviet Union.

Such were the constraints on the administration's ability to ease Jordan's "security problem," deemed essential to the success of the strategic consensus. As for the second requirement, helping Jordan solve its "negotiating problem," it fell victim to Israel's rejection of the Reagan plan and refused to consider putting a freeze on the building of new settlements in the West Bank. The most that the administration was about and willing to try in that regard was "only a promise to urge Israel to freeze further settlements . . . and the argument that once King Hussein comes to the table, pressures will develop in Israel for compromise."[54] Neither Jordan's "security problem" nor her "negotiating problem" was within Washington's capabilities. The "strategic consensus," in fact, suffered from a lack of consensus.

From Special Relationship to Strategic Alliance: The Crisis of Peace   Although Haig's endeavor to forge a consensus among unwilling parties failed, it nevertheless served as a catalyst for the pursuit of "comprehensive security," that is, containment of oppositional forces and ambitious regional leaders, through Israel. No longer would Israel be seen as defending only its own security, even within the pre-1967 border, but the "security" of its major ally as well. Her expanded role required an upgrading of the special relationship and its ingredients including aid, trade, weapons, and diplomatic support. Consequently, Haig's green light for the 1982 Israeli invasion of Lebanon was not surprising.

The evolving strategic alliance, which thwarted the twin objectives of the U.S. policy (comprehensive security and comprehensive peace), was particularly enhanced by President Reagan's anticommunist inclinations and his perception of Israel as a "unique strategic asset." To him, Israel was worthy of U.S. support not because of "altruism on our part," but because of its "combat ready and combat experienced military," which obviate the need for direct U.S. intervention.[55] In fact, after the fall of the Shah, Reagan saw Israel as "perhaps the only strategic asset in the area that the U.S. can really rely on."[56] He concluded an agreement of strategic cooperation with Israel on November 30, 1981, that committed both countries to "provide each other military assistance to cope with threats to the security of the entire region." That was followed by yet another agreement on Strategic Cooperation in 1983, which together with the June 1985 Free Trade Agreement institutionalized the relationship. U.S. economic and military aid was accordingly converted to outright grants and was no longer earmarked for special projects. Israel was also given unique access to U.S. military technology and markets and was accorded the status of a non-NATO ally.

Despite the massive outpouring of U.S. aid, weapons, and technology, combined with increased diplomatic backing, Israel refused to abandon its opposition to an internationally guaranteed territorial settlement. It continued to reject U.S. initiatives, even when such initiatives shielded her from the international scrutiny. Alleging that the Reagan plan of September 1, 1982, had contradicted the Camp David accords, the Israeli cabinet "resolved," on the very next day, not to enter into any negotiations with any party." And following the introduction of the Shultz plan, in response to the Palestinian uprising, *intifada,* in February 1988,

Prime Minister Shamir declared Shultz's signature as "the only acceptable" part of the plan, which he denounced as "bad," "unwelcomed," and "unpractical."[57] The flippant response to the Shultz plan did not stop Shultz from granting Israel a $20 billion debt relief and 80 percent financing of a new ballistic missile system as part of the SDI, better known as the Star Wars program. Moreover, the administration's request of $3.6 billion in military aid for Israel in fiscal 1989, following the demise of the Shultz Plan, represented an increase of $1.8 billion, equivalent to Israeli direct cost of suppressing the *intifada* for one year. An astonished senior Israeli official commented on all this by saying "It almost looked like Shultz gave him [Shamir] a reward for not cooperating."[58]

The period since the 1973 war witnessed the emergence of the United States as the de facto unrivaled super power of the region as well as principal custodian and sole arbiter. Israel has taken the credit for that coup and expected to reap the benefits. The United States concurred in that analysis, because Israel is also dependent on the United States and the state of no war–no peace appeals to both. As long as the conflict persists, Israeli dependence on the United States would also persist and so would Israeli willingness to act as the United States' gendarme. The transformation of Israel from client to surrogate to strategic ally has hastened an ongoing marginalization of Palestinian rights in U.S. policy. By 1983, the Reagan administration had accepted the Israeli view that the Palestine question is not the principal cause of instability in the region. It became secondary, if not indeed tertiary. Henceforth, that issue would not be allowed to interfere in the special relationship between a superpower and its strategic ally.

The United States has effectively conducted its diplomacy in accordance with a symbolic position and a presumed policy. The former accords with Resolution 242, which considers the West Bank and Gaza occupied territories within the meaning of international law as specified in the 1949 Geneva conventions and the 1970 Hague convention. The latter, however, treats the West Bank and Gaza, in effect, as mere territories with two contestants for sovereignty, one of which (Israel) has the superior claim. This marginalization of Palestinian national rights can also be seen in the U.S. plans, which carry the names of Rogers (1969), Reagan

(1982), Shultz (1988), and the current Baker proposals. As long as that foreign policy climate prevailed, Israel was insulated from the pressure for a territorial settlement with the Palestinians, Syria and Lebanon. Its utility in the U.S. global strategy seemed to outweigh its obligations for peace in the region.

The emerging new world order and the end of the Cold War would have by now signaled a glimpse of hope for an Arab-Israeli settlement. That would be congruous with the demonstrable progress already made in Afghanistan, Nicaragua, southern Africa, Cambodia, and the Persian-Arabian Gulf, a fulfillment of the global imperative.

But initially the Bush administration did not feel the same urgency that had driven George Shultz in 1988 to try to rescue Israel from the long-range impact of the *intifada*.. The radical upheavals in eastern Europe and the influx of Soviet Jewish immigration to Israel have decreased the already limited pressure on Israel to show flexibility in its diplomatic posture and on the Bush administration to risk a confrontation involving congressional supporters of Israel.

THE BUSH ADMINISTRATION AND THE ARAB-ISRAELI CONFLICT

Like all its predecessors since the establishment of Israel, the Bush administration's Middle East policy has domestic and geostrategic dimensions. Unlike his predecessors, however, George Bush was the first president who was able to coopt the Soviet Union as an adjunct actor, backing and legitimizing his Middle East policies. The adversary relationship, which permeated the past four decades, was transformed during the late 1980's into a cooperative relationship. This in turn enabled George Bush to invade Iraq and convene a Middle East peace conference to launch Arab-Israeli negotiations.

Today, Washington's traditionally pro-Israel policy is not entangled in the same web of the anticommunist rhetoric and ideological zeal that seemed to be the hallmark of the Reagan posture. But, like the previous administrations, the foreign policy team of George Bush remains fully cognizant of the degree of influence that can be exerted on U.S. policy by Israel's supporters in Congress.

Bush's policy has, therefore, received praise and condemnation, differentially by the various parties to the conflict. That is largely due to the fact that the current era is rather complex and fairly nuanced.

The Domestic Dimension

A principal factor that made peace more elusive in the Middle East than in other regions of the world is the domestic one. The domestic constituencies that support the apartheid regime in South Africa, the Contras in Nicaragua, the Savimbi faction in Angola, and the various competing forces in Campuchea are either nonexistent in the United States or significantly weaker than the pro-Israel lobby.[59]

Traditionally Congress is more responsive to cohesively organized minorities, lobbies, and political action committees (PACs) than to the voters, who make up public opinion.[60] The 47 percent support among the American public for a Palestinian homeland in the West Bank and Gaza is not likely to be reflected in the U.S. Senate, where eighty-eight senators had received pro-Israeli PAC contributions of almost $5 million between 1983 and 1988, according to Common Cause.[61]

The American Zionist lobby continues to share the same perspective of the corporate and military sectors, unlike the situation in 1956, when President Eisenhower ordered Israel out of Egypt. The various constituencies, which ensure the prominence of Israeli priorities on the U.S. diplomatic agenda, continue to operate virtually unopposed in congressional committees, the Christian churches, the labor movement, human rights organizations, the media, and academia, and even among the American Left.

Three recent examples illustrate the extent to which the Bush administration has been hamstrung by congressional stifling of minor initiatives, some of which were explicit whereas others were trial balloons. In the latter category, one example is the proposal by Bob Dole, the Senate minority leader, of January 13, 1990, calling for a reassessment of current U.S. aid programs to accommodate political changes in Eastern Europe.[62] A 5 percent cut affecting the five major recipients of U.S. aid (of whom Israel is one, accounting for nearly one-third of the total aid) provoked a letter on January 30, initiated by Senators Carl Levin and Pete

Wilson and endorsed by seventy-three senators, urging the president to oppose Dole's suggestion.[63] The proposal, which was widely believed to have the president's support, had been shelved.

The second example was President Bush's reminder made on March 3, 1990, that East Jerusalem is part of the 1967 occupied territories and must not be used to house Soviet Jewish immigrants. Bush was the target of some powerful salvos delivered by Senate majority leader, George Mitchell, a top recipient of pro-Israel PAC funds. "Heavy handed blunder" was the way Mitchell referred to Bush's statement.[64] At the same time Senator Daniel Patrick Moynihan (D-N.Y.) pushed a resolution through the Senate securing approval by voice vote on March 22 of a resolution stating that Jerusalem is and should remain the capital of the state of Israel, contrary to long-standing U.S. policy.[65] The House of Representatives passed a similar resolution and the *New York Times, Washington Post,* and the major American-Jewish organization joined the campaign against the president, who finally retreated to safe ambiguity.

The third recent example was the suspension of a token dialogue with the PLO in July 1990, following a relentless campaign in the Congress, over nearly two years, aiming to prove that the PLO has not abided by its November 1988 commitment to "renounce terrorism." The pretext was finally provided in June 1990 when a commando raid was staged by the Palestine Liberation Front, a peripheral faction of the PLO, on the Israeli coast in June 1990.

Now that this strange dialogue has been suspended, the PLO might well be relegated to the periphery of Middle East diplomacy, despite the fact that its participation in it has been more apparent than real. But the fact is that the marginalization of Palestinian national right predates the suspension and has, in fact, been at the center of the U.S. Middle East policy for more than two decades.

The Geostrategic Dimension and the Search for Political Solutions

The peace process in the context of strategic alliance has become less and less viable throughout the Reagan era. After the Shultz Plan was laid to rest, much like its predecessors, the Bush administration prevailed on the Shamir government to propose an initiative that would incorporate the major provisions of the Camp David Treaty. It was contemplated as a response to the Palestinian Declaration of Independence of November 1988 and its corollaries that entailed recognition of Israel and renunciation of terrorism by Yaser Arafat. The Shamir Plan, which was adopted by the Israeli government in May 1989, ruled out a Palestinian state, PLO representation, and "any change in the status of Judea, Samaria and Gaza, other than in accordance with the basic guidelines of the government."[66] Secretary of State Baker, who referred to it as "the only game in town," was subsequently dismayed when Shamir himself disavowed the plan in Spring 1990. Flashing the State Department's telephone number on the television screen, he said, "if interested in peace, call us!"

Baker, however, was granted a second opportunity to persuade Shamir to resurrect his own plan. Soon after the war against Iraq came to an end, he and President Bush made it clear that an Arab-Israeli settlement was near the top of their diplomatic agenda. Bush told a joint meeting of Congress on March 6, 1991, that such settlement would have to be based on the principle of exchanging land for peace. The time was considered most suitable for reactivating Middle East diplomacy, given that so many Arab states including Syria together with Israel were now tacit allies of the United States against Iraq. Meanwhile, the United States has emerged from its war against Iraq as the sole military superpower and the unquestioned diplomatic pacesetter in the region.

Secretary Baker's painstaking efforts to create an acceptable framework for negotiations began in earnest in March and continued through September 1991. Eight Middle East shuttles in seven months, paving the road to Madrid, constituted America's most sustained effort on behalf of an Arab-Israeli rapprochement in nearly a quarter century. Three main reasons account for the presumed relative success in contrast to the failures that permeated U.S. plans beginning with Secretary William Rogers (1969) and extending to George Shultz (1988): the collapse of communism, the Gulf War, and the deliberately ambiguous character of Baker's diplomacy, which devoted considerable time for talks about talks.

The dramatic transformation of the strategic and political landscape of the Middle East, which led, to a virtual recolonization of the Arab East, has provided George Bush with an opportunity to shape a new structure of relationships in which an Arab-Israeli settlement became a U.S. national interest. U.S. strategic planners now envisage a post-Cold War redivision of the world, in which economic rather than military power will be the catalyst for change and in which the Middle East, as a potential source of capital, will rest securely in the North American (USCAN) sphere. Given that U.S. relations with Japan and the EEC will have to consume the larger portion of American energies during the next phase, a settlement of the Arab-Israeli conflict becomes not only desirable but also necessary from the U.S. vantage point.

Baker's second "window of opportunity" was bolstered by objective and material changes occurring at the regional and global levels; it was not dependent, as before, on the imperatives of Israeli domestic politics and Shamir's shifting postures. The Gulf War has effectively demolished the official Arab consensus on Palestine, eroded Arab solidarity, and exposed regime insecurity in the Gulf-Peninsula region. The illusion of Arab defense and the higher Arab interest are now eclipsed by the spectacle of kings, sheikhs, and presidents ingratiating themselves with Washington, thus enabling it to deal with them bilaterally and largely on the basis of narrowly construed interests rather than as a solid bloc with a nationalist and Palestinian agenda. Given these conditions, an Israeli rejection of Baker's initiative would have been difficult to justify.

The Soviet eclipse has reinforced Baker's second opportunity and produced an added imperative for adjusting the U.S.-Israeli special relationship to the post-Cold War, post-Gulf War realities. A diminished Soviet "threat" is less compatible with the notion of a strategic asset or a cheap NATO. In fact, Israel looks more and more now like an expensive liability. The American public is less inclined to give foreign aid now that a Soviet "threat" has been removed from Washington's foreign policy lexicon and as domestic needs assume urgent and renewed concern in the midst of recession. The recent finding of a combined *Wall Street Journal* (15 October 1991) and NBC public opinion poll reveals that the percentage of Americans who would give aid to the Soviet Union (58 percent) exceeds that of those who would give to Israel (44 percent) is rather significant.

All of this implies that Washington's advantageous position vis-à-vis the Arabs and Israel offered it a new flexibility that, if it chooses to utilize, can enhance the desired regional stability. That prospect is linked to America's perception of the roles that Israeli security and Palestinian activism are likely to play in the next phase.

The concept of Israeli security is not likely to continue to constitute the green light that helped entrench the status quo in its favor, sometimes at the expense of America's higher interests and designs. The recent controversy over the $10 billion loan guarantees represents a qualitative change in Washington's diplomatic style. Defying the powerful pro-Israel lobby, President Bush decided in September 1991 to defer a decision on the guarantees for 120 days in order not to "prejudice the outcome of the peace process." Israel's supporters in Congress and at large viewed the decision as tantamount to a link between U.S. aid to Israel and the latter's willingness to accept a territorial settlement. It is also seen as part of a search for an updated basis of the special relationship with Israel. At issue in that process is a possible transformation of Israel from a predominantly global issue to an increasingly domestic matter. The aborted showdown over the loan guarantees represented an initial victory of sorts for President Bush in an arena in which "humanitarian" values were highlighted by American Jewish activists and their legislative representatives while strategic considerations were rendered to the sidelines. The U.S. national security sector is more preoccupied now with the Japanese trade surplus "threat" and the new shape and scope of an integrated Europe as well as with America's role in it. These developments entail a reduced leverage for Israel in Washington; hence its tenacious adhesion to the status quo of "not a single inch," the mad rush to build colonial settlements, and the resultant discord with the United States.

As for Palestinian activism, U.S. strategic planners have already made corresponding reassessments of their estimates of its potential for regional destabilization. The major difference, however, is that unlike the revised estimates of Israel's value, which is subtle, Washington's current estimate of the Palestinian "threat" is rather unequivocal. Deprived of a solid and unified Arab backing in the negotiations; isolated from its constituencies in the occupied territories, the Gulf, Syria, and Lebanon; and faced with economic, ideological, leadership, and governance crises, the PLO is seen by the Bush administration as the weakest link. This low estimation can be readily seen in the structure, framework and style of Baker's diplomacy, which treats the Palestinians as unequal. A deliberate ambiguity in that diplomacy left the various parties considerable room for personal interpretation and even self-delusion; it was designed to secure a unanimous consent for attending the conference. To achieve that goal many substantive issues were thinly camouflaged as procedural arrangements. A few examples suffice:

1. The issue of Palestinian representation is not a matter of procedure; it is substantive par excellence. Baker's acquiescence in Israel's exclusion of diaspora and Jersualemite Palestinians renders Palestinian national rights questionable and negotiable, including their internationally recognized rights of return and self-determination. It also lends a certain credence to the Israeli claim on Jerusalem despite the well-established international position, to which the United States itself is committed. The issue of who represents the Israelis, Syrians, Jordanians, and so on did not arise and could not have arisen.

2. The numerous encumberances on the peace conference, including its designation, participants, the limits of speech, and frequency of meetings, among others, are also substantive in as much as they render the very issue of a belligerent occupation, a recognized status under international law, to the sidelines. The Madrid conference was regional and not the international conference envisaged in the United Nations resolutions. Its main function was to launch the direct bilateral negotiations, in line with Israel's long-standing position. The United Nations presence at the conference was limited to a mute observer, whereas Palestinian participation was within the framework of a joint delegation with Jordan, also in line with Israel's wishes.

3. The "two-track" approach, one to deal with Palestinian affairs and the other for Arab-Israeli differences is also not a procedural issue but a substantive one packaged in procedural wrappings. Although the direction of Mr. Baker's tracks is parallel, the tracks themselves are integal and complementary. That approach, however, was designed to allay Israeli fears that a show of Arab solidarity at the negotiations would weaken its

stance against a territorial withdrawal from the West Bank and Gaza.

For all these reasons, Baker's methodology is already being challenged to become more congruous with the material and objective conditions that rendered the mission necessary in the first place. Although the objective conditions imply a reduction of Israeli influence, the concessions, which permitted the procedural packaging of substantive issues, were made largely by the Palestinians and the Arabs. Such assymetry has already caused Syria to threaten boycotting the third phase, in which multilateral talks would take place, unless progress was made during the second phase of bilateral negotiations on the territorial question.

Meanwhile, the Shamir government, which had already managed to escape the "peace process" in 1990, continues to view the Baker diplomacy as a belated threat to check its ongoing absorption of the land, atomization of the community, and continued efforts to preempt a state-in-formation. The real challenge to Baker and Bush as "catalyst for peace" will be not only to bridge the gap between the Arabs and Israel, but also between the material and objective conditions that propelled U.S. diplomacy towards Madrid and the quality of change Madrid is expected to produce. This is going to depend on the pace at which specific proposals will replace the necessary ambiguity. It will also depend on whether Bush's espousal of peace at Madrid will be followed by the tranfer of the well-known substantive positions of the United States from the realm of the abstract to that of the tangible and the applied. Only then will the real meaning of resolution 242 be known. It would be a real test of the post-Cold War special relationship between Israel and the United States.

NOTES

1. "The Sources of Soviet Conduct," *Foreign Affairs* (July 1947).
2. *Department of State Bulletin* (April 21, 1946), p. 622.
3. *Department of State Bulletin* (June 4, 1951), p. 887.
4. *Department of State Bulletin* (June 15, 1953), p. 831.
5. Charles Cremeans, *The Arabs and the World* (New York: Praeger, 1963), p. 146.

6. Quoted in Donald Neff, *Warriors at Suez: Eisenhower Takes America into the Middle East* (New York: Linden Press and Simon and Schuster, 1981), pp. 439–440.

7. Ibid., p. 107.

8. Moshe Dayan, *Diary of the Sinai Campaign* (Jerusalem: Steinatzky Agency Ltd., 1966), pp. 71–73.

9. *Department of State Bulletin* (November 12, 1956), pp. 745–746.

10. Cheryl Rubenberg, *Israel and the American National Interest* (Urbana: University of Illinois Press, 1986), p. 64.

11. Neff, *Warriors at Suez*, p. 104.

12. See analysis of the doctrine in Fred Halliday, *Arabia Without Sultans* (London: Penguin Books, 1974), p. 54.

13. Quoted in Patrick Seale, *The Struggle for Syria* (London: Oxford University Press, 1965), p. 298.

14. Ibid., p. 296.

15. From a news conference on April 23, 1957. *Department of State Bulletin* (May 13, 1957), p. 768.

16. Melvin Gurtov, *The United States Against the Third World: Anti-Nationalism and Intervention* (New York: Praeger, 1974), p. 14.

17. Rubenberg. *Israel and the American National Interest*, p. 85.

18. Noam Chomsky, *The Fateful Triangle: The United States, Israel and the Palestinians* (Boston: South End Press, 1983), pp. 20–21.

19. Neff. *Warriors at Suez*, p. 441.

20. Malcolm Kerr. "Coming to Terms with Nasser," *International Affairs* (January 1967): 73–76.

21. *New York Times* (June 12, 1966).

22. *Newsweek* (February 17, 1968).

23. *New York Times* (November 4, 1969).

24. Nixon's campaign promise.

25. *New York Times* (December 24, 1969).

26. For a discussion of Israel's counterrevolutionary role, see Israel Shahak, *Israel's Global Role: Weapons for Repression* (Belmont, Mass.: AAUG Press, 1982); also Milton Jamail and Margo Gutierrez, *It's No Secret: Israel's Military Involvement in Central America* (Belmont, Mass.: AAUG Press, 1986).

27. *Boston Globe* (April 2, 1979).

28. Ibid.

29. President Carter's State of the Union Message to the 96th Congress, January 23, 1980. *New York Times* (January 24, 1980).

30. *New York Times* (October 2, 1981).

31. Interview in *New York Times* (April 1, 1976); similar views were expressed in *U.S. News and World Report* (May 24, 1976).

32. *Jewish Telegraphic Agency* (October 18, 1976).

33. *New York Times* (April 1, 1976). Israeli responsibility was documented by Michael Paulmbo, *The Palestinian Catastrophe: The 1948 Expulsion of a People from Their Homeland* (London: Quartet Books, 1987); Simha Flapan, *The Birth of Israel* (New York: Pantheon, 1987).

34. Ibid.

35. Annual Review of U.S. Middle East Policy (Washington, D.C.: Department of State), p. 11; based on a statement by Harold H. Saunders, Assistant Secretary for Near Eastern and South Asian Affairs, before the Subcommittee on Europe and the Middle East of the House International Relations Committee, June 12, 1977.

36. Ibid., pp. 12–13.

37. *New York Times* (January 14, 1977).

38. *New York Times* (February 19, 1977).

39. *New York Times* (February 15, 1977).

40. *The Economist* (January 8, 1977), p. 63.

41. Speech in *New York Times* (March 19, 1977).

42. Interview in *Time* (August 8, 1977).

43. Text in *New York Times* (October 2, 1977).

44. Text in *New York Times* (October 6, 1977).

45. Text in *New York Times* (October 14, 1977).

46. See Haig's testimony before the Senate Foreign Relations Committee and the House Foreign Affairs Committee on March 19 and 20, 1981, in *New York Times* (March 20, 1981). See also "Secretary Haig: U.S. Strategy in the Middle East," *Current Policy,* no. 312 (Washington, D.C.: Department of State, Bureau of Public Affairs).

47. Ibid.

48. Text of the Fez Plan in N. Aruri et al. *Reagan and the Middle East* (Belmont, Mass.: AAUG Press, 1983).

49. Text in Ibid., Appendix A, pp. 79–84; see also *New York Times* (September 2, 1982).

50. See Ze'ev Shiff, "The Green Light," *Foreign Policy* 50 (Spring 1983).

51. *Boston Globe* (February 17, 1982).

52. *Washington Post* (October 15, 1983).

53. See David Newsome, "Hope or Delusion," *Christian Science Monitor* (December 27, 1983).

54. *New York Times* (March 8, 1984).

55. *Christian Science Monitor* (February 2, 1981).

56.   When this quotation resurfaced in the German weekly *Welt am Sanntag*, on February 7, 1982, the White House quickly denied that it represented current policy.

57.   See Secretary Shultz, "A Statement for Palestinians' U.S. Department of State, Bureau of Public Affairs," *Current Policy*, no. 1067; see also Naseer Aruri "The United States and Palestine: Reagan's Legacy to Bush," *Journal of Palestine Studies* 18, no. 3 (Spring 1989): 3–21.

58.   *New York Times* (April 22, 1988).

59.   For an assessment of the power of the pro-Israeli lobby, see Edward Tivnan. *The Lobby: Jewish Political Power and American Foreign Policy* (New York: Simon and Schuster, 1987).

60.   For a discussion of PAC influence on U.S. Middle East policy, see Richard Curtiss, *Stealth PACS: How Israeli-American Lobby Took Control of U.S. Middle East Policy* (Washington, D.C.: American Educational Trust, 1990).

61.   See New York Times–CBS public opinion poll in *New York Times* (July 9, 1990); see Ian Williams "Changing Opinions," *Middle East International*, no. 380 (July 20, 1990): 11.

62.   Bob Dole, "To Help New Democracies, Cut Aid to Israel, Four Others," *New York Times* (January 16, 1990).

63.   Text in *Journal of Palestine Studies* 19, no. 3 (Spring 1990): 192–193.

64.   See N. Aruri, "The Battle over Jerusalem in Washington," *The Return* 2, nos. 8 and 9 (April–May 1990): 29–33.

65.   Ibid.

66.   For an analysis of the plan, see N. Aruri, "The Timed Passivity of Bush and Baker," *Middle East International* (London) no. 363 (November 17, 1989): 16–17.

CHAPTER 5

U.S. Policy and the Palestine Question

Joe Stork

Palestinians and Arabs must have had a bitter laugh when President George Bush declared, on October 9, 1990, that "I hope nobody questions our interest in seeing a solution to the Palestine question, to the implementation of the Security Council resolutions." For more than two decades, the United States policy toward the Palestine-Israel Conflict has been one of irresolution, evasion, and imposition. Washington has vetoed dozens of United Nations resolutions relating to Palestine, often standing alone against the international consensus that has emerged favoring the establishment of an independent Palestinian state alongside the state of Israel. Administration after administration has simply ignored implementing those resolutions it had approved in the past.

The essence of this policy has been to subordinate the issue of Palestinian self-determination to Washington's strategic relationship with Israel and to insist on assigning to Jordan the role of custodian for Palestinian national rights. Within this dynamic, the United States has consistently endeavored to marginalize the Palestine Liberation Organization, occasionally by cooptation but generally by supporting the efforts of Israel to crush the PLO and the efforts of various Arab states, especially Jordan and Syria, to make the organization an appendage of those regimes.

This core policy of denial has been to some extent camoflauged by an elaborate ritual labeled *the peace process*. The ostensible purpose of this mechanism is to bring the parties to the conflict—Israel, the Palestinians, the "frontline" Arab states—to a negotiated settlement. In fact, the so-called peace process is, as one astute

American observer noted nearly twenty years ago, an "illusion of purposeful activity" and functions to forestall any compromise that would meet minimal Palestinian demands of self-determination. The one settlement that has occurred, the Camp David Accords of 1978 leading to the Egyptian-Israeli treaty of 1979, was structured to rule out resolution of Palestinian-Israeli Conflict except on maximalist Israeli terms.

POLICY PARADOX

At first glance, this pattern of U.S. hostility to Palestinian nationalism seems paradoxical. U.S. policy is certainly not constructed on the basis of redressing historic grievances such as those claimed by the Palestinians, but neither is it based on some sentimental attachment to the "shared democratic values" often claimed by Israel's partisans. Over the years, it is true that a well-organized pro-Israel constituency has been developed in the United States, whose influence is particularly great in the Congress. Congressional imprint on U.S. policy toward the Middle East is certainly greater than toward most other parts of the world and it does set parameters on what any administration can achieve, but it is not a determining factor. Its great impact derives from the fact that by and large it is consistent with the direction set by successive executive teams in the White House, State Department, and Pentagon.

U.S. interests in the Middle East, as elsewhere, are determined on the basis of strategic considerations and access to resources and markets. On all these grounds—the strategic location of the region on the southern border of the Soviet Union (which until recently had been the prime adversary of the United States), the concentration of the world's most accessible crude oil reserves in the Arabian Peninsula and Persian Gulf areas, and the extensive market, in terms of population and wealth, for American goods and services—Israel appears to be a relatively insignificant factor; and one would expect a policy more solicitous of Arab, and Palestinian, interests.

It is precisely this paradox that underlies a debate in U.S. policy-making circles that is as old as the Palestine-Israel-Arab Conflict itself. There has always been a segment of the American elite that argues for a mix of policies that would reflect this concentration of American strategic and commercial interests in the Arab part of the Middle East map. It is a position identified most strongly with the giant American oil companies and their Wall Street financiers, a group that has historically been well represented in policy circles. James Forrestal, secretary of defense in the Truman years and a vigorous opponent of U.S. support for the Zionist project, exemplified this stance. The other constituency supporting this tendency is the body of people with direct experience in the region—the "Arabists" of the Foreign Service, churches, and philanthropic organizations represented there—who appreciate the local dynamics and specifics of the conflict.

At critical points, this debate is revived. One recent instance is the period following the October War of 1973, which led to the 1977 efforts of the new Carter administration to formulate a comprehensive set of negotiations that would encompass the Palestinians. A second instance is the period during and immediately following Israel's 1982 invasion of Lebanon, when Alexander Haig was replaced as Secretary of State by George Shultz, a man whose corporate ties seemed to place him well within the "Arabist" orbit. More recently, the Palestinian uprising in the occupied West Bank and Gaza seemed to provide both incentive and opportunity for the new administration of George Bush and James Baker to reorder its priorities in a way that would incorporate Palestinian nationalism, especially as an important segment of Israeli and, in this country pro-Israeli, opinion favored such a move. Not only American interests but even Israeli interests seemed to argue for such a reorientation.

So the debate continues, but policy has moved ever more decidedly in favor of strong U.S. support for Israel against the Palestinians. One explanation with some merit sees a structural and ideological component to U.S. policy that opposes Palestinian nationalism as a part of an endemic opposition to "all Third World nationalism."[1] Certainly the United States has ruthlessly combatted those nationalist projects that directly affected economic or strategic interests. The U.S. interventions against Iran and Guatemala in the 1950s are cases in point. And the U.S. opposition to revolutionary nationalist movements, such as in China and Vietnam, needs no documentation. But this seems insufficient to explain Washington's persistent antagonism toward the Palestinian movement. That movement does not appear to threaten U.S. economic interests, and in fact its cooptation would appear to remove threats of "instability." The Palestinian nationalist movement, although it does contain leftist and revolutionary components, is fundamentally not a revolutionary project; bourgeois and conservative elements play leading roles within the PLO, have encouraged the movement to hitch its fate to the United States and conservative Arab states, and would be immeasurably strengthened by U.S. support for Palestinian self-determination.

President Bush's statement of October 9 will be assessed by Palestinians against the background of the months of fruitless negotiations sponsored by the Bush administration that conform to the pattern of the past several decades—"illusions of purposeful activity." It is that broader, more extensive historical background that I will survey here, drawing on the themes just set out. This will conclude with an assessment of the Bush administration's own record and, finally, some recommendations for fundamental changes in U.S. policy.

WILSON TO TRUMAN

In the aftermath of World War I, President Woodrow Wilson responded to the controversy over the Balfour Declaration, wherein Britain committed itself to support a "Jewish national home" in Palestine, by appointing a fact-finding commission headed by Henry King, president of Oberlin College, and Charles Crane, a wealthy industrialist. The King-Crane Commission urged that "Syria, including Palestine and Lebanon be kept a unity according to the desires of a great majority" and "be under a single mandate."[2]

The rest, as they say, is history. Self-determination as an ideal and a slogan could count for nothing against the very concrete and competetive interests of Britain and France, which favored the division of Syria and colonization project of the Zionist movement. Resolutions endorsing Zionism passed the U.S. Congress, but what mattered was U.S. deference to Britain east of Suez so long as American companies could partake of the scramble for oil concessions in the new countries of Iraq and Saudi Arabia.

This deference to Britain remained rather total until 1943, when President Franklin Roosevelt felt obliged to promise Ibn Saud "that no decision altering the basic situation of Palestine should be reached without full consultation with both Arabs and Jews." This marks the beginning of a formal U.S. position on Palestine.[3] Not just coincidentally, by 1943 the center of Zionist political activities had shifted from Britain to the United States. In the election year of 1944, Palestine became a party issue. At the policy level, Britain still set the agenda. But the bonds of Zionism with Western political culture, bonds of language and ideology, had established a predisposition for Zionist hegemony of perception and interpretation of events in Palestine. There was, for the public and policy makers alike, a Palestine, but there were no Palestinians. In this former Ottoman territory, Zionists battled the British and Jews feuded with Arabs. The struggle there was perceived here not as one between indigenous people and new colonists, but between Britain and the Zionist pioneers.[4]

Roosevelt's response to Ibn Saud was presciently evasive, because the United States would follow its consultations with policies that suited its own perceived interests. It fell to Roosevelt's successor, Harry Truman, to weigh conflicting interests and set policy. Truman initially adhered to the traditional hands-off policy that regarded Palestine as within Britain's sphere of influence. The combination of communal war in Palestine, British abdication of its role there, and growing pro-Zionist political agitation in the United States changed all that. The Truman administration used its leverage in the newly established United Nations to secure passage of the November 1947 partition resolution, and six months later was the first country to recognize the new state of Israel.

Several factors contributed to this decisive American intervention. Truman himself seemed disposed to a "refugee Zionism," supporting the Jewish state project more on humanitarian grounds than out of political commitment. Another element was electoral: the combination of "refugee" and political Zionism had wide popular support. Within the Democratic Party in particular, pro-Zionist Jewish financial contributors helped convince Truman to support partition and then statehood. Truman, though, was not cravenly going after votes and contributions at the expense of "national interest." His pro-Zionist advisors took pains to convince him of the congruence of support for Israel with U.S. interests in the region, and the White House was aware that Saudi opposition would not lead to any break in political or commercial ties.[5]

Truman's policies after November 1948, in any case, would not have been susceptible to electoral considerations. The United States affirmed the UN resolutions calling for repatriation of Palestinian refugees, but made no serious effort to secure Israeli compliance. The combination of Israeli military victories and Truman's strong aversion to dispatching U.S. forces to the region led to a policy of recognizing the balance of forces on the ground and taking steps to align the Israelis in the American camp. In the words of one American diplomat at the time, "underlying US policy there is [a] hardboiled appraisal of elements of Middle East power and prospects for making the best use of them in US-UK defense planning."[6]

EISENHOWER TO JOHNSON

The next phase, running through the 1950s until the 1967 War, remained more or less on the terms set in 1947–49. The United States pursued an "evenhanded" policy toward the Arab states and Israel. The Palestinians had no corporate identity and existed in political terms only as refugees. The conflict was perceived in the region and in the West as essentially a conflict between Israel and Arab states.

In the unfolding context of the Cold War, and developing relations between the Soviet Union and new radical nationalist Arab regimes, the debate over Israel's relationship with the United States intensified. In reality and in hindsight, though, the perception of Israel's role shifted perceptibly from the "liability" to the "asset" side of the ledger.[7]

A set of crises between 1955 and 1958—starting with Egyptian-Israeli clashes touched off by Palestinian guerrilla raids, extending through the Soviet-Egyptian arms deal, the Suez aggression, regime crises in Lebanon, Jordan, Syria, and Iraq—marked the beginning of a dynamic that would determine the elements of U.S. policy toward the Palestine question that still prevail today. The crises of 1955–58 contain the seeds of the alliances and alignments that have characterized the Palestine-Israel conflict ever since. The key ingredients of this redefinition are as follows:

- Out of these crises came a radicalization of Arab nationalism in its various manifestations (Egyptian, Syrian, etc.) and an alignment of these forces internationally with the Soviet bloc.

- The state versus state character of the conflict was reaffirmed, inasmuch as Israel succeeded "in pushing the conflict onto its neighbors' territory, making them fight on its terms, obscuring the Palestinian core of the dispute."[8]

- At the same time, a specific Palestinian nationalism and national movement was born, one that would pave the way for a revision of the central terms of the conflict toward the dynamic of a national liberation movement against foreign (Israeli) occupation. The main constituent organization of the PLO, Fatah, has its origins in the aftermath of Suez, whereas the Nasserist Arab National Movement (ANM) contained the Palestinian forces that later became the Popular Front and Democratic Front.

- Jordan's key gendarme role vis-à-vis the Palestinians—the raison d'être for its creation by the British in the 1920s—was reaffirmed. Palestinians—refugees from 1948 and the population of the West Bank then under Jordanian rule—constituted some two-thirds of the population. In 1957, amid the apparent nationalist victories in Egypt, Lebanon, and Syria, American guns and dollars along with British troops allowed King Hussein to dissolve the elected parliament and political parties, arrest the nationalist prime minister, and impose martial law— a "happy ending" according to a Council on Foreign Relations study published shortly afterward.[9]

- The Eisenhower Doctrine, proclaimed in January 1957, sanctioned U.S. intervention in the region in the name of anticommunism, accomodating an informal U.S.-Israeli political and military collaboration that the formal Baghdad Pact did not. The strategy of building a consensus of regional states to counter the Soviet Union had been replaced by a strategy of anticommunist intervention into Arab politics.[10]

This series of crises thus greatly affected Arab political dynamics, but the appearance of things confirmed the dominant view of "the Palestine question" as an Arab-Israeli Conflict. Neither *Palestine* nor *Palestinian* were part of Washington's political lexicon. The polarization of the Cold War, which had long characterized the "Northern Tier" countries of Turkey and Iran, had fully penetrated the Arab state system by the end of the decade. Although the United States opposed the Israeli-British-French aggression against Egypt, Israel's military accomplishments in that campaign had not gone unnoticed in the Pentagon. In the subsequent crises around Jordan, Lebanon, Syria, and Iraq, according to one pro-Israel analyst, "Israel played a passive but important role" in tying down Egyptian troops.[11] Washington appreciated "this balancing role of Israel" and "began to count on it deliberately" after the demise of the Baghdad Pact.

Thus a decade later, after 1967, when Palestinians had mobilized and established their own corporate identity and national agenda, the perceptual groundwork for the U.S. view of Israel as a "strategic asset" had already been laid. The Kennedy years saw the end of U.S. reluctance to become a major weapons supplier to Israel. The Kennedy administration also backed a UN Conciliation Commission, headed by Carnegie Endowment president Joseph Johnson. Both Israel and the Arab states opposed the commission's effort to devise a plan for implementing the "repatriation or resettlement" aims of Resolution 194 (1949). (The position of the Arab states owed much to the organization, in 1959, of a Palestine Arab Congress representing all refugee groups, which vigorously opposed the "resettlement and economic development" proposals of then-UN secretary-general Dag Hammarskjold.)[12]

The June War of 1967 transformed the military and political balance in the region and confirmed, as a consequence, Israel's utility to Washington. The emergence of the Palestinians as an independent political factor was at first obscured in Washington by Israel's decisive defeat of Egypt, Syria, and Jordan, a severe blow to the prestige and power of the radical nationalist states and their Soviet backers. The hints of the 1950s became a demonstration in 1967 and paved the way for the open collaboration of the 1970s and 1980s.

THE KISSINGER-NIXON PERIOD

In the years that Henry Kissinger presided over U.S. foreign policy, management of the Arab-Israeli conflict became a top foreign policy priority for the first time. This owed nothing to Kissinger's background or inclination. He confessed early on to knowing little and caring less about the specifics of the conflict. It owed rather to the sharp build up of political pressures in the region. How those pressures were dealt with has helped define U.S. policy in the region, and especially towards the Palestinians, to this day.

The collaboration of the United States and Israel in the Black September crisis of 1970 was seminal to the growth of the U.S.-Israeli strategic relationship. Appropriately, the crisis had its origins in the effort of the Palestine Liberation Organization, now controlled by Palestinian guerrilla groups rather than Arab states, to assert its leadership and representational role against that of Jordan's King Hussein. The resulting clashes in Jordan, as well as Palestinian raids against Israel, prompted William Rogers, Secretary of State in the new Nixon administration, to propose negotiations between Israel and the Arab confrontation states on the basis of the land-for-peace UN Resolution 242 passed after the June 1967 War.

Israel opposed Rogers's effort, and the Palestinians were determined to thwart any Arab inclinations to "sell out" Palestinian rights. Palestinian forces hijacked several Western airliners to Jordan in a calculated bid to challenge the king's authority. Hussein responded with a full-scale military crackdown. The question then became whether outside intervention would be necessary to the task. Nixon was keen to crush the Palestinians and reportedly even requested the Pentagon to order U.S. bombing of guerrilla camps and hideouts. U.S. military commitments in Southeast Asia at the time, and no doubt some appreciation in State and Defense Departments of the political aftershocks this would likely create, led defense secretary Melvin Laird to demur.[13]

Henry Kissinger, Nixon's national security advisor, was also determined to see King Hussein prevail: "We could not allow Hussain to be overthrown by a Soviet-inspired insurrection."[14] His solution was to approve Israeli air and ground intervention if necessary to save Hussein. The United States would intervene if necessary to prevent any Soviet or Egyptian attacks on the Israelis.

In the end, the Jordanian armed forces managed to establish control and over the course of the next ten months virtually eliminated the Palestinian military presence in Jordan. In the White House, this outcome and the facilitating role of Israel further elevated Washington's appreciation of Israel's strategic potential in the era of the Nixon Doctrine. It also increased Kissinger's stature and encouraged Nixon to assign him rather than Rogers responsibility for Middle East policy. William Quandt, who served on the National Security Council under Kissinger, described the result as "a new definition of issues in the Middle East, a revised understanding of the political dynamics of the region, in which the U.S.-Israeli relationship came to be seen as the key to combatting Soviet influence in the Arab world and attaining stability."[15] Quandt's own earlier work on Palestinian political dynamics as part of a RAND Corporation contract with the Department of Defense indicates an awareness, at policy-making levels, of the new momentum of Palestinian nationalism under the aegis of the PLO.[16]

This awareness, though, did not filter through the Cold War prism erected by Kissinger in the time-worn tradition of American strategists. A series of agreements with Israel in 1971 dramatically expanded the U.S. military supply relationship and restructured it in ways that made it relatively impervious to potential later challenges based on political or strategic whim.[17]

The October War of 1973 testified to the failure of Kissinger's arrogant and ignorant approach to the region and forced him, now as Secretary of State, to build a strategic framework for the region that included key Arab states as well as Israel (and Iran, the other Middle East pillar of the Nixon doctrine). This effort centered around Egypt and Saudi Arabia.

Under Kissinger's direction, the United States established covert contacts with the PLO, but the U.S. approach to the Palestinians remained one of marginalization of the Palestinian movement, denial of Palestinian demands, and subordination of Palestinian representation to Jordan. In preparation for the first peace conference in Geneva, Kissinger allowed Israel to eliminate all references to Palestinian participation and promised that the United States would veto any PLO participation without Israeli consent.

By all accounts, Kissinger was extremely disturbed when the Arab summit at Rabat in November 1974 recognized the PLO as the "sole, legitimate representative" of the Palestinians. This, and Yasir Arafat's subsequent invitation to address the UN General Assembly in New York City, made Kissinger's task more difficult. In September 1975, as part of the second Sinai disengagement agreement between Israel and Egypt, Kissinger committed the United States not to negotiate with the PLO without Israeli approval, or until the PLO accepted UN Resolution 242 and acknowledged "Israel's right to exist." In January 1976, the United States vetoed a UN Security Council resolution, introduced by Arab states and supported by the PLO, calling for a two-state settlement with security guarantees for both.

Kissinger candidly described his post-1973 goals to a private group of American Jewish leaders in June 1975. They were as follows: "break up the Arab united front"; "insure that the Europeans and the Japanese did not get involved"; "keep the Soviets out of the dipomatic arena"; and create "a situation which would enable Israel to deal separately with each of its neighbors." These neighbors, for Kissinger, do not include Palestinians: "I have left the Palestinian question alone in order to work on frontier questions hoping eventually to isolate the Palestinians." (Kissinger also confirmed a fundamental American tactic when he cited an Israeli request for delay: "So we gave them some time. The United States went into a protracted stall with the Arabs. I took many trips to the area—with no progress of course.")[18]

The year 1975 was also notable for another development that profoundly undermined the ability of the PLO to translate its new regional and international stature into a lever for participation in peace talks. After "Black September," the political as well as military weight of the PLO had shifted from Jordan to Lebanon. The Palestinian presence there became the scapegoat of right-wing Lebanese oppponents of political reform demanded by Lebanese Muslims and progressives. From the first Phalangist attacks of April 1975 through the Syrian military intervention a year later, PLO energies were consumed with matters of physical as well as political survival. Although there is no direct evidence of a U.S. hand in these developments beyond encouragement of the Syrian intervention, it seems safe to presume that Kissinger and his coterie were not unhappy to see the PLO so engaged. It fully coincided with the U.S. view that responsibility to policing Palestinian political behavior lay with the Arab regimes. Interestingly, the special U.S. envoy sent to Beirut in 1976 was none other than L. Dean Brown, who had been ambassador in Amman in 1970.

THE CARTER INTERLUDE

Whereas Kissinger strove to take advantage of the new Arab-Israeli balance following the October War to construct new pro-American alignments in the region, many policy makers, perhaps even Kissinger himself, recognized at least privately that some incorporation of the Palestinians into a negotiated settlement was probably necessary. Saudi Arabia and the smaller, rich, oil-producing states such as Kuwait now had financial leverage over the radical nationalist states, but this brought with it a measure of responsibility for developments regarding the Palestinians. Ratifying Syria's military presence in Lebanon as an Arab League peacekeeping force was one part of this. Political cooptation of the PLO was another.

The transition toward a U.S. position that at least verbally acknowledged the existence of Palestinian claims reached its fullest expression in the first year of the Carter administration (1977). The process began earlier, though. In November 1975, even in the heat of the controversy over the UN General Assembly's passage of the infamous "Zionism is racism" resolution, the United States declined to veto PLO participation in a Security Council debate. That same month, deputy assistant secretary of state Harold Saunders testified to a House Foreign Affairs Committee hearing on "The Palestine Issue in Middle East Peace Efforts" that "the issue is not whether Palestinian interests should be expressed in a final settlement, but how." As for concrete policy steps, though, Saunders was less forthcoming: "It is obvious that thinking on the Palestinian aspects of the problem must evolve on all sides."[19] Those outside of the administration were more daring. The Brookings Institution in 1975 issued a report, whose signatories included a number of prominent appointees to the Carter administration, such as Cyrus Vance and Zbigniew Brzezinski, which signalled a willingness to have Palestinian representation in negotiations and a final settlement. Brzezinski himself, who would succeed Kissinger as national security advisor, wrote that the United States should be prepared to push for an Israeli-Palestinian settlement "which almost certainly means in practice the PLO."[20]

For a very brief period, Palestine and the Palestinians were the focus of an American administration's concentrated diplomatic attention. Jimmy Carter, in the spring of 1977, made several informal references to the need for a Palestinian political entity "in the framework of the nation of Jordan or by some other means." Even vice-president Walter Mondale, in a formal speech designed to "clarify" Carter's remarks, spoke of "some arrangement for a Palestinian homeland or entity—preferably in association with Jordan."[21]

The references to Jordan remain key. Sadat and Hussein had, ever since the Rabat summit recognition of the PLO in late 1974, been pushing to restrict the PLO role to that of "legitimate" but not "sole" representative of the Palestinians; that is, representative of those Palestinians not living in Jordan or the occupied West Bank. In early 1977, the maneuvering among the parties was furious. Sadat publicly urged the PLO to declare a formal link with Jordan and modify the PLO charter. Arafat was looking over his shoulder at Israeli and Jordanian efforts to resurrect Hebron ex-mayor Shaikh Jabari as an alternative interlocutor. The PLO expanded the Palestine National Council, adding delegates representing communities from Jordan, the Persian Gulf and the United States, as a way of solidifying its claim to "sole, legitimate representative."[22]

The chief obstacle to Carter's goal of reconvening the Geneva conference was the question of Palestinian representation. Under pressure in Lebanon, the PLO conducted indirect negotiations with secretary of state Vance through Saudi Arabia. In May 1977, the Saudi foreign minister presented Washington with a PLO "peace plan" restating the centrality of the Palestine question, the role of the PLO, the need for a genuinely sovereign and independent state in the West Bank and Gaza, and willingness to reexamine its charter in the process of transforming it into a state constitution that would have to reflect "existing realities and agreements." When Vance returned to Saudi Arabia in August 1977, it was against the background of little progress in this diplomatic minuet and the rise to power in Israel of Menahem Begin and his hardline Likud Party. Vance had been authorized to offer official meetings with the United States in return for PLO acceptance of Resolution 242, but not an invitation to a peace conference, which the Palestinians insisted on. Begin's "secret peace plan," meanwhile, offered partial Israeli withdrawal from Sinai and Golan and "autonomy" for the occupied West Bank and Gaza.[23]

The final U.S. effort at moving toward comprehensive negotiations was the joint communique issued by Vance and his Soviet counterpart on October 1, 1977, which spoke of "resolution of the Palestinian question, including insuring the legitimate rights of the Palestinian people" and "legal and contractual formalization of decisions" worked out by "representatives of all the parties . . . including those of the Palestinian people."

Israel and its supporters immediately condemned the joint communique and rejected it outright, on the grounds that the concept of Palestinian rights "carries by implication the foundations of a Palestinian state." Israel also objected to the statement's failure to cite UN Resolutions 242 and 338 (1973). "We hang onto those with all our strength because they say nothing about the Palestinians." Carter immediately negotiated with Israeli foreign minister Moshe Dayan to produce a "working paper" that dutifully reduced the Palestinian role to a ceremonial one. Arafat, for the Palestinians, accepted the formulation that Palestinian representatives be "nonprominent" members of a joint Arab delegations, but insisted that they be appointed by the PLO.[24]

All of this was overtaken by Anwar Sadat's dramatic visit to Jerusalem in November 1977 and subsequent Egyptian-Israeli-U.S. negotiations. Any Palestinian temptation to join with Sadat was doused by the Egyptian president's invitation to PLO and non-PLO Palestinians to preparatory talks. All of this was quite congenial to the Carter administration, and PLO rejection of Sadat's move prompted Brzezinski's famous "Bye-bye, PLO" remark. By the end of 1977, Carter himself declared himself opposed to an independent Palestinian state, confining himself to the opinion that what was required was simply "Palestinian participation in the determination of their future."

The protracted and tortuous negotiations that finally produced the Camp David Accords in September 1978 and the Egyptian-

Israeli-U.S. peace treaty in March 1979 did secure an Israeli commitment to complete withdrawal from the Sinai. It was, though, a separate peace, one that allowed Israel to solidify its hold on the West Bank and Gaza and, in the end, facilitated the 1982 invasion of Lebanon. In this it fulfilled Henry Kissinger's goal of isolating the Palestinians. In his off-the-record 1975 remarks cited earlier, Kissinger prophetically characterized Sadat as "an Egyptian nationalist. If you gave him the '67 borders you would never hear from him again."[25]

REAGAN'S REJECTIONIST YEARS

The separate peace of Camp David set the stage for the belligerently anti-Palestinian tone and policy of the Reagan years. Begin was able to turn his intransigence over Palestinians and Palestinian territories into U.S. pressure on Sadat because unfolding revolutionary events in Iran made Washington quite desperate for a pact that would secure both Israel and Egypt in a reconstructed post-Shah strategic alliance. By the time Carter left office in January 1981, the revolution in Iran, the Soviet invasion of Afghanistan, and Israeli intracability on Palestine had thoroughly discredited and disoriented the policy he originally articulated. The renewal of Cold War tensions stemmed in part from developments in and around the Middle East. The Carter Doctrine, with its echoes of "rapid deployment" and "power projection," provided the atmospherics for the entry of Ronald Reagan.

Reagan's campaign proclamation that "Israel is a strategic asset" was more than an electoral slogan. Once Reagan took office, it served as a cancellation notice on Washington's earlier assumption that settlement of the Palestine-Israel conflict was integral to the U.S. mission of maintaining its grip on the Middle East and, especially, the Persian Gulf. Palestine had nothing to do with the Iranian Revolution or the takeover of the Grand Mosque in Mecca. There was little point in making all tasks subsidiary to a Palestine settlement if it is, at best, a secondary factor where things count—in the Persian Gulf. Any solution would require a great deal of political capital, not to mention enormous commitments of aid and arms. Why risk straining Israel with pressures for a settlement that, even if successful, would leave the Arab states of the Gulf vulnerable to insurgency and unrest?

At his first news conference the president declared that Israeli settlements in the occupied territories were "not illegal." Asked if he had "any sympathy toward the Palestinians," Reagan responded with a flat "no." The contrast with Jimmy Carter's talk about the need for "a Palestinian homeland" could hardly have been more striking. Secretary of State Alexander Haig, for his part, announced that "international terrorism will take the place of human rights" on the State Department agenda, and the next day Israeli warplanes launched attacks against Palestinians in several Lebanese cities. Geoffrey Kemp, responsible for Middle East matters on the National Security Council, had recently described the Israeli armed forces and infrastructure as "obvious political assets" and considered it "a real question whether now is the ideal time for Israeli withdrawal from other occupied territory just as these assets are growing in value."[26]

The new administration gave the Begin government extremely wide latitude to pursue its punishing policies against Palestinians in the occupied territories and Lebanon, but a bombing of downtown Beirut in July 1981, which killed hundreds of civilians, proved too much. What followed was a cease-fire between Israel and the PLO, indirectly negotiated via special U.S. envoy Philip Habib. Israel chafed mightily under the cease-fire, because it granted the PLO a kind of de facto recognition and allowed the Palestinians to demonstrate "moderation." For the next ten months, Begin, defense minister Ariel Sharon and ambassador to the U.S. Moshe Arens worked to persuade Washington that any sequel to the Egyptian-Israeli treaty required elimination of the Palestinian armed presence in Lebanon.[27]

Israel finally launched its massive invasion of Lebanon in early June 1982. Virtually alone among the nations of the world, the United States did not issue a single statement deploring or criticizing the invasion. Even the U.S. vote for a UN resolution calling for an immediate Israeli withdrawal was recanted within a week as "no longer adequate to the needs of the situation."[28] U.S. arms deliveries occurred at a pace higher than in previous years. Secretary Haig inadvertently referred to downed Israeli warplanes as losses "we" suffered, appropriately capturing the identity of views in Washington and West Jerusalem.[29] The United States supported the Israeli view that there should be no return to the situation that existed before the invasion—that is, the cease-fire—and the U.S. position on issues like the withdrawal of the PLO from Beirut shifted neatly in tandem with Israel's.[30]

Even after George Shultz replaced Haig at the State Department, U.S. policy varied from Israel's only to criticize from time to time the harsh bombing campaigns against the beseiged Lebanese capital. Habib's mission remained the same: to supervise and facilitate diplomatically Israel's expanded war aims. Among the many illusions shattered by this war was the notion that U.S. policy was driven by popular domestic support for Israel. The problem for the administration was just the opposite: a fear that public revulsion with Israel's conduct might "translate into eroded support for Israel."[31]

On September 1, after the last PLO forces left Beirut, President Reagan unveiled his "Reagan plan," a script crafted by George Shultz in close consultation with Henry Kissinger. In this speech, Reagan for the first time referred to the Palestine problem as "more than a question of refugees," opposed Israeli settlements in the occupied territories, and also for the first time, publicly endorsed the formal U.S. policy since 1967 that a negotiated settlement must involve "an exchange of territories for peace."

The Reagan plan represented an attempt to take advantage of Israel's punishment of the PLO to push for a settlement that would require Israel to forfeit most of the West Bank and Gaza while insisting that the Palestinians accept Jordanian custodianship. The U.S. plan, in other words, called for a restoration of relationships, particularly that between the Arab states and the PLO, that existed prior to June 1967, as if nothing had changed in the interim!

When the Arab heads of state met a few weeks later in Fez, Morocco, they endorsed the land-for-peace formula but reasserted the demand for a Palestinian state and recognition of the PLO as sole, legitimate representative of the Palestinians. They let it be known, though, that the PLO would come under pressure to designate King Hussein to represent Palestinian interests in negotiations with Washington.

After Beirut, the PLO had to maneuver between the crippling embrace of Syria on the one hand and surrendering its "sole representative" role to Jordan and Egypt on the other. Syria's military victory over PLO loyalist forces in Tripoli, Lebanon, at the end of 1983, and Damascus's subsequent uncompromising hostility toward Arafat, had the paradoxical effect of freeing the PLO chairman to move more openly toward Cairo and Amman. Arafat's trip to Cairo in December 1983 was the first for any Arab leader since Camp David and signalled the PLO mainstream's readiness to restructure Arab alignments. The United States wanted Arafat to give Hussein the political cover necessary to initiate "autonomy" talks with Israel. In February 1985, Arafat reached an agreement with King Hussein that called for Palestinian self-determination within the framework of a Palestinian state and a Jordanian-Palestinian confederation. Within months, though, the agreement came apart, as the Palestinians remained unwilling to surrender the two principal provisions of the Rabat summit of 1974: Palestinian statehood and PLO representation. In the course of this struggle, Washington made not the slightest effort to distance itself from Israel, even on questions like settlements, though this would have dramatically altered the balance of forces within the PLO concerning the "Jordanian option."[32]

AFTER THE *INTIFADA*

It is ironical that the Reagan-Shultz team, which had done so much to indulge Israel's desire to eliminate the PLO and Palestinian nationalism as a political force, should have been the administration that ended up, virtually in its last days, initiating a formal dialogue with the very same PLO. This was, above all else, a result of the Palestinian uprising that broke out in Gaza and the West Bank in December 1987 and dominated the politics of the region and U.S. policy there until the summer of 1990. The *intifada* precipitated sharp differences within the Israeli political elite and among its supporters in the United States, creating pressures on the administration to push Israel toward a more compromising position. The 1988 presidential campaign in the United States witnessed a candidate, Jesse Jackson, who spoke forthrightly and favorably about Palestinian rights. Washington saw its major military ally virtually paralyzed politically, while the increasing weight of the inhabitants of the occupied territories in PLO deliberations prompted that organization to declare unequivocally, in the 19th Palestine National Council of November 1988, for a Palestinian state alongside Israel—a resolution based on "possible rather than absolute justice," in Arafat's words.[33]

Despite the enormous changes wrought by the uprising inside Palestine-Israel, as well as the collapse of the "Soviet challenge" in the region, the Bush administration used the "dialogue" with the PLO to stall rather than facilitate any movement toward political settlement. The Pentagon widened and deepened the military relationship between the two countries, and in October 1989 Washington closed off U.S. entry to most Soviet Jews wishing to emigrate, channeling them toward Israel and strengthening the hand of annexationist forces there.

Although Bush and Baker do not have the same visceral attachment to Israel as that exhibited by the Reagan administration, neither have they been inclined to alter radically an alliance that has seemed to advance U.S. interests in the region. Their key State Department and NSC appointments for the Middle East have come almost exclusively from the ranks of Kissinger associates and the Washington Institute for Near East policy, a pro-Israel think tank. It was the Washington Institute that came up with the "Shamir election plan," which has occupied U.S.-Israeli relations for most of 1989–90.

But Shamir did not like the plan that bears his name. It reflects a strategy propounded by Yitzhak Rabin, recently defense minister, and is designed to draw out a team of Palestinian negotiators, with PLO acquiesence, whose existence can then justify marginalization of the PLO itself. Shamir, by contrast, is determined to avoid not only negotiations of substance but also any procedural steps that might have implications for substance. He will not use the bait of interminable talks with the PLO even to undermine the PLO. As long as "his" proposal functions to obstruct "progress," it is working. Any "progress" that would concede the least bit of legitimacy to Palestinian aspirations is the beginning of a slippery slope toward a Palestinian state.

The U.S. approach of tying up Israelis, Palestinians, and Egyptians in issues of procedure reached its apogee in the Baker plan, which proposed a process of exasperating complexity and indirectness: (a) American contacts with the parties to bring about (b) a meeting in Cairo of U.S., Egyptian, and Israeli foreign ministers to select members of a Palestinian delegation that would (c) sit down with the Israelis to discuss the framework of negotiations that would (d) lead to elections in the occupied territories to choose Palestinian negotiators who would (e) decide with Israel on the terms of an autonomy scheme that would, in the fullness of time, produce (f) final status negotiations on issues of substance. By insisting that Shamir was indispensable to this scheme, Washington participated in stopping it dead in the spring of 1990.[34]

Even if Shamir had played along, it would have signified little. All the issues that have bedevilled negotiations so far will be compounded once the meeting commences. Matters of procedure would continue to obscure matters of substance. U.S. funding, and thereby complicity in Israel's occupation, would continue unabated.

LINKING PALESTINE TO THE PERSIAN GULF

Washington's approach to the Palestine-Israel conflict under the Bush administration has been essentially consistent with that of his predecessors. The president's statement of October 9 reflected the dilemmas posed by the glaring inconsistencies in the administration's policies toward Iraq's occupation of Kuwait and Israel's occupation of Palestinian territories, particularly in the aftermath of the October 7 killing by Israeli police of some two score Palestinians at Jerusalem's Haram al-Sharif (the Noble Sanctuary, and one of Islam's most sacred sites).

The fall of 1990 found the United States facing the consequences of its decades-long policy toward the Palestine-Israel conflict. The U.S. response to Iraq's invasion of Kuwait—the military deployment of nearly a quarter of a million troops and the parade of UN Security Council resolutions insisting on immediate and unconditional Iraqi withdrawal—has stirred a deep Palestinian and Arab resentment of Western imposition of a political order that treasures the convenient sovereignty of tiny sheikhdoms where there is oil but sanctions continued dispossession and oppression where there appears to be strategic advantage.

In many ways more typical and indicative of U.S. policy than the press conference response of October 9 was President Bush's statement a week earlier in his address to the UN General Assembly. Iraq's unconditional withdrawal from Kuwait, he proposed, "might" produce opportunities "for Iraq and Kuwait to settle their differences permanently, for the states of the Gulf themselves to build new arrangements for stability, and for all states and peoples of the region to settle the conflict that divides the Arabs from Israel."

This formulation perhaps reveals more than the president intended. First, it clearly subordinates the Palestine-Israel conflict not only to the immediate Gulf crisis but to the construction of "security" arrangements there favoring U.S. interests. Second, the president noticeably avoids even using the words *Palestine* or *Palestinians*. Instead there is the semantic preference for *states* that matches the historical record of U.S. policy. Finally, there is the extremely conditional characterization of "opportunities," a phrase that stands exposed and vulnerable against the sorry record of U.S. deceit, evasion, and manipulation around this issue.

The purpose of the war option in January 1991 was not simply to reverse Iraq's occupation of Kuwait, but to do so in a manner that isolated that crisis from others in the Arab world and from history. Washington claimed that prompt steps toward resolution of the Israel-Palestine conflict would "reward" Iraq's aggression. In the real world, these crises are linked, and a key part of the linkage is U.S. policy itself. The United States imposed its own linkage that deferred, once again, the long-overdue need to apply the principles of self-determination to Palestinians and Israelis.

Washington's military victory in the Gulf crisis was a pyrrhic one. The real threat is political, and it must be met by political means. Washington could have "disarmed" Baghdad politically by moving promptly and persuasively to support the long-standing international consensus behind a two-state solution to the Israel-Palestine conflict. The principles and mechanisms of the campaign to secure Iraqi observance of Security Council resolutions can still serve as a precedent for securing Israeli observance of the Security Council resolutions that apply to it.

Nearly twenty years ago, in the spring of 1973, Malcolm Kerr wrote that

> The Palestine crisis has crystallized the accumulating unhappiness of a whole generation, and continues today to channel it in a rising stream against certain targets that under other circum-

stances would not be so vulnerable: the United States, their own governments and the established buy shaky fabric of institutions and classes in their own society. . . . Americans may well come to wish that their government had taken decisive steps to stem the drift and give the forces of moderation in Arab society a chance to recover their grip on affairs while there is still time.[35]

A few months later, the Middle East again erupted in war, and not for the last time. Henry Kissinger's strategy in the aftermath in one way understood Kerr's concern, but Kissinger sought to build up the moderate Arab regimes by isolating the Palestine question rather than by coming to grips with it. This was the road of Camp David, a road littered with victims. One of them is Malcolm Kerr himself, murdered in Beirut while serving as president of the American University of Beirut.

Another victim has been the U.S. policy to restore the status quo in the Gulf. The juncture of the Gulf Crisis and the Palestine-Israel conflict represented an unprecedented fusion of the politics of oil and the Palestine question. Washington has recognized this with its efforts to arrange negotiations between Israel and the Arab states in the aftermath of the military victory over Iraq. At the end of 1991, though, it was not clear that the United States has substantially altered its determination to marginalize the Palestinians politically and subordinate them to the regimes in place.

NOTES

1.   Cheryl Rubenberg, "U.S. Policy Toward the Palestinians: A Twenty Year Assessment," *Arab Studies Quarterly* 10, no. 1 (1988).

2.   Richard Cottam, "The United States and Palestine," in Ibrahim Abu Lughod, ed., *The Transformation of Palestine* (Evanston, IL: Northwestern University Press, 1971).

3.   Evan Wilson, "The Palestine Papers, 1943–1947," *Journal of Palestine Studies* 2, no. 4 (Summer 1973).

4.   This point is discussed in Edward W. Said, "The Idea of Palestine," *MERIP Reports* no. 70 (September 1978) and in Joe Stork and Sharon Rose, "Zionism and American Jews," *MERIP Reports* no. 29 (June 1974).

5.   Michael J. Cohen, *Truman and Israel* (Berkeley: University of California Press, 1990), pp. 96, 189, 215.

6.   Ibid., p. 273.

7.   See the discussions in Steven L. Spiegel, *The Other Arab-Israeli Conflict* (Chicago: University of Chicago Press, 1985); and Nadav Safran, *Israel: The Embattled Ally* (Cambridge, Mass.: Harvard University Press, 1981).

8.   Rashid Khalidi, "Consequences of the Suez Crisis in the Arab World," in W. Roger Louis and Roger Owen, eds., *Suez 1956: The Crisis and Its Consequences* (Oxford: Clarendon Press, 1989), p. 389.

9.   John C. Campbell, *Defense of the Middle East* (New York: Council on Foreign Relations, 1960).

10.   Spiegel, *The Other Arab-Israeli Conflict,* p. 86.

11.   Safran, *Israel,* p. 360.

12.   Fred J. Khouri, *The Arab-Israeli Dilemma,* (3d ed.) (Syracuse, N.Y.: Syracuse University Press, 1985), pp. 144–46.

13.   Spiegel, *The Other Arab-Israeli Conflict,* p. 197.

14.   Ibid., p. 199.

15.   William Quandt, *Decade of Decisions: American Policy Toward the Arab-Israeli Conflict, 1967–76* (Berkeley: University of California Press, 1977), p. 106.

16.   Published as William Quandt, Ann M. Lesch, and Fuad Jabber, *The Politics of Palestinian Nationalism* (Berkeley: University of California Press, 1972).

17.   This is discussed more fully in Joe Stork, "Israel as a Strategic Asset," *MERIP Reports* no. 105 (May 1982).

18.   The memo was first published in *MERIP Reports* no. 96 (May 1981).

19.   Spiegel, *The Other Arab-Israeli Conflict,* pp. 305–6. See also Marwan Buheiry, "The Saunders Document," *Journal of Palestine Studies* 29 (Autumn 1978).

20.   *MERIP Reports* no. 55 (February 1977): 24.

21.   Spiegel, *The Other Arab-Israeli Conflict,* p. 332.

22.   *MERIP Reports* no. 55 (February 1977): 24.

23.   Joe Stork, "Sadat's Desperate Mission," *MERIP Reports* no. 64 (February 1978).

24.   Ibid.

25.   See note 18.

26.   Stork, "Israel as a Strategic Asset".

27.   Joe Stork and James Paul, "The War in Lebanon," *MERIP Reports* nos. 108 and 109 (September–October 1982).

28.   *Washington Post* (June 15, 1982).

29.   *New York Times* (June 13, 1982).

30.   Stork and Paul, "The War in Lebanon," p. 7. See also Rashid Khalidi, *Under Siege* (New York: Columbia University Press, 1985).

31.   *Washington Post* (June 11, 1982).

32.   The best discussion of this period from a Palestinian perspective is Naseer Aruri, "The PLO and the Jordan Option," *MERIP Reports* no. 131 (March–April 1985). See also Ronald J. Young, *Missed Opportunities for Peace: US Middle East Policy 1981–1986* (Philadelphia: American Friends Service Committee, 1987).

33.   See the articles in *Middle East Report* (formerly *MERIP Reports*) nos. 155 ("The Middle East After Reagan," November–December 1988) and 158 ("Palestine and Israel in the US Arena," May–June 1989).

34.   For a fuller discussion, see Joe Stork and Rashid Khalidi, "Washington's Game Plan," *Middle East Report* nos. 164 and 165 (May–August 1990).

35.   Malcolm Kerr, "Nixon's Policy Prospects," *Journal of Palestine Studies* (Spring 1973): 25.

PART 4

U.S. Policy Toward the Islamic Republic of Iran and the Irangate Fiasco

U.S. Policy toward the Islamic Republic of Iran: A Case of Misperception and Reactive Behavior

Mansour Farhang

Since the fall of the Pahlavi monarchy in February 1979 U.S.-Iranian relations have been plagued with mutual distrust and hostility. This state of affairs cannot be attributed solely to the anti-American tendencies within the Iranian revolutionary movement, for the misperceptions of U.S. policy makers toward the Islamic Republic have had a provocative life of their own. Yet, given the interactive nature of all foreign policy making, any useful effort to comprehend the causes of Washington's failure to come to terms with the new reality in Iran has to include an analysis of the way in which the Iranian regime perceives or reacts to U.S. behavior. This chapter contends that a detailed examination of the admission of the Shah to the United States in October 1979 and the secret U.S. arms sales to Iran in 1985–86 (two policy decisions that exemplify the perplexities of the U.S.-Iranian relations over the past decade) can be used to illustrate how repeated miscalculation and confusion in the U.S. policy on Iran have contributed to the present impasse between the two countries. A candid discussion in Washington of the history of this impasse may well serve as a significant step toward ending it.

151

PRELUDE TO TEHRAN HOSTAGE CRISIS

First and foremost it must be recognized that from its inception the confrontation between Washington and the Islamic Republic was intimately connected to the power struggle among the various forces and persons in the 1978–79 revolutionary coalition. For by the end of the Shah's rule the quarter century of "special relations" between Washington and the Pahlavi regime had caused such widespread resentment in Iran that anti-Americanism had become a potent instrument of mobilization and legitimization in Iranian politics. It was this atmosphere that provoked the first attack on the U.S. embassy in Tehran only three days after the fall of the Shah's last prime minister, Shahpour Bakhtiar.

On that day, a group of armed fedayeen, an independent Marxist-Leninist formation, entered the U.S. embassy compound and took captive ambassador William Sullivan and his staff. However, because Ayatollah Khomeini showed no sympathy for the attack, Ebrahim Yazdi, then deputy premier for revolutionary affairs, managed to end the incident peacefully. According to Sullivan, after the embassy personnel were freed, Yazdi "made a rather eloquent little statement assuring us that the attack had been carried out by undisciplined elements of the revolution, that the government was deeply apologetic for what had happened, and that we would be afforded full protection in the future. He stressed that the government was not ill disposed toward the U.S., but that we would have different relations than we had had under the Shah."[1] Beginning with this episode both the far Left and the militant fundamentalist groups proceeded to exploit the general public's perception of U.S. hostility toward the revolution to discredit the provisional government of Mehdi Bazargan. In this early period Bazargan was able to withstand such attacks because Khomeini supported his conciliatory position toward the United States and rejected the extreemists' call to make anti-Americanism the focus of Iran's foreign policy.[2]

Yet, the challenge of anti-Americanism in postrevolutionary Iran was not a matter of high policy concern in Washington. President Carter and his advisers were informed of the critical nature of the situation in Iran but they had relegated the problem to the public affairs officers of the State Department or the U.S. Information Agency. Such individuals in charge of Iran after the fall of the Shah urged the policy makers to address the anti-American sentiment of the Iranian public as an issue of high priority but they could not impress anyone until it was too late.[3] During the nine months of Bazargan's premiership, February–November 1979, the only Iran-related issue that received constant attention in the Carter White House was whether the Shah should be admitted to the United States. In Iran, however, this was a period in which conflicts among the various supporters of the revolution spread and intensified. The debate over the new constitution became divisive and at times violent. There were also rebellions in the provinces of Kurdistan and Khuzistan. In the midst of these happenings, the extremists of both religious and secular variety were hard at work to portray the United States as the chief instigator of counterrevolutionary plots and accuse Bazargan of tolerating such activities.

This volatile political environment compelled L. Bruce Lanigan, the U.S. charge d'affairs in Tehran, and Henry Precht, head of the Iran desk in the State Department, to advise the White House to at least delay giving the Shah permission to enter the United States. They argued that the adverse effect of the move could seriously hamper the chances of normalizing U.S.-Iranian relations and would provide the extremists with an effective excuse to further weaken or even oust the Bazargan government. In a memo dated August 16, 1979, Lanigan went so far as to warn that the admission of the Shah to the United States could lead to the seizure of the American embassy in Tehran and the taking of embassy personnel hostage.[4] The message certainly was not lost on President Carter, for after reluctantly acceding to the pressure to allow the Shah to come to the United States he addressed his aides in the Oval Office and said: "What are you guys going to advise me to do if they overrun our embassy and take our people hostage?"[5]

According to President Carter's chief-of-staff Hamilton Jordan, when the Shah's request to come to the United States was under consideration, Secretary of State Cyrus Vance told the president, "whatever chance existed for establishing relations with the new government would surely be destroyed if the Shah came to the States. For the supporters of Khomeini, the return of the young Shah a quarter of a century earlier with the help of the CIA was a dark day in Persian history: the Moslem nation exploited by the godless West."[6] At first Carter was in agreement with this perspective. He maintained that "as long as there is a country where the Shah can live safely and comfortably, it makes no sense to bring him here and destroy whatever slim chance we have of rebuilding a relationship with Iran. It boils down to a choice between the Shah's preferences as to where he lives and the interests of our country."[7] The national security adviser, Zbigniew Brzezinski, argued the contrary position. "It is unlikely we can build a relationship with Iran until things have sorted themselves out," he said. "But it would be a sign of weakness not to allow the Shah to come to the States to live. If we turned our backs on the fallen Shah, it would be a signal to the world that the U.S. is a fair-weather friend."[8]

The pressure on President Carter to approve the move was intense and persistent. He writes in *Keeping Faith*:

> The Shah settled upon the Bahamas but later complained about the high prices and moved on to Mexico. Despite his great wealth, he seemed obsessed with the belief that people were trying to cheat him. He still wanted to come to the United States, where he had some enthusiastic advocates. Henry Kissinger called to ask me to let the Shah to come to the United States. David Rockefeller came to visit, apparently to try to induce me to let the Shah come into our country. Rockefeller, Kissinger and my national Security Adviser, Zbigniew Brzezinski, seemed to be adopting this as a joint project. . . . A vocal group of the Shah's advocates approached Vance and Brzezinski repeatedly and on occasion appealed directly to me. They had an ally in Zbig, but could not convince me or Cy. . . . Each time, they went away partially mollified, only to return again. Some were merely representing the Shah's interests, while others, like Zbig, thought we must show our strength and loyalty to an old friend even if it meant personal danger to a group of very vulnerable Americans.[9]

In his memoir, *Power and Principle,* Brzezinski describes the kind of pressure or incentive that might have contributed to his thinking on the subject. He writes, "in late July 1979, I was called by both Kissinger and [James R.] Schlesinger, who urged me to promote a reconsideration of our position on the Shah. Kissinger in his subtle fashion linked his willingness to support us on SALT to a more forthcoming attitude on our part regarding the Shah."[10] In reply to a researcher's inquiry concerning Brzezinski's contention, Kissinger denies the charge and maintains that the claim "is a reflection of his [Brzezinski's] biased perception and not of fact." He further states in the same letter that "the suggestion of my 'pressuring' the administration on the Shah's admission is also a distortion. The facts are that I–along with many others including several top members of the Carter administration—felt early on that the United States owed the Shah, an ally of almost four decades, the option of entering the U.S., at a minimum on humanitarian grounds."[11]

On October 20, when Henry Precht informed Ebrahim Yazdi, then the acting foreign minister, of the impending visit of the Shah to the United States, Yazdi protested the move and told Precht "you are playing with fire."[12] He was genuinely surprised by the decision because only a week earlier he had been personally assured by secretary of state Cyrus Vance, in their meeting at the United Nations headquarters in New York, that the United States had no intention of granting the deposed Shah a visa.[13] Yazdi was aware that many friends of Mohammed Riza Pahlavi were hard at work to obtain such permission for him, and he had repeatedly urged State Department officials to resist the pressure. Yazdi could not openly announce that he feared the Shah's admission to the United States would inflict the final blow to the weakened Bazargan government, but this is exactly what he tried to convey to the American diplomatic representatives in Tehran. Yet, Yazdi did not hesitate to promise, as both Lanigan and Precht reported at the time, that he would do his best "to protect the embassy just as he had in February 1979."[14] What he did not know and could not easily believe was that the judgment and recommendations of Bruce Lanigan and his colleagues had no significant impact on the White House.

The pressures or incentives that finally persuaded President Carter to allow the Shah to come to the United States were totally oblivious to the consequences of the decision either for Iran's domestic politics or for the future of U.S.-Iranian relations. Gary Sick, the principal White House aide for Iran at the time, recalls that

> In the weeks before the attack on the embassy, we had received assurances from Yazdi and Prime Minister Bazargan that the embassy would be protected. They were disturbed—as were many Iranians—by the sudden admission of the Shah to the United States, but they were also men of integrity who took their responsibilities under international law seriously. . . . I took

some comfort in the belief that those charged with the responsibility in the revolutionary regime would exert their best efforts to resolve this new crisis as quickly as possible. And so they did— for thirty-six hours, until they were swept from power in a new swerve of the revolution.[15]

It was only after the anticipated events actually happened that Sick and his colleagues, while gathering in the Operation Center of the State Department, began to ask themselves "the questions that would trouble many Americans in the long months ahead: Why had we let it happen? Could it have been prevented? And especially: Why had the shah been allowed to come to the United States at this delicate moment?"[16]

On October 22, 1979, Mohammed Riza Pahlavi was admitted to the Cornell Medical Center as a cancer patient. The next day, in a lecture at the Feizieh Theology School in Qum, Ayatollah Khomeini made a brief reference to the event and said: "I have been told Mohammed Riza has been admitted to the United States because he is stricken with cancer. I hope it is true." Some observers interpreted Khomeini's remark to mean that he wished the ex-monarch was actually suffering from cancer; others took it to imply that he was doubtful about the truthfulness of the claim. In any case, the statement was not intended to provoke the public to act against U.S. diplomatic presence in Iran. Even *Jumhuri-ye Eslami,* the daily organ of the Islamic Republican Party, did not take a militant position against the move. During this period there was still considerable freedom of expression and assembly for the various political groups that had fought against the Shah. The fundamentalist clerics were not yet powerful enough to effectively contain the activities of their critics and competitors within the revolutionary movement.

The street demonstrations in front of the American embassy in Tehran that immediately followed the Shah's admission to the United States were instigated and organized by Marxist-Leninist groups, particularly the Tudeh Party. The rapid expansion of these demonstrations deeply worried the fundamentalist clerics. This was the first time since the fall of the Shah that the leftist elements were seizing the initiative in a major public mobilization. The only way the clerical leadership could respond to the challenge was to steal the issue around which the mobilization was taking place.

The alternative was to use the Revolutionary Guards to protect the U.S. embassy against popular demonstrations. Such a move would have fulfilled the obligation of the Islamic Republic under international law, but given the Iranian public's pervasive distrust of the American attitude toward the revolution it would have been politically suicidal for the reign of the ayatollahs.

In the crucial two weeks between the admission of the Shah to the United States and the attack on the American embassy on November 4, the fundamentalist university students decided to follow their left-wing competitors in organizing anti-American demonstrations and demanding the extradition of the Shah to Iran. Khomeini's silence and IRP's indecisiveness about the developing situation had compelled the fundamentalist students to act on their own. Their daily arguments with leftist students had made them particularly sensitive to the Marxist-Leninist claim that religious forces could not be genuine anti-imperialist. Thus the attack by fundamentalist students on the American embassy was as much a product of internal power struggle as a show of rage against the United States. For they were convinced that hesitation on their part could only encourage the left-wing groups to enact their own design on the embassy, as they had done on February 14. This suspicion is supported by the fact that initially there were many leftists among the occupiers of the embassy. The first act of the principal conspirators or "students following the Imam's line," as they called themselves, was to expel the leftist and suspicious individuals from the embassy compound and "purify" the occupation.

For three days Ayatollah Khomeini said no word about the incident. On the third day, however, Ahmad Khomeini, the Ayatollah's son, came to the embassy and expressed his solidarity with its occupiers. And, once the holding of U.S. diplomatic personnel became a major crisis for America and television camera crews from around the world came to Tehran to cover the story, Khomeini found it appropriate to describe the seizure of the embassy as "the second revolution, which is more important than the first revolution," meaning the revolution that overthrew the Pahlavi monarchy. It is not an exaggeration to say that in the initial act of seizing the U.S. embassy Khomeini and his lieutenants took the lead from their student followers. Needless to say, they quickly moved to control the situation and use the ensuing hostage crisis to consolidate their power and disarm or discredit their opponents within the revolutionary movement.

The social democratic and progressive religious formations, represented by men like Mehdi Bazargan, Abolhassan Bani-Sadr, and Karim Sanjabi, opposed the hostage taking for moral and legal reasons, but given the general public's perception of the Shah's admission to the United States as a threat to the revolution, they were incapable of facing the issue openly. The People's Fedayeen Organization, the principal Marxist-Leninist group in terms of popular support and ability to mobilize, was paralyzed by the hostage crisis. Since anti-Americanism had the highest priority for the fedayeen, Khomeini's sensational confrontation with the United States robbed them of their supposedly vanguard position. The fedayeen's disorientation in the face of this situation was a primary cause of their fragmentation and their split into several factions. The Tudeh leadership, following the Soviet line, saw the U.S.-Iranian confrontation as a positive development and, thus, did everything in its power to prolong it. The Tudeh leaders also used the opportunity to portray, in sustained and systematic propaganda, the liberal (both religious and nonreligious) critics of the hostage taking as "pro-American" and "counterrevolutionary." This strategy enabled the Tudeh to maintain its legal activities longer than any other secular group. However, once the clerical leaders felt they no longer needed the Tudeh's unacknowledged assistance, they moved against its leaders with an iron fist. Ironically, it was finally on the basis of the information received from British intelligence that the Islamic regime charged the Tudeh leaders with crimes against the state.[17] The presumed members of the military wing of the party were executed; the rest are still in prison.

The Carter administration's economic and diplomatic sanctions against Iran were quite effective and damaging to the Iranian society. The country became so isolated that during much of the crisis it had to buy food, industrial goods, weapons, and other items on the European black market at inflated prices. Some import needs such as raw materials and spare parts could not be found in the black market. Consequently, many factories were shut down, and the resulting unemployment and shortages caused great hardship for the populace. In March 1981 it was estimated that the economic and financial loss to Iran exceeded $10 billion.[18] The freezing of the Iranian assets in U.S. banks brought so many suits against Iran that at least until the release of the hostages in January 1981 the Iranian government had to pay an average of $500,000 a month to the lawyers defending it in its disputes with U.S. companies.[19]

The diplomatic isolation of Iran and its compounding economic problems made the country so vulnerable that President Saddam Hussein of Iraq seized the opportunity to strike militarily at what appeared to be an easy target. Indeed, Iraq would not have dared to invade Iran if the country's economic capabilities and international position were not so weakened by the prolongation of the hostage crisis. At the very beginning of the confrontation many knowledgeable Iranians who were themselves critics of U.S. policy toward Iran warned the authorities about the destructive consequences of the situation for the country's security and economic well-being. Ali-Asghar Haj-Said-Javadi, a popular writer and human rights activist, in an article entitled "The Artillery That Shoots Lies," likened the keeping of the hostages to a rope around the neck of Iran. He courageously argued that the longer the crisis continued, the tighter the rope would become.[20]

Such warnings, however, could not impress Khomeini and his lieutenants because the political and psychological benefits of the episode were proving to be immense for the fundamentalist cause. They concentrated their efforts on the goal of imposing their hegemonic control on the Iranian state and society; economic loss and international isolation did not seem to concern them at the time. In fact, they were quick to use the external pressure on the country to intensify the xenophobic tendencies of their supporters. President Jimmy Carter tells us in his memoirs, *Keeping Faith,* that he decided to let the Shah into the United States for humanitarian reasons. If he had actually stood by this explanation and permitted the Shah to remain in the United States, he might at least have received a more respectful treatment from the Iranian rulers. Instead, only two weeks after the crisis began, Carter decided that the Shah should leave the United States as soon as his medical treatment in New York was over. Brzezinski seemed to have been the only one inside the administration who recognized the serious repercussions of such a quick retreat in the face of the Iranian intransigence. He said,

> frankly, Mr. President, I think that it is disgusting for us to be
> talking about getting the Shah out of the country. As you know, I
> always thought it was a mistake to make his coming to the U.S.
> an issue. But allow him to come here on humanitarian grounds
> for medical treatment and then to hustle him out of the country
> to satisfy some terrorists is not right. I am afraid that it will
> simply be read by Khomeini as another sign of weakness.[22]

In this prediction, unlike his original disconcern about Iran's reaction to the Shah's admission to the United States, Brzezinski proved to be right. For the virtual expulsion of the Shah from the United States could only lend support to the position of the most extremist forces on the scene, including the "students following the Imam's line," who later came to occupy many upper echelon positions in the Foreign Ministry.

More significantly, the Carter administration's seeming confusion and vacilation in facing the grave (and anticipated) implications of the ensuing hostage crisis convinced Ayatollah Khomeini that bold and intransigent action was the only way to deal with the United States. Thus from the perspective of Iran's fundamentalist rulers, as well as their sympathizers throughout the Middle East, hostage taking proved to be a novel and effective method of dealing with their external enemy. As for the cruelty and illegality of their action, the hostage takers rationalized their position by portraying their victims as representatives of evil or by invoking the superior morality of their own cause.

An ironic consequence of the hostage crisis was the convergence of interests between the militant fundamentalists in Iran and the Republican Party in the United States, for they both perceived the episode as an advantage for their own respective agendas. There is little doubt that the confrontation between the Carter administration and the Islamic regime significantly helped the militant fundamentalists in Tehran to consolidate their power. Similarly, it is beyond question that Carter's failure to free the hostages before the 1980 presidential election was a principal cause of his loss to Ronald Reagan. It might appear odd that the hostages were freed on the same day that Ronald Reagan assumed office, but if Ayatollah Khomeini's fixation to humiliate President Carter is taken into account then the coincidence would seem far less strange.[23] For Carter's defeat in the 1980 election was a high priority for the clerical leadership in Iran. During the hostage crisis official Iranian propaganda, taking its clues from Khomeini's public remarks, portrayed President Carter as the personification of the "Great Satan." There is little doubt that in the fall of 1980 Iranian representatives in the negotiations with Carter's envoy Warren Christopher used delaying tactics to make sure that no agreement was completed before the November 6 presidential election in the United States. As Gary Sick, the National Security Council's expert on Iran during the period, explains in his book *All Fall Down,* Carter still expected a breakthrough as late as Sunday, November 2, two days before the election. Sick writes:

> President Carter said that he found the dual-track approach attractive, i.e., keeping his public statement brief and essentially positive while informing the Iranians privately of the limits on U.S. actions. That avoided the risk of provoking an instant rejection from Iran while keeping U.S. options open for serious private negotiations. He noted that the media were interpreting the Iranian action as a transparent attempt to interfere in U.S. domestic politics. He wanted a clear statement that the Iranians would get no better deal before the election than after and that we rejected any such interference.[24]

The truth was that Khomeini had no intention of fulfilling Carter's hope for a last-minute breakthrough in the negotiations. For he was told by his trusted clerical lieutenants, Mohammad Beheshti and Ali-Akbar Hashemi-Rafsanjani, that the release of the hostages before November 6 could dramatically enhance the chances of Carter's reelection. Such a determination to defeat President Carter did not make sense in terms of Iran's national interests, but it certainly enhanced the credibility and prestige of the Khomeini regime among its followers and sympathizers, not only within Iran but also throughout the Middle East region.

THE REAGAN ADMINISTRATION'S ARMS SALES TO IRAN

Even though Ronald Reagan's campaign team and Iran's fundamentalist rulers shared the goal of ending Jimmy Carter's presidency, the Reagan administration's Iran policy did not improve on the performance of its predecessor. In 1981, President Reagan's first act on Iran was to issue a secret presidential order, called *findings,* authorizing the CIA to support pro-Western Iranian exiles opposed to the Khomeini regime.[25] This order included the payment of nearly $6 million to various royalist Iranians based in Europe and financing an anti-Khomeini exile-group radio station in Egypt. A Paris-based group, the Front for the Liberation of Iran (FLI), headed by Ali Amini, the man who negotiated the first post-Mosaddiq oil agreement with the U.S. and British oil companies, received $100,000 a month. In 1983, Oliver North became involved in supervising the FLI after hearing allegations of corruption within the group.[26] (The futility of such activities did not easily penetrate the wishful thinking of Reagan's intelligence operatives.) The Tower Commission Report reveals that as late as 1984 Geoffrey Kamp, Senior Director for Near East and South Asian Affairs on the staff of the National Security Council, reported to Robert McFarlane that "exiled Iranians, with whom he regularly communicated, hoped that, with foreign help, they might install a pro-Western government,"[27] despite all evidence to the contrary.

During the first five years of the Iran-Iraq War the Israelis used similar claims to obtain implicit approval of the Reagan administration for their arms sales to Iran. Of course, Reagan denies this and an Israeli official explains how such a denial can be plausible: "I think there were mixed signals. Let's say we tried to pay more attention to the positive signals. . . . I can't produce a document. I can't produce a letter. . . . It was not the green light. Not the red light. It was the yellow one."[28] Originally, Israeli defense minister Ariel Sharon was instrumental in securing Washington's acquiescence toward Israeli arms sales to Iran. He emphasized the wisdom of arms transfer to Tehran as a means of gaining "influence with moderate Iranian military officers."[29] As early as 1981, long before there were any American hostages in Lebanon, he effectively argued in Washington that arms sales to Iran would enable Israel and the United States "to cozy up to some of these army generals because they are the ones that will knock off these madmen."[30]

The unacknowledged collaboration between Israel and the Islamic Republic began shortly after the outbreak of the Iran-Iraq War in September 1980. From its inception the war was perceived by Tel Aviv as a positive development for Israeli security because it could keep the Iraqi armed forces engaged, divert attention from the Israeli-Palestinian conflict, and destabilize or preoccupy the

Arab states of the Persian Gulf. Thus to prolong the war, as early as December 1980, Israeli-connected arms dealers in the European black markets informed the Iranian authorities of their readiness to sell arms to Iran. When the message reached Khomeini, he decided that it was legitimate for Iran to purchase Israeli arms so long as the actual sellers were not Israelis. The Ayatollah wanted to make sure that his agents would be able to claim that they had never bought any weapons from Israel; he had his own concerns about the need for "plausible deniability."

To understand Khomeini's response to the first Israeli offer of arms sales to Iran, one must recall that at the time Iran was occupied by an intransigent Iraq and Washington had imposed a strict arms embargo on Iran. It is also important to remember that Iran desperately needed U.S.-made spare parts and equipment because the Islamic regime had inherited an American-trained and -equipped military. In the face of these facts, when Iranian purchasing agents started looking for the kind of black market dealers who could satisfy their needs, they soon learned that Israel was the only possessor of the armaments willing and able to bypass the U.S. prohibition. This exclusive position also enabled the Israelis to inflate their prices. There is no public information about the actual costs of the Israeli arms sales to Iran, but it is estimated that the total exceeds $3 billion.[31] Thus in addition to perceived security or strategic advantage, Israeli arms shipments to Iran proved to be a very lucrative business.

Within such a context, one can comprehend the motives and circumstances behind the 1985 Israeli initiative to get the U.S. government involved in its own ongoing arms sales to Iran. President Reagan and his covert operatives were lured into the plan because they were led to believe that the Israelis had useful contact with some anti-Khomeini and pro-Western elements within the Iranian regime. This fantasy was impressed on Reagan and his national security adviser by Israeli officials David Kimche, Yaacov Nimrodi, Amiram Nir, and Adolph Schimmer.[32] From its inception the idea had to be concealed from Iran experts because they could easily recognize it for what it was: a plot with no chance of success aimed at seducing the paramilitary fanatics in the Reagan White House. If the purpose of the arms sales to Iran was limited to the release of the American hostages in Lebanon, it would have been unnecessary for Robert McFarlane and Oliver North to travel to Tehran. Only the expectation of significantly influencing the course of events in Iran could justify such a high-risk undertaking.

There is some evidence that in 1985 the Iranian rulers were interested in a dialogue with the United States. In late July 1985, for example, in a lecture to Iran's ambassadors from around the world, who had been summoned to Tehran to discuss the steps that the Islamic Republic could take to improve its foreign relations, Ayatollah Khomeini hinted that contact with the United States might be permissible if Washington showed a desire to change its policy. He said, "it is clear that if we take one step toward America, they will take one hundred steps in return."[33] A cluster of internal and external reasons, including economic difficulties at home and the need to expand trade with the West, had combined to make Tehran receptive to a gesture of accommodation from Washington. Such a move had to be carried out in a patient, delicate, and gradual manner because, after years of referring to the United States as the "Great Satan," the Islamic regime hardly could change its position in an abrupt way. The clerical leadership needed time and unambiguous expression of respect for their independence from American officials to prepare their popular base for the rapprochement.

However, instead of cautiously testing Tehran's new posture, the Reagan White House impulsively accepted the Israeli proposal of arms sales to Iran in the hope of establishing contact with an anti-Khomeini faction within the Islamic regime. Robert McFarlane told a hearing of the Senate Foreign Relations Committee that the United States had no independent political intelligence about Iran and "relied primarily" on Israel's analysis of Iranian politics when the United States decided to sell arms to Iran.[34] Contrary to the implication that no better advice was available, there are in the United States today many learned and well-informed Iran experts (some of them are present or former State Department employees) who could have provided officials in Washington with a more impressive body of knowledge about the general character, nature of leadership, and the pecularities of the Islamic Republic than either the Israeli arms dealers or their Mossad colleagues. Such information had no attraction for Reagan's covert operatives because it did not offer a buleprint for subverting the government of Iran. The so-called Israeli intelligence was appealing to men like McFarlane, North, and Poindexter because they believed it could help them to gain "access and influence" in the target country.

According to the Tower Commission Report, on July 3, 1985, David Kimche, the director general of the Israeli Foreign Ministry, told Robert McFarlane, then the National Security Advisor, that some "Iranian officials had conveyed to Israel their interest in a discourse with the United States. Contact was to be handled through an intermediary (later disclosed to be Manuchehr Ghorbanifar) who was represented as having good connections to Iranian officials."[35] Then Kimche explained that the Iranians would be willing to demonstrate their "bona fides" by influencing the Hezbollah in Lebanon to release the American hostages. Washington was to show its "bona fides" by approving the sale of U.S. weapons to Tehran. Kimche's suggestions eventually found their way into the January 6, 1986, presidential order that, after referring to the Israeli plan, states: "to achieve the strategic goal of a more moderate Iranian government the Israelis are prepared to unilaterally commence selling military material to Western oriented Iranian factions."[36]

In the January 17, 1986, presidential authorization for direct American arms sales to Iran it is asserted that the U.S. government wants "to establish contact with moderate elements within and outside the Government of Iran by providing these elements with arms, equipment and related material in order to enhance the credibility of these elements in their effort to achieve a more pro-U.S. government in Iran by demonstrating their ability to obtain requisite resources to defend their country against Iraq and intervention by the Soviet Union."[37] In defending what can be described as only a surreal perspective, John Poindexter claims that "once the exchange relationship has commenced, a dependency would be established on those who are providing the requisite resources, thus allowing the provider to coercively influence near term events. Such an outcome is consistent with our policy objectives and would present significant advantages for U.S. national interests."[38]

The missing element in the White House calculation was the fundamental incompatibility of the Israeli initiative with the administration's widely known position and, even more important, the requirements of security in the Persian Gulf region, not to mention the prospect of normalizing U.S.-Iranian relations. After all, the State Department had already pronounced the Iranian regime a sponsor of international terrorism and launched "Operation Staunch" to actively discourage arms sales by other nations to Iran. From 1984 to 1986 "the U.S. government sent more than 400 cables to American overseas missions urging compliance with Operation Staunch."[39] A typical public statement from the State Department, dated May 1985, noted "the U.S. does not permit U.S. arms and munitions to be shipped to either belligerent and has discouraged all free-world arms shipments to Iran because, unlike Iraq, Iran is adamantly opposed to negotiations or mediated end to the conflict."[40] Yet, two months later President Reagan "authorized Israel to sell TOW antitank missiles to the government of the Ayatollah Khomeini, the Hizbullah's spiritual leader. Seven months later he authorized the direct sale of arms to Iran."[41]

The supposed catalyst who brought the disparate parties of the Irangate together was Manuchehr Ghorbanifar, an Iranian whose long-standing association with Israelis was well known to both U.S. and Iranian authorities. Before the 1979 revolution Ghorbanifar was the managing director of an Israeli-connected shipping company. The Iranians had no illusion about Ghorbanifar; they saw him as an Israeli agent who could facilitate their black market arms purchases. North and Poindexter also believed that Ghorbanifar was an Israeli agent or asset. The Minority Report of the Congressional Committees Investigating the Iran-Contra Affair takes the same position and thus infers that "Israel was more than a passive message bearer at the outset of the initiative."[42] Whether through Ghorbanifar or in direct talks with U.S. representatives, the Iranian contacts certainly conveyed the impression to the White House that in exchange for arms they would use their influence to win freedom for American captives in Lebanon. But it is doubtful how much they could do in this regard. The Shi'ites of Lebanon, whether violent or peaceful, have their own agendas and aspirations. Some of them identify with the Khomeini regime because they feel a sense of affinity with its ideology and populist appearance. However, the day Iran begins to treat them as a mere instrument of its own policy, only the mercenary types will remain as the ayatollahs' ally in Lebanon.

Irangate represents a rare occasion in which a Third World

state outsmarted a superpower in a game of deceit and manipulation. Oliver North says: "I lied everytime I met the Iranians."[43] This might be true but on the key issue of arms sales the lieutenant colonel delivered the goods. The rest of what he had to say did not seriously concern his listeners. It was his own sheer naivite to think otherwise. The Iranians who met North nicknamed him *sarhang be-mokh* (the brainless colonel). So long as he could deliver TOW and HAWK missiles, they were willing to hear his lies and reciprocate in kind. North says he believed that Manuchehr Ghorbanifar was "a cheat, a duplicitous sneak. . . . He was widely suspected to be, [among] the people I dealt with at the Central Intelligence Agency, an agent of the Israelis or at least one—if not more, of their security services."[44] Ghorbanifar, on the other hand, accuses North of having misled him by recounting "stories of conversations with the President which were wholly fanciful."[45]

The most significant aspect of Tehran's end of the affair was that from its inception it was supervised by none other than Ayatollah Khomeini. There is no doubt that in pursuing the Iran initiative the White House was dealing with the uncontested authority in the Iranian regime and not, as the Israelis had led Washington to believe, with a pro-Western or anti-Khomeini faction within it. In November 1986, following the disclosures of the Tehran-Washington contacts, Khomeini took the lead in defending and justifying Iran's role in the affair. When eight Majlis (parliament) deputies sent a letter to the Foreign Minister asking him to appear before the legislative body to answer questions, Khomeini attacked them for writing the letter and virtually forbade any criticism of Iran's involvement in the matter. The embarrassed Majlis deputies lost no time in withdrawing their request.

It simply is impossible to imagine that Ayatollah Khomeini would use the service of Israel to seek a genuine discourse with Washington. Even more unthinkable is the assumption that a particular faction within the Iranian regime could buy arms from the United States without Khomeini's approval. Those who assign an independent role to Iran's high-ranking military officers in the affair are simply imagining an Iranian military that has long since vanished. For the prerevolutionary armed forces have been thoroughly transformed and can hardly be regarded as a threat to the Islamic regime. Moreover, in the area of internal security the Revolutionary Guards Corps is by far the dominant institution in the country. Given Tel Aviv's undoubted awareness of these realities, one is left with the inescapable conclusion that Israel and Iran intended to draw the United States into the scheme to achieve their own separate (and mutually exploitative) objectives. As secretary of state George Schultz put it,

> much if not all of the incentive on the Israeli side of the project may well have been an Israeli 'sting' operation. The Israelis used a number of justifications to draw us into the operation— intelligence gains, release of hostages, high strategic goals. . . . Israel obviously sees it in its national interest to cultivate ties with Iran, including arms shipments. Any American identification with that effort serves Israeli ends, even if American objectives and policies are compromised.[46]

President Reagan maintains that his approval of the arms shipments to Tehran was intended to create a "strategic opening" to Iran—a euphemism for the desire to restore American power in Iran. This objective is perceived to be sensible by all elements of official Washington as well as by the mainstream press. Yet, in forty-five days of testimony in the Iran-Contra hearings, no one asked whether "strategic opening" to Iran was a feasible foreign policy goal. Stripped of a rhetoric, the arms deal was not intended to normalize relations with Iran, but, as Reagan said, it was an attempt "to find an avenue to get Iran back where it once was and that is in the family of democratic nations."[47] First of all, pre-revolutionary Iran was hardly "in the family of democratic nations." Second, for better or worse, the fundamentalist rulers in Tehran have so radically transformed the Iranian state and society that any thought of return to where the country once was is an uninformed fantasy. If the American government wished to communicate with Iran on the issues of mutual concern, then limiting the team of negotiators to a gang of arms dealers under the leadership of Oliver North could hardly serve the purpose. And the idea of using Israel as a mediator for legitimate discussion with Iran is too unreal to be taken seriously even by the Reagan White House. The likely truth is that President Reagan agreed to sell arms to Iran because Israeli agents were able to persuade his foreign policy advisors and operatives that the transactions could free the American hostages in Lebanon and, more important, enable the United States to establish contact with an anti-Khomeini faction within the Iranian regime.

CONCLUSION

The secret arms sales to Iran was bound to be exposed. It was simply a matter of time before one of the many strange bedfellows would find it advantageous to blow the whistle. Yet, there is no evidence that the president and his advisors gave any thought to the international implications of adopting the Israeli-instigated Iran initiative. None of them is reported as having wondered about the consequences of pursuing a clandestine operation that was so dramatically opposed to the public policy of the country. In many respects, the decision resembled the admission of the Shah to the United States six years earlier. In both cases the policy makers failed to comprehend the calculation behind the Iranian moves or face the predictable consequences of their own action. In both cases the crucial connection between Iran's foreign policy behavior and its domestic politics was lost in Washington. The hostage crisis, it would seem, taught U.S. policy makers very little in understanding the motives and ciphering of Iran's clerical rulers. Of course, Washington's indifference to the domestic context of Tehran's foreign policy was nothing new. For from the very beginning of its intimate relations with Iran the United States has exhibited a tendency to see the external behavior of the country either as a function of its position in superpower rivalry or as an expression of its leader's idiosyncrasy or ideology. In 1953, Mohammad Mosaddiq, the liberal nationalist prime minister, was seen as pro-communist and theatrical, whereas Mohammed Riza Shah was praised as "an unconditional ally" (in the words of Henry Kissinger) and a modernizer. In both cases the characterization was preposterous. Today, because the label of pro-communist does not fit Ayatollah Khomeini, he is portrayed as irrational and fanatic. It seems that Washington is unwilling to consider the possibility that Iran can have purposeful and indigenously inspired foreign policy of its own. Of course, the normative evaluation of such a policy is entirely a different matter. The point here is that, whereas Khomeini is certainly an obstinate man, such a characteristic does not prevent him from being a calculating actor, as his performance in the hostage crisis and the secret arms deal has clearly demonstrated. The fact that his version of Iran's interests and aspirations is considered repugnant by many of his countrymen hardly makes him alone or unique among the modern national leaders.

Absence of visible political dissent in Iranian politics further complicates the orientation of U.S. policy makers because it reinforces their inclination to neglect the impact of domestic politics on the foreign policy behavior of the country. However understandable such a negligence might be, it nevertheless diminishes the capacity of the United States to pursue a realistic course in its dealings with Iran. For in the contemporary world even the foreign policy of despotic regimes cannot be comprehended or affected without an appreciation for their domestic goals and dilemmas. American policy makers are conditioned to look for politics only in liberal democratic contexts. And they tend to confuse their preference for such a politics with the idea of politics itself. This perceptual flaw often leads to a virtual denial of politics in analyzing the affairs of the Third World, for politics in many Third World countries does not have a liberal democratic form or substance. In the case of the Islamic Republic, although acknowledging both the historical limitations of political action and the autocratic character of the regime, the fact remains that substantive choices concerning the distribution of power and resources are being made by competing actors within the established order. Needless to say, the Iranian state restricts political participation and routinely violates the civil rights of its citizens but it is nevertheless quite conscious of the needs and expectations of its popular constituency.

The sorry state of affairs between the United States and the Islamic Republic represents an instructive case of how the failure of U.S. policy to respect the indigenous choices of a Third World state can produce estragement and destructive behavior. This is not to underestimate the existence of inherent tension between the course of the Iranian revolution and the American interests in the Middle East region. In fact, fundamental conflict of interests between the two countries were bound to emerge after the fall of the Pahlavi monarchy, but these conflicts need not have led to perpetual antagonism. In 1979, shortly after the seizure of the American embassy in Tehran, President Carter was asked whether the U.S. government would be willing to apologize to Iran for the 1953 CIA engineered coup against Prime Minister Muhammad Mosaddiq. Carter replied: "1953 is ancient history." At the time, due to the understandable anger of the American public toward Iran, the insensitivity of this remark was lost on even the most liberal elements of the attentive foreign policy public. For few observers seemed to notice that the U.S. president's "ancient history" was, for the vast majority of Iranians, a vivid reminder that America was hostile to popular rule in their country and that moderation in the face of this hostility was futile.

What needed to be recognized in Washington after the fall of the Shah was that the unavoidable discord between revolutionary Iran and the United States was so closely connected to the Iranian public's memory of the 1953 coup, as well as to the country's unavoidably chaotic postrevolutionary domestic political scene, that any United States move in the encounter was bound to have serious repercussions for the evolving character of the new order in Iran. Yet, instead of initiating a policy of accommodation and maintaining a low profile to alleviate the Iranian distrust, the Carter administration behaved in such a thoughtless fashion that it actually aggravated the estrangement and contributed to the ascendancy of the extremist forces in the revolutionary coalition. Similarly, the Reagan administration's arms sales to Iran in 1985–86 (as well as its approval of the earlier Israeli sales) played into the hands of the most militant and expansionist elements within the Islamic regime.

The failure and frustration of Washington's Iran policy and the abusive intransigence of the Iranian rulers toward the United States have combined to produce a situation in which a new set of myths about Iran and Iranians is being popularized in America. For example, the mainstrem press has come to portray Iranians as a people driven by religious fanaticism and a desire for martyrdom. Such a frame defies the realities of sociopolitical life in Iran and substitutes labels and slogans for reflection and analysis. For a quarter century prior to the 1979 revolution the Westerners who studied Iranian state and society had never observed that Iranians were particularly fanatic or anxious to sacrifice themselves to gain early entry to heaven. But since the establishment of the Islamic

Republic many observers have suddenly discovered that Iranians, as Shi'ite Muslims, exhibit a martyrdom complex and are hostile to reason and fairness in the conduct of their affairs. This image is as fictitious as the prerevolutionary view of Iran—cultivated by official America and reinforced by the mass media—as a land blessed with a modern ruler, economic development, and political stability.

Game metaphors can sometimes help clarify the interplay of international politics. If we assume a spectrum of various games signifying, on the one end, purpose, planning, calculation, and anticipation (i.e., chess); and on the other, impulsiveness, transience, precipitancy, and negligence (i.e., pinball), we can safely say that U.S. policy toward Iran since 1979 has been closer to pinball than to chess. Put simply, those who provoked the hostage crisis and produced the Irangate affair were blind to the intricate challenge posed by revolutionary Iran. They appeared to be more attuned to short-term domestic politics than to long-term foreign policy.

If Washington wishes to break the present impasse in its relations with Tehran, it should begin the process by undertaking a reappraisal of the ends and means to its past Iran policy. It has to acknowledge the fact that Iran as its favorite client state is gone forever, that its ability to determine the course of events in that country has been vanished. What the Islamic Republic expects from the United States is an unequivocal expression of respect for its political and ideological independence. An adequate picture of the new Iran demands delineation and the application of common sense to the complex realities of a society torn by war and revolution. Generalizations and stereotypes derived from either texts on Islam or the ideological rhetorics of clerics in Tehran can only blunt the kind of reflective awareness that is desperately needed if the future of U.S.-Iranian relations is to take a turn toward rationality and accommodation.

NOTES

1. William A. Sullivan, *Mission to Iran* (New York: W. W. Norton, 1981), p. 264. Sullivan, U.S. ambassador in Iran until April 1979 was quite appreciative of Ebrahim Yazdi's intervention to end the seizure of the embassy in February 1979. He is reported to have remarked that Yazdi saved his life in the incident.

2. There was very little specifically anti-American rhetoric in Khomeini's public speeches until the admission of the Shah to the United States. It was not until a week or two into the hostage crisis that Ayatollah Khomeini discovered America was more useful to him as an enemy than as a friend.

3. Gary Sick, *All Fall Down: America's Tragic Encounter with Iran*. (New York: Random House, 1985). Sick's analysis of the early stages of the hostage crisis, particularly in chapters 9 and 10, illustrates the failure of the Carter administration to pay adequate attention to the implications of anti-Americanism in postrevolutionary Iran.

4. Lanigan's memo was among the embassy documents seized by the "students following the Imam's line," on November 4, 1979. Gary Sick also mentions in *All Fall Down* that Lanigan consistently advised Washington that "the entry of the shah [to the United States] would be extremely dangerous for Americans in Tehran," p. 183.

5. Hamilton Jordan, *Crisis: The Last Year of the Carter Presidency* (New York: G. P. Putnam's Sons, 1982), p. 32.

6. Ibid., p. 29

7. Ibid.

8. Ibid.

9. Jimmy Carter, *Keeping Faith: Memoirs of a President* (New York: Bantam Books, 1982), pp. 452–53.

10. Zbigniew Brzezinski, *Power and Principle* (New York: Farrar Straus and Giroux, 1983), p. 474.

11. The letter of inquiry was sent to Kissinger by a Bennington College student, Betsy Dale Treitler, who sought the information for her senior thesis, "The Press And Foreign Policy: A Case Study of Press Coverage of the Issues Surrounding the Carter Administration's Decision to Admit the Shah to the United States," (Bennington, Vt.: Bennington College Library, 1986). Kissinger's letter is attached to the thesis as an appendix.

12. Yazdi recounted the conversation to me in December 1979.

13. I was present at the meeting as Yazdi's adviser.

14. Jordan, *Crisis*, p. 32.

15. Sick, *All Fall Down*, p. 176.

16. Ibid.

17. The source of information was the Soviet vice-consul in Tehran, Vladimir Kuzichkin, who defected to Britain in mid-1982. Kuzichkin provided the British with a list of several hundred Tudeh Party agents operating within various organs of the Islamic Republic. The British passed on the information to the Iranian government.

18. The study of the hostage-related financial loss was conducted by Iran's Central Bank during the presidency of Abolhassan Bani-Sadr.

Ali-Reza Robari, the chairman of the Central Bank at the time, was accused of treason by Iran's clerical rulers for making the study public.

19.   As Iran's ambassador to the United States during the first five months of 1980 I knew of the legal fees paid to the American lawyers who were representing Iran in U.S. courts.

20.   Ali-Asghar Haj-Said-Javadi, *Jonbesh* (Movement) (April 14, 1980).

21.   Jordan, *Crisis,* p. 69.

22.   Ibid.

23.   A number of observers suspect that the common desire of the Reagan campaign team and the ruling Iranian clerics to defeat the reelection effort of President Carter led to contact and complicity between them. There is some suggestive, however circumstantial, evidence to give credence to such contention. See Christopher Hitchens' articles in *The Nation* (June 20, July 4–11, August 1–8, October 24, and November 21, 1987).

24.   Sick, *All Fall Down,* p. 318.

25.   *Washington Post* (November 19, 1986).

26.   Ibid.

27.   *The Tower Commission Report* (New York: Times Books, 1987), p. 104.

28.   *Washington Post* (August 16, 1987).

29.   Ibid.

30.   Ibid.

31.   This estimate was quoted to me in the summer of 1987 by a highly informed member of the Iranian Central Bank.

32.   *The Tower Commission Report,* pp. 22–30.

33.   *Kayhan* (Tehran: June 30, 1985), p. 1.

34.   *New York Times* (January 17, 1987).

35.   *The Tower Commission Report,* p. 24.

36.   Ibid.

37.   *Washington Post* (January 11, 1987).

38.   Ibid.

39.   *Report of the Congressional Committees Investigating the Iran-Contra Affair* (Washington, D.C.: U.S. Government Printing Office, 1987), p. 159.

40.   Ibid.

41.   Ibid., p. 161.

42.   Ibid., Minority Report, p. 527.

43.   Oliver L. North, *Taking The Stand* (New York: Pocket Books, 1987), p. 325.

44.   Ibid., p. 307.

45.   *The Tower Commission Report,* p. 73.

46.   *Report of the Congressional Committees Investigating the Iran-Contra Affair,* pp. 527–28.

47.   President Reagan's televised speech, November 16, 1986.

CHAPTER 7

Irangate:
The Middle Eastern Connections

Stuart Schaar

Much remains unknown about the Middle Eastern connections in the Iran-Contra affair despite the wide availability of books, press reports, trial transcripts, congressional hearings, and other testimony on the subject. Evidence in the public domain reveals glaring contradictions in U.S. and Israeli foreign policy toward the belligerents in the Iran-Iraq War, which ended in a stalemate by 1988. Washington and Israel followed dual tracks in their relations with Iran. While condemning the Islamic Republic publicly as a terrorist state and telling the international community that it was leading a boycott of arms to Iran, the United States, working with Israel, supplied Tehran with weapons. Israel continued to deliver armaments to Khomeini's regime without interruption since 1979, operating with the knowledge of key U.S. officials. The United States also gave its supposed adversary critical military intelligence and negotiated for a presence in the country for American technicians. The same duplicity is seen in the Reagan administration's initial unwillingness to back coups aimed at removing Ayatollah Ruhollah Khomeini, while simultaneously marshalling world opinion against his regime. Rhetorical antiterrorism against Iran helped to build domestic consensus for U.S. intervention into other states, such as Grenada and Libya, but anticommunism made it imperative to ally secretly with the Iranian "terrorist enemy." The contradictions in the policies caught the Reagan administration and several Israeli governments in webs of intrigue.

In examining our lack of information about what transpired and in reviewing contradictions in U.S. and Israeli policy, if much remains unknown this is due to a conscious cover-up by the Reagan administration and Congress. Starting with this premise, this chapter focuses on the following questions: How did the U.S. Iran-Contra investigatory process lend itself to a cover-up? What motives were behind Israel selling Iran arms? To what degree did Israeli political and defense leaders view Iran as a potential ally against Arab Iraq, thereby making it feasible to supply Tehran with arms? Were arms sales policies part of larger U.S. or Israeli strategic planning? Did the sales of U.S.-Israeli military equipment or the supply of sensitive U.S. intelligence to Iran affect the conduct of the Iran-Iraq War? What did the Iranian revolutionary leadership expect to achieve by dealing with Israel and the United States for arms, intelligence, and technical assistance?

THE COVER-UP

When former attorney general Edwin Meese made his stunning announcement on November 25, 1986, linking the diversion to the Nicaraguan Contras of profits from covert arms sales to Iran, he handed Congress a convenient framework for its investigation and set the stage for a cover-up in the Irangate hearings. By stressing the issue of the diversion of Iranian arms sales profits to Nicaraguan Contras he helped to shift focus away from what transpired in the Middle East.

To this day Israel's role in the Irangate scandal remains clouded in secrecy. Two members of the joint congressional Iran-Contra committee remarked that during the inquiry "[m]any questions were not asked or could not be answered" and that "the full story of the Iran-Contra affair has not been told."[1] They admitted that "Israel's role in initiating the opening of the relationship with the so-called Iranian moderates" was one of the "areas that were not fully explored."[2] The Minority Report of the same joint congressional committee also noted limitations surrounding the preceding summer hearings. "The Administration's reliance on Israeli intelligence," they wrote, "has raised questions about Israel's role in the Iran initiative. That role probably will never be fully understood."[3] Stanley Hoffman lamented that in the hearings the "issue of Israel's

influence on American foreign policy and of the extent of cooperation between the countries' secret services was avoided."[4] David
Menashri likewise castigated the superficiality of our knowledge of
what actually happened: "Despite the fact that during the last few
months the Iranian arms deals have occupied a conspicuous position in the international media, there is still more that is not known
about them than is known"[5] While a big story lay in Tehran,
Jerusalem, and Tel Aviv, U.S. attention shifted to Costa Rica, Hon-
douras, and the frontier towns of Nicaragua and to a cast of shad-
owy figures, including some who reportedly were involved over the
years in assassinations, drug trading, gun running, and clandestine
support activities for the Contras.[6]

Most commentators thought that Meese was trying to limit
damage to the president by revealing information before a more
damning story trickled to the press piecemeal.[7] By doing so, was
the attorney general hoping to prevent another Watergate? Did his
disclosures help to set limits for the forthcoming investigations?
Because the fiasco was much too big to conceal, and former president Ronald Reagan's political foes had to derive benefits from a
scandal so large, Meese seemed to have decided to sacrifice momentarily a faltering U.S. Nicaraguan policy for a congressional
finding of presidential innocence in Irangate. Because few members of Congress wished to become embroiled in a scandal involving Israel and none wanted to initiate impeachment proceedings
against a popular president so soon after Watergate, the alternate
path outlined by the attorney general allowed officials to avoid
unwanted confrontations. Congress willingly shifted attention in
the Irangate hearings to Central America.

By November 1986 the Reagan administration had failed to
achieve one of its main foreign policy goals. The president could
not bring down the Sandinistas in Nicaragua by arming the Contras. The $100 million in Contra aid allocated by Congress could
not do the job. These mercenaries were a deadly nuisance, but their
presence in the mid-1980s had provided a rallying point for the
hard-pressed Sandinista regime against the gringo-backed insur-
gents and sparked an antiinterventionist reaction in the United
States. Several hundred millions of dollars needed to inflict severe
damage on the Sandanista state would not be forthcoming from
recalcitrant senators and representatives.

The Vietnam syndrome had held. That was the ideological remnant from the Indochina war through which the liberal center and a smaller Left opposed direct U.S. intervention. The U.S. church movement, this time led by activist Roman Catholics (whose priests and nuns in Central America provided eyewitness counterinformation) and some Protestant denominations, had galvanized a grass-roots movement. These joined forces with segments of the U.S. labor movement and other vestiges of the Vietnam antiwar struggle, to lobby Congress and educate the U.S. public. This groundswell prevented the coalescence of a consensual framework for invading Nicaragua and, more than most people imagine, forced the Executive Branch to adopt covert methods in its Nicaraguan policy. The Republican drive to overthrow the Sandinistas had been momentarily stymied. The Contra cause also seemed compromised.

Two months before the Irangate scandal exploded, Mansour Farhang had raised the issue of Israel selling Iran U.S. arms in contravention of American law. He wondered why there had been no move on Capitol Hill to investigate the matter.[8] The complicity of Congress and the mainstream press in refusing to deal in depth with the Middle Eastern arms supply issues before November 1986 carried over into the Irangate investigative period. With the Central American angle presented by Meese as a critical area of concern, Congress and the press focused mainly on the diversion issue.[9]

The Israelis were expected to remain uncommunicative and not reveal more than necessary about the affair. According to Israeli military analyst Hirsch Goodman, the inner Israeli cabinet received a copy of Meese's November 25 remarks on the diversion issue eleven hours before his announcement, allowing them sufficient time to map out a strategy for their response.[10] Calls from prominent U.S. Jewish leaders warned the triumvirate of Yitzhak Shamir, Shimon Peres, and Yitzhak Rabin not to act as the United States's fall guys.

From the inception of the weapons trade, Israeli officials questioned whether their country would have to absorb criticism for the United States when and if something went wrong. Then-secretary of state George Shultz admitted to the Tower Commission that by January 1986 the administration believed that with

Israel as "the conduit . . . it would be deniable, and we'd just say well, we don't know anything about it, and it's something Israel is doing, and so on."[11] In this way, Israel offered a convenient cover: If caught, what transpired would be hidden under a blanket of Israeli security censorship, and friends of the Jewish state in Congress and the media could be counted on to do their best to conceal facts from the American public. Robert McFarlane had even reportedly told Israeli Irangate figure David Kimche that "[i]f the episode is uncovered, we in the U.S. will deny it. . . . The guilt would be laid at Israel's doorstop."[12]

Thomas L. Friedman in the *New York Times* (November 25, 1986) summarized the Israeli mood on the eve of the diversion disclosure: "[t]he assessment within Israeli leadership circles is that the Reagan Administration will ride out the storm and that Israel should not panic by disclosing information that could add fuel to the controversy." Nevertheless, in a November 28 telephone call from then-Israeli prime minister Shimon Peres to Meese, the latter learned that Israel "was not going to take the blame for the diversion."[13]

The *Tower Commission Report,* the Iran-Contra congressional reports, and the televised hearings lacked analysis relating U.S. and Israeli policies to actual events on the ground in the Middle East. Without that analysis, even an informed public could not be expected to understand the full significance of the Irangate escapade. Although the summary conclusions of the Tower Commission and congressional reports skipped over Middle Eastern matters, these texts nevertheless contained new data. Yet they rarely explained the larger contexts in which events unfolded.[14]

THE UNITED STATES, ISRAEL, AND IRAN

By late 1984 the U.S. National Security Council had begun a major reappraisal of American policy toward revolutionary Iran. A major power shift was taking place within Iran among the forces engaged in the war against Iraq. An earlier shift had occurred in 1982. Then the Iranian military had succeeded in driving Iraqi forces out of Iranian territory, but instead of granting the victorious officers rewards commensurate with victory, the ruling Iranian mullahs decided to reduce the army's role in the war. The army general staff had objected to invading Iraq without careful preparation. They refused to proceed with massive attacks without proper air cover and plentiful supplies of ordnance, both of which Iran lacked. They could not acquire these because of budgetary constraints and the difficulties of procuring spare parts and advanced equipment.[15]

In contrast to the military, the Revolutionary Guards, or *pasdaran,* initially a more informally organized fighting force, had historically opposed fighting for small tactical territorial gains that bogged down the troops in endless small battles of no account. They preferred large-scale massive attacks that demonstrated an ideological commitment to armed *jihad,* or religious crusade. In these endeavors they joined forces with the numerically large *basiij* (militia). Their hope was to defeat the Iraqi regime through heavy assaults. The use of massive numbers in assaults actually cost the Iranian state less money than organized battles that the military planned and fought, because the militia depended on their localities and not on Tehran for sustenance. The state saved scarce funds when the militia joined battles and allowed a depleted treasury to carry on the war without squandering scarce resources. The shortage of revenue due to oil price declines had added to Iranian constraint and led to this shift in policy.

By the beginning of 1984, the mullahs were confronted with deteriorated battlefield conditions and very high war casualties. According to Israeli and British civilian strategic analysts, "failure of the February 1984 offensive, the largest engagement of the war (in which more than 20,000 Iranians died), led the Iranian leadership to abandon its strategy of frontal attacks in favour of 'conventional' operations of the sort that had proved effective in late 1981 and early 1982."[16] That meant that from early 1984 to the summer of 1986 Khomeini's regime allowed the traditional officer corps to regroup and assume major responsibility in the war alongside the Revolutionary Guards and the militia.[17] Officers who had replaced the Shah's generals as military commanders after the 1979 revolution were given enlarged roles in strategic planning and command.

In a Brookings Institution paper, "Ravaged and Reborn: The Iranian Army 1982," William F. Hickman argues "that purges in the Iranian military were not as extensive as many foreign observers believed."[18] Although some 10,000 men were removed, mainly from the high brass, Hickman maintained that sufficient officers remained in the army to serve the revolutionary regime. The purging process probably had some saluatory effects on the morale of the surviving junior officers, for, ironically, the combination of high war casualties and vacancies caused by purging officers opened up possibilities for rapid promotion. Despite the fact that mullahs controlled the armed forces at every level of command, the traditional military continued to function.

A new division of labor also emerged. Schematically, the *pasdaran* tended to use light-weight, hand-carried weapons and heavy-duty Soviet, Chinese, and North Korean equipment bought abroad or captured from Iraq. The military more often employed Western arms left over from the Shah's era or purchased on the open market after 1979.[19] A formal Iranian Navy was reconstituted as a force of 20,000, but it was stripped of its political influence. By 1984, human wave tactics camouflaged the military's carefully orchestrated battles.[20]

The payoff for full professional military integration into the Iranian fighting forces was seen at the Fao Penninsula campaign beginning on February 9–10, 1986.[21] The Iranian general staff had prepared minutely for this offensive, and it turned into the first major victory for the combined Iranian armed forces on Iraq's mainland since 1982.[22] Morale in Iran picked up; Iraq suffered a psychological blow. The victory impressed world chancelleries. But in retrospect, Fao was not a turning point, nor did it provide the pathway to conquest.

Saddam Hussein's air force, which had at least a 4 to 1 aerial advantage, failed at Fao. Iran brought down an unprecedented thirty Iraqi aircraft.[23] Swampy terrain and Iranian antitank missiles prevented Iraq's heavy armored vehicles from counterattacking. Rumors abounded that the United States ordered American-operated Saudi Arabian AWACS to beam out of the war zone during the Fao campaign (as they later did in the summer of 1986), thereby denying the Iraqi general staff critical intelligence normally passed to them by Riyadh.[24] The Iraqis accused the United States of orchestrating a disinformation campaign at Fao that they claimed contributed to their defeat. Although the Reagan administration denied the existence of such a campaign, in Paris officials at the French Ministry of Foreign Affairs, citing Iraqi defense sources with whom they had maintained close relations, believed that the United States did just that.[25]

British newspapers at the time claimed that China and North Korea had sent Iran missile batteries or advisors. The world press, however, remained silent on U.S. and Israeli collaboration with Iran. We now know that by September 15, 1985, Israel had sent Iran at least 504 TOW antitank missiles. In November eighteen Hawk surface-to-air missile systems were also delivered. Seventeen of these were later returned by the Iranians who rejected them because they lacked sufficient range to down Iraqi aircraft. They had been sold outmoded material. The Iranians probably intended to give these batteries to the military for use in their upcoming winter campaigns.[26] On January 6 and 17, 1986, then-president Reagan signed findings retroactively authorizing these and future arms shipments.

Just before the battle over Fao, on January 26 and February 5, 1986, the CIA, in coordination with Lt. Col. North, turned over to the Iranians "a map depicting the order of battle on the Iran/Iraq border" showing units, troops, and tanks and giving the Iranian general staff the wherewithal to plan out a meaningful offensive.[27] The Tower Commission reported that the information was "of potentially major significance to the Iran/Iraq war."[28] Then-deputy CIA director John McMahon had doubts about giving the Iranians such sensitive material and, before releasing segments of a larger map, worriedly cabled overseas to his boss, Director Casey that "[w]e are tilting in a direction which could cause the Iranians to have a successful offense against the Iraqis with cateclysmic results." Casey ordered him to proceed.[29] Intelligence of this sort proved so useful that when the "second channel" to the U.S. National Security Council agreed to meet with his American interlocuters in West Germany on October 6, 1986, he asked for further intelligence that, according to North, was given "a higher priority [by the Iranians] . . . than any other assistance we could provide."[30] Ironically though, the Revolutionary Guards, not the military, benefited from this new intelligence as the guards had already won out in their showdown with the military.[31] The army's objections to launching haphazardly organized large-scale offensives once more led to their reduced participation in the war. Their caution had again triggered the religious establishment's action.

Their removal from strategic planning and command posts thereafter greatly contributed to Iraq's strong showing in the war.

ARMS FOR IRAN AND ISRAEL'S ROLE IN IRANGATE

For several years the United States and the Soviet Union, by manipulating weapons sales through allied states, did not allow either Iran or Iraq to win the war.[32] Over forty-one countries from all blocs sold arms to the belligerents, with some supplying both sides.[33] Arms analysts have estimated that Western countries sold Iran about 20 percent of its defense needs. The estimate seems low because most of the trade was arranged secretly by private arms dealers whose illicit transactions they and Western governments had reasons to hide.[34]

After the Irangate story broke, Elaine Sciolino outlined highlights of this trade in the *New York Times*.

> [T]he Italian authorities have allowed spare parts for [U.S.] Hawk missiles and for helicopters to reach Iran. . . . Iran has also received transports and small trucks from Japan . . . armoured cars, rocket launchers and large amounts of hand grenades from Brazil; artillery and ammunition from South Africa; Fokker aircraft and military electronics from the Netherlands . . . and F-4 and F-5 parts, overcoats and uniforms from South Korea.[35]

In addition to selling ships, airplane engines, armored cars, and spare parts to Iran, Great Britain also concentrated on secretly repairing Tehran's damaged tanks, which were shipped back and forth between the United Kingdom and Iran.[36] Although the French provided logistic as well as major arms aid to Iraq, Paris also armed Iran intermittently and covertly.[37]

According to the Tower Commission, CIA intelligence reports claimed that "the Soviets were discreetly keeping their options open by allowing their East European allies to sell weapons to Iran while the USSR publicly supported Iraq."[38] North Korea reportedly supplied Tehran with 40 percent of its arms imports in 1982. By 1986 military imports from Pyongyang equalled at least $1 billion. The People's Republic of China had also contracted to sell the Islamic Republic billions of dollars worth of arms. North Korea and China together provided about 43 percent of Iranian arms imports in 1985 and close to 70 percent in 1986, while also supplying Iraq.[39] Poland, Czechoslovakia, Lybia, and Syria shipped weapons to Tehran as well.

The public record reveals that Israel continued to supply revolutionary Iran with military equipment, shells, and spare parts for Israeli-made weapons and U.S. tanks, aircraft, and artillery, without interruption from 1979.[40] Israeli explanations for these sales have varied over the years[41] from the desire to aid the fledgling Jewish community in Iran,[42] to helping Iranian military elements overthrow Khomeini or destabilize the Islamic Republic.[43] Other times Israel has claimed an interest in stemming Soviet influence over Tehran.[44] Also in fulfillment of the adage "the enemy of my enemy is my friend," Israelis note that it was logical that they ally with Iran against Arab Iraq, while simultaneously wishing to see both protagonists prolong the war indefinitely and weaken each other.[45] Embarrassment over the Pollard affair, wherein an American spy was caught stealing top U.S. military secrets for Israel in November 1985, led then-Prime Minister Peres to intensify his efforts to help the United States free its hostages in Lebanon.[46] Some commentators also claimed that Israel aimed to drive a wedge between the United States and its moderate Arab allies such as Egypt, Jordan, and Saudi Arabia, all of whom supported Iraq against Iran.[47] Others asserted that Israel hoped to legitimize its own covert arms transfers to Iran by associating the United States with these transactions.[48] Another motive was to gain leverage over the Shi'ites in southern Lebanon.[49] Finally they were eager to reap profits from the arms trade, earn badly needed foreign exchange, barter arms for oil and exotic Iranian foodstuffs, rectify deficits in their balance of payments, and create jobs in a depressed arms export market.[50]

The variety of motives for Israel-Iran arms transfers and changing explanations for that trade hides the fact that, beyond all else, the profit motive and the need for foreign exchange has always been present. Likewise a common thread runs through Israel's Middle East foreign policy since 1948 that strategists again articulated in 1981, at the initial stages of the Iran-Iraq War. Then-Prime Minister Begin's cabinet, meeting with senior intelligence officers, "decided it would be better if the Gulf War continue, and that if Israel had to take a stand in this conflict, it should favor Iran."[51]

Israel's siding with non-Arab Iran remained the core to which other motives for the arms transfers were added as external events changed and as media exposure became commonplace. Siding with Iran was consistent with long-term Israeli strategic doctrine.

The thinking of Israeli politicians and military officers who shaped Iranian policies was rooted in the 1950's. As Benny Morris writing in the *Jerusalem Post* explained,

> The "anti-Iraqi" or "pro-Iranian" lobby, which is led by [former] Defense Minister Yitzhak Rabin and is usually supported by [ex-]Trade and Industry Minister Ariel Sharon and some of the IDF brass, bases its arguments on "history" and past Iraqi performance. Put simply, the "pro-Iranians" say that Israeli policy since 1948 has been to try to forge ties with our "enemy's enemies" or the non-Arab or non-Moslem peripheries of the Middle East—Turkey, the Maronites of Lebanon, the Kurds, Sudan's African rebels, Iran and Ethiopia. That policy, which usefully weakened Israel's enemies (Iraq, Lebanon's Moslems, Sudan), was successful and should remain the basis of Israeli Middle East policy.[52]

Because this pro-Iranian lobby long considered Arabs untrustworthy, they argued that Israel had to look to the periphery of the Arab world, to Iran, Turkey, Ethiopia, and the southern Sudan, and to Middle Eastern ethnic minorities like the Kurds, and particularistic religious communities such as the Maronites and Druze in Lebanon, for potential alliances against the Arabs surrounding Israel. No matter that these regimes and ethnic communities might espouse radical ideologies and vent public hostility against Israel. Private accommodations had to be made with them.[53]

Most Israeli leaders followed the model of Israel's first prime minister, David Ben-Gurion, who identified the Arabs as Israel's perpetual enemy.[54] According to this view, Israel could not make lasting peace with the Arabs. Doing so would entail giving up Gaza, "Judea and Samaria" (the biblical name some Israelis have used for the West Bank), sharing the administration of Jerusalem, and relegating Israel to small power status.

Within the Israeli government during the Irangate period, then-foreign minister Shimon Peres and minister without portfolio Ezer Weizmann publicly expressed doubts about the wisdom of continuing to engage Israel too closely with Iran.[55] In the past their voices were muted, because the governments in which they served in key posts engaged in arms transfers to revolutionary Iran,[56] and it was under Peres's prime ministership that the Irangate operation developed. Israeli weapons transfers to Iran were then coordinated between senior officials in the defense ministry and the prime minister's office.[57] There are also indications that certain key members of the Israeli intelligence community were kept abreast of the transactions. The Mossad (Israel's foreign intelligence agency) bureaucracy apparently refused to get involved.[58] Those operatives brought in, however, included former Mossad officials. Their numbers remained small out of concern that normal intelligence sharing between the CIA and Israelis would tip off lower-level officers in the United States, thereby widening the possibility of leaks.

Available evidence demonstrates that the Reagan administration monitored Israel's arms transactions with Iran and at times even encouraged them, despite official policy that demanded the opposite action. *Time* magazine had already raised the issue on July 25, 1983.

> The underlying problem is that the U.S. has shown little zeal in enforcing the ban on arms sales to Iran. Concedes a high-level State Department official: "it is true that we have not done all we can to stop Israel's re-export of U.S.-made equipment to Iran." The unofficial Administration attitude seems to be that the sale of arms to Iran does little damage to U.S. interests.

One section of the congressional Irangate report focused on the issue of Israeli-U.S. complicity in supplying Iran with arms prior to 1985 and queried whether the United States violated its own embargo much earlier. It concluded that "Operation Staunch," a campaign initiated by the United States on December 14, 1983, to stop the flow of arms to Tehran from U.S. allied states, had too many loopholes; Israelis, in collusion with U.S. officials, seemed to violate the policy from its inception. The Majority Report stated:

> [r]eports persisted that Israel still actively supplied the Iranian military despite U.S. efforts to stop arms sales through Operation Staunch. Other reports hinted that U.S. and Israeli representatives met regularly to discuss Tehran's war needs. Widespread reports, particularly from the Middle East, also suggested that the United States was violating its own arms prohibitions.[59]

The Republican-inspired Minority Report of the joint House-Senate committee agreed that Israel had requested permission from the United States to ship weapons to Tehran, but contrary to the majority's contention, the minority claimed that the United States never gave a green light. This implied that Israel violated U.S. law and deceived the United States. The Minority Report quoted a State Department memorandum which asserted that

> in 1981 and 1982. . . . the Government of Israel asked the United States to approve shipment of certain military items under U.S. control to Iran. . . . The United States stated that certain types of U.S. controlled items could be shipped if specific U.S. Government approval were obtained, but no shipment of such items was ever approved.[60]

But as *Le Monde* pointed out on April 27, 1986, it was unlikely that Israel would have risked its relationship with the United States unless it had a secret agreement with the Reagan administration to help Tehran.[61]

It seems inconceivable that steady shipments of war materials from Israel could have escaped U.S. surveillance. Even if military equipment sailed under false bills of ladings and were transferred to third country vessels, the cargos would have been very difficult, if impossible, to hide from American satellites, AWACS and other intelligence-gathering sources. Pentagon worldwide computer tracking of U.S. military equipment stockpiled by allied states, even if inventories were inaccurate and out-of-date—as often is the case—would have picked up sufficient discrepancies and shortages to raise questions in Washington. Indeed, David Shipler of the *New York Times* on November 23, 1986, corroborated that "State Department officials . . . knew about Israeli shipments for at least five years before President Reagan authorized Israeli weapons deliveries as a way of reopening ties with Iran."

Some members of Congress had to know about the Israeli trade and implied American complicity in that trade. Yet, as previously noted, no congressional committee deemed it worthy of investigation before the story broke in Lebanon on November 3, 1986. The lack of congressional interest dates back a long way and stems from widespread pro-Israeli sentiment on Capitol Hill and the leadership's unwillingness to publicize Israel's role in perpetuating apparent illegalities.

Was it coincidence that Wolf Blitzer, former *Jerusalem Post* Washington correspondant before becoming the Pentagon correspondant for the U.S. Cable News Network, bragged about congressional support for Israel at the moment that the Irangate scandal broke in early November 1986? Blitzer wrote:

> The next Congress promises to be even more pro-Israel than the last . . . [and] is seen as a built-in guarantee that the Republican administration will not be in a position to lean too hard on Israel. . . . Virtually all of Israel's best friends in the Senate were reelected. . . . In the House, there will be about thirty Jews, roughly the same number as in the last session. All of Israel's best friends there were also reelected. . . . Returning to the Head of Appropriations Subcommittee on Foreign Operations will be Daniel Inouye of Hawaii. . . . [who is] seen as very pro-Israeli.[62]

The practice of turning a blind eye to apparent violations of U.S. law by Israel carried over into the congressional hearings that Senator Inouye cochaired. One of my Israeli interlocutors had been impressed with Inouye when he visited Israel. "He was tough on us in private and asked very difficult questions," I was told. "As a diligent senator, he will try to dig out the facts in the hearings, but we are not too worried, since he will probably bury major criticism of Israel in the body of the final report, which few will read." Israel's congressional allies, like Inouye, have worked hand in hand with Israel's military-industrial complex to protect that country's interests in the United States.

ISRAEL'S MILITARY-INDUSTRIAL COMPLEX

The increased militarization of Israeli society since 1971 has created strong internal lobbies for policies based on narrowly defined defense interests tied to arms sales. As a quantitative indicator of this militarization, between 1948 and 1970 Israel received from the United States a total of $277.3 million in military loans. Between 1971 and 1983, the total of U.S. military loans and grants soared to $16.8 billion. This exponential growth followed the U.S. government's aim under the Nixon Doctrine of arming allied states (Iran and Israel in the Middle East) to police strategic regions following the American debacle in Vietnam.[63]

Israeli scholar Alex Mintz provides another quantitative indicator of growing militarization of the society by examining Israeli investment patterns: "during the late 1960's, investments in the textile industry reached 15–18 per cent of total investments in industry in Israel, investments in chemicals and plastics 19–20 per cent and in defense-related branches 31–35 per cent. By the late 1970's, however, the respective percentages were 8, 14 and 50 percent."[64] Defense industries have employed about 25 percent of Israel's labor force and about half of all industrial workers, and in the late 1980s between one-fifth to one-third of Israel's non-diamond-related exports were defense related. Indeed, "Israel's ratio of defense exports to total exports is the highest in the world"[65] As one Israeli scholar has noted, "[d]efense, encompassing defense sales, is, after all, the biggest business in Israel."[66] Ze'ev Schiff in a harsh assessment of the role of defense industries in Israeli society has written:

> With time, Israel's defense industry became one of the largest pressure groups in the country. It dictated moves to the Defense Ministry and the three IDF [Israel Defense Forces] branches. In order to maintain itself the defense industry—or parts of it [—] acts as if it were in the "underground," even toward the Defense Ministry administration. . . . Responsibility is borne by the entire Cabinet, since defense ministers have themselves become hostages of the defense industries.[67]

Even kibbutzim and Histadrut labor union—federated subsidiary industries (tied to the Labor Party) manufacture weapons for export.[68] There are also more than 100 private companies producing for the military sector.[69] These frequently press for indiscriminate overseas military equipment sales, numbing the moral debate over such transactions.[70]

Ze'ev Schiff has estimated that the Israeli armaments industry had external sales of about $1.2 billion in 1986.[71] This sector expanded annually by 25 percent between 1968–75 when growth began to taper off.[72] Crises developed in the 1980s due to growing competition from other producers, especially Pacific rim countries, Brazil and Argentina, whose production costs were much lower than Israel's. In the realm of salaries alone "[t]he price of one hour's labor at IAI [Israel Aircraft Industries, owned by the Defense Ministry], which used to average $24, jumped to $34."[73] Servicing Third World debt also cut into the purchasing power of potential customers; such debtors also found it increasingly difficult to float loans for armaments imports.[74] Israeli defense circles sought new export markets to save jobs. By 1988 weapons exports soared to $3.4 billion only to fall by over 50 percent in 1989 when signed contracts for exported weapons amounted to $1.6 billion.[75]

The Israelis have specialized in manufacturing hand-tailored weapon systems for their large and reliable customers. Such had been the case with Pahlavi Iran. In many cases, shells and spare parts for these weapons could be purchased only in Israel.[76] The quantity of Israeli weapons, spare parts, and shells supplied to Iran after 1979 were only a small part of Tehran's military related imports. But because they were tailor-made and *formed the core weaponry* for the Iranian infantry since the days of the Shah, they were indispensable for the smooth functioning of the Iranian revolutionary armed forces.[77] The latter had conserved large quantities of stockpiled Israeli small arms and ordnance that the Shah had previously purchased. When the Iranian Revolution erupted, Israel also had in its warehouses significant inventories of undelivered orders for military equipment, ammunition, and spare parts designed specifically for Iran and that no other country could use.[78]

ISRAELI-AMERICAN CONNECTION TO IRAN: PLOT TO OVERTHROW KHOMEINI

Between 1984 and the summer of 1986, while the traditional army fought as equals alongside the Revolutionary Guards, opportunities opened for Israel and the United States to influence Iranian events. Whereas the United States had cultivated the top brass of the Shah's armed forces, most of whom had been eliminated, the Israelis had maintained contacts with Iranian arms dealers and some middle-level officers who had earlier served the Shah. As the Tower Commission observed, "[t]he Israelis represented that they for some time had had contacts with elements in Iran. The prospects for an opening to Iran depended heavily on these contacts."[79] Israel's arms deals with Tehran, which had continued unabated after 1979, had solidified some ties.[80] Since early 1984 the Israelis were aware of the shift in relationship between the Iranian army and the *pasdaran*. Armed with this knowledge and their contacts, the Israelis provided the United States with an indispensable means to reach out to the Iranian military and through them to targeted political leaders.

Both the Tower Commission and the *Congressional Report* stressed the importance that Israeli operatives and the U.S. national security staff placed in initially bolstering the Iranian military. In the strangest and least discussed scenario of the Irangate escapade, members of the U.S. National Security Council working with Israelis, contemplated using perceived allies within the Iranian military to overthrow the Khomeini regime.

The episode seemed like a partial rerun of events in the early 1980s when media reports claimed that Israel had considered helping friends from the Shah's days in the Iranian armed forces who hoped to stage a coup d'etat against Khomeini and replace him with the son of the late Shah. Yaacov Nimrodi, then appearing on the British "Panorama" program, which was broadcast in Israel on February 8, 1982, told viewers about the planned coup and added that the United States vetoed the plan. David Kimche, when asked by the interviewer on the same program "if this meant that . . . [Israel] wanted an Iranian military takeover[,] replied 'Possibly yes.' . . . On the following day he denied he had said any such thing."[81] On the same program Uri Lubrani, Israel's unofficial ambassador in Tehran between 1974 and 1979, recommended a military coup wherein "Tehran could be taken by a hundred tanks, with 'only' ten thousand dead." He, like Nimrodi, pointed out that the U.S. opposed the scheme.[82] In October 1982, the *Boston Globe* published an interview with then-Israeli ambassador to the United States, Moshe Arens, who, although admitting that Israel supplied arms to Iran in coordination with the United States, added that the aim "was to see if we could not find some areas of contact with the Iranian military to bring down the Khomeini regime."[83]

These statements by three of Israel's leading spies and a seasoned diplomat, make no sense. Why would these men publicize a failed coup against the same Iranian regime that they were supplying with millions of dollars worth of arms and ammunition and with which they expected to continue doing business? Nimrodi, Kimche, and Lubrani, three behind-the-scenes operatives who excelled at remaining closemouthed, and Arens, who, like most diplomats, lied as a matter of policy, most likely planted this news to lessen the public shock over leaks disclosing Israel's ongoing weapons trade with Iran. The manufactured ulterior motive for these sales—overthrowing Khomeini—would be viewed by Israelis and Westerners as a noble enterprise. But if such a plot had existed and failed, we never would have heard about it from any one of these four normally tight-lipped men.

The more intriguing aspect of these "disclosures" was the Israeli contention that the United States refused to countenance overthrowing Khomeini in the early 1980s. That claim actually corresponded to U.S. Iranian policy in the autumn of 1981. In planning a plot against Khomeini, organized with the Iranian air force, Sadiq Qutbzadeh, who had served as foreign minister in Tehran, sent an emissary to Washington to elicit support. The U.S. administration scarcely paid him attention.[84] The United States would not then support a coup against the Iranian regime because Khomeini was sufficiently anticommunist. On April 8, 1982, Qutbzadeh was arrested in Tehran, a prelude to his execution on September 15, 1982.[85]

As Eqbal Ahmad has noted, U.S. government strategists know the difference between real and rhetorical revolutions. Ahmad argues that Iran has had a profound cultural revolution, but has stopped short of transforming its productive forces through wide-scale land distribution or by introducing socialist structures into state-controlled industries.[86] The Iranian revolution therefore has posed no fundamental threat to U.S. interests as the leader of the capitalist world, nor to local oil potentates in the region. A consensus had formed in the Reagan administration that Khomeini, as an anticommunist, should be left alone and even supported. This consensus held until the Irangate period.

The former chief of SAVAK[87] under the Shah and a self-admitted covert agent for the CIA, Mansur Rafizadeh, writing in 1987 has claimed that CIA Director William Casey proposed selling arms to Iran as early as September 1981. "The reasons Casey gave," he wrote, "were that this would enable the United States to gather intelligence inside of Iran, to initiate contacts with the Iranian Army, and to discover Iran's military deficiencies."[88] Casey reportedly also proposed funding Iranian opposition groups to discover their membership and "offer this information to Khomeini in order to instigate a relationship."[89] At his behest, former President Reagan signed a finding that legitimized such CIA activities.[90] We now also know that in 1983, with information provided to him by the British, the Ayatollah purged his bureaucracy of communists and ushered in a reign of terror against them, to Washington's delight.[91]

Only in 1985–86, when a seemingly propitious moment arrived, with the resurrection of the military as a major fighting force, did a military coup leading to Khomeini's overthrow seem plausible to the CIA director and a limited group within the National Security Council. By then it appeared realistic to some that a still more malleable and anticommunist regime than Khomeini's could be installed in Iran. Rightly, the Secretaries of State and Defense viewed the entire matter as absurd. The problem was that Casey seems to have sold the idea to then-President Reagan. The scenario appears to have permeated the top levels of the U.S. intelligence community, as reflected in the November 9, 1986, *Washington Post* column by William Colby, CIA director under Presidents Nixon and Ford. "The United States," he wrote, "should actively encourage the appearance of a new Riza Shah [founder of the Pahlavi dynasty] probably and preferably out of the army rather than the clergy."

The Ayatollah, confident in the parallel structures that the revolution had created to control the population and military, allowed some officers to play along with the subterfuge. The mullahs controlling the military had standing orders to watch, listen, and report. Through them Khomeini had to be informed about U.S. and Israeli machinations, and found it convenient to milk his ostensible enemies for weapons that he could not buy on the open market.[92] Khomeini in his confrontations with the United States over the hostage issue had learned that the U.S. fear of communism could be used to Iran's advantage. Likewise, Israel's anathama toward Arabs could be exploited for Persian profit.

Although the *Tower Commission Report* and the joint *Congressional Report* of November 1987 mentioned the plot, few commentators took these allegations seriously and none have probed the issue.[93] Samuel Segev, in *The Iranian Triangle: The Untold Story of Israel's Role in the Iran-Contra Affair,*[94] a semiofficial Israeli record based on still classified documents and interviews with some of the participants, claimed that by February 1983 Israel accepted the Khomeini government and no longer explored possibilities for overthrowing his regime. This corresponded with the moment when "it seemed that the U.S. had accepted Khomeini's revolution as an established fact."[95] He nevertheless quoted from the Congressional *Iran-Contra Report* citing a communication from then-National Security Council director Robert McFarlane to the CIA director in which McFarlane claimed " 'that the Israelis intend[ed] to supply arms to certain elements in the Iranian army ready to overthrow their government.' "[96] Instead of investigating the matter, Segev left his readers with the impression that Israeli government leaders rejected participation in any such initiative. Most other commentators have dismissed the scenario as another wild scheme of former Lt. Col. Oliver North. Yet this failed plot has to be taken seriously at least from the U.S. and Israeli side of the triangle.

Ex-President Reagan testified that he understood that the Israeli arms deliveries to Iran were meant to shore up certain officers within the traditional military forces as well as their political allies.[97] Manuchehr Ghorbanifar,[98] the Iranian exiled businessman working with the Israelis and U.S. National Security Council operatives, on July 25, 1985, regarding 100 TOWs being sent to Iran by Israel, said that these missiles "would . . . win the support of the [Iranian] military."[99]

According to McFarlane, when David Kimche saw him on August 2, 1985, "Kimche said. . . . The Iranians were more concerned about . . . whether or not we would provide weapons right away . . . for the expansion of and consolidation of . . . army elements."[100] When Israel delivered 96 TOW missiles to Iran on August 20, 1985, "no hostages were released. Ghorbanifar had an explanation: contrary to his plan, delivery of the missiles was taken by the Commander of the Iranian Revolutionary Guards rather than by the Iranian faction [the military] for whom they were intended." Rectifying that mistake, a second shipment of 408 TOWs was sent by Israel to Tabriz on September 15, 1985. "Tabriz, rather than Tehran, was used as the Iranian delivery point to prevent this shipment from falling into the hands of the Revolutionary Guards."[101] Actually just that happened.[102]

By November 14, 1985, McFarlane told CIA director William Casey of the "Israeli plan to move arms to certain elements of the Iranian military who are prepared to overthrow the government."[103] On December 4, 1985, in a computer note to the new national security advisor, Vice-Admiral John Poindexter, Lt. Col. Oliver North listed as the first of "our three objectives . . . support for a pragmatic . . . army oriented faction which could take over in a change of government."[104] In another computer memorandum from North to Poindexter, on December 5, 1985, the former lieutenant colonel argued that it was in the interest of the U.S. and Israel that "a change of government in Iran is most likely to come about as a consequence of a credible military establishment which is able to withstand the Iraqi onslaught and deter Soviet adventurism/intimidation. The Iranian army (not the Revolutionary Guards) must be capable of at least stalemating the war."[105]

North sent Poindexter another memorandum on January 4, 1986, which contained his suggestions for the contents of a presidential finding authorizing retroactive and future sales of U.S. military equipment to Iran by Israel. In the covering memorandum for the president that Poindexter attached to the finding of January 6, 1986, but that Reagan claimed never to have read, North outlined former Israeli Prime Minister Peres's plan "to bring about a more moderate government in Iran" as follows:

> The Israeli plan is premised on the assumption that moderate elements in Iran can come to power if these factions demonstrate their credibility in defending Iran against Iraq and in deterring Soviet intervention. . . . The Israelis are prepared to unilaterally commence selling military material to Western-oriented Iranian factions. It is their belief that by so doing they can achieve a heretofore unobtainable penetration of the Iranian governing heirarchy [sic]. The Israelis are convinced that the Iranians are so desperate for military material, expertise and intelligence that the provision of these resources will result in favorable long-term changes in personnel and attitudes within the Iranian government. Further, once the exchange relationship has commenced, a dependency would be established on those who are providing the requisite resources, thus allowing the provider(s) to coercively influence near-term events.[106]

When the Revolutionary Guards emerged victorious during the summer of 1986 (and it was with this group that McFarlane was forced to negotiate on his famous trip to Tehran during July 1986) instead of calling off all deals, as McFarlane then recommended, the United States continued negotiating and supplying arms. At this point, getting the hostages out of Lebanon took precedence over plans for coups or long-term strategic concerns. As the Israeli Amiran Nir told Vice-President Bush at their meeting in Israel on July 29, 1986, "we are dealing with the most radical elements. . . . We've learned they can deliver and moderates can't."[107]

The Tower and joint Congressional committee reports reveal an Iran desperate not only for arms and spare parts but also for technical advice and U.S. intelligence. The Iranians were driven to solidify ties with Israel and the United States while both countries continued to be targets of the regime's anti-Zionist and antiimperialist propaganda. Realpolitik won out over rhetoric. The United States noted this and, later in the Irangate affair, U.S. officials, embellishing their fantasies, expected to be able to place CIA officials in Iran with the agreement of the Khomeini regime. The dream of reestablishing a U.S. listening post on the Iranian side of the Soviet border, they believed, would have been the pay-off for this secret aid. Disclosure of the McFarlane trip to Tehran by opponents of Iranian Assembly Speaker Rafsanjani curtailed all collaboration and opened up the pandora's box of Irangate.

Once Irangate exploded, Khomeini easily stymied any efforts at investigations or questioning by the Iranian National Assembly. After the United States and Israel had publicly been exposed as arms suppliers to Tehran, it was easier for Iran to acquire arms from other countries, such as China, which continued its sales without worrying about international condemnation. Who would take U.S. protestations seriously after Irangate?

The United States, caught in policies of duplicity, had to face the wrath of allied Arab states. In a knee-jerk reaction it used the pretext of Kuwaiti wooing of the Soviets to send a major fleet into the Gulf. Once caught, the United States then adopted Iraq's war aims and Iran became America's bête noir in the Gulf. Such policies may have been consistent with U.S. shifts toward the underdog throughout the Iran-Iraq War, but the irony of the situation was that by the spring of 1988 the tilt to Iraq gave that country a decided edge in the war and led to a cease-fire. Iraq's strength after the cease-fire held, ultimately led to confrontation between the United States and Iraq over Kuwait and control of Persian Gulf oil by August 1990.

NOTES

I owe thanks to the Blue Mountain Center and its director Harriet Barlow for a winter writing residency in 1988. The Israeli Government Press Office and Professor Israel Shahak provided me with their useful back files of English translations from the Hebrew press. Discussions with Dr. Chris Giannou, Professors Eqbal Ahmad, Hooshang Amirahmadi, Renate Bridenthal, Richard Falk, and Nikki R. Keddie, helped clarify some points of analysis in earlier drafts of this chapter.

1. Senators William S. Cohen and George J. Mitchell, *Men of Zeal: A Candid Inside Story of the Iran-Contra Hearings* (New York: Viking Penguin, 1988), pp. 3–4.

2. Ibid., p. 7.

3. U.S. House of Representatives Select Committee to Investigate Covert Arms Transactions with Iran; U.S. Senate Select Committee on Secret Military Assistance to Iran and the Nicaraguan Opposition, H. Rept. No. 100-433; S. Rept. No. 100-216, 100th Congress, 1st Session, *Report of the Congressional Committee Investigating the Iran-Contra Affair with Supplemental, Minority and Additional Views* (Washington, D.C.: U.S. Government Printing Office, November 13, 1987), p. 526; henceforth cited as *Congressional Report*. See also Walter Pincus and Dan Morgan, "High-Level Cover-up Shown in Irangate Testimony," *Manchester Guardian Weekly* (July 5, 1987).

4. Stanley Hoffman, "The War for Washington," *New York Review of Books* (October 8, 1987), p. 8.

5. David Menashri, "The American-Israeli-Iranian Triangle," *New Outlook* 30, no. 1–2 (January–February 1987), p. 11.

6. For a review of covert activities since 1959 of some Iran-Contra operatives, see United States District Court Southern District of Florida, Case No. 86—1146-Civ-King, "Amended Complaint for RICO Conspiracy, etc.," Tony Avirgan, and Martha Honey, Plaintiffs *v.* John Hull *et al.* (October 3, 1986) and *Affidavit of Daniel P. Sheehan,* Filed on December 12, 1986 (Minor Revisions January 31, 1987) (The Christic Institute, Washington, D.C.). See also Johnathan Marshall, Peter Dale Scott, and Jane Hunter, *The Iran-Contra Connection: Secret Teams and Covert Operations in the Reagan Era* (Boston: South End Press, 1987), especially chs. 3, 4, and 6; Leslie Cockburn, *Out of Control: The Story of the Reagan Administration's Secret War in Nicaragua, the Illegal Arms Pipeline, and the Contra Drug Connection* (New York: Atlantic Monthly Press, 1987), chs. 9 and 10; and Johnathan Kwitny, "Money, Drugs and the Contras," *The Nation* (August 29, 1987).

7. See Dave Lindorff, "Why Meese Spoke," *The Nation* (March 21, 1987).

8. Mansour Farhang, "Iran-Iraq Conflict: An Unending War Between Two Despots," *The Nation* (September 20, 1986). For details on this trade, see Segev, *The Iranian Triangle: The Untold Story of Israel's Role in the Iran-Contra Affair* (New York: Free Press, 1988), passim.

9. See Elizabeth Drew, "Letter from Washington," *The New Yorker* (August 31, 1987), pp. 71–89, which summarizes the record on the diversion issue. My argument does not imply that the diversion issue was a frivolous matter, but rather equally serious violations were committed in the Middle East by Israel and members of the U.S. administration that the congressional investigators glossed over. Peter Kornbluth noted that in the congressional reports following the televised hearings, "there is not one word about congressional complicity in allowing . . . illegal activities to go on as long as they did. In the report, as during the hearings, no mention is made of how inexplicably inattentive Capitol Hill was to Reagan administration's skullduggery before Attorney General Edwin Meese's dramatic disclosure on November 25, 1986 embarrassed the legislative branch into action. The Iran-Contra committees never pose the question, How did we let this happen?" Peter Kornbluth, "The Iran-Contra Scandal: A Postmortem," *World Policy Journal,* (Winter 1987–88): 133. Rowland Evans and Robert Novak, accused the joint congressional investigative committees of canceling the public testimony of Michael Ledeen (a key factor in the early stages of Irangate who served as intermediary between National Security Advisor Robert McFarlane and then-Israeli prime minister Shimon Peres) "so as to protect and not embarrass Israel." Mark Belnick, Deputy Chief Counsel for the Senate committee "vigorously denied a suggestion of conspiracy." See *The Jerusalem Post International Edition* (henceforth cited as *JPI*), Aug. 8, 1987).

10. Interview, Hirsch Goodman, Jerusalem, January 5, 1987. Goodman claimed that he had been shown the telegraphed message.

11. *The Tower Commission Report, The Full Text of the President's Special Review Board, John Tower, Chairman, Edmund Muskie and Brent Snowcraft, Members,* "Introduction" by R. W. Apple, Jr. (New York: Bantam Books and Time Books, 1987), p. 225; henceforth cited as the *Tower Report.*

12. Yossi Melman, *Davar* (December 16, 1986).

13. *Congressional Report,* p. 318.

14. "What is missing, perhaps inevitably in a bipartisan congressional investigation, is any serious attempt to situate the dense description of events in history and politics. But because the *Report* offers such a rich detail, a deeper understanding may be drawn from its 690 pages. . . .

Like the hearings that preceded it, the report omits much important background." Joe Conasen, James Ridgeway, and Murray Waas, "The Right Stuff: What the Iran-Contra Report Leaves Out," *The Village Voice* (December 1, 1987). For further analysis of the cover-up, see Marshal *et al., The Iran-Contra Connection,* pp. 123–124; and Johnathan Marshall, "Cover-up and Blowback: What Congress Left out of the Iran-Contra Report," *Middle East Report* [MERIP] (March–April 1988): 40–42.

15. See George Joffé and Keith McLachlan, *Iran and Iraq: The Next Five Years* (London: The Economist Publications Limited, 1987). See also *Economist Intelligence Unit,* Country Report, Iran, no. 3, 1986, p. 12, and no. 3, 1987, p. 11.

16. Efraim Karsh and Ralph King, "The Gulf War at the Crossroads," *The World Today* 42, no. 10 (October 1986): 168; see p. 167.

17. Ibid., p. 168, recognized the significance of this shift: "The regular army was once more placed in control of war operations. During 1984 Iran made considerable efforts to turn the Pasdaran into more 'conventional' units and to re-establish the working relationship between the Pasdaran and the regular army." Drew Middleton, *New York Times* military analyst, reporting from Tel Aviv on January 24, 1984, also noted that "[a] civilian analyst said one secret behind what he believed to be Iranian successes was that the leaders of the old regular army and air force and the new generals of the Revolutionary Guards had composed their differences and were now planning and directing operations in harmony." Shahram Chubin, "La conduite des opérations militaires dans le conflit Iran-Irak," *Politique étrangère,* no. 2 (Summer 1987): 307 and 309, also noted: "the professional [Iranian] officers concentrated on practical problems, like strategic planning, logistics, coordination, orders of command, etc. Their attention to detail was demonstrated in March 1985 during the Howeizah offensive, [which was] minutely prepared before it began. . . . Contrary to what happened between 1982 and 1984, large [military] operations were launched only after probing operations succeeded, coordination was better [and] a synthesis was worked out between the spirited fighting masses and professionalism."

18. Quoted in *The Guardian* [U.K.] (February 8, 1983). See also Haleh Afshar, "The Army," in Haleh Afshar, ed., *Iran: A Revolution in Turmoil* (Albany: State University of New York Press, 1985), p. 190, who claims that Khomeini sacked or executed over 13,000 of the Shah's 25,000 officers.

19. Dilip Hiro, in a personal communication, pointed out that the revolutionary guards primarily employed Soviet weapons, whereas the regular army used Western weapons.

20.   For details see *The Middle East* (December 1984): 26. See also Dilip Hiro, *Iran Under the Ayatollahs,* rev. ed. (London and New York: Routledge and Kegan Paul, 1987), p. 374.

21.   "the offensive [at Fao] inaugurates a [further] change in tactics, the General Staff having renounced the practice of sending waves of twelve–fourteen year olds on suicide missions. Instead they stress greater technical prowess. The Revolutionary Guards, the spearhead of the offensive, are older (twenty to twenty-five years) and much better equipped than during their previous offensives: well turned out uniforms, boots, [and] gas masks." Paul Balta, *Iran-Irak: une guerre de 5000 ans,* (Paris: Éditions anthropos, 1987), p. 182.

22.   *The Economist Intelligence Unit,* Country Report, Iraq, no. 2, (London, 1986), p. 7.

23.   Dilip Hiro, *Iran Under the Ayatollahs,* p. 388, citing the British press, asserts that within a two-week period the Iranians claimed to have shot down fifty-five Iraqi airplanes and helicopters. During the crisis following Iraq's invasion of Kuwait in August 1990, experts estimated the number of Iraqi pilots at 100. In light of those figures, Iraq suffered a major loss at Fao.

24.   See *Le Monde* (November 12, 1986); and Niles Latham, "AWACs Shocker! U.S. Ordered Spy Jets out of Iran-Iraq War in Hostage Deal," *The New York Post* (November 13, 1986). See also Dilip Hiro, ibid., p. 388.

25.   Multiple interviews, *Quai d'Orsay* [Paris] (January 28, 1987).

26.   Manuchehr Ghorbanifar, the Iranian businessman working with the Israelis and the United States, repeatedly claimed that Hawks were destined for the Iranian military. He was fearful that they would fall into the hands of the Revolutionary Guards. See Segev, *The Iranian Triangle;* pp. 174–175 and 204–205.

27.   *Congressional Report,* p. 222. The *Tower Report,* p. 240 ff., asserts that the intelligence reached Tehran in time for integration into Fao campaign planning.

28.   *Tower Report,* p. 73. Segev, *The Iran Triangle,* p. 240, writes: "It later became clear that this intelligence was of limited value and could not affect the situation at the front." He cites no sources for his misleading conclusions.

29.   *Tower Report,* p. 222; see also pp. 239–40.

30.   *Congressional Report,* pp. 259–60. Segev, *The Iran Triangle,* p. 252, identifies this "second channel" as Sadegh Tatabai, Khomeini's son-in-law.

31.   "In July, the commander of the Iranian ground forces, Colonel Ali Seyyed Shirazi, and the commander of the Revolutionary Guards,

Mohsen Rezaie, clashed violently over policy. Khomeini called them to his residence on July 19, 1986, where he enjoined them to 'seek unity'. . . . Shirazi and Rezaie were appointed members of the Supreme Defense Council, but three weeks later Shirazi was relieved of his post as commander of the ground forces, while Rezaie maintained his operational command. It appeared that Shirazi had been kicked upstairs and the Revolutionary Guard was once again in the ascendancy." Gary Sick, "Iran's Quest for Superpower Status," *Foreign Affairs* 65, no. 4, (Spring 1987): 705–6.

32.   See *The Middle East* (November 1987): 17–19. For conclusions of the Stockholm International Peace Research Institute (SIPRI), see the *Daily Telegraph* (March 3, 1984) and *The Middle East* (June 1984): 19.

33.   "The Reagan Administration listed no fewer than 41 countries that had provided Iran [alone] with weapons since the start of the war." *Congressional Report,* p. 159.

34.   According to Francis Tusa of the British Royal United Services Institute for Defense Analysis quoted in *The Middle East* (November 1987): 19.

35.   *New York Times* (November 5, 1986).

36.   Interview, Yehuda Litani, former editor *Jerusalem Post,* Jerusalem (January 12, 1987). See also Anthony H. Cordesman, "Arms to Iran: The Impact of U.S. and Other Arms Sales on the Iran-Iraq War," *American-Arab Affairs,* no. 20 (Spring 1987): 20–21.

37.   See *International Defense Review* (September 1984); *Sunday Telegram* (September 23, 1984); *New York Times* (November 25, 1986).

38.   *Tower Report,* pp. 114–15.

39.   Cordesman, "Arms to Iran," p. 19; Michael R. Gordon, "War in Gulf Spurs Chinese Arms Export Role," *New York Times* (May 19, 1987); Micahel Weisskopf, "China Secretly Selling Arms to Iran," *Washington Post* (April 3, 1984); and Patrick Seale, "North Koreans' Gulf Role," *The Observer* (February 23, 1986). Also the *New York Times* (November 28, 1986) and *The Middle East* (June 1984): 19.

40.   See Michael A. Ledeen, *Perilous Statecraft: An Insider's Account of the Iran-Contra Affair* (New York: Charles Scribner's Sons, 1988), p. 99; Stephen Engelberg, *New York Times* (November 8, 1986); Francis X. Clines, *New York Times* (November 9, 1986); Dan Fisher, *Philadelphia Inquirer* (November 23, 1986); *The Daily Telegraph* (March 3, 1984); Segev, *The Iran Triangle,* pp. 4–6.

41.   "Information about these arms deals has been published often by the world media, and time after time Israeli sources gave explanations: before the Iranian-Iraqi war it was the desire to strengthen the status of

Iranian officers who are supposedly in opposition to the Ayatollah, then it was the Israeli interest to engage Iraq in a long war, and get her out of the 'Eastern front' against Israel, then it was the national and humanitarian desire to protect Iranian Jews from internal terror, and now it is the need and necessity to help the Americans to release their hostages held by the extreme Shiites in Lebanon." R. Kislev, *Ha'aretz* (December 4, 1986).

42.   "In 1980 . . . when the Iraq-Iran war began, Iranian representatives met in Paris with Israel's deputy defense minister and worked out a 'Jews for arms' deal. Iran permitted Jews to emigrate and Israel sold Iran ammunition and spare parts for Chieftan tanks and US-Made F-4 Phantom aircraft. Channeled through a private Israeli arms dealer, this particular agreement appropriately ended in 1984, when Iran was slow in paying its bills." Jane Hunter, "Israeli Arms Sales to Iran," *The Washington Report on Middle East Affairs* (November 1986): 2. Then-vice prime minister and foreign minister Shimon Peres disclaimed any connection between Irangate, i.e., transactions in 1985 and after, and the needs or interests of the Iranian Jewish community in a speech before the Israeli Knesset (Parliament) after attorney-general Meese broke the diversion story: "Who said we did this out of concern for the fate of Iranian Jewry? This is not so. None of us said so. This, too, is incorrect." State of Israel, Government Press Office, From the Knesset, no. 32, *Foreign Minister's Knesset Statement* (November 26, 1986).

43.   Edward W. Said, "Irangate: A Many-Sided Crisis," *Journal of Palestine Studies* 16, no. 4, 64 (Summer 1987): 27–29.

44.   Yitzhak Shamir in June 1986 said that he was in favor of Western normalization of relations with Tehran. While in Paris he said "Iran is an important country of the Middle East that the West cannot ignore and abandon to the influence of the U.S.S.R." Paul Balta, *Iran-Irak,* p. 220, also p. 221; and *Ha'aretz* (November 9, 1986).

45.   *The Jewish Press* (December 5–11, 1986) lead story began: "Israel and the United States have a clear interest in seeing the Iraq-Iran war continue for as long as possible." See Segev, *The Iran Triangle,* pp. 140 and 151.

46.   "From the Israeli point of view, there was a strong desire . . . to help the U.S. on the issue of hostages kidnapped in Lebanon in order to get the 'Pollard affair,' which exploded in Washington with ear-piercing noise, out of the headlines." Shmuel Segev, *Ma'ariv* (December 19, 1986). See also Segev, *The Iranian Triangle,* pp. 208–9; Yoel Marcus, *Ha'aretz* (December 5, 1986). Regarding arms for hostages, former National Security Advisor Zbigniew Brzezinski confirmed in his memoirs that the Carter administration offered spare parts to Iran in return for release of the forty-four U.S. hostages held in Tehran. The practice did not

therefore begin in 1985. See *Time* magazine (July 25, 1983). In early April 1988 *The Miami Herald* confirmed Brzezinski's contention, but former president Carter denied knowing anything about such negotiations. Gary Sick, *All Fall Down: America's Tragic Encounter with Iran* (New York: Random House, 1985), pp. 310 ff., details what transpired at a secret meeting in Bonn between Warren Christopher and Iranian Minister of State Sadegh Tabatabai during the hostage crisis on September 16 and 18, 1980, just days before the outbreak of the Iran-Iraq War. "When Tabatabai alluded to the question of military spare parts, Christopher acknowledged that approximately $50 million worth of military spares . . . that Iran had ordered and paid for were in storage in the United States. Christopher said that the inclusion of military equipment would complicate any agreement, but this material could be made available to Iran once all other aspects of the [hostage] dispute were resolved" (p. 312). Later Sick reports that the "core group" in the United States responsible for the hostage issue on October 11, 1980, prepared "a draft message . . . for President Carter's approval offering [Iran] a military package of about $150 million . . . that would be made available upon release of the hostages." Sick transmitted the message to Camp David and after the "president approved the draft, it was sent out that evening" (p. 314). See also Cockburn, *Out of Control,* ch. 10.

47. Ze'ev Schiff, *Ha'aretz* (November 26, 1986). Also Rowland Evans and Robert Novak, *New York Post* (November 10, 1986).

48. According to Secretary of State Shultz, "I felt that one of the things Israel wanted was to get itself into a position where its arms sales to Iran could not be criticized by us because we were conducting this Operation Staunch and we were trying to persuade everybody not to sell arms. That is what all this is about." *Congressional Report,* p. 213.

49. Cordesman, "Arms to Iran," p. 23.

50. *Newsweek* (November 17, 1986). On the profit motive and the need to create jobs see Marshall *et al., The Iran-Contra Connection,* pp. 171 and 176. On the needs for foreign exchange and offsetting the Israeli trade deficit through intensification of military equipment exports, see Aharon Klieman, *Israeli Arms Sales: Perspectives and Prospects* (Tel Aviv: Jaffee Center for Strategic Studies, Tel Aviv University, 1984), pp. 8 and 21.

51. Y. Melman, *Davar* (December 7, 1986). Z. Schiff confirmed that this meeting occurred and what transpired. Interview, Tel Aviv (January 12, 1987).

52. Benny Morris, *JPI* (November 28, 1987).

53. "Despite the tremendous change which occurred in Iran, its involvement with and influence on the Shi'ites in Lebanon, and its part in

terrorism, it seems that Israel has not freed itself from the belief or the delusion that it will return to Iran. In the face of this notion is a minority conception which argues that Israel has an opportunity which absolutely cannot be missed to forge a link with Iraq and effect a change in that country's direction. The advocates of the Iranian conception believe that . . . [i]f any prospect for a strategic dialogue does exist, it is with Iran, as Tehran has several interests in common with Israel." Ze'ev Schiff, *Ha'aretz* (November 28, 1986). For discussions of the periphery strategy, see Benjamin Beit-Hallahmi, *The Israeli Connection: Who Israel Arms and Why* (New York: Pantheon Books, 1987), pp. 8–9, Uri Lubrani, "Open Options," *New Outlook* 30, nos. 1–2 (January–February 1987): 12–13; Menashri, "The American-Israeli-Iranian Triangle"; and Segev, *The Iran Triangle,* pp. 30–31.

54.   For roots of Israel's strategic doctrines, see Michael I. Handel, *Israel's Political-Military Doctrine* (Cambridge, Mass.: Center for International Affairs, Harvard University, 1973).

55.   Inga Doitchkron *Ma'ariv* (November 28, 1986), quotes Weizman that contacts with Iraq are preferable to those with Iran, because "Iraq is connected to Jordan and Egypt, with which we also have ties." See also Menashri, "The American-Israeli-Iranian Triangle," p. 13.

56.   "Weizman, reacting to foreign news reports that Israeli arms shipments were initiated during the Begin administration, stated that no such transactions had taken place when he was Defense Minister in Begin's Government." *Ma'ariv* (November 24, 1986). Weizman did not resign over the Irangate scandal in 1986–87, although he served in the cabinet while the arms transfers took place.

57.   Ze'ev Schiff, *Ha'aretz* (December 15, 1986).

58.   Ledeen, *Perilous Statecraft,* pp. 130–31.

59.   *Congressional Report,* p. 159. The *New York Times* (November 26, 1986) reported that "[a] former American official who routinely reviewed intelligence reports said . . . that the Reagan administration made at least two attempts in 1984 to use Israel to circumvent a Congressional ban on military aid to the contras."

60.   U.S. Department of State, Memorandum from Richard W. Murphy to Secretary of State Shultz, "U.S.-Israel Discussions on Arms Sales to Iran—1980–82, Nov. 21, 1986 . . ." quoted in *Congressional Report,* footnote, p. 526.

61.   Ledeen, *Perilous Statecraft,* p. 99, confirms that "there was no stern American condemnation of the practice [of Israel selling arms to Iran]."

62.   Wolf Blitzer, "Congress Likely to Be Even More Pro-Israel," *Jerusalem Post* (November 6, 1986).

63. Source: Library of Congress Research Service, printed in "U.S. Aid to Israel," in *AAUG Newsletter* 16, no. 5 (September–October 1983), Special Report no. 6, p. 14.

64. Alex Mintz, "Civilianization of the Military or Militarization of Society? Arms Production in Israel," *The Jerusalem Quarterly*, no. 42 (Spring 1987): 94.

65. Alex Mintz, "The Military-Industrial Complex: The Israeli Case," in Moshe Lissak, ed., *Israeli Society and Its Defense Establishment: The Social and Political Impact of a Protracted Violent Conflict* (London: Frank Cass, 1984), p. 112. See also Reuven Pedatzur, *Ha'aretz* (September 17, 1986). Alex Fishman, *Hadashot* (December 10, 1986), reported on "a survey published in 1984 [which] reveal[ed] that 25% of all the workers employed in industry . . . [we]re employed in the military industries." Yitzhak Deutsch, *Ha'aretz* (November 2, 1986), maintained that military exports had been 25 percent of all Israeli industrial exports (excluding diamonds), but declined to 20 percent by November 1986.

66. Klieman, *Israeli Arms Sales*, p. 36. Yoram Peri and Amnon Neubach, *The Military Industrial Complex in Israel: A Pilot Study* (Tel Aviv: International Center for Peace in the Middle East, 1985), pp. 52 ff. describes the growth of Israeli military industries to the point where the combination of arms dealers, armaments factory managers, and defense–military-intelligence service bureaucrats form a growing and significant force within the Israeli state. For the preponderant role of Israeli defense forces in decisions, see Yehuda Ben Meir, *National Security Decision Making: The Israeli Case* (Boulder, Colo.: Westview Press, 1986), pp. 84 ff. Also Yoram Peri, *Between Battles and Ballots: Israeli Military in Politics* (Cambridge: Cambridge University Press, 1983) and Yoram Peri and Moshe Lissak, "Retired Officers in Israel and the Emergence of a New Elite," in Gwyn Harries-Jenkins and Jacques van Doorn, *The Military and the Problem of Legitimacy* (Beverly Hills, Calif.: Sage Studies in International Sociology, 1976).

67. Ze'ev Schiff, *Ha'aretz* (December 17, 1986).

68. Ze'ev Schiff, *Ha'aretz* (April 29, 1986).

69. Mintz, "Civilianization of the Military," p. 90.

70. A. Abramovich, *Ma'ariv* (December 5, 1987), a foe of Israel's Labor Party, points out that "[a] considerable portion of the arms industry is centered around Koor and other Histadrut enterprises. This is the reason, he argues . . . which prevents the Labour party from raising their voice [against this commerce]."

71. Ze'ev Schiff, *Ha'aretz* (April 29, 1986).

72. Yitzhak Deutsch, *Ma'ariv* (November 2, 1986). See also Marshall *et al.*, *The Iran-Contra Connection*, p. 87.

73. Ze'ev Schiff, *Ha'aretz* (November 21, 1986). See Klieman, *Israeli Arms Sales,* pp. 51–52.

74. Yitzhak Deutsch, *Ma'ariv* (November 2, 1986).

75. *Yedioth Ahronet* (June 6, 1990).

76. Dan Fisher, of the *Los Angeles Times,* reprinted in *Philadelphia Inquirer* (November 23, 1986), reported that informed sources in Jerusalem told him that, of the weaponry sent to Iran since 1979, "the shipments consisted almost entirely of shells for artillery pieces, mortars and recoiless rifles. . . . All the ammunition is Israeli produced, and some is available only here."

77. "The Uzi has . . . become the standard issue for the Revolutionary Guard under Khomeini." Beit-Hallahmi, *The Israeli Connection,* p. 11. Radio Tehran (September 23, 1986) reported that Iran's defense minister, Muhammad Husayn Jalali, announced that an assault rifle meant to replace the Uzi had reached the production stage. In BBC shortwave broadcast (September 25, 1986) (Persian). Monitored in the Israeli *Mideast File* 6, no. 1 (March 1987), no. 721, pp. 63–64.

78. Interview, Hirsch Goodman, Jerusalem (January 5, 1987).

79. *Tower Report,* p. 68. "U.S. officials accepted Israeli assurances that for some time they had an extensive dialogue with high-level Iranians." *Tower Report,* p. 83. Jeff Gerth, *New York Times* (November 30, 1986) reported that "Israel had ties of its own to Iranian military officials through Israeli arms dealers."

80. See Segev, *The Iran Triangle,* chs. 1 and 5; and Ledeen, *Perilous Statecraft,* pp. 97 seq.

81. *Arabia: The Islamic World Review* (March 1982), no. 7. See also Yoel Marcus, *Ha'aretz* (November 18, 1986).

82. Beit-Hallahmi, *The Israeli Connection,* p. 13. For details about the alleged plot, see Segev, *The Iran Triangle,* pp. 6 seq.

83. The *Boston Globe* story was sent over the Associated Press wire and reprinted in *Chicago Tribune* (October 22, 1982).

84. See Ledeen, *Perilous Statecraft,* p. 95.

85. "Qutbzadeh and his . . . supporters in the military would kill Khomeini by hitting his Jamran residence and offices with rockets, and assassinate the members of the Supreme Defense Council. Qutbzadeh and his associates would [then] blame the outrage on the Tudeh, and seize power in order to avenge the killings." Hiro, *Iran Under the Ayatollahs,* p. 218, see also p. 219.

86. Eqbal Ahmad, unpublished public lecture at Hampshire College, early December 1986. See also *The Middle East* (April 1985): 51–53; *Economist Intelligence Unit,* Country Study, Iran, no. 3 (July 17, 1987): 13–14; and Farhang Rajaee, "The Islamic Cultural Revolution

and Pre-Revolutionary Iranian Society," in Shireen Hunter, ed., *Internal Developments in Iran* (Washington, D.C.: The Center for Strategic and International Studies, Georgetown University, 1985), pp. 49–61. In the same volume also see Djavad Salehi-Isfahani, "The Iranian Economy Since the Revolution," pp. 42–43 and 45–46; and Haleh Afshar, "An Assessment of Agricultural Development Policies in Iran," p. 75 seq.

    87.   The Iranian secret police.

    88.   Mansur Rafizadeh, *Witness: From the Shah to the Secret Arms Deal, An Insider's Account of U.S. Involvement in Iran* (New York: William Morrow and Company, 1987), p. 366.

    89.   Ibid.

    90.   See Mansour Farhang's chapter in this book for further details on this episode.

    91.   See Ledeen, *Perilous Statecraft*, p. 96; and Segev, *The Iran Triangle*, p. 129.

    92.   For further discussion of this issue, see Mansour Farhang's chapter in this book.

    93.   Said, "Irangate," pp. 27–29, argues that Israeli and Americans probably intended to provoke prolonged instability in Iran or overthrow the Khomeini regime.

    94.   P. 11.

    95.   *Tower Report*, p. 128.

    96.   Quoted by Segev, *The Iranian Triangle*, p. 194, from *Congressional Report*, p. 176. See also Segev, ibid., pp. 209 and 212.

    97.   *Tower Report*, p. 39. Repeated on p. 231.

    98.   "Ghorbanifar . . . prior to the 1979 revolution, had been the managing director of an Israeli-connected Iranian shipping company. According to rumors, Ghorbanifar also was an informant for SAVAK, the Shah's intelligence service, and had a relationship with Israeli intelligence; but those relationships have never been confirmed." *Congressional Report*, p. 163. The *Village Voice* (December 1, 1987) claims that "[m]embers of Ghorbanifar's family were involved in an unsuccessful coup against Khomeini in 1980, and thereafter he sought repeatedly to curry favor with U.S. intelligence agencies." By 1985 Ghorbanifar had established relationships with several factions of the Iranian leadership. Though many in the U.S. with whom he came in contact did not trust him, key players in the Irangate venture continued to use his services over several years. For a more sympathetic view of Ghorbanifar, see Ledeen, *Perilous Statecraft*, passim.

    99.   *Congressional Report*, p. 167.

    100.   *Tower Report*, pp. 137 and 140–41.

    101.   *Congressional Report*, pp. 168–69.

102.   Ledeen, *Perilous Statecraft,* p. 131.

103.   *Congressional Report,* p. 176.

104.   *Tower Report,* p. 165.

105.   "Special Project Re Iran," apparent North memo to Poindexter dated December 5, 1985, in ibid., p. 180.

106.   Ibid., p. 215.

107.   Ibid., p. 388.

PART 5

U.S. Strategic Policy Toward the Middle East and the Persian Gulf War

CHAPTER 8

United States Strategic Policy toward the Middle East: Central Command and the Reflagging of Kuwait's Tankers

Elizabeth J. Gamlen

The last decade has seen a dramatic resurgence in U.S. capabilities to deploy its military forces around the world. Crisis interventions such as those against Grenada (1983), Libya (1986), and Panama (1989) have caught widespread attention, but the centerpiece of this U.S. strategy has in fact been the area denoted *South West Asia* (SWA) by the United States.

Calls for U.S. military intervention to solve the 1973–74 oil crisis developed by the late 1970s into plans for "quickly deployable forces" to defend U.S. interests throughout the world. However, these plans, which received little funding or attention until the Soviet invasion of Afghanistan, prompted Carter to declare the Persian Gulf an area of "vital interest" to the United States, which would, if necessary, be defended militarily (the Carter Doctrine).

This chapter, following a brief overview of U.S. policy toward the Gulf region since World War II, traces the development of Central Command (the military instrument designed to implement the Carter Doctrine) and details its first major application, the escort of Kuwait's reflagged tankers during the latter phase of the Iran-Iraq War.

It assesses the strategic implications of Central Command and in particular the undertaking of these escorts, examining them in the context of the U.S. reliance on military action to protect its interests during the 1980s, and concludes that there are severe limitations to such a policy, especially in its application to the Middle East region.

U.S. STRATEGIC POLICY TOWARD THE PERSIAN GULF REGION SINCE WORLD WAR II

The U.S. prime concern in this region, as elsewhere, has been to contain the Soviet Union. Indeed, the reluctance of the Soviet Union to withdraw its troops from Iran in 1946 was one of the opening salvoes of the Cold War. However, prior to 1971 the Gulf region was of secondary importance to U.S. strategic planners when compared to Europe and the Far East.

The principal reasons for this lesser status were first, that the region, although contiguous with the Soviet Union, was not seen to be in the front line of the fight to contain communism because, unlike parts of Europe and East Asia, the ideology was not widely welcomed; and second, that the extensive British presence in the region constrained the United States, and at the same time minimized the necessity for a U.S. presence. Britain and the United States had a number of common interests in the region—notably containment of the Soviet Union and preventing local regimes from asserting control of their national assets; and therefore the United States was generally content to accept this situation while it lasted.

The major exception was the U.S. influence in Saudi Arabia. By the beginning of World War II the United States had already forced the British to concede oil interests in Kuwait, Bahrain, Iraq, and Saudi Arabia to the United States. During the war the United States then took advantage of its wartime position in Saudi Arabia to build a long-term strategic presence.

The other notable in-road that the United States made into this British sphere was the establishment of the U.S. Navy "Middle East Force" in 1949. This small naval contingent, based in Bahrain and restricted to two warships and a command vessel for most of the next thirty years, was a largely symbolic assertion of U.S. power directed against the Soviet Union. On the whole, however, the United States concentrated on diplomatic means such as bilateral treaties and the Baghdad Pact, backed by threats of nuclear retaliation, rather than on U.S. conventional forces, to constrain Soviet actions.

U.S. global concern with the threat of the spread of communism was overlain in the Middle East by two more specific regional concerns: (a) the protection of Israel (although until 1973 the connection between Israel and the Gulf states was considered rather tenuous by the United States), and (b) the protection of oil supplies.

Global oil consumption rose steadily throughout the 1950s and 1960s, and although U.S. domestic production also expanded rapidly, the West as a whole became increasingly dependent on imported oil, most of which came from the Middle East. Despite disruptions caused by the attempts of oil-producing nations to regain control of their resources and to raise its price, prior to the 1973–74 oil crisis U.S. concerns regarding oil supplies focused on the potential for the Soviet Union to interfere with them, rather than disruptions arising from within the region.

By the end of the 1960s, public disillusionment with the human and financial costs of the Vietnam war had fuelled general revulsion of interventionist policies, particularly those involving U.S. troops. Consequently when the British announced in 1968 that they were withdrawing their forces "East of Suez" it was politically (and financially) impossible for the United States to consider directly replacing them.

Reluctant to damage U.S. prestige by withdrawing to isolationism, in 1969 Nixon announced a new U.S. doctrine, based on three central themes:

> —First, the U.S. will keep all of its treaty commitments.
>
> —Second, we shall provide a shield if a nuclear power threatens the freedom of a nation allied with us or of a nation whose survival we consider vital to our security.
>
> —Third, in cases involving other types of aggression, we shall furnish military and economic assistance when requested in accordance with our treaty commitments. But we shall look to the nation directly threatened to assume the primary responsibility of providing the manpower for its defense.[1]

As a result of the coincidence of the British withdrawal and the extension of Soviet naval operations into the Indian Ocean the Persian Gulf became the model area for application of the Nixon

Doctrine, with Saudi Arabia and Iran as the twin pillars to support it.

The 1973 Arab-Israeli War contributed to a major revision of U.S. strategy. Arab oil-producing states coordinated production cutbacks and price rises as a protest against the Israeli occupation and instituted total embargoes of the Netherlands and the United States for their overt support for Israel. The economic disruption accompanying this oil crisis clearly demonstrated the potential for U.S. (and Western) security to be threatened by non-Soviet, non-military means and the inadequacy of Western strategic policy to meet such threats.

In consequence, U.S. policy makers were forced to recognize the direct connection between Gulf oil supplies and a resolution of Arab-Israeli disputes. Although the subsequent lack of Arab cohesion has since enabled this link to be largely ignored, its existence was acknowledged by both the Carter and Reagan administrations. In addition, the leading role that Saudi Arabia played in imposing political constraints on oil supplies and the Shah's support for higher oil prices (already demonstrated by the 1971 Tehran agreement) were clear indications of the inadequacies of the Nixon Doctrine, as the twin pillars on which it rested could themselves directly threaten U.S. security.[2]

The use of oil embargoes for political purposes was viewed with great alarm in the United States, and there were threats of military action if "strangulation of the industrialised world" became a serious prospect.[3] Although Secretary of Defense Schlesinger claimed that such military action was feasible, a study by the authoritative Congressional Research Service concluded that the United States did not have the military capability to forcibly seize and operate the oil fields, because the collateral damage, particularly if the oil-producing states chose sabotage as a form of defense, would cause worse disruption to the oil supplies than the Arab embargo.[4] The political repercussions of such blatant intervention would also be long-lived, indeed even the suggestion that the United States might have resorted to such measures continues to hinder U.S. relations with the region.

Rather than minimize the dangers of a similar oil crisis, by paying a reasonable price for oil and seriously tackling the Arab-Israeli dispute, the United States remained preoccupied with Soviet containment and continued its reliance on the Nixon Doctrine. However, the crisis had rekindled calls for U.S. intervention forces as the only totally reliable instrument for protecting U.S. interests, and despite serious skepticism as to its feasibility, consideration was given to developing the military capability to rapidly respond to crises in the Persian Gulf.

In the general climate of superpower detente there was little impetus for major military changes, but the events of 1979 caused a radical change in both public and governmental U.S. attitudes.[5] U.S. self-esteem was severely damaged; there were a number of alarmist claims about a Soviet "grand strategy" for seizing control of the region; and a general consensus arose that a new tough approach, backed by major investment in military programs was needed to reassert U.S. preeminence.

Carter's announcement in March 1978 that a "rapid deployment force" was to be formed, intended to enable the United States to take prompt military action to resolve crises, had received little attention but his declaration in January 1980 that: "An attempt by any outside force to gain control of the Persian Gulf region will be regarded as an assault on the vital interests of the United States of America, and such an assault will be repelled by any means necessary including military force"[6] was recognized as a major policy initiative (and one that has subsequently been endorsed by Reagan and Bush). In the light of the Afghanistan invasion, *outside force* was generally assumed to refer to the Soviet Union, and as U.S. capabilities to prevent Soviet incursions into the region were extremely limited, *any means necessary* was assumed to include nuclear force. The instrument chosen to implement this Carter Doctrine was the new "rapid deployment force" (later Central Command).

CREATION AND DEVELOPMENT OF THE "RAPID DEPLOYMENT FORCE"

The idea of a reserve of forces, kept in the United States to be rapidly deployed to areas of crisis is by no means new. The Marine Corps was traditionally associated with foreign interventions (for example, its use in Lebanon in 1958) and supplemented the Navy's capacity for "gunboat diplomacy," based on its aircraft carriers, but in 1961 selected U.S.-based Army and Air Force units were joined together to form Strike Command (STRICOM). This new unified command was intended "to provide an integrated, mobile, highly combat-ready force . . . instantly available for use as an augmentation to existing theater forces under the unified commanders, or as the primary force for use in remote areas."[7] STRICOM was never able to fulfill its intended potential. Seriously weakened by the refusal of the Navy and Marines to participate,[8] and the demands of the Vietnam war, it was replaced in 1971 with Readiness Command. Although this command retained theoretical responsibility for limited war reinforcement (in general rather than with the Middle East emphasis of STRICOM) it was not a combatant command and concentrated on planning and training.[9]

The origins of the current rapid deployment capabilities can be seen in the 1977 review of U.S.-Soviet strategic balance that formed the basis of Presidential Review Memorandum (PRM)-10, and its confirmation as official policy, Presidential Directive (PD)-18. This latter ordered the formation of a "deployment force of light divisions with strategic mobility independent of overseas bases and logistical support" and "moderate naval and tactical air forces which could be used in the Middle East, Persian Gulf, Korea, or elsewhere."[10]

As early as March 1978 Carter announced that "the Secretary of Defense, at my direction, is improving and will maintain quickly deployable forces—air, land, and sea—to defend our interests throughout the world."[11] Four months later, press reports leaking details of the secret PD-18 disclosed that this rapid deployment force (RDF) could consist of "approximately 100,000 troops, including two Army airborne divisions and a Marine Amphibious Brigade, backed by two to four aircraft carriers and up to three Air Force wings totaling about 200 planes."[12] However, controversy over the policy caused by opposition from the U.S. State Department (which was promoting Indian Ocean arms limitation talks with the Soviets), and interservice rivalry prevented significant progress on these proposals until after the Iranian Revolution.

The Rapid Deployment Joint Task Force (RDJTF) finally became officially operational on March 1, 1980, with overall responsibility to "plan, jointly train, exercise and be prepared to deploy and employ designated forces in response to contingencies threatening U.S. vital interests."[13] The initial global application of RDJTF was subsequently narrowed to Middle East contingencies,[14] but responsibility for U.S. operations in this region remained divided between European and Pacific commands. As with STRICOM, the RDJTF was assigned forces that it could call on in times of crisis, but that were normally under the control of other commands, although this time the RDJTF could call on forces from all four services. One consequence of the bureaucratic struggles involved in the creation of RDJTF was its extraordinarily complicated command structure. The new Reagan administration attempted to rectify this in April 1981 when it announced that the RDJTF was to be upgraded to the status of a unified command (Central Command).

In January 1983 the RDJTF was converted to Central Command (CENTCOM). The first new unified command with specific geographic responsibilities to be created in thirty-five years, CENTCOM's "area of responsibility" (AOR) stretched from Kenya to Pakistan, incorporating nineteen countries, and was denoted *South West Asia* (SWA) by the United States. In keeping with U.S. attempts to segregate Gulf issues from Palestinian ones, Israel, the Occupied Territories, Lebanon, and Syria were excluded from SWA. The forces allocated to the RDF on a contingency basis have expanded alongside its command structure. PD-18 reportedly referred to a RDF of around 100,000 troops, but CENTCOM can now call on up to 400,000.[15]

At the time that the RDJTF was created, its ability to deploy in the Middle East was seriously constrained by lack of transport and logistical support. Proposals by President Carter to rectify this were implemented with vigor by President Reagan, alongside more ambitious programs of his own.[16] Consequently there has been a dramatic increase in U.S. force projection capabilities over the last decade, even though a number of projects are yet to be completed.

ENHANCEMENT OF U.S. FORCE PROJECTION CAPABILITIES

The major expansion of U.S. nuclear capabilities during the early 1980s has received considerable attention because of the simultaneous surge in "peace movements," especially in Europe. Less widely recognized is the equally dramatic expansion in U.S. conventional capabilities, much of which was directed toward interventionist strategies, or in current-day parlance "force projection." Whereas many of these programs have global application (for example, an aircraft carrier can be sent more or less anywhere), they have also directly enhanced the U.S. ability to intervene militarily in the Middle East and therefore assume a particular significance in the context of the Carter Doctrine and the creation of CENTCOM.

The expansion of military capabilities ranges right across the spectrum of military requirements, from the readiness of the U.S. forces to fight, the means to communicate with and transport them, and the equipment that they use on arrival. Particularly significant programs include the following:

1. *Strategic Mobility* Strategic mobility (i.e., the means of getting armed forces from A to B) relies on three forms: airlift, sealift, and prepositioning of equipment. Since 1980 U.S. capacity for airlift has almost doubled (and will be increased substantially more when the $35 billion fleet of the new C-17 aircraft becomes operational during the 1990s), sealift has tripled, and large stocks of equipment have been prepositioned in both Europe and SWA.[17] The United States can now transport a heavy Army division, including most of its support, to SWA in about a fortnight (i.e., half the time previously required) and has two sets of ships stationed off Diego Garcia loaded with enough equipment to support a 16,500 Marine expeditionary brigade and various Air Force and Army units for a month.[18] The troops that would use this equipment would be flown in from the United States to meet up with their equipment, which will take about five days to arrive in the Gulf from Diego Garcia.

2. *Amphibious Lift* The service that has benefitted most from renewed interest in rapid deployment is the Marines. Although, unlike the Special Operation Forces (SOF), they have not been enlarged they have been rejuvenated with a wide range of new equipment, such as two new types of amphibious shipping (LHD and LSD 41) and a new kind of hovercraft (LCAC) that will revolutionize their mode of operation.[19]

3. U.S. Navy The U.S. Navy, alongside its subsidiary the Marines, bears primary responsibility for U.S. military forces projection. The expansion to a 600-ship Navy (from 480 in 1980) involves a substantial upgrading of its capabilities. In particular the addition of two extra operational aircraft carriers, the replacement of old carriers by considerably more powerful new ships, and the reactivation of four battleships provides the Navy with vessels well-suited to force projection.[20]

4. Special Operations Forces (SOF) The SOF, having been substantially cut back after the Vietnam war are now being expanded again. The number of active duty personnel will have been almost doubled by 1990, a new unified command for special forces has been created, and as with the Marines, major improvements in their equipment are being implemented.[21]

5. Logistic Support As part of the RDF concept the Carter administration sought to negotiate agreements with countries in SWA for U.S. use of bases in the region. The negotiations were largely unsuccessful because of the reluctance of most countries in the region to be publicly involved with the U.S. RDF concept, and only three written agreements for contingency access have been signed (those with Oman, Kenya, and Somalia).[22] Nevertheless the United States has spent some $1.4 billion during the 1980s on improving facilities in and en route to the SWA region, and it also benefit from the U.S.-directed construction programs in Saudi Arabia, which were paid for by the Saudis.[23]

MILITARY OPERATIONS OF CENTCOM

During an interview with the *Marine Corps Gazette* in December 1986, Commander-in-Chief (CINC)CENTCOM Crist, was asked when CENTCOM forces had responded to world crises. He cited five occasions:

1. The deployment of AWACS to Egypt in 1983 to help prevent a Libyan sponsored coup attempt against Sudan.
2. Deployment of AWACS in response to the bombing of a Sudanese radio station in March 1984.
3. Mine sweeping in the Red Sea in 1984.

4. Searching, unsuccessfully, for the Israeli submarine *Dakar,* which has been missing since 1968.

5. Protection of U.S. merchant shipping in the Persian Gulf.[24]

Excluded from this list, although it has been acknowledged elsewhere that the forces are under CENTCOM command,[25] was the deployment of AWACS to Saudi Arabia in October 1980. The U.S. AWACS are still operating from Saudi Arabia and played an important role in the escort operations for the reflagged tankers.[26]

As with other sections of the armed forces, the ability of CENTCOM to meet its strategic requirements is periodically tested with military exercises, ranging from those on paper (or computer simulated) through to operations involving thousands of troops. The biggest of these exercises is the Bright Star series. The first of these, held in Egypt in November 1980, involved about 1,400 troops, but the exercise becomes larger and more complex each time it is conducted. Bright Star 87 involved 27,700 U.S. and 15,375 "host nation" personnel and included ground force maneuvers in two countries.[27]

The first major operation of CENTCOM was the escort of the reflagged Kuwaiti tankers. In consequence then CINCENTCOM, Crist, was able to claim in his 1988 report that: "1987 was the year USCENTCOM came of age. We deployed—we exercised—we operated—we fought. Theory turned into reality in twelve short months. USCENTCOM has become the premier US military force and presence in Southwest Asia, on a par with our sister unified commands."[28] Details of this operation, and its political implications are considered later in this chapter.

U.S. STRATEGIC POLICY AND THE IRAN-IRAQ WAR

In parallel with the development of CENTCOM the United States has sought to protect its interests in the region by establishing close relationships with "friendly" regimes, relationships based largely on lavish military assistance (training, construction programs, arms sales, etc.). In the aftermath of Afghanistan, emphasis was initially placed on the Soviet threat to the region, despite obvious skepticism from regional states,[29] but internal unrest in producer nations and regional disputes (particularly the Iran-Iraq War) have since been identified as far more likely causes of oil supply disruption.

Concern that the Soviet Union would take advantage of the war to increase its influence in the Gulf was mollified by a meeting in September 1980 between the U.S. secretary of state and the Soviet Foreign Minister Gromyko in which both governments pledged neutrality in the war.[30] This joint declaration reflects the fact that neither the Soviets nor the United States had overriding reasons for giving clear backing to either side, and indeed wished to refrain from doing so.

The outbreak of the war caused serious concern in the West generally that oil supplies would be disrupted and that this could cause a return to the economic depression of the 1970s. Accordingly within three weeks of war breaking out approximately sixty Western warships were deployed to the region,[31] including a U.S. Navy aircraft carrier battle group based on the *Nimitz*.[32] In fact, despite the destruction by Iran of the Iraqi oil terminals at Fao and the institution of a naval blockade preventing Iraqi access to the Gulf,[33] oil supplies were not substantially affected and most of these ships were soon redeployed.

Serious concern erupted again in 1982, when Iran, having expelled Iraq from Iranian territory, launched its own invasion. Concern that Iran would be able to crush Iraq and that this would be the first stage of implementing Iran's ambitions of exporting its revolution, prompted both superpowers to increase their support for Iraq, while maintaining their official neutrality. Soviet arms supplies reaching Iraq were substantially increased, and the United States removed Iraq from its list of terrorist states. Although U.S. arms sales remained prohibited, sales of militarily useful equipment such as transport planes were made and credit loans extended to Iraq.[34] In return, Iraq noticeably moderated its opposition toward Israel, and in August 1982 Saddam Hussein announced his acceptance of Israel's right to exist.[35] Diplomatic relations between Iraq and the United States, broken off since the 1967 War, were resumed in November 1984.

Alongside U.S. concerns to minimize Soviet influence in the Gulf and secure oil supplies was an attempt by the United States to reassure the Gulf states through diplomatic support and arms supplies. The most significant assistance was provided within weeks of the war breaking out and was in response to a request from the Saudis for "American military protection."[36] Four U.S. AWACS, accompanied by ground radar, communications equipment, and 400 U.S. personnel to operate it were hastily dispatched. The rapidity of the decision contrasts sharply with the tortuous passage through Congress of the proposed sale of five AWACS to the Saudis, which was not finally approved until October 1981.[37]

The AWACS assistance was provided out of U.S. concern that oil supplies would be disrupted if the smaller Gulf states became embroiled in the conflict and largely disregarded the extent to which Saudi Arabia and Kuwait in particular had compromised their neutrality by aiding Iraq, although one of the conditions of supplying the AWACS was reportedly that the Arab Gulf states should not permit Iraq to use their air bases.[38] At least some of the intelligence data collected by the AWACS appears to have been passed onto Iraq, with the agreement of the United States. This was confirmed by Saddam Hussein in May 1984.[39]

The "Tanker War"

The danger to Gulf shipping became the focus of international attention once again in late 1983, with Iranian threats to prevent oil being exported from the Gulf if Iraq used its new French Super Etenard aircraft to attack Iranian tankers and oil facilities.[40] Despite the fact that Iran is almost totally dependent on exporting its oil through the Straits of Hormuz and so would not have made any attempt to close them unless it was unable to use the Straits itself, these threats were taken seriously by the West, and considerable debate ensued about the possibilities of Iran either mining the Straits or blocking them with sunken ships.

Iraq, under stress in the land war, had a dual purpose in threatening to launch this first phase of the "Tanker War." In addition to damaging Iran economically it hoped to attract international interest in ending the war. It was, therefore, encouraged rather than deterred by this Western concern, especially as this was directed almost entirely against Iran, and it began seriously targeting tankers in the Gulf in February 1984.

Because Iran had closed off Iraq's access to the Gulf in the initial stages of the war, it was unable to retaliate against Iraqi oil exports. After ten weeks and some fifteen tanker attacks by Iraq, Iran began to retaliate against shipping dealing with Saudi Arabia and Kuwait, on the grounds that the aid they had been providing to Iraq (financially and the use of their ports as transshipment points) negated their neutral status.[41]

Despite the leading role that Iraq played in the attacks, international condemnation concentrated on the threat emanating from Iran. The United States announced that it was determined to keep the Straits open and to reinforce this message dispatched a naval task force to the Indian Ocean, while the White House also announced that the United States was prepared to send armed forces, including ground troops if necessary, to the area to protect oil exports.[42] In January 1984, U.S. warships in the Gulf were placed on alert after reports that they might be attacked by Iranian suicide missions and a five-mile territorial exclusion zone around U.S. ships was announced.[43] Contingency plans were drawn up for mine sweeping and the armed escort of ships to neutral ports—convoys in which Britain agreed to participate.[44]

The United States used the opportunity to press the Arab Gulf states for greater military cooperation, but met stiff resistance; and at a meeting of the Gulf Cooperation Council (GCC) the Kuwaiti defense minister, while deploring the shipping attacks, affirmed that the GCC would "resist any foreign intervention at all levels."[45] In response to the Iranian reprisals in May 1984, the Gulf Cooperation Council held an emergency meeting to discuss how to deal with the situation. They rejected the idea of asking for direct U.S. involvement in the Gulf (although assistance with air cover had reportedly been offered[46]) and favored instead an approach to the UN Security Council.[47]

Plans were also drawn up to improve protection of tankers dealing with the Arab side of the Gulf by routing them close to the coast and improving air cover.[48] Despite Arab reluctance to rely publicly on direct U.S. help, this air cover was based on the U.S. operated and controlled AWACS. A direct consequence of this U.S. supported air cover was the shooting down, by a Saudi F-15, of an Iranian F-4 Phantom jet on June 5, 1984. Immediately prior to this, the Reagan administration had used the presidential waiver to respond positively to an urgent Saudi request for Stinger missiles to deal with the new shipping threat. Four hundred Stinger missiles and 200 launchers were immediately dispatched, although a similar request from Kuwait was refused.[49]

In addition to this close cooperation with Saudi Arabia, the United States considered independent plans for action to protect shipping. These options reportedly included air patrols, based either on an aircraft carrier in the northern Arabian Sea, or from Gulf state air bases, escorting ships in convoys, or surgical strikes against Iranian airfields. Air patrols were considered impractical because the long distances involved precluded the use of carrier-based aircraft, and the Gulf states were not willing to cooperate. U.S. Navy escort ships were considered vulnerable to attack, tankers would be difficult to protect while loading, and a huge supply network would be needed in the Gulf. Strikes against Iranian airfields would risk shooting down U.S. planes and would eliminate only one of several threats from Iran.[50] This National Security Council review provides an interesting forerunner to the events of 1987–88, as do the preconditions of any U.S. action. These were reported to be

1. Any security arrangements would have to involve a multinational force with allies of the USA.

2. The Gulf states would have to invite US protection.

3. The Gulf states would have to make available necessary ground facilities for the support of aircraft in order to make them ready at a moment's notice.[51]

Despite the widespread alarm during the first few months of the "Tanker War," once it had been realized that oil supplies were not seriously threatened, the outside world began to show remarkable indifference to the tanker attacks. The first phase of the "Tanker War" petered out because although it had affected Iran economically, Iraq was incapable of severely curtailing Iran's exports nor was it achieving the other objective of internationalizing the war. The importance of Saudi Arabian and Kuwaiti aid to Iraq meant that they were well placed to persuade it to refrain from tanker attacks, which were provoking retaliation against them. It is also possible that similar pressure was placed on Iraq by the United States, as part of the negotiations for the resumption of diplomatic relations in November 1984.

The second phase of the "Tanker War" began in 1986, when Iraq was again under severe pressure in the land war following the Iranian capture of the Fao peninsula. Concerned to ward off the expected Iranian assault on Basra in early 1987, Iraq substantially increased its attacks on economic targets, including tankers serving Iran. Iran responded with missile and shelling attacks against Iraq, pressing for changes in OPEC, issuing stronger threats against the GCC states for their support of Iraq, and to reinforce these messages, increasing its attacks on tankers serving them.

The pattern of the first "Tanker War" was repeated, with Iraq being the prime instigator of attacks and Iran receiving most criticism internationally. A substantial difference on this occasion was that Iran, since its capture of the Fao peninsula, appeared to be clearly dominant in the land war, and consequently Iraq was applying considerably more pressure in the Gulf. In August 1986 Iraqi planes succeeded in attacking Sirri Island for the first time; in October Kharg Island was temporarily completely closed; and in November Iraq extended its attacks to Larak.[52]

THE U.S. REFLAGGING AND ESCORT OF KUWAIT'S TANKERS

In anticipation of severe retaliation from Iran because of this major escalation, and threatened by the proximity of Iranian troops, Kuwait sought protection from outside the Gulf. In late 1986 it approached first the superpowers and later the other members of the UN Security Council with a request for help in protecting its exports. The nature of Kuwait's request, protection of Kuwaiti ships, despite the fact that a large proportion of Kuwait's trade is carried on ships using "flags of convenience," and the minimal disruption actually caused to its exports at the time, are clear indications that the request was motivated by security concerns rather than physical problems with its exports. The intention was to draw international attention to the war and thereby bring pressure for its termination.[53]

Kuwait simultaneously approached both the United States and USSR in December 1986,[54] seeking the protection of their flags. The U.S. response, though positive in principle provided U.S. regulations were met, did not include an offer to provide naval protection for the reflagged ships. By contrast the Soviet response was an immediate offer of full cooperation. The Soviets lacked the larger tankers Kuwait needed and agreed to a Kuwaiti suggestion that it reflag some Kuwaiti tankers. Only when these talks were made known to the US did then US Secretary of Defense, Caspar Weinberger, declare U.S. willingness to reflag all eleven Kuwaiti vessels and provide them with naval protection.[55] The United States appears to have refused to help Kuwait if any of the tankers were reflagged by the Soviet Union. The Kuwaitis compromised by accepting the U.S. reflagging of all eleven tankers and limiting the Soviet role to chartering three vessels.

The approach was adroitly planned. By inviting help from both superpowers Kuwait could profess to be upholding its "neutrality" between them and simultaneously force the hand of the United States. To emphasize this "neutrality" Kuwait subsequently requested similar help from the other permanent UN Security Council members, but only Britain responded in any way positively, announcing that registration was a matter of "commercial and procedural arrangement," not one that required a governmental policy decision.[56]

The official rationale for the United States agreeing to the reflagging was twofold: "First to help Kuwait counter immediate intimidation and thereby discourage Iran from similar attempts against the other moderate gulf states; and second to limit to the extent possible, an increase in Soviet military presence and influence in the gulf."[57] Although the U.S. action of reflagging demonstrated a political commitment to Kuwait (and by implication the other GCC states), the reflagging itself did not, as was implied, contribute greatly to Kuwait's security as the majority of its exports continued to be carried on foreign-flagged ships (which remained unprotected until April 1988). The second element refers to the Kuwaiti invitation to the Soviet Union to assist in protecting their exports. This is part of a long-standing policy of the United States to deny that the Soviet Union has reason to be concerned about affairs in the Gulf, despite its close proximity to the region. The policy is unrealistic as the Soviet Union has been visiting ports in the Gulf since 1968; and the United States could not expect to substantially expand its presence in the Gulf, as would obviously be necessitated by the reflagging action, without the Soviets also increasing their deployments there.

In reality the U.S. reflagging worked out extremely well for the Soviet Union, because it was able to quietly establish patrols in the region, while criticizing the U.S. handling of the consequences of its high-profile reflagging operation. It used the opportunity to call for the withdrawal of all outside naval powers from the region, for the establishment of a UN naval peace-keeping force, and to further its relations with Iran, at the expense of the United States.[58]

Three other factors that are widely thought to have played important parts in the U.S. decision, although they were rarely officially acknowledged, were the need to regain the confidence of Arab states in the wake of "Irangate," U.S. concern that Iraq might be defeated, and the desire to improve access to regional bases.

The revelation in November 1986 that the United States had been secretly selling arms to Iran undermined the whole framework of U.S.-Arab relations because it demonstrated that Arab interests could be supplanted not only by Israel but also by U.S. attempts to open a dialogue with Iran and free U.S. hostages.[59] Clearly the United States needed to reassert its commitment, especially to the Gulf Cooperation Council states, but in view of its potential impact on relations within the region, the wisdom of using the reflagging to achieve this objective is questionable.

A number of statements by the U.S. administration have indicated that the possibility of an Iraqi defeat, which was being seriously muted in 1986, would not have been acceptable to the United States. For example, a report of the House Armed Services Committee, claimed that: "while the Administration has proclaimed a policy of strict neutrality [in the Iran-Iraq War] . . . a minimal requirement of its strategy is to see that Iraq does not collapse. If it did, radical Islamic fundamentalism could well spread to Iraq itself, and quite possibly to the moderate Gulf states and beyond."[60] The U.S. decision to reflag the Kuwaiti tankers and its subsequent actions against Iran in the Gulf are consistent with this policy, which appears to date back to at least October 1983, when a National Security Council study was reported to have concluded that an Iraqi collapse would not serve U.S. interests.[61] Consequently the Reagan administration reportedly encouraged the GCC states to sustain, or increase, their aid to Iraq, while attempting to curtail the supply of arms to Iran through Operation Staunch (with the major exception of the Irangate sales).[62]

One of the major problems for CENTCOM in planning for military action in the region has been the reluctance of "friendly" regimes to become too publicly associated with the United States, and in particular to provide the United States with base facilities. The request by Kuwait appeared to offer a unique opportunity to increase U.S. access to the region and was therefore an additional incentive for the United States to agree to it. However, in practice even Kuwait remained wary, and the long-sought-after land bases, which were initially cited as being essential for the effective operation of U.S. forces, were not made available.[63] As a result of Iranian threats most of the assistance provided to the United States was kept secret, especially after the agreement to extend coverage of the Saudi-based AWACS was almost cancelled by Saudi Arabia due to the extensive publicity it was given in the United States.[64] Other assistance provided included free fuel, some degree of aircraft landing rights, assistance in mine sweeping, transhipment of supplies, and increased surveillance flights.[65]

Although, prior to the USS *Stark* attack, the reflagging plan proceeded smoothly, and congressional approval was granted with little publicity,[66] subsequent events in the Gulf suggest that the final U.S. decision to reflag and escort the tankers was taken hastily, and with little assessment of the military and political consequences. No formal interagency assessment of the risks involved was requested, and although consideration was given to the possibility of shipping lanes being mined, little was done to mitigate the threat.[67] Ignorance of the political implications involved was demonstrated when U.S. Under-Secretary of State Armacost, in answer to a query about the danger of the United States being drawn into the conflict as a result of the reflagging testified that: "[he did] not see that it [reflagging the Kuwaiti tankers] qualitatively changes the situation, other than just to increase the numbers slightly."[68]

The Iraqi attack on the USS *Stark* brought to public attention for the first time the dangerous conditions under which U.S. naval forces were operating in the Gulf and the potential consequences of protecting Kuwait's tankers. To counter the resulting public and congressional skepticism about the reflagging policy, the Reagan administration launched a major publicity drive claiming that the reflagging was necessary to uphold freedom of navigation and protect oil supplies, and that the United States, as a superpower, had a responsibility to fulfil these duties.[69]

However, these were empty claims being used to deflect attention from the partisan nature of the U.S. actions. Reflagging and protecting eleven ships out of the hundreds using the Gulf every week is not a very effective means of promoting freedom of navigation, and no attempt was made to prevent Iraqi tanker attacks. Prior to the reflagging, oil supplies had not been significantly disrupted. This was partly because only about 1 percent of all the ships in the Gulf had been affected by the war and most of these incurred only minor damage, and partly because a considerable proportion of oil is exported from the Gulf using overland pipelines, not through the Straits of Hormuz.[70] In fact, the level of disruption of Gulf shipping considerably increased after the expansion of naval forces in 1987, and far more tankers were attacked.[71] Following the U.S.-Iranian clashes in April 1988, shipping and oil commerce in the southern Gulf virtually ceased for two days, so this action, initiated by the United States, created the situation that the policy was supposed to prevent.[72]

Considerable emphasis was placed on the threat posed by Iran's newly acquired Silkworm missiles but as the U.S. administration had known about the Iranian purchase since summer 1986 and expressed little concern until the reflagging issue attracted public attention, this would also not appear to have been a major factor.[73]

The political decision to reflag the tankers caused a major change in the military environment for the United States in the Gulf. The U.S. Middle East Force was originally established in 1949, but for the next thirty years consisted of just two small warships and a command vessel. An extra three warships were added in February 1979, following the seizure of the U.S. embassy, and by the time of the attack on the USS *Stark* there were seven in total, although news reports suggest that up to twelve U.S. warships deployed in the Gulf during the first phase of the "Tanker War."[74] Official figures acknowledge that at its peak in 1987 twenty-five warships were deployed in the Persian Gulf–North Arabian Sea, but this is a serious understatement. The

Washington-based Center for Defense Information calculated that at one time forty-eight naval combat ships and their support were in the region, and this figure still excludes, for example, small special-purpose patrol boats, large barges used as floating sea bases, and European vessels that contributed both directly and indirectly to the U.S. efforts.[75] In total the number of U.S. personnel in the region is believed to have reached a peak of at least 25,000.[76]

The escalation of hostilities between Iran and the United States was a predictable consequence of the reflagging policy. Iran was being prevented from responding to Iraqi attacks on tankers and oil facilities in the Gulf, the economic and psychological damage were constraining Iran's war effort. Iran attempted to circumvent U.S. rules of engagement by, for example, the "anonymous" mining of the *Bridgeton,* the attack on the *Sea Isle City* in Kuwaiti waters (where Kuwait, not the United States was responsible for its protection), and concentrating attacks on the numerous ships trading with Kuwait and Saudi Arabia that were not being protected by Western-Soviet navies.[77] The United States reacted by continuously amending its rules of engagement to punish Iran, and the situation was in grave danger of escalating completely out of control.

The most significant incidents to occur were the major naval battle in April 1988, when the US Navy destroyed a substantial proportion of the Iranian Navy, and the shooting down by the USS *Vincennes* of an Iranian civilian airliner.[78] Although it seems clear from U.S. investigations into the latter that the airliner had been mistakenly identified as an attacking aircraft, it is hardly surprising that such a mistake occurred given the extremely tense situation in the Gulf, arising directly from the reflagging. Although there are precedents, such as the major conflict between Britain and Argentina in 1982, it seems remarkable that modern warfare has so outpaced traditional laws of war that these incidents could occur without any declaration of war.

These, and other, clashes between the United States and Iran caused a dramatic worsening of the situation in the Gulf and sent shock waves throughout the United States and its allies about the potential dangers involved. For example, Iran responded to the attacks in April by targeting a U.S.-operated, but United Arab Emirates–owned, oil platform, and a UK-registered tanker. The

United States was not operating in a vacuum—its actions had implications for its friends and allies, although they had few means of influencing U.S. or Iranian behavior, which by July 1988 had deteriorated to a state of virtual undeclared war.

Iran was left with stark choices. Persuade, either by threats or promises, the outside powers to leave the Gulf and hope that the "Tanker War" would defuse as before; seek support elsewhere; or call an end to the war. The only means by which Iran was likely to persuade the United States to leave the Gulf was by provoking domestic pressure on the U.S. administration to protect the lives of U.S. service personnel by withdrawing U.S. forces, as had occurred in Lebanon four years earlier. This seems to have been the Iranian motive in the April 1988 naval battle, because the Iranian forces could not possibly have expected to defeat the far larger and better equipped U.S. forces through direct confrontation.

Unfortunately for Iran the stakes for the United States were considerably higher than they had been four years earlier, in part because of the need to prove its staying power after Lebanon, and in part because the alleged purpose of the U.S. presence in the Gulf (protection of oil supplies) was far more popular in the United States than involvement in the Lebanese civil war. In addition the legacy of the Iranian Revolution and hostage crisis is a deep-rooted public antipathy toward the Islamic regime of Iran, and this would probably have sustained support for very heavy-handed retaliation against Iran (for example, destruction of land targets) rather than led to pressure for withdrawal.

Iran was in an impossible position. As a result of Iran's international isolation, there was little pressure on the United States to constrain its actions, and even the terms of a negotiated settlement through the United Nations (Resolution 598) were weighted heavily against Iran.[79] Iraq could exercise complete control over the Tanker War, because Iran was no longer able to prevent attacks by retaliating against Iraq's allies; and the international backing given to Iraq reinvigorated its efforts in the land war, leading to a series of Iranian defeats.[80]

It might have been possible for Iran to seek greater support from the Soviet Union to counter these pressures. However, Soviet options were constrained by their relations with Iraq and their limited ability to deploy naval contingents in the Gulf. It would have been a very major step for the Soviet Union to publicly distance itself from Iraq, in favor of an alliance with an unpredictable Iran; and in reality Soviet actions would probably have been limited to quietly curtailing Iraqi arms supplies and blocking anti-Iranian moves at the United Nations.[81]

Despite appearances to the contrary Iran had been negotiating since 1987 for a settlement based on a modified version of UN Resolution 598,[82] but the demoralization of Iran following its battlefield defeats and the shooting down of the airliner precipitated its humiliating acceptance of the original resolution in July 1988.

CONTRIBUTION OF THE REFLAGGING TO U.S. POLICY GOALS

The reflagging and escort of Kuwait's tankers is generally considered a success by U.S. policy makers and military personnel. A number of difficult logistical problems were solved, the GCC states were reassured of U.S. commitment to them and (to some extent) of U.S. resolve in pursuing its policies. U.S. access to base facilities and regional cooperation was greatly increased; and the U.S. actions, whether justifiable or not, undoubtedly contributed a great deal to Iran's acceptance of a cease-fire. The U.S. Navy now operates at a much higher tempo in and near the Gulf than would have been accepted prior to the reflagging.[83]

However, the longer-term consequences of U.S. actions seriously challenge these claims to have successfully furthered U.S. interests, particularly in view of the grave risks of uncontrollable escalation of the Iran-Iraq War resulting from the reflagging.

Four serious risks are easily identified. First is the danger of directly involving the GCC states in the war, something that had been avoided for eight years. Iranian missile attacks on Kuwaiti territory and the rupture of Iran-Saudi relations demonstrate the seriousness of the problem, particularly as Saudi Arabia has bilateral defense pacts with all the other GCC states.[84] Direct involvement of the GCC would have had major consequences for the United States both because of the widespread disruption of oil supplies that would have resulted and because of implicit U.S. security guarantees to the GCC states.

Second, although, despite strong congressional pressure, the US War Powers Act was never actually invoked,[85] the U.S. Navy was clearly operating on a wartime basis and at least forty-nine U.S. personnel (and an unknown number of Iranians) were killed.[86] Had the Iranian Navy missiles succeeded in breaching U.S. defenses there could have been a considerable number of U.S. casualties from the April naval battle. Iran also demonstrated the vulnerability of the high-tech U.S. Navy to World War I mines, and the long-standing U.S. policy of relying on its European allies for mine countermeasure vessels could have seriously constrained the United States if these allies had continued their refusal to cooperate.[87] The political repercussions of a large number of U.S. service personnel being killed, particularly in a presidential election year, could have forced an ignominious departure by the United States with serious consequences for its relations with GCC states.

Third, one of the few options left to Iran in the face of overwhelming U.S. military capability was to resort to terrorism. For example, the Lockerbie bombing may have been direct or indirect retaliation for the downing of the Iranian civilian airliner.[88] The problem for Iran would have been to make the connection sufficiently obvious to catalyze U.S. domestic pressure to bring the U.S. Navy home, without provoking U.S. retaliation for "state sponsored terrorism." The determination of the United States to use military means for this was demonstrated against Libya in 1986 and was also recently reaffirmed by the Presidential Commission report on the Lockerbie bombing.[89] An easier option for Iran would have been sabotage in the GCC states, to pressurize them to distance themselves from the United States.

The fourth important risk was demonstrated by the shooting down of the Iranian civilian airliner. The Gulf waters were crowded with combatant ships all trying to ensure their own survival against a variety of threats, while coexisting with large numbers of commercial ships and aircraft. A number of near accidents occurred before July 1988, and any one of these confrontations could have escalated out of control, particularly if say, both Soviet and Western warships were involved.

The longer-term consequences of the U.S. actions are equally worrying. In general the GCC states appear to have accepted that they must coexist with Revolutionary Iran; and therefore their best defense is to improve the circumstances of their people who might be influenced by Iran, in particular Shi'ites and minimize the level of hostilities between themselves and Iran. The Kuwaiti reflagging achieved the opposite of this. The other GCC states appear to have been taken by surprise by the Kuwait initiative; and although the incidents surrounding the reflagging (notably the Silkworm attacks on Kuwait and the July 1987 disturbances in Mecca) combined with the greater U.S. involvement encouraged the GCC to temporarily harden its position against Iran, the southern GCC states remained reluctant to antagonize Iran. The southern states and Kuwait have sought to rebuild relations with Iran since the cease-fire, but the breach of diplomatic relations between Saudi Arabia and Iran cannot be so readily healed.[90]

Nor did the reflagging clearly advance U.S.-GCC relations. The military support offered by the GCC states to the United States was limited and highly secretive, and although the United States did demonstrate considerable resolve by continuing the escorts in the face of Iranian opposition, it also caused concern with its high-handed and uncontrollable (by the GCC) actions.[91] There is also evidence of concern about the heightened U.S. presence in the region since the cease-fire, and the slow withdrawal of U.S. ships when compared with its European allies. Although Kuwaiti officials have said that Western assistance in clearing mines from the Gulf would be welcome, the defense minister has also stated Kuwaiti intentions to "seek to reduce the foreign military presence in Gulf waters,"[92] and Kuwait has attempted to encourage the United States by returning six of the U.S. "reflagged" tankers to the Kuwaiti flag.[93]

The GCC has reverted to its more traditional policy of promoting self-reliance and is attempting to improve its indigenous naval and air defense capabilities. For example, Saudi Arabia has ordered six Sandown mine hunters from Britain as part of a £10 billion deal agreed in July 1988.[94] A number of arms deals have recently been concluded between GCC states and a range of arms suppliers, indicating their intention to diversify their options and reduce reliance on an unpredictable superpower.[95]

Although a comprehensive peace settlement looks unlikely the cease-fire has led to a readjustment of positions both within the Gulf and the wider Arab arena. In Iran, Khomeini typically tilted the balance back from the "pragmatists" who had accepted a humiliating cease-fire, toward the "radicals," with a renewed emphasis on Iranian independence and the controversial edict on Salman Rushdie. Since Khomeini's death the "pragmatists," led by Rafsanjani appear to be in reasonably firm control, but it is impossible to predict how long this will last, and they are seriously constrained by rival factions from seeking the outside help that Iran desperately needs to rebuild its economy.

In Iraq, Saddam Hussein lost no time in eliminating the threat from the Kurds. The major offensive immediately after the cease-fire caused widespread surprise due to its ferocity, and the use of chemical weapons.[96] The leading role of Iraq in inter-Arab affairs has been firmly reasserted. Egypt has been rewarded for the support it gave Iraq during the war by its reintroduction to the Arab League, and temporarily at least, the two are forging close links, for example within the framework of the new Arab Cooperation Council. Meanwhile Syria is being roundly punished for its maverick role in supporting Iran by the withdrawal of Arab support for its occupation in Lebanon, a situation aggravated by the increased involvement there of Iraq.[97]

Clearly, although the threat from Iran was considered dominant, both Saudi Arabia and Kuwait were willing to ensure Iraq's survival, but now that threat has abated, earlier concerns about Iraqi domination of the Gulf region have resurfaced. There appears to be no question of Iraq joining the GCC, and suggestions, for example, that Iraq may attempt to divert the flow of the Shatt-al-Arab River to solve its boundary dispute with Iran are not welcome in Kuwait, as this might give added impetus to Iraq's unwelcome territorial claims on Warba and Bubiyan Islands.

The intervention of the United States in the war enabled Iraq to emerge in an artificially strong position. This complicates the negotiations for a full peace settlement, without which the entire region remains unstable, but a confident Iraq also creates wider problems for the United States. Not only is it a potential direct threat to the GCC states, it is in a position to seriously challenge Israel, and U.S. policies toward the Palestinian issue.

The lack of international condemnation of Iraq's widespread use of chemical weapons may well prove to be one of the most serious long-term consequences of the Iran-Iraq War.[98]

Less directly, the U.S. actions in the Gulf during 1987–88 showed little regard for international law. Responsibility for upholding international laws, such as freedom of navigation, rests with the United Nations, not with superpowers or ad hoc multinational forces. Incidents, such as the destruction of Iranian oil platforms, the sinking of the *Iran Ajr,* and the April naval battles have dubious legitimacy in international law and set precedents for more outrageous floutings by the United States (such as its invasion of Panama[99]) and by other states. The partisan actions of the United States (and other states) during the Iran-Iraq War raise important questions about the acceptable conduct of non-belligerents during a war.[100]

Finally, the U.S. actions should be considered in the context of the basic U.S. goals in the Middle East: protection of oil supplies; protection of Israel; and containment of the Soviet Union. The short-term impact of the reflagging was considerably greater disruption of oil supplies than any previous time during the war, and if the war had widened to include direct GCC involvement this would have been far worse. The reflagging escorts also demonstrated the impracticality of protecting oil supplies militarily. Not only was it physically impossible to prevent tanker attacks, the Iranian missile strike on Kuwait's main offshore oil terminal (Mina Al-Ahmadi), which disabled it for a month, demonstrated the vulnerability to oil supply disruption at other transit points.[101]

In the longer term, the emergence from the war of a strong Iraq, particularly in view of reports of major new oil discoveries in Iraq, its leverage over the GCC states, its past uncompromising record on Israel, and its extremely well-equipped armed forces does not auger well for the security of future oil supplies or regional stability.

Israel was, perhaps, the only beneficiary of the Iranian refusal to seek an early end to the war, owing to the preoccupation of one of the main Arab military powers (Iraq) and the diversion of Arab League attention from Palestinian issues to the Gulf War (particularly at the November 1987 summit). Although by no means intending to suggest this as an acceptable reason for U.S. inaction over the Iran-Iraq War, the ending of active hostilities, the readmission of Egypt to Arab circles, and the improved status of the Soviet Union have all contributed to greater insecurity for Israel.

Since the Iranian Revolution the United States has had to balance its desire to contain and punish the Islamic regime, against driving it into close cooperation with the Soviet Union. The U.S. actions against Iran, flirted with the danger that Iran would turn to the Soviet Union for support. In addition to the substantial improvement in relations between Iran and the Soviet Union,[102] the nonprovocative style of the Soviets in the Gulf compared with the US, and their justifiable claim to be the only major power on reasonable terms with both parties to the conflict, further undermined U.S. claims of a Soviet military threat to the region. One of the prime reasons for the United States reversing its policies and agreeing to the reflagging was learning of Soviet agreement to do so. The United States concentrated on attempting to prevent greater Soviet naval involvement in the Gulf, but the cost of doing so was contributing to increased Soviet involvement both in Iran and on Palestinian issues.

CONCLUSIONS

U.S. policy toward the Gulf since World War II has been based on three clear and overriding principles: security of oil supplies, containment of the Soviet Union, and protection of Israel. These commitments override that to any particular regime in the Gulf and explains some of the apparent inconsistencies in U.S. policy toward states in the region. The dilemma for the United States is to identify the best means to protect these interests in both the short and the long term.

Over the last decade the United States has made massive investments in improving its capabilities for rapid military intervention in the Middle East. These capabilities now dwarf all regional forces and, in the unlikely event of Soviet invasion of Iran, would be able to seriously harass and perhaps halt Soviet forces.[103]

The concept of rapidly deployable forces is not new, but the wide-ranging series of improvement programs and the creation of an effective command structure (Central Command and Special Operations Command) form an unprecedented capability that is of serious concern to all those who may become its target. Although the U.S. effort has been directed particularly toward the Middle East, many of the capabilities involved would be suitable for use anywhere in the world and are part of a general reinvigoration of U.S. interventionism as the memory of Vietnam fades.[104]

The principal use of Central Command to date was the escort of the reflagged Kuwaiti tankers. In early 1987, when Kuwait's request to reflag its tankers was being considered by the United States, the scandal of Irangate was at its height, and the prospect of the Soviet Union being invited into the heart of an area the United States considers its exclusive preserve was sufficient to panic the United States into agreeing to the reflagging. This agreement resulted in direct intervention in the Iran-Iraq War that, legitimately or otherwise, considerably benefited Iraq.

It seems, with hindsight, that both Kuwait and the United States should have adopted a more cautious strategy, because within a few months it was clear that Iran was unable to muster its threatened major offensive, and U.S. allies were reluctant to support the new U.S. policy, which proved considerably more difficult and dangerous to implement than was expected. Although the U.S. Navy predictably displayed overwhelming superiority in a direct battle with Iranian naval forces, the confined, crowded waters of the Gulf are unsuited to the U.S. Navy force—mix, and without European assistance it would have been unable to deal with the mined waters.

Although the policy did contribute to the current cease-fire this followed a substantial worsening of the "Tanker War" and inter-Gulf relations and has encouraged Iran to seek support from the Soviet Union. The U.S. actions in the Gulf were not controlled by the United States, but by Iraq's dictation of the tempo of the "Tanker War" and by internal Iranian politics. Alternative policies that addressed Kuwait's motive of attracting international pressure to end the war, without escalation to virtual war between Iran and the United States, would have been more appropriate.

For example, the United States could have refused to get involved militarily and with some expectation of success, in view of the Soviets difficult position between Iran and Iraq, could have sought to persuade the Soviets to do the same. Because Kuwait's prime interest was attracting attention to the war, rather than protection of its exports, it should have been possible to seek alternative means of satisfying Kuwait, such as diplomatic initiatives or, as had been done in the past, boosting the self-defense capabilities of the GCC states. If naval escorts were considered necessary the possibility of multilateral action could have been explored, such as the creation of a UN naval force. A number of proposals were made for this, but none of them were developed in any detail largely because of the total refusal, particularly by the United States and United Kingdom to consider the idea.[105] Alternatively the United States could have pursued a more evenhanded approach toward a diplomatic settlement of the war. UN Resolution 598, which was supposedly an attempt to seek a fair settlement to the war, was reportedly discussed with Iraq in advance, and Iraq was expected to accept the resolution and Iran to reject it.[106]

There are two fundamental flaws in current U.S. strategic policy toward the Gulf: the unwarranted emphasis on the supposed Soviet threat to the region, and the misplaced confidence in U.S. ability to protect its interests militarily. However capable of rapid deployment the U.S. armed forces become, they cannot alter the basic geographical fact that the Persian Gulf is on the opposite side of the world from the United States. Consequently, there will inevitably be a significant delay in deploying large scale forces to the region from the United States. Even if it was politically and economically realistic to deploy large numbers of troops in the region during peacetime, in readiness for a crisis then the United States would find it difficult to militarily prevent the kind of political action on oil supplies that occurred during 1973/1974, and any military action in the region is likely to result in significant collateral damage and/or sabotage to oil supplies, particularly if Saudi Arabia was involved, which would frustrate the fundamental goal of securing U.S. oil supplies.

Preoccupation with the Soviet Union was a general trait of the Reagan administration, reinforced in the Gulf region by the proximity of Afghanistan. Although the Soviets have an obvious interest in oil supplies from the region, both for their own use and potentially controlling Western supplies, it is ludicrous to suggest that they will attempt to seize the fields militarily, outside a global war scenario. Far more plausible is the opportunist expansion of Soviet influence by nonmilitary means. Nevertheless, a Soviet large-scale invasion of Iran remains the basis for Central Command planning. The distorting affect of these assumptions is clearly demonstrated by the fact that the only major use of

CENTCOM forces so far was for a *naval* operation, whereas U.S. military planning for CENTCOM has concentrated on improving the ability to deploy ground forces in the region.

Central Command hinders rather than helps containment of Soviet influence because it encourages resentment against the U.S. The countries in the region do not want to become a battleground for the superpowers in either a hot or a cold war, and the extensive US military build-up invites a Soviet response.

Protection of oil supplies is seen as being synonymous with protecting the GCC states, particularly Saudi Arabia, yet CENTCOM is ill-equipped to deal with their most likely threats. Probably the most serious of these is the resumption of active hostilities between Iran and Iraq. Renewal of hostilities between Iran and Iraq will not be prevented by Central Command, but by international pressure at the UN negotiating table.

The second most likely serious threat to the GCC states is renewed fighting over the Arab-Israeli dispute. The proliferation of ballistic missiles in the region places the GCC well within range of direct combat, and despite consistent U.S. attempts to separate the two regions, their intrinsic linkage has been proved on numerous occasions since the 1973 War. The whole strategy of Central Command will be torn apart by the divided loyalties of the United States, although based on its past behavior the United States will unquestionably support Israel. Kuwait faces the additional problem of aggressive Iraqi claims on its territory, notably the islands of Bubiyan and Warba, with their strategic location overlooking the Shatt-al-Arab, while Saudi Arabia is potentially threatened by its sour relations with Iran.

During the Iran-Iraq War the GCC ideals of self-reliance and regional cooperation fell well short of reality, and although, with the exception of Oman, the GCC states refused to sign formal agreements with the United States it was clearly seen as an ultimate guarantor of security. However, contrary to the general assumption of the United States, such guarantees need not necessarily take the form of direct military assistance.

The GCC regimes are well aware that security extends well beyond purely military considerations and that the convergence of U.S. and Arab interests is limited. Major arms purchases, designed to improve their defenses against any extension of the Iran-Iraq

War, were sought from the United States because this was the easiest way to rapidly build up cohesive defenses. However, now that most of the infrastructure is in place, and there is less urgency while the cease-fire holds, they are diversifying their sources, particularly as Zionist lobbying of the U.S. Congress has made U.S. purchases so embarrassing for them.

U.S. attempts to directly involve itself in the Gulf region coincided with an eight-year-long war between its most powerful states. If the United States is to seriously pursue its prime goal of securing oil supplies from the Gulf region it must take advantage of the cessation of hostilities to review both its military and non-military strategies. In particular, it must resolve the dilemmas over its relations with Iran. The oscillation between overtures such as Irangate, followed within months by virtual war are helpful to no one.

NOTES

1.   C. A. Kupchan *The Persian Gulf and the West: the Dilemmas of Security* (New York: Allen and Unwin, 1987), p. 32.

2.   A. Acharya "US Strategy in the Persian Gulf: The Rapid Deployment Force as an Instrument of Policy," Ph.D. thesis, Murdoch University, Australia, 1986, p. 37.

3.   Ibid., p. 37.

4.   U.S. Congressional Research Service, *Oil Fields as Military Objectives: A Feasibility Study* (Washington, D.C.: Government Printing Office, 1975).

5.   Four events in the Gulf area can be identified as catalysts of this change of attitude: the Iranian Revolution; the occupation of the Grand Mosque in Mecca; the seizure of the U.S. embassy in Tehran; and the Soviet invasion of Afghanistan.

6.   Jimmy Carter, "State of the Union speech," January 1980.

7.   U.S. House Committee on Armed Services, *Hearings on Military Posture and HR 9751, FY 1963*, p. 3296, cited in Acharya, "U.S. Strategy in the Persian Gulf," p. 123.

8.   Ibid., p. 94.

9.   Ibid., p. 104.

10.   U.S. Joint Chiefs of Staff, *Military Posture FY 1982*, p. 55.

11.   Carter, "Wake Forest Speech," 1978.

12.   Acharya, "US Strategy in the Persian Gulf," p. 131.

13.   HQ RDJTF factsheet, cited in A. Acharya, *US Military Strategy in the Gulf: Origins and Evolution Under the Carter and Reagan Administrations* (London and New York: Routledge, 1989), p. 65.

14.   R. Haffa, *The Half War: Planning US Rapid Deployment Forces to Meet a Limited Contingency, 1960–83* (Boulder, Colo.: Westview, 1984), p. 126.

15.   G. Crist, commander-in-chief CENTCOM, statement before the Senate Armed Services Committee (March 11, 1986), p. 39.

16.   The incoming Reagan administration increased the proposed fiscal year 1982 budget for the RDJTF by 85 percent to $4.5 billion and proposed spending $17.5 billion over the next five years. However, a congressional committee report reportedly estimated that the proposal would in fact cost $25–30 billion (see "A Ballooning Bureaucracy: RDF Is Not Ready to Fight," *Defense Week* [November 2, 1981]). It is impossible to make any meaningful assessment of the costs of CENTCOM because many programs will benefit both CENTCOM and other U.S. forces.

17.   See Secretary of Defense and Commander-in-Chief CENTRAL COMMAND annual reports to Congress.

18.   These two groups of ships are the maritime prepositioned ships (MPS) and the near-term prepositioned force. Note there are two other MPS squadrons, one in the Atlantic and one in the Pacific, providing in total sufficient equipment for one-third of the U.S. Marine Corps.

19.   W. Donko, "US Navy Amphibiosity: LHDs and LCACs a Perfect Symbiosis," *Navy International* (January 1986): p. 35.

20.   For use of aircraft carriers, see, for example, R. Stumpf, "Air War with Libya," *US Naval Institute Proceedings* (August 1986). For battleships, see R. O'Rourke, "Born Again Battleships," *Navy International* (February 1986): 73–78; and S. Terzibaschitsch, "The US Navy's Iowa Class Battleships," *International Defense Review* (March 1987): 283–87.

21.   J. M. Collins, *Green Berets, Seals and Spetsnaz* (London: Pergamon Brassey, 1987); and Center for Defense Information, "America's Secret Soldiers: The Build-up of US Special Operations Forces," *Defense Monitor* 16, no. 2 (1985).

22.   A. Acharya *US Military Strategy in the Gulf*, ch. 5.

23.   C. Crist, Commander-in-Chief, CENTCOM, Statement before the Senate Armed Services Committee, 27 January 1987, p. 62.

24.   *Marine Corps Gazette* (December 1986).

25.   U.S. Senate Armed Services Committee Hearings, *National Security Strategy*, S-HRG 100-257 (1987), p. 553.

26.   E. Gamlen and P. Rogers, "The Reflagging of the Kuwaiti Tankers by the US: Reasons and Implications," *Proceedings of the International Conference on Aggression and Defence,* held in Tehran, August 1988 (Tehran: War Propaganda Headquarters, 1989).

27.   Department of Defense 1989 Appropriations Hearings before the House Department of Defense Subcommittee of the Committee on Appropriations, Part 2, p. 263.

28.   Ibid., p. 218.

29.   Acharya, *US Military Strategy in the Gulf,* p. 114.

30.   R. King, "The Iran-Iraq War: The Political Implications," Adelphi Paper No. 219, IISS (1987), p. 47.

31.   Ibid., p. 51.

32.   *Defense* (March 1984).

33.   E. O'Ballance, *The Gulf War* (London: Brasseys, 1988), p. 45.

34.   U.S. Senate, Committee on Foreign Relations, Staff Report, *War in the Gulf,* 1984.

35.   R. Preece, *US Policy Toward Iran: 1979–86,* CRS Report for Congress, 87-974 (December 1987), p. 20.

36.   Z. Brzezinski, *Power and Principle: Memoirs of the National Security Adviser, 1977–1981* (New York: Farrar Straus and Giroux, 1983), p. 452; cited in Acharya, *US Military Strategy in the Gulf.*

37.   Kupchan, *The Persian Gulf and the West,* p. 144.

38.   Preece, *US Policy Toward Iran,* p. 11.

39.   A. Cordesman, *The Iran-Iraq War and Western Security 1984–87* (London: Janes, 1987), p. 36; King, *The Iran-Iraq War,* p. 53.

40.   *International Herald Tribune* (October 12, 1983).

41.   A detailed chronology of tanker attacks from the start of the war until January 1987 is provided in UK House of Commons, *The Protection of British Merchant Shipping in the Persian Gulf,* 3rd Special Report of the UK Defence Committee (HMSO, May 13, 1987).

42.   E. Karsh "The Iran-Iraq War: A Military Analysis," Adelphi Paper No. 220 (1987), p. 29. *Philadelphia Inquirer* (February 23 and 24, 1984).

43.   Preece, *US Policy Toward Iran,* p. 24.

44.   *Navy International* (April 1984); *Daily Telegraph* (February 3, 1984), p. 5.

45.   *The [London] Times* (February 21, 1984), p. 7. Kuwait's attitude did fluctuate according to the degree of threat perceived, see also *The [London] Times* (May 22, 1984), p. 36.

46.   *New York Times* (May 17, 1984), cited in King, *The Iran-Iraq War,* p. 53.

47.   *The [London] Times* (May 22, 1984), p. 36. The approach led to UN Security Council Resolution 552, which demanded an end to attacks on ships trading with nonbelligerent states.

48.   *Navy International* (August 1984), p. 484.

49.   Testimony by Richard Murphy, House Committee on Foreign Affairs, *Developments in the Persian Gulf* (June 1984), pp. 26–27, cited in Acharya, *US Military Strategy in the Gulf,* p. 131.

50.   *Newsweek* (May 28, 1984).

51.   *Navy International* (July 1984), p. 435.

52.   Cordesman, *The Iran-Iraq War and Western Security,* ch. 5.

53.   *Overview of the Situation in the Persian Gulf,* U.S. House of Representatives, Committee on Foreign Affairs (May and June 1987), p. 214.

54.   C. Weinberger, *A Report to Congress on Security Arrangements in the Persian Gulf* (June 15, 1987), Table 1. Note: according to Kuwaiti sources cited in *War in the Persian Gulf: The US Takes Sides,* staff report to the Senate Committee on Foreign Relations, S PRT 100-60, p. 37, the original request was in September 1986.

55.   Ibid.

56.   *The [Manchester] Guardian* (July 16, 1987). Three Kuwait Oil Tanker Company (i.e., government owned) vessels were reregistered in Britain, but the Royal Navy continued its practice of quietly accompanying ships rather than adopting the high profile style of U.S. operations.

57.   U.S. Under Secretary Armacost, *US Policy in the Persian Gulf and Kuwaiti Reflagging* Dept. of State, Current Policy 978 (June 1987).

58.   *Janes Defence Weekly* (November 28, 1987).

59.   See, for example, F. Axelgard, "Deception at Home and Abroad: Implications of the Iran Arms Scandal for US Foreign Policy," and A. Cordesman, "Arms to Iran," *American Arab Affairs,* no. 20 (Spring 1987).

60.   *National Security Policy Implications of US Operations in the Persian Gulf,* Report of the Defense Policy Panel and Investigations Subcommittee of the House Committee on Armed Services (July 1987), p. 25.

61.   Preece, *US Policy Toward Iran,* p. 20.

62.   Ibid.

63.   *Philadelphia Inquirer* (June 6, 1987).

64.   *Washington Post* (June 19, 1987).

65.   R. O'Rourke *Persian Gulf: US Military Operations,* CRS Report IB87145 (updated March 24, 1988), p. 9.

66.   *War in the Persian Gulf: The US Takes Sides,* p. 38.

67. *Washington Post* (July 5, 1987), p. 13; *New York Times* (May 29, 1987); *Washington Times* (July 2, 1987); *The [Manchester] Guardian* (July 3, 1987).

68. *Overview of the Situation in the Persian Gulf,* p. 205.

69. For example, *Baltimore Sun* (October 23, 1987), p. 2; *Washington Times* (June 1, 1987), p. 3. For a more detailed account of these claims and their inaccurate portrayal of U.S. motives, see E. Gamlen, "US Military Intervention in the Iran-Iraq War 1987–8," Peace Research Report No 21 (School of Peace Studies, University of Bradford, March 1989).

70. *War in the Persian Gulf: The US Takes Sides,* p. 42.

71. R. O'Rourke, "The Tanker War," *USN Institute Proceedings, Naval Review* (1988).

72. *New York Times* (April 21, 1988), p. 8.

73. *The [Manchester] Guardian* (June 17, 1987).

74. *The [London] Times* (June 8, 1984).

75. *National Journal* (January 23, 1988).

76. *Washington Post* (August 10, 1987), p. 1.

77. Gamlen, "US Military Intervention."

78. R. O'Rourke, "Gulf Operations," *US Naval Institute Proceedings, Naval Review* (May 1989).

79. G. Sick, "Slouching Toward Settlement: The Internationalization of the Iran-Iraq War," in N. Keddie and M. Gasiorowski, eds., *Neither East nor West: Iran, the United States and the Soviet Union* (New Haven, Conn.: Yale University Press, 1990), pp. 219–47.

80. *Financial Times* (August 16, 1988), p. 12.

81. Soviet prevarication on the proposed UN arms embargo against Iran is one example of its ability to assist Iran in this way.

82. Sick, "Slouching Toward Settlement."

83. See, for example, *International Herald Tribune* (September 19 and December 8, 1988); and *Janes Defence Weekly* (August 13, 1988).

84. There were also reports of attempts at direct attacks by Iranian forces against GCC territory for the first time in the war. For example, against the Saudi Arabian oil island of Ras al-Khafi (see *Washington Times* [October 5, 1987], p. 8) and against the Kuwaiti island of Bubiyan (see *The [Manchester] Guardian* [March 31, 1988], p. 8).

85. Gamlen, "US Military Intervention," pp. 35–36.

86. Thirty-seven were killed in the Iraqi attack on the USS *Stark,* and at least twelve in various helicopter crashes; see *Janes Defence Weekly* (November 19, 1989), p. 1251.

87. Gamlen, "US Military Intervention," pp. 40–42.

88. "Unholy Plot to Destroy Flight 103," *Observer* (July 30, 1989), pp. 8–9.

89. *The [Manchester] Guardian* (May 16, 1990), p. 1.

90. For example, condolences were sent after the death of Khomeini, and a plan was drawn up in November 1988 for all eight Gulf states to cooperate in clearing the Gulf of war debris; see *The [London] Times* (November 2, 1988), p. 9.

91. For example, in early 1988 when the Tanker War had quieted down the Secretary-General of the GCC openly encourages the United States to "lower the profile of its operations"; see *Washington Post* (February 24, 1988), p. 20.

92. *International Herald Tribune* (December 8, 1988).

93. *Janes Defence Weekly* (January 28, 1989).

94. *Janes Defence Weekly* (March 11, 1989).

95. Most notable of these was the Saudi Arabian purchase of Chinese ballistic missiles; see *Los Angeles Times* (May 4, 1988), p. 1.

96. *The [Manchester] Guardian* (September 16, 1988), p. 1; G. Roberts, "The Winds of Death," *Dispatches* Channel Four TV Documentary (November 23, 1988).

97. There have been a number of reports of Iraq supplying arms to the Lebanese Forces, and at the Arab League meeting in May 1989 Iraq claimed rights equal to those of Syria to deploy troops in Lebanon (*The [Manchester] Guardian* [May 26, 1989]).

98. "Controlling the Poor Man's Nuclear Weapon," *Financial Times* (August 19, 1988), p. 12. At the Paris Conference on chemical weapons in January 1989, a number of Arab countries openly asserted for the first time that they saw chemical weapons as a legitimate deterrent against a potential Israeli nuclear attack; see *The [Manchester] Guardian* (January 11, 1989), p. 10.

99. Gulf incidents, see Gamlen, "US Military Intervention," pp. 55–60; Panama invasion, see M. Gellhorn, "The Damned of Panama City," *The [Manchester] Guardian* (June 30, 1990), Weekend Section, pp. 4–6.

100. Gamlen, ibid., pp. 4–8.

101. *Washington Post* (October 23, 1987).

102. This improvement continued after the cease-fire, with an exchange of letters between Khomeini and Gorbachev (January–February 1989) and the signing of a pact on "good neighborliness" during Rafsanjani's visit to Moscow in June 1989; see *The [Manchester] Guardian* (June 22, 1989), p. 8.

103. J. Epstein, *Strategy and Force Planning the Case of the Persian Gulf* (Washington, D.C.: Brooking Institution, 1987).

104. See, for example, "Discriminate Deterrence," the Report of the Commission on Integrated Long-Term Strategy (Washington, D.C.: Government Printing Office, January 1988).

105. *The [Manchester] Guardian* (September 25, 1987), p. 6. Although it is true that a large-scale naval peace-keeping force has never been used before, there are some limited precedents of UN naval action; for example, from 1966–75 the "Beira Patrol" was formed by Britain, at the request of the UN, to enforce the oil embargo against "Rhodesia," and the U.S.–led UN command operating in Korea in the 1950s included a naval component.

106. Sick, "Slouching Toward Settlement."

CHAPTER 9

The Persian Gulf War: Myths and Realities

Eric Davis

A fundamental flaw of U.S. foreign policy in the Middle East, and the Third World generally, lies in the propensity to support authoritarian rather than democratic regimes. In its support of exclusionary regimes that oppose political, economic, and social reforms, the United States has become identified as standing against social change. Nowhere in the Middle East is this policy more pronounced than in the Persian Gulf, where the United States has backed some of the area's most authoritarian and reactionary regimes. One of these was the Iraqi regime of Saddam Hussein and the Baath party with which the United States began to forge closer ties in 1982. Yet following Iraq's August 1990 invasion of Kuwait, George Bush "drew a line in the sand" and proclaimed a great moral crusade against Saddam Hussein, whom he compared to Hitler, and his forces of aggression.

What was largely ignored throughout the crisis was the extensive support that had been given to the Baathist regime. Not only was United States duplicity in its dealings with Saddam and the Baath almost totally neglected by the institutions of the state and the media but both promoted a mythology surrounding the crisis. This mythology has served to reinforce rather than challenge the shortcomings of U.S. policy in the Middle East. Rather than reduce instability as the Bush administration asserts, the Persian Gulf conflict may actually increase the possibility that the United States will face many more such crises in the region. Given the crisis's impact on the Middle East and the larger world community, the myths and realities surrounding the crisis require extensive analysis.

The mythology surrounding the crisis asserts that the United States intervened in the Persian Gulf to rescue a small, defenseless state from a bellicose neighbor that scorned all norms of international law. Not only did the United States act swiftly to protect neighboring Saudi Arabia and liberate Kuwait, it also protected the Middle East as a whole from a Hitlerian tyrant bent on subordinating the region through the use of military force, including chemical, biological, and nuclear weapons. Faced with an enemy who shunned all diplomatic efforts to solve the crisis, the United States and the global community were forced to go to war after having tried every possible avenue to solve the conflict peacefully. Having successfully defended Kuwait from aggression, the United States has sought nothing in return. The mythology emphasizes that the successful repulsion of aggression in the Gulf will not only bring greater stability to that area and the larger Middle East but represents the first building block in the development of a "new world order" and a stronger role for the United Nations in world affairs.

Contrary to these assertions, it is the argument proffered here that the portrayal of the Gulf Crisis in the United States, both by the Bush administration and the media, represents a distortion of reality. United States intervention in the Persian Gulf involved a complex set of motives. These entailed a desire to offset its declining power in the global economy, an effort to maintain access to oil reserves and the integrity of its alliance structure in the Middle East, and the desire to send a message to the Third World that it now lives under a pax Americana.

The Gulf Crisis must also be situated within the context of the end of the Cold War. As the Soviet threat to American interests has diminished, the attention of the United States has increasingly turned toward its relations with less developed countries. Because power relations among the advanced industrialized states of North America, Europe, and Japan as well as the Soviet Union (and now the emerging commonwealth of nations) are increasingly determined by economic rather than military factors, economic ties to Third World countries have assumed greater importance. It is in the Third World that multiple opportunities exist for expanding markets, for obtaining much needed raw materials such as oil, and for sources of cheap labor for American and other Western industries that seek to reduce production costs at home. It is in this arena that the three great economic powers—the United States, a united Europe, and Japan—possess the best opportunities to increase their respective competitive advantage.

The recent dramatic changes in international politics underline the importance of the deception and mythology surrounding the Persian Gulf Crisis because they signify a pivotal change in the international political order and political economy. The main political and economic cleavage has shifted from one that has pitted the West against the Soviet Union to one pitting the "North" or advanced industrialized countries against those of the underdeveloped nations of the "South."

In terms of hegemonic ideology, the crisis is likewise significant because the Gulf Crisis represents an enormous lesson in political socialization for Western mass publics. This is especially true for the middle and lower-middle classes in the United States who, throughout the crisis, provided the core of support for military action against Iraq. Given the declining economic fortunes of the American middle and lower classes, the state's mythologizing of the Gulf Crisis has fallen on receptive ears. Thus, George Bush's "new world order" can be seen as a model of how Americans will be expected to react in the future to either real or imagined aggression by Third World states. Simultaneously, it is intended to make Americans feel more optimistic about their political and economic future. The symbols and terminology associated with the crisis can thus be "recycled" in future crises in an effort to evoke similar support among the American populace against Third World countries deemed hostile to American interests and to offset domestic problems. The mythology surrounding the Persian Gulf Crisis thus extends far beyond the Middle East. It provides a model of thought and behavior for Western mass publics that can be trotted out in future crises for both foreign and domestic ends.

UNITED STATES POLICY IN THE GULF: THE MYTH OF MORAL IMPERATIVES

One of the most important elements that distinguishes an authoritarian from a democratic society is the free flow of information based on freedom of speech and opinion. These two freedoms were among those constantly emphasized by political leaders and the media in the United States to distinguish the American from the Iraqi political system during the Persian Gulf Crisis. However, an overview of the newspaper of record in the United States, *The New York Times,* the broader print media, and the major television networks points to a historical amnesia surrounding U.S.-Iraqi relations that belies the meaning of these freedoms. Put differently, how was it possible for the state to sustain the notion of freedom of information during the crisis while simultaneously expunging from the record its long involvement and complicity with the Baathist regime in Iraq? Likewise, how was the state able to avoid any serious discussion of the potential wider ramifications of its military confrontation with Saddam Hussein and the Iraqi Baath?

A better understanding of the answers to these questions requires an examination both of the reasons offered by the Bush administration for its policy during the crisis as well as the possible unintended consequences of the war that have not been addressed by the political leadership in Washington. A more realistic analysis of the motivations behind both American and Iraqi policy might contribute to "bringing history back in," thereby better educating the American public as to the real dynamics of the crisis. Such an awareness might also provide some of the analytic tools to those who opposed both Iraq's seizure of Kuwait as well as U.S. conduct of the crisis, especially its use of military force, to prevent such crises from recurring in the future.

U.S. policy in the Persian Gulf, particularly the use of massive military force against Iraq—a level of force that far exceeded the United Nations mandate under Resolutions 660 and 678—promises to have widespread ramifications both for the West and the peoples of the Middle East. One of the problems in critically assessing this policy is the ignorance of the majority of the American populace of the region. Very few people had heard of Iraq, Kuwait, or Saddam Hussein prior to August 1991. Prior to the war's onset, only one in four Americans could correctly locate the Persian Gulf. This "tabula rasa" facilitated the Bush administration's ability to set the structure and parameters for thinking about both the crisis and the new relationship with the Third World subsumed under the term *the new world order.*

The reasons for American involvement in the Persian Gulf Crisis underwent a number of changes following Iraq's invasion of Kuwait on August 2, 1990. The Bush administration's first response was largely an economic calculation in arguing that Iraq's control of 20 percent of the world's oil threatened "our way of life." The initial concern was to protect an even larger oil producer, Saudi Arabia, as indicated by the term, *Operation Desert Shield*. Once Iraq's invasion of Kuwait moved to the United Nations, the issue was no longer just about oil but rather about one nation's aggression in absorbing a neighboring sovereign state and the need to restore that country's legitimate government. This was understandable in light of the Bush administration's efforts to forge an international coalition against Iraq. If it had argued that the main significance of Iraq's invasion was its impact on the American economy, this probably would not have been a compelling enough reason to attract the support of other nations. It was at this point that George Bush began to articulate the concept of a "new world order."

By November 1990, the Persian Gulf Crisis had broadened still further. Now the Bush administration argued that Iraq represented a threat to global stability because, not only did it possess chemical and biological weapons, it was approaching development of a nuclear capability as well. Iraq's military might had grown from a threat to the Persian Gulf to one with global implications.

Which of these stated motivations really explains American foreign policy in the Persian Gulf? Or can United States involvement be attributed to other factors that have not been widely reported in the media? Perhaps the clearest statement of United States policy came in a speech by Secretary of State James Baker entitled, "Why America Is in the Gulf," delivered before the Los Angeles World Affairs Council on October 29, 1990.[1]

Baker outlined three reasons for American involvement in the Gulf. First, he stated,

> Iraq's aggression challenges world peace. . . . Saddam Hussein's aggression shatters the vision of a better world in the aftermath of the Cold War. . . . The rest of the world is trying to go forward with the 1990s. But Saddam Hussein is trying to drag us all back into the 1930s. . . . In the 1930s, the aggressors were appeased.

In 1990, the President has made our position plain: This aggression will not be appeased.

Second, Baker argued that,

> Iraq's aggression is a regional challenge . . . the Middle East is already disturbed by unresolved conflicts, sectarian and social strife, and vast economic disparities. When you add weapons of mass destruction and much of the world's energy supplies, it becomes an explosive mix. . . . There can be no hope of resolving other problems in the region unless peaceful change becomes the wave of the future in the Middle East and the gulf. . . . If [Saddam's] way of doing business prevails, there will be no hope for peace in the area.

As the third and final reason, he asserted that, "Iraq's aggression challenges the global economy . . . for better or worse, the health of the global economy will depend for the foreseeable future on secure access to the energy resources of the Persian Gulf. Neither we nor the international community can afford to let one dictator control that access."

On the face of it, Secretary Baker's speech sounded very reasoned. However, his arguments for why the United States became so heavily involved in the Persian Gulf belie a number of problems. First, there is the issue of world peace, particularly the argument invoking appeasement. Although the Hussein-Hitler analogy is discussed in greater detail later, clearly George Bush and members of his administration attempted to equate Saddam Hussein with Adolf Hitler and his Nazi regime during the crisis. If this was the case, why, for eight years, had the United States been one of his strongest backers? For example, during the Iran-Iraq War, the United States actively pursued a policy after 1982 designed to help prevent Iraq from being militarily defeated by Iran. When the war began, the United States adopted a neutral posture content to see two potential regional powers destroy one another. As Henry Kissinger put it so bluntly in 1981, "the ultimate American interest" was that "both sides lose." However, when it became evident in 1982 that Iraq might lose the war to Iran, the United States stepped in to actively support Saddam Hussein's regime. Clearly, its intent was to stop the spread of Islamic radicalism from Iran and the subversion of Saudi Arabia and the other Arab oil-producing states of the Gulf region. Having lost the Shah of Iran as a policeman for its interests in the Gulf, the United States now hoped that Saddam Hussein might occupy that role.

What did the United States do to assist Iraq? First, in February 1982 Iraq was removed from the State Department's list of terrorist nations. Second, the United States began to allow Iraq to purchase American technology and some military equipment, such as helicopters, transport planes, and vehicles. Third, having removed Iraq from the list of states that were "supporting international terrorism," Iraq was now given access to trade with the United States. Fourth, in 1984, Iraq and the United States resumed full diplomatic relations, which had been cut off since the 1967 Arab-Israeli War; this gave Iraq the benefit of receiving United States intelligence data, particularly data from American AWACS reconnaissance aircraft and satellites indicating Iranian troop strength and movements.[2] Fifth, with the collapse of oil prices in 1986, the United States, France, and other Western nations offered Iraq commercial and agricultural credits and helped it reschedule the large debt it had amassed during the war.[3] If Saddam Hussein was the functional equivalent of Hitler, why was he given such favorable treatment by the United States, France, Great Britain, and other Western nations that ultimately were to forge a military coalition against him?

Other dimensions of American-Iraqi relations prior to Iraq's invasion of Kuwait also undermine the high moral tone taken by the United States following the seizure of Kuwait. For example, when in May 1987 Iraqi aircraft attacked the USS *Stark* with exocet missiles killing thirty-seven American sailors, the United States not only failed to condemn Iraq but issued a statement whose main focus was to blame Iran for the continuation of the war.[4] Furthermore, when Saddam Hussein ordered his air force to drop poison gas on the Kurdish village of Halabja in northern Iraq, killing anywhere from 3,000 to 20,000 Iraqi Kurdish civilians, the Reagan administration did little to punish Iraq. Whereas the U.S. Congress passed an economic sanctions bill against Iraq in September 1988, the bill was never signed into law due to the Reagan administration's lack of support. Subsequently, the Department of Agriculture advanced Iraq over a billion dollars in credit in 1989.[5] In the spring of 1990, Secretary of State Baker forced the Voice of America to cease broadcasts criticizing Saddam. A subsequent visit to Baghdad by five prominent United States senators, including Bob Dole, produced a further apology to Saddam for the critical broadcasts.[6]

Finally, in July 1990, the Bush administration was still working to prevent the U.S. Senate from condemning Iraq for trying to develop nuclear weapons. In a famous interview on July 25, 1990, as the Iraqi army was massing along the Kuwait border just a little over a week before the invasion, the American ambassador in Baghdad, April Glaspie, met with Saddam Hussein and conveyed ambiguous messages to him regarding what the U.S. position would be should Iraq use force against Kuwait.[7] Given its nature, why did the U.S. government fail to take action against the Baathist regime prior to August 1990? Could one not argue that U.S. policy toward Iraq prior to the Kuwait invasion was in fact a form of appeasement, precisely what Secretary of State Baker so roundly condemned in his October 29 speech? All the actions just cited clearly sent a message to the Baathist regime that it was being courted by the United States.

In light of this background, it is difficult to accept Secretary Baker's arguments that the United States sent troops to the Persian Gulf because Saddam Hussein represented a threat to world peace paralleling that posed by Adolf Hitler during the 1930s. Indeed, his assertion is itself an implicit criticism of the U.S. government for not realizing who it was dealing with prior to August 1990. How could it be intimately involved with Saddam and the Baath for almost a decade and not be aware what type of a regime ruled Iraq?

If the United States was so concerned with aggression and oppressive regimes in the Middle East, its efforts to obtain the participation of the Syrian regime of Hafez al Assad in the Arab coalition opposing the Saddam Hussein regime were particularly curious. Assad's armed forces have occupied a substantial portion of Lebanon since 1976, and his regime has one of the worst human rights records in the region. In an attempt to suppress a local uprising of the Muslim Brotherhood, Assad ordered the indiscriminate bombing of the city of Hama in 1982, killing an estimated 20,000 Syrian citizens. Although Assad is no less ruthless than Saddam Hussein, President Bush met with him in Geneva in

November 1990, bestowing further legitimacy on him and his repressive regime. Why did George Bush meet with Hafez al Assad despite the fact that Syria is on the United States government's list of states sponsoring international terrorism? Simply because Syria agreed to send troops to the Persian Gulf and because the United States was keen on giving the impression that the military alliance facing Iraq was not just a Western coalition but one supported by Arab forces as well.

It is likewise strange that little has been said about repression in Kuwait and Saudi Arabia, which American troops were sent to protect. While human rights abuse in these two countries in no way parallel those in Iraq or Syria, they are still disturbing. In Kuwait, the ruling Amir abolished the Kuwaiti parliament in 1986 after it became too critical of lack of democratic freedoms and corruption in government. Numerous critics of the Kuwaiti regime have been either imprisoned or banished from the country. Only about 10,000 eligible men out of a total population of 1.5 million people are allowed to vote in elections and only 40 percent of the country possesses Kuwaiti citizenship. Prior to the crisis, all of the menial labor in the country was performed by non-Kuwaitis. The Amir, whom coalition forces returned to his throne, has dozens of offspring with young women whom he temporarily marries. The country's massive oil wealth, of which over $1 trillion is invested abroad, much of it in the United States, is almost the exclusive preserve of the ruling al-Sabah family. In fact, the royal family makes more from its overseas investments than from domestic oil production.

Events in postwar Kuwait are even more disturbing. Middle East Watch has documented a pattern of torture and summary executions of Iraqis, Palestinians, and other third party nationals from countries that sided with Iraq by the Kuwaiti military and police. Apparently, these actions are being overseen by U.S. Special Forces personnel who wear Kuwaiti rather than U.S. Army insignias.[8] Martial law has been imposed, and the prospects for democratization by the ruling monarchy appear dim. Indeed, a sharp cleavage has already developed between those Kuwaitis who stayed behind and formed the backbone of the resistance to the Iraqi occupation, many of whom were poorer Shi'ites, and the returning al-Sabah family and its supporters. As those Kuwaitis who resisted the occupation refuse to accept a return to the status quo ante and the Sabahs seem equally intent on reimposing their rule in its autocratic form, political instability seems certain to characterize postwar Kuwaiti politics.

Unlike Kuwait, Saudi Arabia has never even made a pretense of being democratic. Parliamentary institutions are nonexistent. Floggings for failure to conform to religious prescriptions are enforced by al-mutawa', a morals police. Public amputations and beheadings still take place in major cities on a regular basis for crimes ranging from theft to murder. However, the standards applied to the poorer classes of society are not those by which the Saudi royal family and its rich and powerful allies who regularly flaunt the state's strict moral codes have to live.

Saudi Arabia is also a society in which women are not allowed to drive cars, cannot attend the same classes in school or the university as men, and have virtually no role in the country's political life. The types of regimes that the United States has sought to protect in Kuwait and Saudi Arabia may be less oppressive than the regime in Baghdad but they are dictatorial and authoritarian nevertheless. As one commentator put it, whereas in World War II the Western alliance was fighting to make the world safe for democracy, in the Persian Gulf it has fought to make the region safe for feudalism.

The second argument offered by Secretary Baker is that the United States sent troops to Saudi Arabia and the Persian Gulf to counter a regional challenge posed by Iraq. Here his arguments likewise lack credibility. First, if regional stability is the United States' main concern, why has it sold massive amounts of arms to the region? The list of states in the Middle East that have been the recipient of American weaponry and military technology include Iraq, Iran, Israel, Egypt, Saudi Arabia, Kuwait, the United Arab Emirates, Oman, Bahrain, Turkey, the Sudan, and Morocco. Furthermore, the United States is preparing to ship even more arms to the Middle East now that the Gulf War has ended.[9]

Second, if regional security is its goal, why has the United States failed to enforce UN Security Council resolutions other than those enacted during the crisis, such as Resolution 678 authorizing the use of "all necessary means" to force Iraq to withdraw from

Kuwait? For example, Resolutions 242 and 338 call for a settlement to the Arab-Israeli dispute. They call for Israeli withdrawal to its pre-June 1967 borders, the recognition of secure borders for Israel by the states of the region, and the creation of a Palestinian state. The United States has not pursued the implementation of these resolutions with anything near the vigor of Security Council resolutions regarding Kuwait.

It is also noteworthy that, when Iraq invaded Iran in September 1980 and occupied portions of the country, the United States said and did little. While it provided Iraq with military and financial assistance following 1982, the United States did not engage in efforts to help bring about an end to the war. The prevalent attitude seemed to be that, as long as neither side was gaining the military advantage, the war could go on. The United States demonstrated little concern for the hundreds of thousands of lives being lost on both sides. In Lebanon, Syria and Israel have illegally occupied portions of the country since 1976 and 1982, respectively, yet the United States has done little to force them to withdraw. Morocco's seizure of the former colony of Spanish Sahara after Spain withdrew brought no American troops to that area. These actions suggest that there must be more than just world peace and regional stability to explain current American policy in the Gulf. In fact, the United States has been applying a double standard in the Middle East and has not been at all consistent in opposing the seizure of territory or aggression in the region.

Secretary Baker's third reason for the U.S. response to Iraq's seizure of Kuwait seems closer to the truth. Iraq's seizure of Kuwait represented a threat to the global economy, a potential "stranglehold on gulf energy resources." This then was a war about oil and its economic and political consequences. It seems clear that, if Kuwait did not possess large oil reserves, it is highly doubtful that U.S. troops would have been used to rid it of foreign occupation.

THE MYTH OF IRAQ'S THREAT
TO THE GLOBAL ECONOMY

Among commentators who have agreed that the Gulf Crisis was indeed about oil, many argued that the United States still should have responded militarily because oil is the lifeblood of the Western economy. However, did Saddam Hussein's control of Kuwaiti oil really constitute a stranglehold on world oil supplies? During the crisis, the world was completely cut off from Iraqi and Kuwaiti oil; not only was there no shortage but the world was awash in oil. Although oil prices initially rose during the crisis, once it became clear that the United States and its coalition partners would use force against Iraq, prices dropped precipitously reflecting actual market conditions. Following the end of the Gulf War, prices were actually lower than they had been prior to Iraq's invasion of Kuwait. Estimates are that it will be at least two years before Kuwait and Iraq are producing substantial quantities of oil for the world market and five to seven years before prewar production levels are reached. Nevertheless, no one is predicting substantially higher oil prices in the near future.[10]

If oil was at the center of United States concerns—that is, concern with adequate supplies at reasonable prices—it can be argued that it was not in the U.S. national interest to wage war against Iraq. This is especially true given the potential negative consequences of the war for U.S. interests in the Middle East *in the long run*. To make this argument does not mean that Iraq's invasion of Kuwait should have been ignored by the world community. However, there were other means by which to force Iraq to withdraw from Kuwait and to bring about the downfall of Saddam Hussein. In November 1990, CIA-head William Webster testified before Congress that nine to twelve months of sanctions would substantially reduce the effectiveness of the Iraqi air force and army.

THE MYTH OF IRAQI MILITARY MIGHT

Because such emphasis was placed on Iraq's control over global oil supplies due to the power of its military, it is necessary to situate Iraq within a proper economic and military perspective. To do so, let us briefly review some salient historical and geopolitical characteristics.

Roughly the size of the state of California, Iraq has a population (17 million people) the size of the Netherlands and a gross national product the size of Portugal. These figures are important because they underline Iraq's status as a small, relatively under-developed country as opposed to the image promoted in the West prior to the war of a country possessing a powerful military machine (the fourth largest army in the world) that presented a credible threat even to U.S. forces. Contrary to another stereotype held by many Westerners, Iraq is not primarily a desert. Incorporating ancient Mesopotamia (Greek for the land between the two rivers, or what is also known as the Fertile Crescent, the rich agricultural land that lies between the Tigris and Euphrates Rivers), Iraq is far more agricultural than industrialized. Iraq is literally the cradle of civilization because the oldest recorded human societies were to be found in the Tigris and Euphrates River basin dating back, in some estimates, to 10,000 B.C. In ascribing military and economic power to Iraq, it would be far more accurate to see such power residing in the ancient Mesopotamian kingdoms rather than the contemporary state.

Iraq only appeared as a modern state in 1921. Prior to the end of World War I, it was a province of the Ottoman Empire which, allied with Germany, collapsed following the war's end. Having invaded Iraq in 1914, Great Britain created modern Iraq but did so by drawing artificial boundaries and imposing an alien ruler. For example, the British drew a red line across the southern portion of the country that created yet another state, Kuwait. However, under the Ottoman Empire, Kuwait had been part of Iraq as a subdistrict of the province of Basra. The British also imposed a foreign ruler on the new nation-state, Faisal, the son of Sharif Hussein, the guardian of the two most holy cities of Islam, Mecca and Medina, in what is present-day Saudi Arabia.

Why did Great Britain impose an alien monarchy on Iraq in 1921? As is well known, the British promised the Sharif of Mecca that, if he and his forces were to rise up against the Ottoman Turks, the British would reciprocate by establishing an Arab state following the war that would encompass the Hejaz, Palestine, and Greater Syria. Of course, at the same time that the British were promising the Arabs a state, they were also promising the Zionist movement in Europe a national home in Palestine, a concept that would ultimately lead to the establishment of the state of Israel. Meanwhile, during the war, the British and French foreign ministers, Sykes and Picot, were dividing the entire Middle East into respective spheres of influence as codified in the 1916 Sykes-Picot Treaty. Placing Faisal on the Iraqi throne, especially after the French ended his short two-year rule in Damascus in 1920, represented a means of repaying Sharif Hussein and the Hashimites for their wartime revolt against the Ottomans in the Hejaz, Palestine, and Syria. More important for Great Britain, Faisal not only represented a leader who might be acceptable to the Iraqi population but one who would not be hostile to British interests.[11]

As a result of artificial boundaries, an alien monarchy, and control of the country's wealth by a small class of landowners and merchants, Iraq was beset by tremendous instability during the period of the monarchy between 1921 and 1958. Furthermore, its oil wealth was largely controlled by the British-owned Iraq Petroleum Company that dominated oil production in the country until it was nationalized in 1972. Thus, many of the problems that beset the Middle East today were caused, in part, by British and French colonial policies.

Not only does recurrent instability help explain the rise to power of despots such as Saddam Hussein, but more important it points to an important source of weakness of the Iraqi state. The image of a powerful Iraqi state poised to seize control of the oil wealth of the Arabian Peninsula and to dictate the world price of oil was just that, an image. It was one thing for Iraq to successfully conduct a war against Iran, whose armed forces had just suffered massive purges following the overthrow of the Shah and which was forced to fight a war with little or no air support. It was another for it to confront the sophisticated military technology of the U.S. Armed Forces as well as those of its Western and Arab coalition allies. The creation of the myth of the Iraqi war machine was part and parcel of a policy of deception by the Bush administration designed to prepare the American public for war.

THE MYTH OF THE HITLER-HUSSEIN ANALOGY

A corollary to the myth of Iraqi military might was the analogy between Saddam and Adolf Hitler, which was a particularly conspicuous element in the U.S. efforts to isolate Iraq. Although Saddam is a brutal dictator, to what extent is this comparison valid? Saddam Hussein, whose full name is Saddam Hussein al-Takriti, reflecting the town of Tikrit, northwest of Baghdad from which he and many of Iraq's top leaders are recruited, came to power in a coup d'etat in 1968. Because the period following the overthrow of the monarchy in 1958 and Saddam's rise to power in 1968 was one of great political unrest, many Iraqis looked favorably on the new regime, which was the first to be able to bring political stability to the country in over a decade. This was largely possible not only because Saddam was a shrewd and ruthless politician, but also because oil prices began to rise during the 1970s. The tremendous impact of oil wealth can be seen in the rise in revenues from oil sales from $1 billion in 1972 to $26 billion in 1979.[12]

Although Saddam was a brutal ruler, killing and imprisoning all those who were either actual or potential challengers to his rule, he also took much oil wealth and used it to develop the country. New schools, universities, health care clinics, illiteracy centers, childcare facilities, industrialization, and agricultural projects as well rural electrification and expansion of the country's infrastructure dramatically transformed Iraq and the populace's standard of living.[13]

This populist development policy and Saddam's efforts to exploit the gap between the "haves" and the "have-nots" helps explain the popularity that Saddam enjoyed among some sectors of the Iraqi populace prior to the Iran-Iraq War and among the lower classes in the Arab world during the Gulf crisis. Support for Saddam represented less affection for him as an individual leader than a reflection of the tremendous resentment many Arabs felt that the oil wealth generated by the oil states of the Arabian Peninsula and the Gulf, countries that have very small populations, has not been shared with the poorer Arab states. During the crisis, Iraq came to represent for many Arabs, as well as for Turks, Iranians, and other peoples in the Third World, a force that would help bring a better standard of living to the masses. Even if it was an unrealistic expectation, Saddam came to be seen as a sign of hope for many in the Third World.

What type of regime rules Iraq? Although Saddam Hussein is president, the country is run by a Revolution Command Council all of whose members are drawn from the Arab Socialist Baath (Renaissance) Party. Founded in the Levant during the 1940s, the Baath party advocates Pan-Arabism (i.e., unity of the entire Arab world from the Atlantic Ocean to the Persian Gulf) and a mild variant of socialism. However, socialism in Baathist ideology means a vaguely defined redistribution of wealth rather than Marxism, and Iraqi Baathists are hostile to communists. Indeed, when it first came to power in 1963, the Baath party executed over 3,000 Iraqi communists and sympathizers.

Although the founders of the Baath party, Michel 'Aflaq and Salah al-Din al-Bitar, were influenced by fascist thought during their education in France during the 1930s, there is no evidence that Saddam and the Iraqi Baath ever entertained the notion of conquering the Arab world or Middle East along the racial lines advocated by Hitler and the Nazi Party. Even though Iraqi Baathist ideology contains racist elements, especially against Persians, Jews, Kurds, and other minorities, Saddam and top members of the Baath began to downplay much of traditional Baathist ideology during the 1980s. This was especially true once the country began to move to the right following the Eighth Party Congress of the Baath Party in 1974. While a virulently anti-Persian campaign accompanied the onset of the Iran-Iraq War, it was concerned less with facilitating the conquest of Iran than with fostering nationalist fervor within Iraq and dissuading Iraqi Shi'ites from contemplating the creation of an Islamic republic in Iraq.[14] As I have argued elsewhere, Iraq's invasion was less a response to Iraqi-Iranian antagonism than a reflection of state-building efforts on the part of the Baath.[15]

Neither was the invasion of Kuwait motivated by ethnic or religious hostilities. Indeed, there is much evidence to support the idea that the Baathist regime initially thought of seizing only part of Kuwait but, facing no resistance, occupied the entire country.[16] An even more plausible argument can be made for the thesis that the occupation of Kuwait was never intended to be permanent. Rather Saddam and the Baath sought to plunder Kuwait of its resources and then offer to withdraw in exchange for concessions from Kuwait. These concessions would have included a restructuring of the Iraqi-Kuwaiti border that runs through the Rumailia oil field and access to the Warba and Bubiyan Islands that separate

Kuwait and Iraq at the head of the Persian Gulf.[17] Clearly, if based on ideological criteria, the analogy between Saddam Hussein and Adolf Hitler does not hold.

If the analogy is simply meant to refer to brutality, then Saddam is by no means alone in this regard. In neighboring Syria, President Hafez al Assad has at least as bad a human rights record as his Iraqi counterpart, as indicated earlier. Whereas Saddam is referred to as a modern-day Hitler, Assad was invited to join the anti-Iraq coalition. Many other brutal dictators that the United States has supported come to mind ranging from "Papa Doc" Duvalier in Haiti to Ferdinand Marcos in the Philippines to Augusto Pinochet in Chile to Manuel Noriega in Panama. In none of these instances was the analogy of Hitler invoked.

If seizure of territory is the principle guiding the characterization of Saddam Hussein in Hitlerian terms, then this likewise does not stand the test of rational analysis. Hafez al Assad's forces control 70 percent of Lebanon and have occupied much of the country since 1976. In early 1991, Israel announced that it was strengthening its own self-proclaimed "security zone" in southern Lebanon. This followed its annexation of East Jerusalem, a portion of Syria in the form of the Golan Heights, and the consistent assertion by Likud government that there will be no Israeli withdrawal from the West Bank and the Gaza Strip. Morocco seized former Spanish Sahara, and Libya has, on several occasions, occupied portions of Chad. South Africa illegally occupied Southwest Africa (Namibia) for many years as well as portions of Angola. Indonesia engaged in a particularly brutal invasion and seizure of East Timor. In collusion with the Nazis, the Soviet Union annexed three Baltic states during the early 1940s. China seized Tibet. In none of these instances did the U.S. government draw an analogy to Hitler and his Nazi regime. The point is that none of these interests so directly affected what the United States defined as its national interest as did the Baathist regime's seizure of Kuwait with its substantial oil production. Furthermore, the seizures of territory just mentioned occurred prior to an era in which United States began to confront relative economic decline in the global economy.

To summarize, Saddam Hussein is no Hitler. He is, however, a brutal dictator with whom the United States maintained increasingly close ties throughout most of the 1980s. The cruelest irony of all is that, once the Persian Gulf War ended, all of the Bush administration's references to Saddam as Hitler ceased as quickly as they had begun. At the same time, the United States has refused to support the Iraqi Democratic Opposition that has sought to topple Saddam and the Baath through armed uprisings in the northern and southern portions of Iraq. This stance runs counter to George Bush's call in a February 15, 1991, speech for the Iraqi people to overthrow Saddam. It seems clear that, despite the rhetoric of democracy, self-determination, and freedom from oppression, the Bush administration prefers the continuation of authoritarian rule in Iraq to democratic elections. This policy can best be characterized as "Saddamism without Saddam." In other words, what the United States prefers in Iraq is another autocrat, albeit one shorn of a powerful army and chemical, biological, or nuclear weapons. Ideally, this would be a military leader who would prevent the "Levantization" of Iraq. However, as one analyst asked: "If the goal is to obtain a smarter but not necessarily less authoritarian regime in Baghdad, did American policy carry through on its philosophical underpinnings: the rule of law, self-determination, democratic reform?"[18]

THE MYTH OF THE WAR FOR THE LIBERATION OF KUWAIT

The obverse of the myth of Iraqi military might and the Saddam-Hitler analogy is the notion that the Persian Gulf War was fought to liberate Kuwait. The United States constantly emphasized terms such as *legitimate rule, democracy,* and *the right to self-determination* during the crisis. However, rule by the al-Sabah family has never been subject to democratic elections. Its rule over the modern state of Kuwait is largely the result of British actions rather than those of the indigenous population. As indicated earlier, the ruling Amir has followed neither the country's 1962 constitution nor the will of the elected (and now dissolved) parliament.[19]

Prior to the Iraqi invasion, the Kuwaiti regime had, to its credit, established a comprehensive welfare state that offered free education and health care to most residents of the state regardless of citizenship. However, the fact that the expatriates, especially the

400,000 Palestinian residents, who contributed so significantly to the development of Kuwait, had not been given the right of citizenship, even after having lived there in some instances for more than forty years, represented a source of deep resentment and helps explain the cooperation some of them gave to the Iraqi occupation forces.

In Kuwait, all menial labor, indeed most labor, has been performed by non-Kuwaitis such as Palestinians, Egyptians, Algerians, Pakistanis, Indians, and most recently, East Asians. Much of this labor is composed of little more than indentured servants, who surrender their passports upon entering the country and become the virtual slaves of their Kuwaiti employers.[20] A country ruled by an autocratic monarchy, that precludes women from political participation, and that severely limits citizenship and the franchise to a small segment of society can hardly be spoken of in terms such as legitimacy and democracy.

Because the country is dependent for its development on foreign labor, one of the problems that will plague postwar Kuwait is the lack of a suitable work force. This is especially true as most foreign labor has left the country and most Palestinians residents will sooner or later be forced to leave. It is highly unlikely that the Kuwaiti aristocracy will undergo the extensive cultural transformation that would be required for it to fill this need. Given the behavior of expatriate labor during the Iraqi occupation, it is highly likely that such labor will be even more tightly controlled in the future. Kuwaiti leaders have already expressed a preference for Egyptians to fulfill this role because they are considered "docile" and desire to return to their native land once they have accumulated savings. The harsh treatment of many expatriate laborers by the Kuwaiti military and security forces following the war is not only intended to send a message to such workers but is also indicative of the type of political regime they will face in the future.

THE MYTH OF DIPLOMATIC EFFORTS TO END THE CRISIS

Of all the myths propagated by the United States and its coalition allies none was as blindly accepted by the Western mass media and public as the argument that the United States was forced to resort to war due to Iraq's refusal to consider a diplomatic solution to the crisis. The truth is that Iraq did offer to consider a withdrawal from Kuwait in exchange for a comprehensive discussion of political problems facing the Middle East including the Palestinian issue and regional arms proliferation. On numerous occasions, Saddam tried to open discussions with the U.S. and British governments.[21]

It is very possible that none of these proposals were serious. Nevertheless, the United States still should have explored Iraq's offer in light of the tremendous destruction and human suffering caused by the subsequent war and its aftermath. Not only did the United States make little or no effort to negotiate with Iraq, but little support was given to efforts by Arab states, the Soviet Union, and France to find a peaceful solution to the crisis. Both George Bush and Saddam Hussein came to personalize the crisis through the constant stream of epithets that they threw at one another. The many publicized efforts by the United States to force Iraqi forces to withdraw through diplomatic means were, in fact, rigid dictates whose real intent was to humiliate Saddam Hussein rather than draw him into negotiations and offer him a way to withdraw from Kuwait and save face. Perhaps the most touted example of the U.S. approach to negotiation can be seen in the January 9 meeting between Secretary of State Baker and Iraqi Foreign Minister, Tariq 'Aziz. Baker refused to let what was an excellent opportunity for undertaking negotiations to become that in fact. Instead, he refused to allow the meeting to become anything more than the articulation of yet another U.S. ultimatum to Iraq.[22]

It seems that George Bush made the decision to go to war with Iraq very early in the crisis. In this sense, all the purported diplomatic efforts on the part of the United States were directed at isolating Saddam and his regime. Why the United States adopted such an inflexible position with regard to Iraq's seizure of Kuwait is still not clear. It might be argued that the invasion of Kuwait presented the United States with the perfect opportunity to construct another enemy, this time in the form of a violence-prone, irrational Third World country, which could replace the "international communist conspiracy" that had preoccupied American policy makers and the American public for so long.

Having dealt with the core of the mythology surrounding the Persian Gulf Crisis, what constitutes a more realistic approach to understanding U.S. foreign policy in the Persian Gulf? What are some of the possible long-term ramifications of this policy, particularly in light of the use of military force against Iraq? How are we to understand the origins of the Persian Gulf crisis. Let us begin with Iraq.

ALTERNATIVE EXPLANATIONS OF THE CRISIS: IRAQI MOTIVATIONS

From the Iraqi leadership's standpoint, no one outside Saddam Hussein's small circle of advisors can say with certainty what were the exact reasons behind the invasion of Kuwait. Nevertheless, a number of causal factors are clear. Iraq began its eight-year war with Iran with a $35 billion surplus. Due to Iran's destruction of much of Iraq's export capacity in the form of tanker loading platforms early in the war, Iraqi sales of crude oil declined drastically; by the war's end in 1988, it had amassed a huge debt, probably in excess of $65 billion. Although some of this debt is owed to Western countries and banks, much of it was owed to Saudi Arabia, Kuwait, and other wealthy Arab oil states in the Persian Gulf.

During the Iran-Iraq War, considerable resentment developed among the Iraqi military at the fact that Saddam, a man with no military training, attempted to dominate military planning. The result was disastrous. By 1986, Iraq was on the verge of losing the war to Iran. It was only when Saddam finally turned over military operations to his officer corps that the Iraqi army performed up to its potential, thereby preventing an Iranian victory. Nevertheless, many of Iraq's top generals were either imprisoned or even executed during the war whenever Saddam feared that one of them was becoming too popular. Indeed, Saddam had the minister of defense, 'Adnan Khayrallah Tulfa, who was both his cousin and brother-in-law, killed by planting a bomb in his helicopter, which was made to look like an accident. These actions prompted several attempted military coups d'etat toward the end of the war and immediately following it.[23] Thus, from Saddam and the Baath's viewpoint, one purpose of the invasion was to keep the military preoccupied and out of domestic politics. Given a history of Iraqi military involvement in politics that extends back to 1936 and the overthrow of the first Baathist government by the military in 1963, an overriding concern of the current regime is to prevent a military coup d'etat.

An equally important consideration influencing the Kuwait invasion was Iraq's depressed economic situation following the 1988 truce with Iran. During the war, the Iraqi people suffered great material deprivation and over 100,000 casualties. The Baathist regime promised that living conditions would improve once the war ended. However, oil prices began to decline once Iraq and Iran resumed exporting oil in the world market following the war's end. Because Iraq depends on oil for 95 percent of its foreign currency earnings, Iraq was unable to repay its loans much less offer its citizens a higher standard of living. Saddam Hussein's decision to initiate a number of expensive development projects after the war only made economic conditions worse.

It was within this context that the policy of Saudi Arabia, Kuwait, the United Arab Amirates, and the other Arab states of the Persian Gulf toward Iraq after the truce with Iran must be situated. During the Iran-Iraq War, these states were terrified at the prospect of an Iranian victory as the Khomeini regime had vowed to overthrow them because of their close ties to the West and replace them all with "Islamic republics." Although Iraq did not defeat Iran militarily, by the war's end it was clearly the more powerful of the two states despite a much smaller population. Consequently, following the truce, the fears of the Arab oil states shifted from Iran to Iraq. Knowing that Iraq could not assert itself if it were economically destitute, two states in particular—Kuwait and the United Arab Amirates—began to exceed their OPEC production quotas. As a result, world oil prices began to fall still further, reaching their lowest levels in almost a decade in June 1990. At this point Iraq began to accuse Kuwait and other Arab oil states in the Persian Gulf of conducting economic warfare against it.[24]

Nevertheless, Iraq's invasion of Kuwait was not a result of moral outrage at the actions of the Arab Gulf oil states. Kuwait's refusal to forgive some or all of Iraq's war debt and lower its output of oil provided a convenient pretext for Saddam Hussein's regime to seize a wealthy neighbor, thereby strengthening Iraq's economy. Because the United States had not sent definitive signals to Iraq prior to the invasion that it would oppose Iraqi actions along the border with Kuwait (the United States probably believing that, at most, Iraq would only seize the disputed Rumailia oil field that straddles the Iraq-Kuwaiti border), Saddam Hussein probably believed that he would meet little or no opposition.

Another justification that Iraq gave for its action was to help the Palestinian people. According to this logic, the invasion of Kuwait represented a step forward in the process of unifying and thus strengthening the Arab nation. A strong Arab nation would be a crucial step in regaining Palestine for the Palestinian people. In exploiting the issue of Palestine, Saddam Hussein and the Baath Party generated considerable support among Palestinians, especially poorer ones, in the West Bank, Gaza, and Jordan. Despite this support, Iraq did not invade Kuwait to help the Palestinians. The underlying reason for stressing the Palestinian issue was to gain wider support in the Arab world and develop a bargaining tool to use against the West. If the West used UN resolutions to pressure Iraq to withdraw from Kuwait, then Iraq could in turn demand implementation of prior resolutions calling for Israeli withdrawal from the occupied territories of the West Bank and the Gaza Strip.

The final and perhaps most compelling reason that Iraq gave for its invasion of Kuwait was that it constituted territory unjustly severed from Iraq following the breakup of the Ottoman Empire at the end of World War I. Kuwait was a subdistrict of the Ottoman province of Basra in southern Iraq. The British, having signed a treaty with the al-Sabah's in 1899, sought to use their close ties with the family to increase their influence in the area. This was especially true following the discovery of oil. Hence they separated Kuwait from Iraq when the latter was established as a state in 1921. One of the aims of the British in establishing Kuwait as a separate state was also to shorten Iraq's coastline, which is only 34 miles long and is blocked by two islands that the British also gave to Kuwait.

In 1962, a large Iraqi expeditionary force massed along the Kuwaiti border demanding that the country be returned to Iraq. The British sent troops to Kuwait, and an expected invasion never occurred. In 1963, a new Iraqi government renounced Iraq's claims to Kuwait. Therefore, it is possible to argue that Iraq no longer has any right to claim Kuwait as its own. During my own research in Iraq, I never met any Iraqis who thought that Kuwait should be incorporated into Iraq. Although many Iraqis may have resented the Kuwaiti government for having tried to undermine the Iraqi economy after the Iran-Iraq War, very few supported the idea of annexing Kuwait by force.

ALTERNATIVE EXPLANATIONS FOR THE CRISIS: UNITED STATES MOTIVATIONS

U.S. policy was motivated by a number of considerations. First, Saddam and the Baath had upset the regional balance of power through the seizure of Kuwait. Put differently, Iraq had become too strong a regional power. Full comprehension of this point requires an understanding of the variety of alliances that the United States maintains with states in the Middle East. Of all these alliances, none is as important as that between the United States and Israel. Alliances with Arab states such as Egypt and Saudi Arabia and with non-Arab states such as Turkey are important but secondary to that with Israel, which stands at the apex of the U.S. alliance structure in the Middle East. This structure of alliances was intended, until recently, to prevent the spread of Soviet influence in the Middle East and protect U.S. access to the region's oil reserves.

Until 1982, Iraq was beyond the Pale having been relegated to the position of an enemy state promoting international terrorism. Between 1982 and 1990, Iraq was in the process of transforming itself from an enemy to becoming part of the U.S. alliance structure in the Middle East. However, Iraq was not content to assume a role such as that occupied by Egypt or Saudi Arabia, two countries that tacitly accepted a secondary role to Israel as long as, in the Egyptian case, the United States gave it economic aid, and, in the Saudi case, the United States gave it military technology and military protection (which paid the necessary dividends under Operation Desert Shield).

Saddam and the Baath Party wanted to make Iraq the most powerful state in the region, thus challenging Israel's military dominance. To this end Iraq developed one of the strongest armies in the world, with sophisticated tanks, artillery, and aircraft. The Baathist regime also embarked on a concerted effort to develop chemical, biological, and nuclear weapons. Once Iraq began to openly threaten Israel during 1990 with chemical weapons, should Israel attempt to repeat its 1981 attack on Iraq's nuclear reactor, the United States began to change its attitude toward Iraq. Relations that had become especially warm after the 1988 truce with Iran now began to cool. If it was to be a choice between Israel and Iraq, the U.S. government would certainly choose the former.

When George Bush stated that Iraq could not be allowed to control 20 percent of the world's oil supplies, this statement should be taken to mean more than just oil narrowly defined. In this sense, some Arab commentators are correct when they argue that the United States does not want to see any powerful states or alliances develop in the Arab world. Thus the war was really concerned with the structure of power in the Arab world and the larger Middle East. An Iraq that was able to become a dominant power in the Arab world would have represented a challenge to U.S. dominance in the region.

WHAT ARE THE POSSIBLE CONSEQUENCES OF THE WAR?

What has been particularly disturbing about the Persian Gulf Crisis has been the lack of attention given to the postwar era. Did the U.S. government really believe that it would be able to restore the Kuwaiti government to power and then bring all the troops home? To pose this question assumes that, once armed hostilities ended, the United States wanted in fact to withdraw all its troops from the area. Many commentators have argued that the United States has sought to establish a military presence in the Persian Gulf for years. However, Saudi Arabia, Kuwait, and other Arab Gulf states have refused to allow the positioning of large numbers of American troops or naval vessels in the region. Prior to the crisis, the United States possessed rights only to a small naval base in the island nation of Bahrain in the northern Gulf off the coast of Saudi Arabia.

Why would the United States want to maintain a military presence in the Gulf? One key reason is the fact that in the Arabian Peninsula and the Persian Gulf lie well over 60 percent of the world's proven oil reserves. Second, a U.S. military presence would undercut any efforts by Iran or Iraq to assert control over these resources. Furthermore, a number of analysts have argued that once the European Common Market becomes a unified currency zone in 1992, the United States' competitive position with the global economy—a position that has been weakening in relation to Germany and Japan—will be weakened still further. Through a military presence in the Gulf, the United States would presumably also enjoy closer economic ties with the wealthy oil producing states of the region thereby strengthening its competitive position vis-à-vis Europe.[25] Some analysts have argued, therefore, that the United States sought, in the Persian Gulf War, to achieve militarily what it could not achieve economically.

It is not surprising that one of the first acts of the Amir of Kuwait following the Iraqi invasion was to suggest that the United States might have access to military facilities in his country once it was retaken from Iraq. One result of the war will undoubtedly be an increased military presence for the United States in the Persian Gulf. Even if the United States were not interested in expanding its military presence in the Persian Gulf, the war with Iraq has made that a necessity. Given the massive destruction of Iraq's infrastructure, its roads, bridges, communications network, and industrial base, the question of how will Iraq feed and rebuild itself now that the war has ended is a pressing one.

The possibility of internal instability in Iraq resulting from its defeat was predicted by many observers conversant with the repressive nature of the current Baathist regime. That possibility subsequently came to pass with a vengeance. The Kurdish population of northern Iraq, which had been promised greater political and cultural autonomy by successive regimes in Baghdad, has been subject instead to continuing repression. The Shi'ite population in the south has been denied its cultural heritage despite the fact that the Baathist regime has invested considerable funds in development projects in southern Iraq.[26] During a visit to the al-Ahwar region, the level of this repression was clearly evident.[27]

Although the United States has argued that it is not in its mandate to support the Kurds, Shi'ites and other groups opposed to Saddam Hussein and the Baath, such considerations did not seem to have bothered it while it was destroying Iraq's infrastructure during over 200,000 air sorties. Estimates are that perhaps as little as 7 percent of the bombs dropped actually hit their targets, meaning that the bombing probably caused much wider civilian and property damage than reported in the Western media.[28] Not only do the Kurds, Shi'ites and other opposition forces now face the tanks and heavy artillery of the remainder of the Iraqi army still loyal to Saddam and the Baath—primarily Republican Guard units—they also are suffering from lack of food and medicine. During the refugee crisis that developed in March 1991, the White House and the Department of State issued hypocritical statements deploring the violence afflicted on the Kurds but asserting that the "current unrest" was an internal matter and that it was "for the Iraqi people to decide their future leadership." Helicopter gunships dropped phosphorous, sulfuric acid, and napalm on Iraqi civilians yet U.S. forces were prevented from intervening. The fact that concern with chemical weapons was not invoked once they were used against Iraqi civilians can only serve to undermine the credibility of U.S. policy in the eyes of the broad masses of Middle Easterners.

U.S. actions both during and following the war with Iraq point to an underlying attitude toward not just Iraqi but Third World peoples in general. They seem largely invisible unless they threaten U.S. interests in a particular region of the world. Following the war, preventing the "Levantization" of Iraq was far more important than Iraqi suffering or assisting those who rose up against the regime in bringing some modicum of political participation and democracy to their country. In refusing to have contact with leaders of the Iraqi Democratic Opposition until April 1991, the Bush administration sent a symbolic message not only to Iraqis but to other peoples of the Middle East that, extensive rhetoric notwithstanding, the United States is not really concerned with bringing democracy to the region.

The development of a widespread civil war in Iraq raises the possibility that Iraq's neighbors, Iran, Turkey, Syria, and Saudi Arabia may become embroiled in Iraq's internal politics.[29] Given the debilitation of Iraq's armed forces as a result of the war, civil unrest, and massive desertions, one or more of Iraq's neighbors may try to use the continuing civil unrest to seize parts of Iraq under the pretext of maintaining regional order. Turkey still maintains claims to the oil-rich area surrounding the city of Mosul in northern Iraq. During the civil war that followed the ousting of Iraq from Kuwait, Turkey argued against arms being sent to the Kurdish Pesh Merga rebels fighting the Baathist regime. It thereby made clear its own unease at the prospect of Kurdish rebels gaining greater autonomy within Iraq because an autonomous or semiautonomous Iraqi Kurdistan might encourage its own Kurdish population to demand greater freedom as well.[30] Iran would like to increase its influence among the Iraqi Shi'ites as well as its control over the area around the Shatt al-ʿArab waterway formed by the confluence of the Tigris and Euphrates Rivers in southern Iraq. Syria, one of Iraq's arch rivals, would like to see a regime installed in Baghdad that was sympathetic to its own variant of Baathism. A lengthy civil war could lead to the fragmentation of the country. Any of these eventualities would greatly increase instability in the Gulf region, which was precisely what the initial U.S. intervention was intended to prevent.

In other words, the instability of Iraq and Kuwait caused by the war makes it naive to think that United States forces will be able to withdraw from the region in the near future. Indeed, the opposite assumption is much more valid. That is, it is far more likely that the United States may be required to retain a significant troop presence in the Gulf, either on its own or under the rubric of a UN peace-keeping force, for an indefinite period of time. Taking as examples World War II and especially the Korean war (which has perhaps the greatest similarity to the Gulf War), large numbers of American troops were required to remain in both theaters of operation.[31]

Another outcome of the war is the exacerbation of the Israeli-Palestinian dispute. If Israelis and Palestinians distrusted each other prior to Iraq's invasion of Kuwait, that distrust was greatly magnified by strong Palestinian support for Iraq. This support was foolish because Saddam Hussein and the Baath would no more like to see a democratic Palestinian state independent of external influence than would the right wing Israeli Likud government of Yitzhak Shamir. Support for Iraq was more an indicator of the hopelessness felt by many Palestinians at the prospects of ever achieving self-determination through a state of their own than genuine affection felt for Saddam Hussein. Despite his hypocritical stance, Saddam was the first Arab leader since Gamal Abdul Nasser to place the Palestinian issue at the forefront of the Arab political agenda. Through SCUD missile attacks on Tel Aviv, Haifa, and other areas of Israel, he was also the first Arab leader to ever bring the Arab-Israeli conflict so directly to the Israeli populace, even though the missiles were a terror weapon with little military significance.

With the war's end, the Palestinians are even more bitter and frustrated and the Likud government finds little incentive to make any meaningful concessions to them. Indeed, greater restrictions have been placed on Palestinians from the Occupied Territories working in Israel and the crackdown on Palestinian violence, such as deportations, has intensified. Middle East peace negotiations seem to have had little impact on improving Israeli-Palestinian relations.

Another consequence of the crisis has been to deepen the cleavage in the Arab world between the oil-rich and oil-poor countries, the so-called haves and have-nots. It has also widened the political distance between wealthy political elites and the mass populace within many Arab countries, such as Egypt. During the war, there were massive demonstrations in some of the poorer and mostly non-oil-producing Arab states such as Jordan, Yemen, Morocco, Algeria, and the Sudan. Demonstrations also occurred in Egypt, which was the most prominent Arab state outside the Gulf in the anti-Iraq coalition. Even though public opinion had initially been largely anti-Iraq, the massive American bombing turned Egyptian attitudes against the war. The government was forced to ban pro-Iraqi demonstrations and the mid-year vacation for high school and university students was lengthened to prevent student demonstrations. In Syria, prominent intellectuals called on the government to pull its troops out of the coalition forces. Given the authoritarian nature of Syrian politics, this overt criticism of the state was unprecedented.

In Jordan, King Hussein, who in the past has been one of the most pro-American rulers in the Middle East, even to the point of having been on the CIA payroll, threw his support to Iraq against the United States—led coalition. During the war, he strongly attacked the bombing campaign against Iraq. This attack, which was in large measure a response to the large Palestinian population that constitutes over 60 percent of Jordan's population, indicates the extent to which the crisis has radicalized segments of Arab public opinion. Even in Saudi Arabia, the most vociferously anti-Iraq Arab state, conservative religious figures sharply criticized the presence of U.S. forces in the country. Attacks on American service personnel, although limited in number, also indicated underlying hostility to the policies followed by the royal family during the crisis.

Although it is too early to predict the possible long-term effects of the crisis on Arab politics, it is noteworthy that prior crises that were perceived as major humiliations in the Arab world—such as the Anglo-Egyptian Treaty of 1936, the defeat of the Rashid 'Ali coup in Iraq in 1941, the Arab-Israeli Wars of 1948 and 1967, and the Israeli invasion of Lebanon in 1982—all had significant ramifications. These events were critical in the spread of Arab nationalism during the 1940s and 1950s, the rise to power of such leaders as Gamal Abdul Nasser and Saddam Hussein and, more recently, the spread of Islamic radicalism. Thus the real impact of the Persian Gulf crisis will probably not be fully felt for years to come.

CONCLUSION

From the U.S. perspective, the worst case scenario is that the Persian Gulf war, as have many wars in the past, will undermine the very objectives for which it was fought. Although Iraq is militarily defeated, an even worse prospect is the overthrow of regimes in the Middle East that support the United States. This is especially true of Jordan. The cut-off of United States military aid to Jordan in March 1991 only underlined its status as a loser in the Gulf crisis. Coupled with the cessation of aid by Saudi Arabia and the other states of the Gulf Cooperation Council and discrimination against Jordanian workers in the Gulf, which will cut the flow of remittances, the country's economy has been strained to the breaking point. Political discontent emanating from Iraq's defeat and a worsening economy could lead to massive street demonstrations and the abdication of the king. The establishment of a Jordanian regime dominated by leaders sympathetic to the Palestine Liberation Organization or radical Islamic groups could provoke Israeli intervention. Such intervention would force Syria to adopt an even more radical posture toward Israel and disrupt what ties have already been forged with the United States and the ongoing peace negotiations. Such a scenario would surely pressure Egypt to adopt a more critical posture toward Israel as well. In other words, one of the eventual outcomes of the Persian Gulf Crisis may be a greater polarization of the Arab-Israeli conflict.

Although the breakup of Iraq is a possibility, as the civil war that erupted after the war's end indicates, it is far more likely that continual strife may lead to a breakdown of central authority. Because the Baathist regime has shown no inclination to accommodate any of the demands of disaffected elements in Iraq, there is every likelihood that the Kurds, Shi'ites and other opposition groups will continue their struggle. Whereas the Baathist regime was successful in curtailing the first uprising of disaffected elements during February and March 1991, the onerous terms of the cease-fire imposed on Iraq, especially the garnisheeing of its oil revenues for war reparations, will no doubt weaken the central regime. If fissures develop within the Baath Party or army, a further wave of uprisings could be successful. The breakdown of central authority in Iraq will only encourage neighboring countries such as Iran to become involved in Iraq's internal affairs.

Even in Saudi Arabia, whom the United States troops were originally ostensibly sent to protect under Operation Desert Shield, religious leaders criticized, in Friday sermons, the presence of Western troops in the country, site of the holiest shrines of Islam. In Turkey, leftist organizations have claimed responsibility for bombing several American-Turkish associations and the assassination of Americans in the country. Thus another impact of the war has been the strengthening of Islamic radicals (sometimes referred to as Islamic fundamentalists) and leftist forces throughout the Middle East, both of whom are hostile to American interests in the region.

Of course, it is possible that an Iraqi government that succeeds Saddam Hussein might be more sympathetic to American interests in the Persian Gulf and the Middle East generally. If these conditions were to be met, it is possible that the impact on pro-Western states in the region, particularly Arab states, would be minimal. It is also possible that the defeat of Iraq may lead the United States and other European powers to pressure Israel to implement a peace plan that would facilitate a solution to the Israeli-Palestinian dispute. As for the Israeli-Palestinian dispute, the Likud government of Yitzhak Shamir has already made it clear that it will not look favorably on attempts by the United States and Europe to pressure

Israel to come to a settlement with the Palestinians. Will the United States use financial aid or other mechanisms to force Israel to come to the bargaining table with Palestinian representatives (either from the West Bank and Gaza or the Palestine Liberation Organization) and make territorial concessions in exchange for peace? If past history is any indicator, the answer is no; and therefore the crisis will be no closer to a settlement than it was before the conflict.

All indicators are that long-term outcomes favorable to U.S. interests are unlikely. Although there is a good likelihood that Saddam Hussein will be overthrown, he will probably be replaced by military leaders no less hostile to the United States. Oddly enough, the United States has to date shown little interest in the Iraqi Democratic Opposition, which is headquartered in London. Because this movement includes a wide ideological spectrum, including communists and Islamic forces as well as business interests and Western-style liberals, the U.S. government apparently feels that such a coalition could not effectively rule Iraq. Instead, the preference seems to be for another dictator, although one with fewer regional pretensions than Saddam Hussein, a "mini-Saddam" if you will. Having seen the problems of supporting dictators such as Trujillo in the Dominican Republic, Batista in Cuba, Somoza in Nicaragua, Marcos in the Philippines, Diem in Vietnam, Saddam Hussein in Iraq, the question arises as to when the United States will learn that, although democracy may be a less predictable form of government, it is much more stable than dictatorships in the long term.

Lastly, there is the impact of the war on the West itself. In the United States, it is clear that the war created an artificial euphoria that was amplified by the emphasis on the technologies of war. As a conservative publication such as *U.S. News and World Report* could note, what Americans saw during the war, especially during the final day of the war when the remains of the Iraqi army was fleeing north from Kuwait City, was destroyed buildings and machinery.[32] The human face of war was almost entirely absent from Western images of it. The term *nintendo war* became an entirely appropriate metaphor to apply to the ultimate outcome of the crisis. It became a game in which buttons were pressed and imaginary targets disintegrated in the face of precision bombing. It is not difficult to imagine that in the eyes of many young adults and children, there was little difference between fighting the war in the Persian Gulf and playing "war games" at the local penny arcade. In terms of political socialization, particularly the desensitization of American and Western youth to the horrors of war, the impact of the war will not be seen for years if not decades. In this instance, the parallel with the Arab world is striking, as the war's full impact will also not be felt there until the next generation of political leaders begins to make its influence felt. The United States won the battle in forcing Iraq to withdraw from Kuwait, but whether it will win the war for the hearts and minds of the peoples of the Middle East is still an open question.

NOTES

1.   James Baker, "Why America Is in the Gulf," *Dispatch* 1, no. 10 (November 5, 1990). This is a publication of the Bureau of Public Affairs, United States Department of State.

2.   Amatzia Baram, "Iraq: Between East and West," in Efraim Karsh, ed., *The Iran-Iraq War* (London: Macmillan, 1989), pp. 80–81.

3.   Shahram Chubin and Charles Tripp, *Iran and Iraq at War* (London: I. B. Tauris and Co., 1988), p. 194.

4.   Thomas L. McNaugher, "Walking Tightropes in the Gulf," in Karsh, *The Iran-Iraq War,* p. 175.

5.   Baram, "Iraq," p. 91.

6.   Adel Darwish and Gregory Alexander, *Unholy Babylon* (New York: St. Martin's Press, 1991, p. 252.

7.   Darwish and Alexander, ibid., pp. 267–270. Ambassador Glaspie's testimony before the U.S. Senate and House of Representatives in February 1991, over seven months after the crisis began, represented an attempt to dispel the notion that she and the Bush administration had sent ambiguous messages to Saddam and the Iraqi Baath. However, her protestations to questions suggesting she was not firm enough with Saddam notwithstanding, Glaspie still defended the Reagan and Bush policy of accommodation with Saddam and the Baathist leadership as the right course. In the context of this entire debate, it is important to note that State Department spokesperson, Margaret Tutwiler, responded to a reporter's question during a July 21, 1990, briefing that, "We do not have any defense treaties with Kuwait and there are no defense or special security commitments to Kuwait." Ibid., p. 266. This latter comment is

perhaps the better indicator than Ambassador Glaspie's testimony as to the messages that the Bush administration sent to Iraq prior to the crisis.

8.   *The New York Times* (March 10, 1991); and *The Nation* (January 21, 1991), p. 44.

9.   See, for example, Patrick E. Tyler, "As the Dust Settles, Attention Turns to New Arms Sales," *The New York Times* (March 24, 1991).

10.   Youssef M. Ibrahim, "Slow Recovery Is Seen for Kuwait and Iraq Oil," *The New York Times* (March 21, 1991).

11.   David Fromkin, *A Peace to End All Peace: The Fall of the Ottoman Empire and the Creation of the Modern Middle East* (New York: Avon Books, 1989), p. 506.

12.   Eliyahu Kanovsky, "Economic Implications for the Region and World Oil Market," in Efraim Karsh, ed., *The Iran-Iraq War,* p. 232.

13.   It should also be noted that oil wealth also spawned a new bourgeoisie that 'Issam al-Khafaji has referred to as "parasitic." See *Tatawwur al-ra'smaliya al-wataniya fi-l-'iraq, 1968–1978 [The Development of National Capitalism in Iraq, 1968–1978]* (Cairo: Dar al-Mustaqbal al-'Arabi, 1983), especially pp. 45–63, 165–184; it has also been alleged that Saddam Hussein's family has skimmed as much as 5 percent of Iraq's oil wealth since the early 1970s.

14.   See, for example, *Al-sira' al-'iraqi al-farisi [The Iraqi-Persian Conflict]* (Baghdad: Dar al-Huriya li-l-Tiba'a, 1983).

15.   Eric Davis, "State Building in Iraq During the Iran-Iraq War and the Gulf Crisis," in Manus I. Midlarsky, ed., *The Internationalization of Communal Strife* (New York: Routledge, 1992), pp. 69–92.

16.   Darwish and Alexander, *Unholy Babylon,* p. 280; the authors also argue that the much-cited threat to Saudi Arabia was a fiction: "once Kuwait had been secured, Iraqi deployments were entirely defensive and the much-cited move towards the Saudi border was merely the extending of front lines and fortifying defensive positions. . . . In fact, American officials have since admitted in interviews that there was no evidence to suggest that Saddam Hussein was going to invade Saudi Arabia" (p. 286).

17.   Ibid., pp. 282–83, 290–91.

18.   Andrew Rosenthal, "What the U.S. Wants to Happen in Iraq Remains Unclear," *The New York Times* (March 24, 1991).

19.   Interview with Ahmad al-Khatib, *Middle East Report,* no. 168 (January–February 1991): 8–9. Prior to the Iraqi invasion, al-Khatib was a member of the former Kuwaiti parliament and one of the country's most prominent opposition leaders.

20.   On this problem, see the excellent article by Denis MacShane, "Gulf Migrant Labor: Working in Virtual Slavery," *The Nation* (March 18, 1991), pp. 325, 342–44.

21. Darwish and Alexander, *Unholy Babylon*, pp. 291–92, 301.

22. Ibid., p. 307.

23. Efraim Karsh, "In Baghdad, Politics Is a Lethal Game," *The New York Times Magazine* (September 30, 1990), p. 100.

24. Darwish and Alexander, *Unholy Babylon*, p. 263.

25. Thomas Ferguson, "Bush's Big Gamble: The Economic Incentives for War," *The Nation* (January 28, 1991), pp. 73, 76–77, 92.

26. On the efforts of the Baath to impose a uniform historical memory and cultural interpretation on Iraqi society, see E. Davis and N. Gavrielides, "Statecraft, Historical Memory and Popular Culture in Iraq and Kuwait," in E. Davis and N. Gavrielides, eds., *Statecraft in the Middle East: Oil, Historical Memory and Popular Culture* (Miami: Florida International University Press, 1991), pp. 116–148.

27. During a trip to the village of Chibayish and the surrounding region in May 1980, I had the opportunity to discuss the political situation with several villagers while on a boat ride through the marsh region apart from the "companion" (*rafiq*) assigned by the Ministry of Culture and Information. I was told that communists and their sympathizers and Shi'ite radicals were summarily executed by local party officials and that the families of those killed were forbidden to mourn or even mention the departed family member.

28. See, for example, Tom Wicker's column, "An Unknown Casualty," *The New York Times* (March 20, 1991).

29. Indeed, Saudi Arabia has already become actively involved in preventing dissident Iraqi groups from mounting a successful campaign against the Baath because such an eventuality "would be a threat to their own undemocratic regimes." *Middle East International* (March 8, 1991), p. 4.

30. Turkey's Kurds are treated as badly as those in Iraq. They are forbidden to use their native tongue, and the Ankara government refuses to even recognize their ethnic distinctiveness, referring to them as "mountain Turks."

31. Jae Won Kim, "The Gulf War Could Be Another Korea," *The New York Times* (January 29, 1991).

32. John Leo, "Lessons from a Sanitized War," *U.S. News and World Report* (March 18, 1991), p. 26.

PART 6

U.S. Middle East Policy, Media, and Education on the Middle East

CHAPTER 10

Media, Public Discourse, and U.S. Policy Toward the Middle East

William A. Dorman

For a society with such high self-regard for its openness, the United States since World War II has held remarkably few public debates on foreign policy issues. When these debates do occur, such as with the Vietnam war, they usually come far too late in the day, that is to say long after official Washington has committed the nation to a frequently disastrous course of action. And of all the policy concerns facing the United States today none has been less frequently or vigorously debated than those regarding the troubled Middle East.

Why public discourse on vital foreign policy issues and in particular those concerning the Middle East should be so circumscribed has much to do with the nature of contemporary American mass media, which after all is the modern forum for public debate. Like so many other segments of society, ranging from the academy and science to commerce and industry, however, the media—both entertainment and information—have been transformed by the Cold War and its implicit requirement that civil society subordinate its usual interests in the name of national security. Such a subordination on the part of the media is of particular concern if for no other reason than they provide most Americans with their generalized day-to-day sense of the world and how the United States is faring in it.

To the degree that public opinion matters in the foreign policy process, and I will argue that it matters a great deal, this sense of the world—of who is enemy and who is friend, of who deserves our support and who does not, of when diplomacy has failed and when military action is called for—has everything to do with how far policy makers feel they can go.

Researchers in the mainstream of social science, to be sure, are uneasy with such generalizations that assume great media effects on opinion or behavior. A minimalist approach, expressed in the sentiment that some media can have some effects some of the time under some conditions on some people, began to dominate media studies in the 1940s, held sway until the 1970s, and still holds a slight edge in mainstream scholarship. This school of thought was a reaction to the highly unscientific, usually oversimplistic kind of research that had gone before and that suggested a simple stimulus-response model of media effect.

Despite the valuable caution and greater rigor that the new approach brought to studies of media and society, investigators tended to focus their efforts, as had their predecessors, on that range of media effect most easily measured: effects that cause immediate change in individual attitude or behavior. As well, the premier studies usually concentrated on short-term effect on (1) electoral behavior or (2) violent behavior. Finding no dramatic, immediate impact of media within these realms on most people, the new consensus among researchers was that media have a far more modest impact than was popularly assumed.

The problem with this general conclusion, at least as it applies to the realm of foreign affairs, is that the phenomena under investigation were usually the most resistant to short-term cognitive shift. In the first case, the realm of voter behavior usually involves well-defended and complex opinions. In the second case, researchers frequently fail to distinguish between acquiring behavior that is within socially acceptable boundaries as opposed to acquiring deviant behavior that can earn punishment, censure, or disapprobation. Thus, whereas enlistment in the U.S. Navy seemed to increase briefly as a result of the movie "Top Gun," the number of murders by chainsaw following "Texas Chainsaw Massacre" did not.

The point here is that to the extent the news media may have an effect on opinion about foreign affairs—assuming the absence of prior strong feelings or long-running news events such as Vietnam or the Arab-Israeli conflict—such effect is likely to involve attitude creation rather than change and does not concern behavior that is subject to social sanction.

The caution in mainstream social science about assuming great effects of the press on public opinion is even more pronounced where the assumed effects on foreign policy are concerned. Until very recently, the prevailing belief in political science, foreign policy studies, and international affairs seemed to be that the press did not count for much in the policy-making process. After all, the argument ran, the policy process is dominated by elites with special interests and special knowledge. A public preoccupied with domestic concerns is disinterested, and debate among attentive publics is carried on at a higher level.

As a result, little serious academic attention has been paid to the link between the press and policy until the past ten years or so. For instance, only one full-length scholarly study of the press and the broad policy process has been published by a university press, and that was in 1963.[1]

There can be little doubt that the link between the press and policy is enormously complex and subtle. Hardly is there a simple cause-effect relationship. But if the press does not make foreign or defense policy, in some important ways it helps establish the boundaries within which policy can be made. In this respect, journalism is usually affecting in the policy process, rather than determining.

Why the press may count for more than social scientists usually give it credit for has everything to do with the changed nature of the world after World War II. As historian Robert Dallek has noted: "Burdened with the defense of the 'free world,' touched in countless ways by the rise of a 'military-industrial complex,' charged with securing U.S. interests abroad, Americans could no longer turn their backs on world affairs."[2]

Moreover, the rise of television, the country's only truly national medium, and its capacity to dramatize worldwide events visually, created an unprecedented immediacy for the postwar citizenry to foreign affairs and entered enthusiastically into the task of convincing Americans that they faced great peril from an intractable enemy.[3]

Above all else, the introduction of nuclear weapons and the

idea of species threat into the calculus of world affairs created a sense of perpetual crisis that demanded closer attention to the world. In a sense, what existed for many Americans was a garrison state of the mind, and citizens living in a garrison state cannot help but be concerned about external events.

The fact is that in a democracy an aroused or frightened public, which in the final analysis must bear the material and human costs of foreign policy, cannot be ignored.

Assuming a system of checks and balances is healthy in foreign policy, there are two fundamentally important effects that journalists can have in today's foreign policy arena. The first effect derives from the capacity of the press to provide an alternative source of information for, and a reality check on, those elites that become directly or indirectly involved in the policy process. As the foreign policy initiative has tended to concentrate more and more in the executive branch since World War II, so has the power to regulate, shape, even dictate intelligence information. Through executive powers of security classification and by gaining control over or politicizing the usual intelligence apparatus, the presidency often is able to control the information with which the foreign policy community has to work.

To the extent that journalists provide elites with analysis and reportage that confirms or challenges an administration's version of reality, they make a significant contribution. The news media, therefore, if they are authentically autonomous, can serve as an important corrective for all levels of the foreign policy community, as well as the general public.

A second vitally important, if less obvious, way in which the news media may figure in the foreign policy arena involves the portrayal of dissent from policy. Whether an ember of public dissent from official policy ever becomes a threatening flame has much to do with how the dissent is presented in the media. Is a criticism given legitimacy by the press, or is it ignored, denigrated, or framed in such a way that there is no opportunity to persuade decent opinion? Are dissenters, either here or abroad, portrayed as worthy of a fair hearing, perhaps even admiration? Or are they depicted as political outlaws whose complaints are as dangerous as they are unfounded? All of these questions loom large in a consideration of past and present media performance where the Middle

East is concerned, yet the record of the American media in this region is hardly reassuring.

Put simply, Middle Eastern peoples (other than Israelis) are portrayed as Indo-Europe's slow learners, people who can survive only in the custodial care of a Westernized power or a Westernized dictator; they are portrayed in a racist context, that is, in such a way that they do not appear to have the capacity for self-rule, for consensus politics, for peaceful coexistence. They do not have politics, only fates. They are portrayed as having inherently violent and unstable cultures, and this despite centuries of European warfare.

Perhaps the most serious outcome of the American media's reductionist treatment of non-Israeli peoples in the Middle East is that it frequently cuts them off from the support of the nominally liberal, nominally suspicious element in American society that was forged from the Vietnam war experience.

But there are other consequences as well. For instance, the media's dehumanization can serve to pave the way for interventionist policies. Such treatment can also excuse support of such unpopular client regimes as that of Shah Pahlavi's, justify arms sales to the region, and last but hardly least, provide legitimacy for economic exploitation. Certainly, the performance of the media has served to protect the "special relationship" between the United States and Israel.

Anyone with even the slightest familiarity with the topic of mass media and the Middle East will know immediately that the judgments just offered are in stark disagreement with advocates for Israel, who argue to the contrary that it is the Arabs—particularly the Palestinians—who receive favored treatment by the media.

Typical of this point of view was a piece by syndicated columnist Don Feder, who used the 1990 Iraq-Kuwait Crisis as an opportunity to ask:

> Will Iraq's Saddam Hussein cause the media to re-evaluate its entrenched anti-Zionism? Probably not.
>
> Recall how the Fourth Estate howled when Israel blew up Iraq's nuclear reactor. Now imagine what the Butcher of Baghdad would be like with nuclear weapons?
>
> Though its actions often further U.S. interests, the Jewish state is far and always the media's favorite international target. The *Boston Globe* ritualistically datelines stories from the

"Israeli-occupied West Bank." Readers will search in vain for reports from "Soviet-occupied Vilnius" or more to the point, "U.S.-occupied Arizona."[4]

Ignore the fact that under the Geneva Convention the West Bank has been declared a territory under military occupation, whereas Lithuania and the state of Arizona have not. What is important here is Feder's further claim:

> The poison seeds of bias, so carefully cultivated over the past decade [by the media] are at last bearing bitter fruit. Along with their [the media's] allies—Yasser Arafat, Saddam Hussein, and assorted ayatollahs—the media can be justly proud of its contribution to the Middle East Piece [sic] Process: the piecemeal dismemberment of Israel.

A far more sophisticated view is offered by scholar Daniel Pipes, who has argued that the American press overemphasizes Israel to the detriment of our understanding of the region:

> The truth is that Israel does not account for the volatility of Arab politics, the anti-Western policies of OPEC, the Iran-Iraq war, the civil war in Lebanon, or the pro-Soviet alignment of the Syrian government. Were not the media so preoccupied with Israel, Americans would have a more correct and balanced view of its role in the Middle East.[5]

According to Pipes, media preoccupation with Israel leads to exaggeration of the importance of the Palestine Liberation Organization (PLO) and results in attention being paid the Palestinian refugees out "of proportion to their numbers or distress."

It is a truism of media studies that conflicting claims to bias are inescapable. Because of the phenomenon of selective perception, human beings have no difficulty whatsoever detecting bias in the media on practically any side of any issue. The press for many people is objective when it portrays reality according to their view of the world; it is biased when it does not. Does this mean that useful judgments about media performance are impossible. Hardly.

As with a case at law, among other things, one can examine the credentials or expertise of the person doing the study, including past work; the representativeness and proponderance of the evidence; the internal consistency of the evidence; whether the investigator accounts for contrary evidence; the logical consistency of the argument; and whether the conclusions agree with the world as most reasonable people know it.

By these tests, the argument that the American media are pro-Arab and anti-Israeli simply does not hold up. To begin with, it is virtually impossible to find criticism of the American media's handling of Israel before 1982 and the invasion of Lebanon. For a variety of complex reasons, not the least of which was a strategic disagreement between the United States and Tel Aviv over Israeli goals in Lebanon, the American press for the first time in an Israeli-Arab War began to accord Arabs a human face.[6] Ardent supporters of Israel's foreign policy became alarmed, and began for the first time to express apprehension about media performance. This concern would revive when the *intifada* began to attract the attention of journalists, for reasons that will be examined later in this analysis. The important point here is that until the invasion, supporters were generally satisfied with the treatment Israel received.

Equally significant, if the press was staunchly anti-Israel as a number of observers have claimed since 1982, how does one explain the continued high rate of military and economic assistance to Tel Aviv—the highest amount given to any country by Washington—an amount that has increased over the years, not decreased? There is not one single post-World War II instance in which the U.S. government was able to indefinitely continue assistance, particularly at such a high level, to a country toward which the press was relentlessly hostile. Feder and Pipes are silent on these matters.

Finally, a position that the American media are somehow pro-Arab completely ignores the realm of popular entertainment, where the evidence is overwhelming that Middle Easterners other than Israelis are portrayed in a incessantly negative manner. Whether in popular fiction, television, or films, Arab-Muslim life is reduced to "a special malevolent and unthinking essence."[7]

Although critical attention has been paid for some time to Orientalist scholarship, it has only been relatively recently that scholars have turned to the function of popular culture. One such investigator is Laurence Michalak of the University of California at Berkeley, who has argued, "Our misconceptions about Arabs probably come at least as much from informal as from formal education. Our negative stereotype of Arabs begins with and is nurtured by what has been called 'popular' or 'folk' culture—songs, jokes, television programs, cartoons, comic strips, movies and the like."[8]

Michalak and others[9] make an irrefutable case that the Arab is now the villain of choice in American media. The results are predictable. David Lamb, *Los Angeles Times* Middle East correspondent and author of *The Arabs,* writes of the time at a suburban Washington costume party, when eight of the children showed up dressed as Arabs. Their accessories included toy guns, knives, big noses, oil cans, and moneybags. "In the past forty years, few ethnic groups have been more vilified and inaccurately stereotyped in the imagination and news media of the West than Arabs," Lamb has written.[10]

The result is that many Americans hold in their minds a malignant—if muddled—equation to the effect that all Middle Easterners are Arabs, all Arabs are Muslims, and all Muslims are terrorists.

Certainly, anti-Semitism directed toward Jews was and still is an element of American society. But even at their most vicious, in the period before World War II, stereotypes of Jews in the American popular media never matched the violence and systematic negativity that characterizes Arab stereotyping in the contemporary context.

Moreover, sufficient social conventions and sanctions exist today that an American television network, say, would never consider airing a series that portrayed Jews as relentlessly avaricious or engaged in a plot to take over the world. To the contrary, Hollywood and New York have compiled an impressive list of sensitive films and television programs dealing with the Jewish experience, particularly during the Holocaust, and have time and again used Israeli military and intelligence exploits as grist for the romantic adventure mill.

Just one popular novel, *Exodus,* and the film on which it was based, have had a tremendous impact on American understanding of Israel. "When the moment came in the film for 'Ha-Tikvah,' the national anthem of Israel, to be played, people danced in the aisles of movie theaters. . . . The Israel of most Americans, including Jews, is still the *Exodus* version."[11]

Similarly, such movies as *Cry Freedom* presumably have had at least some salutary effect on American popular opinion about the plight of the minority black population in South Africa. Yet while there is enough drama, tragedy, heroism, and repression in the Palestinian experience in general and the *intifada* in particular to provide films, television docudramas and popular novels sufficient to a decade, Palestinians still await their *Exodus*.

Indeed, television series, films, and popular novels in the 1970s and 1980s used an astonishing range of stereotypes for Arabs, routinely associating them with "theft, abduction, rape, knives, fighting, murder," unrepressed sexuality, and anti-Western attitudes.[12] Palestinians or what appear to be Palestinians, of course, are popular media's favorite terrorists.

As Michalak has observed, "Middle East specialists sometimes deplore American ignorance about the Arab World. . . . Strictly speaking, however, this is not true. Americans know a great deal about Arabs. The problem is that so much of what is known is wrong."[13]

Were it only the popular arts in which this kind of kitsch-cum-orientalism existed, the problem might be less severe. But what of the more serious print media, the information media, on which the educated classes presumably base their informed opinion. The picture is hardly brighter.

Systematic study after study shows a pattern of stereotypes, frames, historical inaccuracies, and so on that have placed Arabs at a considerable disadvantage in American public opinion.[14] And although mass public opinion may or may not matter much in the policy equation, elite opinion certainly does; and there is a considerable body of evidence to indicate that decision makers and members of the attentive policy publics get much of their information from the press.[15]

It is through the process of *framing* that the news media achieve their effect. *Framing* is simply a term used to describe how media, by using certain phrases or images, can construct a particular kind of social reality for a reader or viewer. By putting things in a certain context, journalists *create ideas* for their audience; they help us to arrange our minds.[16]

For instance, consider how the PLO has been portrayed or framed over the years up until and including the present. There was, for example, the lead to an AP account of Yasser Arafat's May 1990 speech to the UN Security Council, which began not with a summary of what he had to say—but with a rebuttal by Israel's prime minister, Yitzhak Shamir, who charged Arafat's speech was "full of lies and distortions." The usual journalistic sequence in speech stories is the reverse: details of the speech come first, then rebuttals.

Or what of another AP dispatch from Jerusalem that reported on the release of three Jewish settlers who were freed after serving less than seven years for killing three Arabs and maiming two Palestinian mayors in car bombings. Part of a group that carried out attacks in the West Bank in the early 1980s, the three were referred to throughout the AP article as either *radicals* or *members of the Jewish underground*. The only use of the word *terror* occurred when the correspondent wrote that the leader of the group had justified its actions "because of the government's failure to combat Arab terror."[17] This is the process of framing, then: it results from what you put in, what you leave out, the words and images you choose, and what you emphasize.

Framing, in short, was the practice during the Iranian Revolution of routinely referring to religious figures as "black robed." Would it occur to American reporters covering the Vatican to so describe Catholic priests? Framing also consists of the throw away lines that appear as authoritative background in news reports, such as this example taken from *Newsweek* nine years after the invasion and the history should have been clear: "PLO shelling of northern Israel from southern Lebanon [led] to a fullscale Israeli invasion."[18] This assertion is despite all evidence to the contrary, including UN truce violation reports, that the PLO had observed the cease-fire for almost a year prior to the invasion.

And what of the commonplace journalistic explanation of religious fanaticism to explain unrest in the region. Might it not be the case of too many contemporary observers paying too "little attention to the impact of uneven economic development and class conflict on the internal dynamic of dominant and repressed groups" and a preference for "the know-nothing explanation of primitivism"?[19]

Whereas the influence of the ideology of the national security state has been the constant in coverage of the Third World throughout the Cold War, an important dependent variable is ethnocentrism. In this regard, cultural myopia on the part of the press frequently has served political ends, the most important of which is to convince an American audience that Third World peoples are incapable of self-governance and the best they can hope for is life under a Westernized ruler. Whether intentional or not, through ethnocentric reporting and the ethnocentric reactions such reporting triggers in readers and viewers, American journalism has often paved the way for a particular policy choice, even intervention.

All societies, of course, are prone to varying degrees of ethnocentrism and a sense of cultural superiority. The important question in journalism as in international relations is whether such tendencies are restrained by the political culture and rendered effectively harmless, or whether they are encouraged and pressed into service by the state to subtly justify ill-conceived policy. The record of U.S. journalism in this respect is not encouraging.

A close analysis of coverage of Iran's 1978 Revolution, for instance, provided ample evidence that American journalists found it extremely difficult to rise above Western prejudices, particularly in dealing with the religious symbolism employed in the revolt.[20] Whether it was repeated references to "religious fanatics" or descriptions of grief-stricken women as "wailing" for their lost sons, the overwhelming tendency was to use words and frames that would never be employed in a European setting. The focus was on seemingly exotic ritual rather than on the validity of political claims. For the most part, opponents of the Shah were pictured variously as religious zealots and opponents of modernization or "Islamic-Marxists" or some combination, thereby cutting off those resisting the Shah from the sympathies or serious consideration of the educated-liberal forces in the United States. After all, how could Western liberals be expected to support a people who were supposedly antiprogress, anti-land reform, and antiwomen—all of which the press insisted they were.

As a result, Carter was able to continue material support of the Pahlavi regime at the same time public opinion forced him to cut off such support from Somoza in Nicaragua, where for a variety of reasons reporters did a far better job of presenting revolutionary grievances. Moreover, a case can be made that had public opinion been alerted to the true nature of the Shah's regime over the years, no political figure would ever have argued that he be admitted to the United States for medical treatment, thus perhaps heading off the hostage crisis.

One outcome of the media's dehumanization of foreign peoples or denigration of their political aspirations is to persuade Americans to look the other way at the overthrow of leaders at odds with Washington. An ABC News–Harris poll taken in early 1979 after a year's intensive journalistic hammering of the revolutionary movement showed that Americans by an impressive 52–24 percent favored a military government in Iran no matter what Iranians preferred.[21] Unlike in 1953, such an attempt was never made, but the poll results came at the moment when the Carter administration was actively considering assisting a military coup to overthrow the revolutionary Iranian government.

The press performed a similar service preceding the coups in Guatemala in 1954 and Chile in 1973, and in advance of or during interventions ranging from the Bay of Pigs[22] to the Dominican Republic,[23] and more recently, Grenada and Panama, except that in these cases the elements who challenged American interests were discredited as much on political grounds as cultural.

With the beginning of the *intifada* in late 1987, for the first time since the Israeli invasion of Lebanon, American journalists began to more routinely portray Palestinians in a much different light than had historically been the case. The uprising in the occupied territories meant that at the risk of their lives, health, and property, a good number of Palestinians, many of them very young, for the first time were able to command space and time in the American media, and there seemed to be a new, far more tough-minded attitude taken toward Israel.

Major television news programs ranging from CBS "60 Minutes" to ABC's "Nightline" aired balanced and insightful looks at the conflict and the protagonists. Among broadcast outlets, National Public Radio (NPR) in particular produced a number of interesting and humanizing features. For instance, on New Year's Day 1989, the public network aired a segment on the music of the uprising, dealing with some of the songwriters who have employed their art in the service of the *intifada*. Interestingly enough, the commentator took pains to point out that the songs very much reminded him of the Zionist songs of his boyhood that were common among the people when Israel had been seeking a homeland.

And several weeks later, NPR aired a devastating report on the new Israeli policy of dynamiting homes of rock throwers and of soldiers having been given new license to fire at fleeing stone throwers. The program dealt with the dramatic increase in severe head and chest wounds among Palestinians as a result of the change in policy.[24]

As the uprising neared the end of its first year, the editors of *Middle East Report* could write, "Israel's ability to dominate media discourse is becoming more difficult as the Palestinians persist . . ."[25]

Still, there was hardly cause for partisans of Israel to charge that the media had gone completely over to the other side. Double standards in coverage continued to abound. For instance, if the Sandinista government had placed the same restrictions on foreign journalists that Israel has frequently imposed on those covering the *intifada,* it is safe to assume a storm of editorial protest would have followed judging from the reaction to the Sandinista suppression of *La Prensa.*

Yet similar outrage was totally absent at the suppression of West Bank newspapers, or the imprisonment without specific charge or trial of Palestinian journalists, or the suspension of the Palestine Press Service in March 1988. As well, there was the case of Abie Nathan, an Israeli peace activist who ran an offshore radio station called *Voice of Peace* and who began serving a six-month jail sentence in October 1989, charged with violating the 1986 law forbidding Israelis to have contact with the PLO.

Finally, what of the move in the summer of 1989 by the Israeli military to place a ban on the unauthorized use of FAX machines in the Gaza strip, an action that can only be compared to the Ceausescu regime in Romania, which before its fall required all typewriters to be registered.[26]

Beginning in late 1989, coverage of the uprising began to fade if not disappear altogether. The typical explanation for the diminished coverage is one offered by a National Public Radio correspondent, who argued the American media have an attention span of only about one year. Israel understands this, he said, and has simply outwaited the uprising.[27]

This argument might be more persuasive were it not for the media's record on covering uprisings that meet the ideological needs of the national security state, say, in Afghanistan. Similarly, American journalists kept the plight of Soviet and Polish dissidents alive for years through sheer commitment and under reporting circumstances every bit as restrictive as those imposed by Israel. The point here is a simple one: the media's attention span is precisely as long as media decision makers decide it should be.

Perhaps the central question in all of this is why does the American press, which prides itself on being fair and objective and an adversary of the state, persist in a pattern of behavior that better serves Israel's interests than the American public's right to know. There are a number of explanations, some more common than others.

First, there is the possibility of cultural bias. American reporters are from a nominally Christian culture but they are also quite used to Judaism. Islam and or Arab culture is much more exotic, mysterious, and finally, threatening. Too, although there is no doubt that popular anti-Semitism has been a major problem in this society, for a variety of reasons such anti-Semitism is no longer socially acceptable, at least among the educated classes. No such social sanctions exist for anti-Arabism.

A second factor, and a very significant one, is the Israeli lobby. There has been no more effective political pressure group in the realm of foreign policy, including the China lobby of the 1950s and 1960s, than the Israeli lobby. Over the years it has built a formidable political machine.[28] This lobby operates by putting pressure not just on politicians, however. It is equally powerful when it comes to the media. For instance, the lobby has been directly or indirectly responsible for killing or delaying several important documentaries on the Palestinians and the *intifada*, witness the furor surrounding the PBS film, "Days of Rage."[29]

Following the downturn in approval of Israel after the 1982 invasion of Lebanon, the American Jewish Congress sponsored a conference in Jerusalem chaired by the chairman of the American advertising agency responsible for the Miller Lite Beer ads. The conference drew, among others, the literary editor of the *New Republic* and the former vice-president of public relations for Pepsi Cola.

Out of the conference grew the Hasbara Project, which among other things provided for an internship program to train Israeli career diplomats in communication and public relations techniques. The interns also got to meet the top editors at the *New*

York Times, the *Washington Post,* and the three network evening news shows. To my knowledge, this is the only such training program on behalf of a foreign power of which I am aware, and the degree of cooperation that it received is uncommon for a program of this sort in any event.[30]

If elements of the pro-Israeli lobby have had significant influence over the American information and entertainment media, however, this does not mean that a Jewish cabal owns or dictates to the media in this country, a charge frequently made by the far-right wing and by some Arabists.

Rather, the case is that groups uncritical of Israel's foreign policy have managed to have a disproportionate share of influence over media policy on stories concerning the question of Palestine, largely because Israel has a potent constituency in this country that understands how to apply pressure point advocacy on behalf of (1) a nation-state that figures importantly in U.S. geopolitical strategy; (2) a people that are admired by many Americans, Jewish and Christian alike, for their military success at a time when that of the United States seems limited; and (3) a people that underwent terrible pain in Europe during World War II while the world, including the United States, stood by.[31]

Indeed, support for Israel comes from both Christian and Jewish journalism. As Ben Bradlee, managing editor of the *Washington Post,* has said, if polled privately, the reporters in his newsroom "would say they are pro-Israel. Not pro-Syria. Not pro-Palestinian. I think that's probably a fact of life."[32]

It is also the case, as Steve Mallory, a veteran broadcast journalist who covered the Middle East for ten years for NBC, has said: "TV news executives in New York figure that the American public cares less and less about what happens to people the darker their skin is."[33]

Important as cultural factors and the influence of the Israeli lobby may be to an explanation of why the press and entertainment media behave as they do, the critical factor, as suggested at the beginning of this chapter, is the ideology of the national security state and its forty-year hold over the U.S. media system.

Throughout the Cold War, only just recently said to have ended, the media, particularly the serious press, have more often than not tended to validate rather than challenge a whole string of arguably disastrous assumptions of official Washington. Case studies of how the press has covered nuclear weapons, the Soviet Union, and much of the Third World bear this contention out.[34] There is a persuasive body of evidence that foreign affairs comes to us from a system of news gathering that is deeply flawed by the subtle influence of a world-view that favors policy makers. The result is a journalism of deference to the national security state.

What is meant by *journalism of deference* is the willingness of the press in most situations most of the time to defer to Washington's perspective on the world scene, particularly where the Soviet Union and international conflict are concerned. In the Middle East, of course, this has meant deferring to Washington's judgment that Israel ought to be the centerpiece of American strategy in the region, particularly after 1973.

The media's deference on national security matters is directly rooted in the establishment in this country of a sense of continuing crisis since World War II. Consider what has happened during what is called the *Cold War*. The United States ended 150 years of isolationism and struck out in a search for world power. As well, the United States acquired a permanent enemy, the Soviet Union, for the first time in its history. Never before have Americans had to endure perpetual anxiety. Always before they went off to war, won it, came home, and went back to business as usual. This did not happen after 1945. Third, the world's peoples for the first time in history faced "species threat," a threat made possible by nuclear weapons. Such weapons do not just spell the possibility of military defeat, but instead promise defeat of the species.

If the American press has always served the state during times of hot war, why should we be surprised when the press serves the state during a Cold War, particularly one that if things go wrong promises total warfare against the homeland and devastation of the species; but if things go "right," in the definition of power elites, there is a promise of unprecedented power.

In sum, the problems with press coverage of the Cold War in general and the Middle East in particular are bound up in some forty years of antagonism, fear, and anxiety. Journalism, like other major institutions, has been operating on a wartime footing in what conventional wisdom holds is a life-and-death world struggle.

In the case of the Middle East, Jewish influence and American ethnocentrism simply are not necessary and sufficient explanations for why the press behaves as it does. Statist goals more than anything else have dictated Israel's place in the scheme of things, and those goals, goals that are discussed elsewhere in this volume, as they have throughout the Cold War, have been well served by the press.

To be certain, nothing in this analysis should be taken to mean that the American press is a monolith or that journalists or television producers or film directors work on orders from Washington, D.C. The press can come to criticize the state under certain circumstances—the breakdown of elite consensus, for instance—and the effects of ideology work their way more through cultural osmosis than directive. As a journalist who covered the Middle East during the 1950s once remarked about the subtle effects of Cold War ideology on his work, "Is a fish aware of water?"

If this analysis is correct and the American mass media are operating largely within the ideological confines of the national security state, the prospects for improving media performance are not particularly good—unless there is a significant shift in the ideological direction of the larger society. For instance, there is definitely a need for journalists covering the region to have more of an educational and language background than is typical. However, area studies alone will not alter a journalist's perspective if his or her training consists of exposure to largely Orientalist scholarship. And note how many career diplomats can speak fluent Arabic and still make culture-bound assumptions about Middle Eastern people that conveniently serve U.S. policy goals. Similarly, simply providing journalists with a solid background in international relations will matter little if it is based on conventional understandings of the United States as essentially an actor with nothing more than high moral purpose as its only motivation in the world.

Certainly, university journalism and media studies programs need to pay far more attention to the challenge of reporting about the Third World than they do at present. Various foundations, councils, and the like concerned with international affairs would also do well to move more systematically into the area of education for journalists. The quality of public knowledge about the region, for instance, might benefit from a university- or foundation-sponsored Institute of Middle East Reporting, but only if the program is not associated with any particular regional interest—economic or political.

Educationally, perhaps the greatest need of all is for a vastly improved regular elementary and secondary school curriculum. Journalists after all are socialized long before they enter the profession. Their world-views do not form at their first assignment.

There is some possibility that the media themselves, as they approach the twenty-first century and finally are freed of the obsession with the Soviet Union, may now focus on North-South issues, which have long gone untended. Since 1985, for example, ABC has had an academic advisor on Middle East coverage. However, to do this, the conventions of journalism will need a serious overhaul—if not reinvention. For instance, the practice of using a narrow range of sources for information about foreign affairs because it is safe, convenient, and fast must give way to a broader range of opinion. So long as the circle of acceptable sources remains as small as at present, there is little hope for greater understanding of policy options in the region.[35]

If indeed the Cold War is over, there is no reason that the American media can not move to gain the vitality that it has always claimed. Yet until non-Israeli peoples in the Middle East are accorded a human dimension in the media, and debate is opened up, American policy makers will remain free to export far more pain to the region than hope.

NOTES

1. Bernard C. Cohen, *The Press and Foreign Policy* (Princeton, N.J.: Princeton University Press, 1963).

2. Robert Dallek, *The American Style of Foreign Policy: Cultural Politics and Foreign Affairs* (New York: Alfred A. Knopf, 1982; Mentor, 1983), p. 143.

3. On the role of television during the Cold War, see J. Fred MacDonald, *Television and the Red Menace: The Video Road to Vietnam* (New York: Praeger, 1985).

4. Don Feder, "Unfair Media Beat up on Israel," *Sacramento Union* (August 15, 1990).

5.   Daniel Pipes, "The Media and the Middle East," *Commentary* (June 1984), p. 30. For an Israeli critique of American press coverage of the Middle East, see Ze'ev Chafets, *A Double Vision: How the Press Distorts America's View of the Middle East* (New York: William Morrow and Company, 1985). Interestingly, this book by the one-time director of Israel's Government Press Office was widely and respectfully reviewed in the American print media, despite its harsh criticism of American journalism for distorting Israel's case (see, for example, Elie Abel, "Who Weakened the Case for Israel?" *New York Times Book Review* [November 4, 1984]). By contrast, *Double Vision: The Portrayal of Arabs in the American Media*, edited by Edmund Ghareeb, received not nearly so much attention in the press.

6.   William A. Dorman and Mansour Farhang, "The U.S. Press and Lebanon," *SAIS Review* (Winter–Spring 1983).

7.   Edward W. Said, *Covering Islam: How the Media and the Experts Determine How We See the Rest of the World* (New York: Pantheon Books, 1981).

8.   Laurence Michalak, *Cruel and Unusual: Negative Images of Arabs in Popular American Culture, ADCIssues* 19 (January 1984): 3.

9.   For example, see Jack G. Shaheen, *The TV Arab* (Bowling Green, Ky.: Bowling Green State University Popular Press, 1984).

10.   David Lamb, "Other Stereotypes Fade, but Negative Arab Image Stays," *Los Angeles Times* (June 10, 1984).

11.   Edward Tivnan, *The Lobby: Jewish Political Power and American Foreign Policy* (New York: Simon and Schuster, 1987), p. 51.

12.   Michalak, *Cruel and Unusual,* p. 11.

13.   Ibid., p. 3.

14.   For analyses of the media, Arab peoples, and American public opinion, see Janice Monti Belkaoui, "Images of Arabs and Israelis in the Prestige Press," *Journalism Quarterly* 55 (Winter 1978); R. Curtiss, "A Changing Image: American Perceptions of the Arab-Israeli Dispute" (American Education Trust, 1982); C. DeBoer, "The Polls: Attitudes Toward the Arab-Israeli Conflict," *Public Opinion Quarterly* 47, 121 (1983): 31; Edmund Ghareeb, ed., *Split Vision: The Portrayal of Arabs in the American Media* (Washington, D.C.: American-Arab Affairs Council, 1983); Shelley Slade, "The Image of the Arab in America: Analysis of a Poll on American Attitudes," *The Middle East Journal* (1981); Edward Said, *Covering Islam;* M. Suleiman, "National Stereotypes as Weapons in the Arab-Israeli Conflict," *Journal of Palestine Studies* 3 (Spring 1974); R. Trice, "The American Elite Press and the Arab-Israeli Conflict," *Middle East Journal* 33 (1979).

15.   See, for instance, Craig H. Grau, "What Publications Are Most

Frequently Quoted in *Congressional Record?*" *Journalism Quarterly* 53 (1976).

16. For a discussion of journalistic frame analysis, see Gaye Tuchman, *Making News: A Study in the Construction of Reality* (New York: Free Press, 1978).

17. Associated Press (27 December 1990).

18. "A Heritage of Humiliation and Defeat," *Newsweek* (August 27, 1990), p. 27.

19. Micah L. Sifry, "Sermon From the Mount," *The Nation* (November 28, 1989), p. 605.

20. William A. Dorman and Mansour Farhang, *U.S. Press and Iran: Foreign Policy and the Journalism of Deference* (Berkeley: University of California Press, 1987), ch. 7.

21. ABC News–Harris Survey (January 30, 1979), p. 1.

22. See Neal D. Houghton, "The Cuban Invasion of 1961 and the U.S. Press—in Retrospect," *Journalism Quarterly* (Summer 1965), p. 424.

23. Theodore Draper, "Contaminated News of the Dominican Republic," in Alan Casty, ed., *Mass Media and Mass Man* (New York: Holt, Rinehart and Winston, 1968), pp. 212–14.

24. National Public Radio (January 17, 1989).

25. "From the Editors," *Middle East Report* (September–October 1988), p. 2.

26. See *CPJ Update 37* [newsletter of the Committee to Protect Journalists] (December 1989), p. 12. See also, Eric Goldstein, "As Palestinian Uprising Continues, Israel Gets Tough with Journalists," *CPJ Update* 33 (May–June 1988), p. 1.

27. National Public Radio, "Morning Edition" (January 3, 1990).

28. One of the best discussions of the history and impact of the lobby is provided by Tivnan, *The Lobby.*

29. Steven Emerson, "The System That Brought You 'Days of Rage'," *Columbia Journalism Review* (November–December 1989): 25–30.

30. Robert I. Friedman, "Selling Israel to America: The Hasbara Project Targets the U.S. Media," *Mother Jones* (February–March 1987), pp. 21–26, 52.

31. For a discussion of how the American press downplayed or ignored the Holocaust, see Deborah E. Lipstadt, *Beyond Belief: The American Press and the Coming of the Holocaust, 1933–45* (New York: Free Press, 1987).

32. Friedman, "Selling Israel to America," p. 22.

33. Ibid., p. 22.

34. See William A. Dorman, Robert Karl Manoff, and Jennifer

Weeks, *American Press Coverage of U.S.-Soviet Relations, the Soviet Union, Nuclear Weapons, Arms Control, and National Security: A Bibliography* (New York University: Center for War, Peace and the News Media, 1988).

35. For discussion of the narrow range of sources used by American news organizations in foreign policy and national security stories, see Daniel C. Hallin *et al.*, "National Security Sourcing Project" (New York: Center for War, Peace, and the News Media, New York University, 1991).

CHAPTER 11

Middle East Studies and
U.S. Foreign Policy

Richard B. Parker

The American foreign policy process suffers from an essential irrationality. This realization is not new. Graham Allison, in his classic *Essence of Decision,* described John F. Kennedy's decision to impose a selective blockade against Soviet shipping to Cuba in 1962 as follows: "part choice and part result, a melange of misperception, miscommunication, misinformation, bargaining, pulling, hauling, and spurring as well as a mixture of national security interests, objectives, and governmental calculations recounted in more conventional accounts."[1]

When such disparate factors as Allison lists result either in a policy success or a policy with which we agree (and the two may not coincide), we tend to think of it as an act of brilliance or high principle by the chief of the state and his close advisors. When it miscarries or we disagree with it, we see it as irrational, stupid, or even malevolent on the part of the same people.

Miscalculation is not peculiar to the Americans or to the Middle East. It is endemic to human condition. Everyone does it—the Americans, the Soviets, the Israelis, the Egyptians, the Iraqis, the Iranians, indeed, any people you care to name. I am currently writing a series of essays on miscalculation in the Middle East, looking at the mistakes made by the Soviets and Egyptians in 1967, by the Israelis and Americans in the so-called Canal War in 1970, and by the American in Lebanon in 1982–83. A common thread that runs through all of these cases is that people hear what they want to hear, and this is being brought home to us vividly as the 1990 crisis in the Gulf unfolds.

We like to think that students and scholars of Middle Eastern affairs are above such misperceptions because as scholars they know better. Unfortunately, they often do not. They are all too human and have the same difficulty everyone else does in divorcing themselves from their backgrounds and the past and in being completely objective about events that touch people they know and may even love, or hate.

Middle Easterns usually recognize their own ability to miscalculate, but often find it difficult to believe that a country with America's technological skills and practical approach to problems can also make stupid mistakes. They tend to see a dark and hidden purpose, carried out with often malevolent skill, behind the most obvious policy misjudgment or miscarriage. Although they are aware that many of their own decisions spring from emotional reactions, they do not recognize the importance of the same phenomenon among Americans. (As I write this, I am waiting for the first expose of the emotional content in President Bush's reaction to the Iraqi invasion of Kuwait.)

In this vein, someone this morning asked what the United States would rather have had happen during the past fifty years, as a result of its Middle East policies, than what actually happened. The implication was that things had gone pretty well for us, and that in the long run our policy had been successful, in terms of American interests, narrowly perceived. A number of things occurred to me immediately as developments we would have wished to avoid, and could have—the blowing up of our embassy in Beirut, the slaughter of our marines there, the hostage problem in Iran, having Iran be instrumental in the destruction of one presidential administration and threaten another. On reflection, and thinking more broadly, I would add our failure since 1945 to come to terms with Arab and Iranian nationalism, our inability to deal successfully with the problem of Palestine, and our overidentification with regimes and rulers that too often have legitimacy problems.

We have had a series of disasters in the Middle East, and as David Newsom remarked in an article in the *Middle East Journal* some years ago, what is remarkable is that we are not worse off than we are.² In spite of everything, we still seem to have a good deal of influence in that area, and theoretically we still have the capability of playing a role, even the honest broker role, if we can find it within ourselves to play it (although we seem not to have done very well in the dialogue with the Palestine Liberation Organization). One questioner said he did not know whether it was that we were *unable* or that we *would not,* or whether they were the same thing, but that we had a certain paralysis in our foreign policy which meant that things are settled or done by default rather than by long-term thinking. To me, this is one of the great differences between Americans and the Soviets, who are more methodical. But the Soviets, with their supposedly much more careful and much slower process of thinking things through, make just as many mistakes as we do, and for the same reasons. Thus, current research on the origins of the Six-Day War indicates no coordinated planning by the Soviets, or realization of what they were starting, before they took the step that provoked that crisis. The same was true of Khrushchev's installation of nuclear missiles in Cuba in 1962.³ We can add Afghanistan to the same list, I am told.

My subject in this chapter is Middle Eastern studies and U.S. foreign policy. What is the connection between the two? The short answer is: very little. Professor X goes down to Washington to be consulted by the Department of State. He comes back and is insufferable to all his colleagues because he has been invited and they have not. The bureaucrats are sincerely interested in hearing what the professor has to say, because he is known to be an eminent authority. They hope the scholar is going to say something new— something that would enable them to initiate effective action rather than reacting or letting things happen by default. Most of the time they are disappointed, because the professor is unlikely to know anything that is really new. In terms of what is happening on the ground at the moment, the bureaucrat, the country desk officer, is likely to know more than the academic does, because the desk officer is getting classified telegrams from post in the field about what is going on. As a result, the desk officer knows details the professor has never dreamed of. Nevertheless, the officer wants to hear what the professor has to say, and the most useful task the latter can perform is to point out in what respect the accepted wisdom is wrong. The professor has the advantage of a historical perspective, which the desk officer usually lacks totally. That perspective often enables the former to see and to articulate the fallacies that may underline a given policy, such as the Eisenhower Doctrine, which had as a basic tenet the belief that Egypt was under the domination of international communism. This was widely believed in Washington in the late 1950s. We now recognize that to have been absurd. (Few people did at the time, however; I can recall no one important who came, from academia or elsewhere, to argue forcefully that Nasser was not under Soviet domination and that the secretary of state and the director of the CIA did not know what they were talking about in that respect. My memory is probably faulty, but I was impressed at the time by the apparent unanimity on the subject in Washington.)

The academic may also convey something of the complexity of the situation, and point out that you cannot accept a black and white version of events, that there are only various shades of gray and can suggest other people we should be talking to. This often leads to more fruitful exchanges. Indeed, the Department of State has a regular program of bringing in academics, to listen to them and to have them spend time at the Department of State to learn how the policy process works and to teach the practitioners something about those subjects that they know best. This connection is made difficult sometimes by the academic's suspicion of the government—MESA's perennial resolutions about not doing any research for the CIA or the Defense Intelligence Agency and so forth. I understand the scholar's reluctance to get involved in intelligence, but it means that this channel of communications is choked off. As a result, we do not get anything like what we should from the academic community, which merely carps from the sidelines and makes little direct contribution to policy discussion in Washington.

The preceding is the simple answer. The reality of the impact of Middle Eastern studies on foreign policy is more complex. For one thing, Middle Eastern area studies have produced a number of people who have ended up in key positions in our foreign policy structure over the years, and the Foreign Service has made a continuing effort to train specialists in Middle Eastern area studies. I was once one of them; and although this is a very frustrating experience and area specialists in general usually conclude that over the years they have very little real influence, occasionally they do get to inject a note of sanity. The point is, however, that the foreign policy establishment does have people in it who are familiar with academic views on the area and are often in direct contact with the academic community. There is frequent exchange of views between them.

Middle Eastern studies have also been an important source of expertise, of people who are sometimes able to tell the bureaucrats what is actually going on, as opposed to what real-time intelligence shows. Some scholars have had a more direct impact than others. For instance, a Brookings Institution study some years ago was instrumental in shaping the Carter administration's approach to the Palestine problem.[4] An attempt at a repeat performance in 1988 had considerably less impact, in part because the study was too tepid.[5] The difficulty with selling such a study to the power brokers is, very simply stated, that the decision makers, the people at the top floor of the Department of State, in the National Security Council (NSC), and the White House and the Pentagon, have no time for complexities. They are too absorbed in crises to sit down and listen to some outside "experts" tell them what they should do about this phenomenon or that. In particular, the fact that the outside expert has no responsibility for what happens if his or her advice is followed means that he or she is often seen as irresponsible.

Policy makers must deal with what they see as reality, with the situation on the ground, with the domestic political situation, with the electoral situation, and with public opinion. All of these are in constant disequilibrium and flux. Nothing is constant. More important, they must deal with them now, not tomorrow or next week. They must make a decision before the close of business or it will be too late. And most important, they are responsible for what happens, even though they may not control the process.

Of these factors, public opinion is perhaps the most immediate concern of every political appointee. Paradoxically, the government itself is the strongest single influence in changing or affecting that opinion. Positions taken by the president, the secretary of state, and the secretary of defense are, in the first instance, usually what tell the public what is right and what is wrong in the field of foreign affairs. These officials are subject to battering by Congress, criticism by opponents and so forth, but they have first claim on the media and whatever they say is followed closely. The classic example of this was President Eisenhower's election-eve speech on Suez in 1956, which set forth a position of strong opposition to the Tripartite invasion of Egypt. He was very critical of Israel, Britain, and France. This was not expected that close to an election and was considered a risky step in view of pro-Israeli sentiment in the United States, but everyone accepted it once it had been made. It did not affect the election. One often wishes we had more presidents like Eisenhower, who was willing to stand up and be counted for what he thought was right. But then think of some of the mistakes he made, such as the Eisenhower Doctrine of 1957. Nobody is perfect.

Public opinion is also strongly affected by the media, of course, but they in turn are often responding to what the administration says. One morning in 1987 I was to appear on the CBS morning news to talk about the anniversary of the Tripoli raid. The question that I knew would be asked was, "Has the raid been effective in reducing Libyan support for international terrorism?" The day before, I talked to the director of North African affairs at the Department of State and to a man who was deeply involved in planning for Libya raid. Both said that the raid had made Qaddafi realize how vulnerable he was, and that as a result he had pulled in his horns and adopted a lower profile and to that extent it had worked. I read the same thing in the *Washington Post* and the *New York Times* and knew their reporters must have talked to the same people I had. All of us were drinking from the same source—the administration. I personally thought the raid was a mistake, that we should not get involved in trying to kill chiefs of state, and that the reduction in terrorist activities was more the result of increased security measures in Europe and changing attitudes in the Arab world than of the Tripoli raid itself. The media, however, accepted the official line, and today I am not sure they were not right in doing so. The point of this anecdote is that the opinion of the officials in question was accepted, in part because they had access to information the rest of us did not have, and they controlled its dissemination.

The media process of forming public opinion depends heavily on pundits, however, as well as on the official line. *Pundit* comes from the Sanskrit *Pand,* to pile up, and means a person of great learning. In Washington today it means anyone who is allowed to pontificate in the media—whether in a twenty-second sound byte on ABC television or a scholarly paper at a think tank. At the risk of some oversimplification, three classes of pundit are discernible today. At the top is a small group who hold world-class status. They are free to comment on any subject they choose, they make a good living by doing so, and they will be listened to by the administration. The prototype of this class was Walter Lippman. There is nobody of his stature on the scene today, although Walter Cronkite played a similar role in the 1960s and 1970s. More recently, during the Reagan period, Jeanne Kirkpatrick held a similar status, and so did George Will, but both lost it when Bush came in.

At the second level are the pundits who are free to comment on all subjects and earn a comfortable living at it, but who have little impact on the administration or policy. In this category are George Will today, Evans and Novak, William Safire, and so forth.

The distinguishing aspects of the first two categories are (1) they earn a good living from being a pundit, and (2) they do not need actually to know anything at all about the subject they are discussing. The world is their oyster, and they are free to comment about any aspect of it they choose.

At the third level is a rather large group of people who are invariably referred to as "experts" and who tend to be academicians or involved in academic-related activities. They are in the universities, think tanks, and the public affairs organizations; and they generally spend their time working in some way on a particularly area. They write books or organize conferences or get themselves hired as consultants, and so on. They are to be found throughout the country, but the largest single concentration is Washington. That is where the action is. My informed estimate is that there are about seventy-five so-called Middle East experts functioning as pundits in Washington today. As distinguished from the first two categories, they are restricted to Middle Eastern subjects, and few of them actually earn a living from being pundits (although they often get paid useful honoraria) and, although nobody at the top of the government listens to them directly, they collectively provide most of what often becomes the accepted wisdom. In particular, the first two categories draw their information from them. Many of these people in the third category have had little real exposure to the Middle East. They have not lived or worked there, and they do not know its language or history. They have nevertheless established niches for themselves by dint of work experience or association and can comment with apparent authority on their specialty with very little advance notice. At times of crisis, as in the summer of 1990, they are constantly appearing in this media.

The Middle East experts can usually expect no serious rejoinders from the public to whatever they may say because the level of understanding in this country of foreign affairs in general and of the Middle East is particular is often abysmal. The public is willing to believe almost anything it is told by authoritative-sounding people with direct answers. It shows a certain healthy skepticism about things like Irangate, but if President Reagan had played it right he could have sold it almost anything. In fact, some would say he did.

This phenomenon has to do with many aspects of the American outlook, which starts with a concentration on domestic concerns and with little time for geography. People do not know where these countries are and have little knowledge of foreign cultures and languages. They find complexity fatiguing and they want short, clear answers. They want to read it in *USA Today* and they want it in one paragraph. The public is instinctively anti-intellectual. It distrusts university professors and others who give long-winded, complex answers.

Public ignorance is less than it was, but it is still profound. Most Americans automatically assume, for instance, that all Muslims are Arabs: that the Iranians and Turks are Arabs. I do not know which party is offended the most by this linkage, the Persians, the Turks, or the Arabs. None of them is happy about it, and all are a little incredulous that anyone would confuse them.

A number of studies have illuminated the extent of public ignorance, such as Michael Suleiman's *The Arabs in the Mind of America*.[6] There was also a survey on unfavorable American attitudes toward the Arabs compiled by Shelly Slade and published in the Spring 1981 issue of the *Middle East Journal*.[7] It has been widely reprinted in the Arab press. It has been devastating to Arabs to read in the Slade article what their image is, and they are incredulous that anyone could see them thus, but this is the reality we have to deal with. A similar survey of attitudes toward Iranians would probably put them even lower on the scale, given lingering resentment over their treatment of American hostages, although Saddam Hussein may change that.

On the other hand, there has been much progress in education on the Middle East in this country. The December 1983 *MESA Bulletin* and the Winter 1987 issue of the *Middle East Journal* both had long articles on progress in Middle Eastern studies in the United States, the first by Michael Bonine and the second by the late Bayly Winder.[8] The growth in the number of universities and colleges offering courses of some sort in Middle Eastern studies is remarkable. The number has gone from a handful in 1953 to almost 600 in 1989. We have also had a great increase in the number of Middle Eastern organizations in Washington, to the point that the Middle East Institute now publishes a booklet, *Middle East Organizations in Washington,* which lists them and describes their purpose, affiliation, and programs. There are over 100 in the current issue, where there were three or four thirty years ago.

Similarly, membership in MESA has gone from 51 in 1966 to 2,100 in 1990[9]—a tremendous increase. The number of study centers and programs abroad has also increased. Twenty-five years ago, there was the American Research Center in Egypt. Today we also have such centers in Tunis, Sanaʿa, and Istanbul. There are numerous regional studies associations within MESA; and there has been a proliferation of visits, conferences, exchanges and publications on all sides. The number of studies that come out every year on the Middle East is astounding—we are well ahead of the British and Soviets and everyone else. We are even ahead of the Iranians and the Arabs. Visit the Arab world today and you find very little in the way of what we would call "Arab" studies at Arab universities. Arab academicians explain, "we do not have to have Arab studies as you need to have American studies. We study the history, the language, and the literature, and that's enough." One Arab professor told me the Arabs in the Arab world were not yet ready to study themselves; and indeed judging by book titles and presses, most serious study of the Arabs by Arabs today seems to be done abroad.

At the same time the media have also made great progress, too.

They are much more sophisticated about the problems of the Middle East than they were twenty years ago. There are very good correspondents in the field, people like Tom Friedman, David Shipler, and Yussef Ibrahim, who report things in a way they never would have been reported, or published, in 1967.

Paradoxically, all of this expansion of knowledge seems to have little immediate impact on policy. Although people can read critical articles about Israel that never would have appeared before, relations between the United States and Israel have a sacred quality about them, whereas Arab influence has never been weaker than it is today.[10] This is perhaps because there is less understanding of the complexities of the issues within the administration than there was twenty or thirty years ago. You can say what you like about Foster Dulles, but he never would have gone along with the Israeli invasion of Lebanon in 1982. He would have understood just how dangerous that was. Alexander Haig, on the other hand, apparently accepted General Ariel Sharon's view of that operation because of his own ignorance of the area.

Secretary Baker has shown a good deal more sense about the area than his two predecessors, but at the upper levels of the U.S. government, aside from cynicism, there has been a good deal of ignorance; and that is one reason why Arab influence is so low in Washington today. (The more important reason, though, is the Arabs' inability to get their act together.) People at the top do not know much about the area, they have no time to listen to specialists, and anyway, the specialists never agree. They cannot agree about the details; and they can be just as blind as everybody else when it comes to predicting what is going to happen.[11] Policy makers need a practical recommendation in two short paragraphs. It must be clear. They want it now. They don't want it tomorrow. You have fifteen minutes in which to explain it, and there can be no elaborate explanation based on an analysis as to whether *vilayat-e faghih* is heretical. That is something policy makers do not care about. They do not want to know all that. They want to know which direction we should move in tomorrow.[12]

Go back and read the briefing memo Allen Dulles took to the White House on July 14, 1958. It is unclassified and in the microfiches. It describes how the CIA saw the crisis in Lebanon as a result of the coup in Baghdad. It is a very superficial document, and it was probably instrumental in our decision to land the troops in Lebanon. That is the degree of sophistication you find among the policy makers, who have the entire world on their minds.

In these situations, when suddenly we have to make a decision, we do not go to a university professor who is going to tell us why we should not do this. We go to a Robert McFarlane or an Ollie North who will salute and go out and get things done. They are not going to ask a lot of questions, and they will do it immediately. This is not going to change. It is not going to get any better until there is a lot more sophistication in this country among the public, among people who are not Middle Eastern specialists, about the complexities of that area. It must start in primary and secondary schools, in Sunday schools, in popular literature, not with graduate theses on Abbassid court etiquette and things like that, but with progress in making the public aware of the issues and some of their complexities. It is very good, it is very important, to have people up in the stratosphere looking at these questions, but they have little impact on popular attitudes today. The battle goes by default to ignorance and to those who do care, who are willing to go into the high schools.

In my view there must be a revision of attitudes in universities in this respect. Most Ph.Ds. do not want to teach in high schools. They want to teach in a university. Well, somebody has got to go out and have some impact on high schools. This is not a new idea with me. A good deal has already been done in this respect in places like Arizona and Texas, but it is a very touchy subject. The Arizona experience shows that you must be very careful. You must take everybody's sensitivities into account. But this is a vineyard that must be tended, otherwise the American public will never be educated. So my final word is, do not send your professors to Washington. Send them to Dubuque.

NOTES

1. Graham Allison, *Essence of Decision* (Boston: Little, Brown and Company, 1971), p. 210.

2. David Newsom, "Miracle or Mirage: Reflections on U.S. Diplomacy and the Arabs," *Middle East Journal 55*, no. 3 (Summer 1981): 297–313.

3. See James G. Blight, *On the Brink: Americans and Soviets Re-examine the Cuban Missile Crisis* (New York: Hill and Wang, 1989), pp. 291–305.

4. Brookings Middle East Study Group, *Toward Peace in the Middle East: Report of a Study Group* (Washington, D.C.: Brookings Institution, 1975).

5. Brookings Study Group on Arab-Israeli Peace, *Toward Arab-Israeli Peace: Report of a Study Group* (Washington, D.C.: Brookings Institution, 1988).

6. Michael Suleiman, *The Arabs in the Mind of America*, (Brattleboro, Vt.: Amana Books, 1988).

7. Shelly Slade, "The Image of the Arab in America: Analysis of a Poll on American Attitudes," *Middle East Journal* 35, no. 2 (Spring 1981): 143–62.

8. Michael Bonine, "MESA and Middle East Studies: An International Perspective from North America," *MESA Bulletin* 20, no. 2 (December 1986): 155–70; and Bayly Winder, "Four Decades of Middle Eastern Studies," *Middle East Journal* 41, no. 1 (Winter 1987): 40–63.

9. The Statistics for 1990 MESA membership was provided to the editor by the MESA headquarters in University of Arizona, Tucson.

10. This was written before the Gulf crisis of 1990, which is likely to change most of the givens in the Middle East equation before it is over.

11. As indicated earlier, this is not unique to the Middle East. See Blight, *On the Brink*.

12. For a good discussion of decision making in a crisis situation, see William B. Quandt, *Decade of Decisions: American Policy Toward the Arab-Israeli Conflict* (Berkeley: University of California Press, 1977).

CHAPTER 12

Middle East Studies and Education in the United States: Retrospect and Prospects

Hooshang Amirahmadi
Eliane C. Condon
Abraham Resnick

During the last decades, the crises recurring in the Middle East have been a source of serious concern for all nations, for they represent a threat to the world peace and economy. The United States, in particular, perceives any disturbance in that geographical area as a danger signal which activates its responsibility, as a world power, to intervene in a potentially explosive situation. The United States–led war against Iraq in 1991 was the latest and most significant episode in modern Middle East history in which the Americans were directly involved.

Unfortunately, as Middle Eastern experts have noted repeatedly, American policies toward the region have not been always overly effective, nor have they been tailored to the cultural expectations, assumptions, prescriptions, and values of those diverse Arab, Iranian, and other nations that constitute the Middle East. Even the successful and destructive war against Iraq has not yet produced any tangible positive results beyond forcing Iraq out of Kuwait for the time being. Indeed, the war has created additional economic, environmental, and political problems on top of the problems that existed in the region. The inefficacy of U.S. Middle East policies may be attributed to two major causes, one of which is the prevalence of an anglocentric orientation among those responsible for international relations in the United States, which leads them to disregard the existence of other world-views and function strictly in accordance with their own culture-bound standards in all international negotiations.[1] This unfortunate chauvinistic attitude, which is bitterly resented by overseas societies, and interpreted by them as a display of American arrogance, is further aggravated by another factor—the deplorable and widespread ignorance of the general public and many American government officials about the Middle East, its cultures, and its people. This lack of knowledge has resulted in a proliferation of stereotypes, misjudgments, and distorted expectations, aptly summarized in a 1978 study by Szalay et al., who equated the American image of Arabs as "camel, desert, oil" and to which one must now add that of "terrorist."[2]

The majority of the American people tends to be uninformed, as well as only marginally interested in international affairs. Furthermore, the information available to the public in this area is likely to be inaccurate, for it is derived primarily from tainted sources—the biased presentations of "facts" carefully edited by mass media specialists intent on achieving a maximum emotional impact on their viewers or readers.[3] This distortion factor was specifically highlighted in the results of a 1977 study, conducted by Mir-Djalali, that compared American and Iranian cultures, and from which the researcher concluded that "the American image of Iran indicates little substantive knowledge of the country but appears to a large extent stereotypical."[4]

It is worthy to note, at this point, that the sources of international information available to the mass media both here and in the Middle East are by their very nature biased in their approach to world affairs. Currently four major news agencies control overseas information: AP, UPI, AFP, and Reuters—all of which are based in Western countries; namely, Great Britain, France, and the United States. Their determination of what is newsworthy is culture bound and Eurocentric, both in terms of quantitative—a minimal amount of time and space devoted to non-Western news—and qualitative representations—stereotyped treatment of such countries.[5] An excellent example of "filtered" news management, which results in a misrepresentation of a world event taking place in the Middle East, was cited by a renown linguist, Noam Chomsky, in a recent article reviewing the concepts of terrorism and retaliation, as they are defined by key individuals and institutions in this country. Referring to the statements made in 1984 by Arafat, "calling for negotiations between Israel and the PLO, leading to mutual recognition," this scholar pointed out that the *New York Times,* a newspaper commonly praised for its high professional standards, failed to include in its issues at that time even one mention of this occurrence while, at the same time, continuing to denounce Arafat's alleged "unwillingness to pursue a diplomatic course."[6] What is interesting here is the fact that the *New York Times* chose not to report a statement that they saw as out of character for the PLO leader, rather than acknowledging it and simply discrediting it as pure rhetoric or even the "ravings of a madman."

Quite clearly, any slanted news coverage (whether through omission or distortion) is obstructive to international understanding, for it not only generates misinformation about other parts of the world, but also reinforces the ethnocentrism of those exposed to it, a dangerous attitude to maintain at a time when the economic hegemony of the United States is on the wane and Third World countries are increasingly gaining access to full membership in the international community. For evidence on this changing balance of power, one need only look at the unassailably dominant position in world trade attained by Japan, an event predicted some twenty years ago by Kahn who anticipated that country's emergence as a superstate that would some day surpass the United States.[7] Typically, however, this meteoric rise is viewed by most Americans as the product of "unfair trading practices," rather than the natural outcome of a specific cultural orientation. In this respect, the only valid interpretation of Japanese business practices must consider that society's basic concern for harmony which, logically, results in the favoring of firms and individuals with a long-established track record of positive interactions. Both this modus operandi and the Japanese perception of trade competition as a form of war are inconsistent with American business ethics and expectations.[8]

In world affairs as well, the tenor of international relations is dictated to a large extent by the relative ratio of cultural commonalities and incongruence that may unite or separate different nations. With respect to the Middle East, for instance, the balance between these positive and negative factors tends to weigh in favor of the latter, when one considers the far-reaching implications of crucial religious divergences: Islam, which has dominated the Arab world for centuries and prescribes every aspect of public and private life, on the one hand; and Western faiths, which abide by the separation of church and state, on the other.[9] Such seemingly diametrically opposed outlooks are further complicated by other disparities in Middle Eastern and American world-views and accentuated by the U.S. media's biased presentation of Middle Eastern affairs. Indeed, the outcome of such ethnocentric clashes was amply illustrated during the Iran hostage crisis, when the United States chose to confront the issue publicly, in accordance with the tradition of "openness" established for such matters in the country. In doing so, government leaders and negotiators overlooked the crucial importance of *abrus* (literally translated as "the color of one's face", i.e., one's reputation) to Iranians, thereby triggering, on their part an immediate response of enraged shame.[10] This reaction was further intensified by the latter's own misinterpretation of American democracy that, according to the unconfirmed reports of students who had visited the country recently, had led them to expect a mass uprising of U.S. citizens in protest against the antagonistic stance of their government against Iran.

The entire history of humankind is fraught with such examples of crises resulting from mutual misunderstandings between two or more nations but, today, world affairs have become infinitely more complex than they were fifty years ago. As noted in the introductory and concluding chapters by Amirahmadi, the distinctively bipolar orientation after World War II (based on the U.S.-USSR axis) has given way to a "multipolar system" in which all nations may be expected to interact on a relatively equal basis both politically and culturally. Given this egalitarian situation, any attempt on the part of any country to rule by fiat, through sheer economic or military pressure, no longer qualifies as an acceptable or even overly effective means of influencing the course of international events in favor of a particular nation and for any significant length of time. Instead, the expectations of contending governments are likely to be fulfilled only to the extent of their representatives' proficiency in what may come to be known as "the new diplomacy," a negotiation process mediated by multinational world organizations such as the United Nations and grounded in a solid combination of crosscultural communication skills, bilingual fluency, and a comprehensive knowledge of both societies and their cultures.

Although the innovations mandated by the "new diplomacy" may be challenging, they are by no means insurmountable in a country, such as the United States, which has been characterized as ethnically diverse, competitive, and change oriented. These pluralistic, ethnoracial conditions have created microcosms of crosscultural encounters throughout the nation, in every area of human interactions that have, in turn, stimulated research on culturally induced factors causing interference in interpersonal and intergroup communication. These efforts have culminated in the creation of a new field of specialization, known as Intercultural–Cross-Cultural Communication, which gained momentum from the time of publication of Hall's seminal work on the human dimensions of time and space, *The Silent Language,* in 1959.[11] Since then, its development has been nothing short of phenomenal, and its impact, at first restricted to education, has gradually been extended to other areas, such as civil rights, law enforcement, medical care, social services, media advertisement, and multinational trade. Presumably, it is also an integral part of government training programs for all appointees and employees scheduled for overseas or overseas-related assignments.

With respect to the latter, however, the effectiveness of the provided cross-cultural instruction may be somewhat in doubt, when it is assessed in the light of implemented American foreign policies (imbued, at best, with limited vision and, at worst, with imperialistic overtones). Such a state of affairs immediately raises questions concerning the adequacy of professional preparation prior to entry into the civil service, particularly in the liberal arts sequence of internationally oriented courses of study, intended to nurture a cadre of foreign relations experts with concentration on a specific world region, such as the Middle East.

From an educational standpoint, the concerns that have been raised in connection with the limited scope and accuracy of the international perspectives internalized by American officials, on the one hand, and the American public, on the other hand, are particularly significant. They suggest the presence of a potential deficiency in the coverage of such subject matter at institutions of secondary and higher education. If American schools and universities are to continue to fulfill their mandated responsibility for intellectual development and leadership, now and in the future, in a country that has assumed the role of a major world power, this deficiency must be corrected and with some urgency.

THE STATE OF MIDDLE EAST STUDIES IN THE UNITED STATES

When members of a technologically advanced society exhibit a manifest ignorance in an area of knowledge that cannot be defined as esoteric or culturally taboo, the origin of the problem is usually traceable to a deficiency in the educational system. As noted earlier, such a state of affairs exists in this country with respect to the Middle East. To assess the extent to which university courses of study meet the needs of students and, by extension, those of the general public for accurate information on this particular region, the authors of this chapter initiated a project at Rutgers, the State University of New Jersey, in 1987 to survey existing programs and course offerings at accredited institutions of higher education throughout the nation. Its aims were, first, to determine the place and state of Middle East studies at undergraduate and graduate levels and, second, to utilize these findings as a basis for the restructuring, expansion, and improvement of the course of study in place in the university's Middle Eastern Studies.

To accomplish this objective, a comprehensive questionnaire consisting of thirty-nine items was constructed and disseminated, with a letter of explanation, to all universities listing this subject matter in their catalogues. Some of the queries contained therein were intended to collect basic information on course offerings, majors, and degree programs; on faculty size and composition; and on student recruitment and enrollment. Others sought to clarify the contents of instruction, its objectives, its underlying philosophy, and the pedagogical strategies and resources prevailing in this area. Finally a number of items attempted to identify those culture-based judgments, misconceptions, and stereotypes commonly manifested by American and Middle Eastern students toward each other and their respective countries, as noted by their instructors. This information would be treated as strictly confidential.

A total of forty-one survey forms, duly filled out, were returned to the investigators out of the ninety-eight that had been initially disseminated; these responses included all contacted major universities, as well as a representational sample of smaller institutions. The corpus was analyzed and the results recorded; wherever deemed appropriate, an item analysis was performed that yielded frequency distributions. The data were subsequently organized into six categories: program information, faculty, students, course contents, course methods, and cultural interference in instruction. The outcome of this classification was then examined in each group to detect potentially prevailing trends within specific areas, and the findings derived from this analysis were described in a report; they are summarized in the next section.

THE NATURE OF MIDDLE EASTERN STUDIES IN THE UNITED STATES

If any general conclusion may be drawn from the survey conducted at Rutgers, it is that Middle East studies have not proliferated in the United States and that significant variations do exist among programs now in existence throughout the nation.

Most of the programs appeared to have been established in the 1970s, with one notable exception, a course of study initiated in 1788, and reorganized in 1978. Very few of these offerings had been revised since their inception, and none appeared to have been subjected to periodic review. Although there were some indications of planned expansion at selected universities, a majority of the contacted institutions stated that, at the present time, they intended to maintain a status quo in program size and curriculum content (a ratio of 2.25 to 1).

When these results were examined in the context of the relatively low rate of responses obtained in the survey, they hinted at the potential presence of lacunae (gaps) in academic programs that could account, at least in part, for the lack of public interest and knowledge about the Middle East in the United States. This particular observation was found to be consistent with current scholarly assessments of international education in this country as minimal and relatively ineffectual in counteracting the parochial world-view of American students. The implications of such a state of affairs were outlined by Woyach in 1982, who felt that U.S. citizens were ill prepared on world matters because they held[12] "an elementary conceptual map of the world coded primarily in terms of whether other people or foreign events are good, bad, relevant, or indifferent to American welfare. And the conceptual maps are often based on misperceptions, distortions, and gross simplifications" (p. 18). This scholar attributed the narrowness of this outlook to the inadequacies of public school instruction, which he saw as a combination of ill-trained teachers, undifferentiated textbooks, and institutional resistance to change.

That this undesirable status quo persists today was made clear by Derek Bok, former president of Harvard University in his 1990 Annual Report, where he highlighted the need to "emphasize foreign languages and international studies in order to prepare students for an interdependent world."[13] In so doing, Bok identified once again a significant flaw in American education.

Existing Programs in Middle East Studies

The survey yielded the following information on available options for specialization in Middle East studies: six universities were found to possess a fully fledged program, both at the undergraduate and graduate levels, with a Ph.D. alternative in only one case; three others included a course of study leading to a Bachelor of Arts degree; and an additional two listed a Master of Arts degree in this field. All but two of the remaining institutions offered courses on the Middle East as a component of related programs such as International Relations, Asian Studies, Political Science, and Social Studies among others. It seems logical to assume, subject to further verification, that the curriculum of those colleges that failed to participate in the study did not encompass any specialized offerings related to the subject matter under investigation.

The oldest program in existence had been created in 1788 (reviewed in 1978), and the most recent one had been set up in 1983 (unchanged to date). Elsewhere, revisions had occurred after periods ranging from eight to eighteen years at the undergraduate level, and from six to ten years in graduate schools. Most of the courses of study were located in liberal arts programs, and the primary reasons cited for their initiation included the need to diversify offerings or to fulfill a need and special interest on the part of a faculty member. The comprehensiveness of course offerings reported by each respondent varied considerably: for full programs, the listings ranged from seven to forty-six courses for a Bachelor's degree, and from two to thirty-three for a Master's degree in Middle East studies. For related programs, the lowest number of catalogue entries was three, and the highest was twenty-eight. Two out of three universities indicated the possibility of expanding offerings "at a future date," but they did so without reference to a specific time frame. As for subject content, Middle East history, languages, and politics constituted the basic requirements for a major in the field.

This information may be taken to serve as a confirmation that the academic community has not, on the whole, exhibited more than a minimal interest in disseminating knowledge about an area of the world that has been viewed as a constant source of unrest in international circles. At the time of the study, the extent of this inactivity could be gauged by the fact that only one new Middle East program had been initiated in the last decade, in 1983. When this fact is viewed in the context of global issues affecting the world community, it is somewhat surprising, given the recurrence of Arab-Israeli conflicts, international and civil wars, and "terrorist" activities associated with the Middle East; it is moreover incomprehensible, given the impact of the Iran hostage situation that involved the U.S. government and its people directly with a seemingly hostile revolution. In light of this fact, one cannot help but wonder what effect, if any, and with what time lag the Iraqi annexation of Kuwait and the subsequent United States–led war against Iraq will have on American education, despite the increased American involvement in the region.

Faculty Members in Middle East Studies Program

An individual's perception of world events and other societies is both culture-bound and ethnocentric by virtue of one's upbringing in a specific environment. Thus, an American's view of Jordan's position today vis-à-vis Iraq will differ considerably from that of a

Jordanian, as well as that of other citizens in Arab countries. In the field of international studies, as well as that of foreign language education, the need to present multiple viewpoints to the students has long been recognized as means of providing them with the "multinational perspective" advocated by Banks to ensure mutual understanding among the people of earth.[14] In university programs, these ideal conditions may be achieved through the size of professorial staff, to ensure a sufficiently diverse presentation of interpretations on world events, and through the implementation of "bipartisan" faculty appointments, that is to say individuals of Middle Eastern as well as American backgrounds in the case at hand.

To obtain information in this area, the questionnaire sought to determine the number of full-time and part-time personnel appointed to Middle East programs, their respective national origins, their professional background, and the extent of their international experience. Responses indicated that one university maintained a faculty of seventy full-time specialists to serve the needs of students enrolled in both graduate and undergraduate courses of study; other institutions combined a staff of full-time instructors (ranging in number from one to seventeen), with teaching assistants (one to six), and part-timers.

At the undergraduate level, none of the faculty members had been born and educated strictly in the Middle East; however, 20 percent of those who had originated from that region had studied there as well as in the United States. Another 10 percent of the professors, all of whom were native-born Americans, had attended universities in both the United States and the Middle East.

Graduate programs were handled by a mixed team of individuals born and educated in this country and Middle Easterners educated here and in their native lands; the two groups were approximately equal in numbers. Three instructors had come from Europe. Similar situations existed in institutions where course were offered and no Middle East program existed.

This information would tend to indicate that staffing may be an area of weakness only at the undergraduate level. There, instruction may suffer from a monocultural, anglocentric bias that is likely to be detrimental to the achievement of an objective international outlook on world interaction in general, and U.S.-Middle East relation in particular.

Student Bodies in Middle East Studies

Personal experience with another way of life is commonly thought to be enriching. Although the ideal situation would be a total immersion in the day-to-day existence of members of a foreign society, a viable alternative may also be found in the interactions that take place on campus between American and foreign students, especially among those who are enrolled in the same programs. To ascertain the nature of student experiences in an informal context, the researchers requested data on the size of the student body and on their national origins.

The collected data revealed that the ratio of learners enrolled in Middle East programs to the total school population was generally low, ranging from .01 to 1 percent at the undergraduate level, and from 0.7 to 4.5 percent in graduate divisions. In actual numbers, these percentages represented 100 to 1,300 individuals pursuing a Bachelor's degree in this field, as opposed to 10 to 300 young men and women earning a Master's degree. In the former case, the predominant nationality of the enrollees was American (89 to 100 percent), with a minimal contingent of Middle Easterner (5 to 10 percent), and a sprinkling of other foreign nationals. Statistics were somewhat different in the latter situation, where a larger proportion of students came from the Middle East (5 to 50 percent); the American group ranged from 30 to 100 percent of the total student body, with other countries represented as well, but only in scattered numbers.

All but one university planned to increase local enrollment, primarily by means of a systematic recruitment campaign, scholarships, career-oriented courses, and featuring guest lecturers from the Middle East. The method most frequently selected by the respondents as a particularly effective means of attracting new applicants included word-of-mouth advertisement and dissemination of recruitment literature, such as brochures and catalogues.

The distinct university interest in expanding the size of their American enrollment in Middle East studies, combined with the greater exposure of those enrolled in the graduate programs than those engaged in undergraduate studies to bipolar perspective on the Middle East (ensured by the presence of both Americans and Middle Easterners on the faculty) may be taken as positive factor that should, ideally and eventually, result in the propagation of more accurate information concerning this part of the world than has been heretofore available in this country, both to the general public and public officials.

Course Content in Middle East Studies

The region known as the Middle East suffers from what may be defined as an ambiguous identity. There are, indeed, very few Americans who would be able to name more than six to eight of the most well-known nations located in that area. In fact, some of the "lesser" countries may be overlooked at times by specialists in the field. This fact was noted in the survey, where Afghanistan, Cyprus, and Pakistan were frequently omitted from the respondents' definitions of the Middle East.

Given these circumstances, a comprehensive coverage of the target area is hardly to be expected in university programs. This assumption was tested in the survey. Four key issues in 1987, which the researchers considered to be especially significant to international relations, were selected for inclusion in the questionnaire to serve as an index of course content: the Iranian Revolution, the Iran-Iraq War, recent (since the late 1970s) developments in Middle East–U.S. policies, and the Lebanese-Palestinian question. The Arab-Israeli conflict was omitted not only because it had received disproportionate attention, but also to allow these other issues to stand out in the questionnaire.

Institutional responses showed the first issue to be addressed in at least one and, at most, three courses, the second and third ones in one to four courses, and the last in one to seven courses. The latter topic was clearly the one most thoroughly treated in existing curricula. This was partly because of the impact of the Arab-Israeli conflict on the Lebanese-Palestinian question. Similar trends were noted in those college offerings outside of a specialized degree program, except for the fact that their syllabi stressed new developments in Middle East–U.S. policies over the Lebanese-Palestinian question as a major area of concern.

In terms of subject content, all undergraduate programs highlighted history, and all but two checked Political Science and Religion as essential to an adequate understanding of the Middle East; some also included Language–Area Study but seemingly reluctantly and only as a last choice. Graduate programs, as well, assigned their priority to History, Political Science, and Religion, but they also added Art to their listing, whereas Language–Area Study was omitted entirely by four institutions. Considered of least importance across the board were the disciplines of Psychology, Philosophy, and Geography. Course offerings elsewhere placed an emphasis on Religion and Political Science at the undergraduate level, and History and Religion at the graduate level.

Worthy of note is the fact that responses to the question on which four courses were most significant for Middle East specialization diverged somewhat from the identifications outlined in the previous paragraph. Here, survey participants cited Middle East Languages and International Relations (or Cultural Anthropology) as being of equal importance to History or Political Science and Religion. There was no reference remotely suggestive of International Communication, Human Relations, or Geography. The preeminence assigned by universities to the disciplines was evidently a reflection of the primary objectives of their programs, which was to impart to the students an "understanding of Middle East policies," rather than a more global comprehension of the assumptions and expectations underlying these decrees, and the mode of reasoning followed by those responsible for their definition and implementation.

The Emerging "Expanded" Approach

The inclusion of Middle East Languages and Cultural Anthropology among the four courses prioritized by participating institutions is particularly interesting, for it suggests a possible shift in professorial orientation from the narrow, traditional study of foreign nations, based strictly on concrete aspects of civilization, to a more inclusive one that would consider as well those psychosocial factors reflective of the basic world-view of a given society, which determine its modus operandi in international relations. This change in scholarly approach is, indeed, long overdue in a country that has pioneered research in intercultural communication and, as noted earlier, actually established it as a legitimate field of knowledge worthy of scholarly interest.

To illustrate this point, one need only consider the immediate implications of a culture-bound evaluation of contending positions in the current crisis in the Middle East. For U.S. citizens, the American presence in Saudi Arabia and on the Iraqi border was an exercise in brinkmanship conveying a sense of doom, which cannot be easily assuaged as a result of the stereotyped "terrorist" frame of reference associated with anything "Arab" or Muslim in this country. Such misgivings are amply justified, given the equivocal nature of past American foreign policies toward, and transactions with, other governments in that part of the world.

An objective assessment of the situation may be attained, however, through the application of cross-cultural communication principles. Basically, such an approach entails a radical shift in human perception, from a purely ethnocentric, monocultural viewpoint to a broad-based, multinational consideration of all relevant factors, one grounded on a careful examination of the respective positions adopted by all the nations (including Iraq and the United States) involved in the event, *as perceived and interpreted by them*. Without a clear understanding of those internal and external conditions likely to affect the crisis and its outcome, no action should have been taken. Such conditions should encompass both intangible elements, such as the national character and status of each country in the world community, and concrete factors, such as estimates of military capability, based on personnel and armament statistics.

In this respect, a case in point may be derived from past history through a pursual of a perceptive analysis of the Nazi defeat in World War II, featured in an unusual text on intelligence factors affecting foreign relations, written by Platt, a retired Army Brigadier-General, in 1961.[15] In this landmark document, the writer ascribed the Allies' victory to Hitler's decision not to invade Great Britain after Dunkirk. He further attributed this ill-fated verdict to the German High Command's erroneous perception of the British as "a thoroughly defeated enemy" who would, according to Teutonic logic, inevitably sue for peace in the face of overwhelming odds. It was, he noted, a military error traceable to the generals' failure to factor the English national character (the "bulldog mentality") in an, otherwise, realistic assessment of their opponent's defense capability. This faulty evaluation was, in fact, an ethnocentric blunder that eventually tolled the death knell of the Nazi regime.

Given the cross-cultural limitations of government leaders at present, exemplified in the recurrent frictions characterizing foreign relations, a short-range prognosis on future events in the Middle East would not be overly favorable, were it not for one single redeeming factor—the global nature of international reactions to the Persian Gulf Crisis. If any approximation of cross-cultural understanding may be achieved in the current situation, it will arise from a consensus in the United Nations on what constitutes an equitable solution to the problem, for such an agreement may be reached only through public articulation, consideration, negotiation, and resolution of culturally diverse positions on the issue at hand. To this extent, then, the United Nations Organization is a unique force in the world community: by virtue of its heterogeneous membership, it has been led to assume an unanticipated and much needed role in international relations, that of "cultural mediator," whose primary function is to interpret and reconcile the divergent world-views, assumptions and expectations of contending countries.

The expanded role of the United Nations, however, does not release individual countries from their respective responsibilities in the formulation of viable foreign policies. And for those occupying a privileged position among their peers, there is the added obligation of providing guidance for the needed changes in international relations. Such modifications should include a redefinition of *leadership*, a shift in world-view from a monolithic to a pluralistic outlook on world events, and more important still, the creation of a new framework for the determination of international policies consonant with the egalitarian conditions of an interdependent world. Most assuredly, these major changes in the traditional modus operandi of national governments are unlikely to be implemented overnight, even in the United States where the maintenance of a status quo in any human endeavor tends to be equated with fossilization.

In terms of long-range planning, education clearly offers the best opportunity to foster a measure of international sophistication among American citizens. At the university level, there is a need to initiate a comprehensive course of study, designed to develop within selected groups of individuals the cross-cultural skills and language-area expertise that will be required of professionals involved in overseas interactions, if they are to represent the nation's interests effectively in an international community of equals.

If one examines the state of Middle East studies from this premise, the "expanded" approach noted in the responses to the Rutgers University survey may be judged as a step in the right direction. Should this trend persevere, the continued diversification of such programs may be expected eventually to produce graduates endowed with "bicultural or multicultural literacy"—the ability to perceive and interpret foreign events from possibly divergent perspectives and to anticipate the alternative outcomes of policy decisions made in response to these events. Middle East experts empowered with such skills would be of priceless value to international relations, for they would become the cornerstones of the "new diplomacy" in the United States, one truly expressive of democratic ideals.

Instructional Methods and Resources in Middle East Studies

The most common methods of instruction associated with existing Middle East programs included class discussions, individual projects, lectures, collateral readings, and media presentations, in that order, at the undergraduate level; they centered on individual projects, collateral readings, lectures, class discussions, and seminars in the graduate divisions. These preferences for flexible classroom approaches (particularly in advanced studies), which are known to stimulate learner participation in the instructional process, were less evident in courses offered under related majors: there, lectures still prevailed, although some allowances were made by professors for the inclusion of occasional group discussions, collateral readings, and media presentations as an adjunct to teacher-directed presentations. Guest speakers, as a rule, were accorded a low ranking on the survey, a finding that may, perhaps, be ascribed to budgetary restrictions.

Somewhat less progressive tendencies were evidenced in the responses with respect to instructional resources, which placed textbooks unanimously at the head of the list, followed by more diversified options, such as journal articles, trade publications, and monographs.

Given the inflexible nature of time-honored scholarly tradition, the very fact that a variety of instructional strategies are apparently implemented at universities participating in the survey is encouraging, for it points to an awareness, on the part of faculty members, of the need to expose their students to multiple viewpoints to prevent them from developing a monolithic conception of the Middle East, one that would serve only to reinforce their ethnocentrism and perpetuate their biased interpretation of U.S.–Middle East interactions.

CULTURAL INTERFERENCE IN INSTRUCTION

One of the major problems encountered by university instructors in courses on the Middle East was that of coping with those misperceptions and stereotypes that students bring to bear on the study of the subject matter, most of which are derived from their exposure to the distorted portrayal of foreign nations prevailing in the mass media. Both American and Middle Eastern individuals enrolled in the surveyed programs displayed similarly discriminatory tendencies toward each other's nations. An outline of some of the common misconceptions reported in the collected data follows. They are equally outrageous, regardless of their origin.

First, from the American viewpoint came the following misconceptions:

Misinformation about the Middle East

The Middle East is populated by Arabs and Jews.

All Arabs are Muslims; and Palestinians are a sort of tribe.

All Israelis are Zionists and are of European stock; there are no Arabs in Israel.

The Middle East is anti-American.

The Middle East sees only the Arab side in the Arab-Israeli conflict.

The United States is always right.

Stereotypes of the Middle East

All Arabs are devious, lascivious; they are terrorists and religious fanatics.

The Middle East is a backward, fabulously wealthy area, fraught with violence.

Arab men oppress women.

From the Middle Eastern viewpoint came the following misconceptions:

Misinformation about the United States

The United States is a country without religion.

The United States is controlled by Jews and by Zionist propaganda.

All Americans have a strange family life.

The United States has an incomprehensible political system.

The United States is anti-Middle East.

The United States sees only the Israeli side of the Arab-Israeli conflict.

Stereotypes of the United States

All Americans are naive and unfriendly; they are uninformed about international events and obsessed with sex; they are materialistic and have little spiritual life.

The United States is a hostile country and treats the Middle East in an unfair manner; it is an imperialistic country.

American men are controlled by women.

What is particularly striking about these misjudgments is the fact that they illustrate a well-known phenomenon in cross-cultural communication—the mirror-image effect noted by Bronfenbrenner in her study of U.S.-Soviet interactions.[16] In this process, the mutually negative feelings of two societies toward each other are frequently complementary and parallel in nature. Thus, in the case at hand, both Middle Easterners and Americans hold reciprocal views that "the others" are permeated with violence, hostility, and sexual obsession, and that they treat the other nation in an unfair manner. What is significant is the fact that neither side perceives the irrationality and injustice of such summary judgments, nor do they consider the possibility of accepting part of the blame for their failure to interact positively and productively with each other.

The misconceptions and stereotypes listed in the questionnaire responses are particularly meaningful, for they reveal the depth of ignorance and confusion found among American and Middle Eastern students about their respective countries. This confirmation of cultural illiteracy on the part of individuals who belong to the intellectual elite of both societies, further substantiated the researchers' premise that had originally prompted the study—that the unsuccessful nature of U.S.–Middle East relations over the years could be traced to a combination of natural ethnocentrism and inadequacies in international education.

In all fairness, however, it should be pointed out that the world-views and ways of life found in the Eastern and Western parts of the world are so radically different and mutually incompatible that they can neither be mutually understood, nor easily accepted without assistance. As Fisher noted in his study of international negotiations, there is too much "noise" in cross-cultural encounters to permit an accurate exchange of information, for it interferes with a person's ability to see others as they really are.[17]

To explore this notion in the target area, the researchers included an item in the questionnaire seeking to identify specific concepts associated with Middle Eastern and American cultures that would be particularly difficult to understand from an alien frame of reference.

Those Middle Eastern concepts alien to American comprehension included the following:

General Concepts

The mixture of religion and politics.

The religious structure, and the pervasiveness of religion (Islam and others) in daily life.

The legitimacy of martyrdom for religious and political beliefs.

The antiimperialism and nationalism of the people.

The Arab-Israeli problem.

The goals of the Palestinians.

The Middle Eastern resentment at being unable to rule without external interference.

Cultural Patterns

Individual roles in society (mediator, male-female).

Public modesty.

The stress on appearance at the expense of honesty.

The greater concern for good relations than for efficiency.

The ability to live with ambiguity.

The flexible concepts of time and space.

Those American concepts alien to Middle Eastern Comprehension included the following:

General Concepts

The separation of church and state.

The status of religion as a private matter.

U.S. foreign policies.

U.S. support of Israel.

The U.S. government's inability to understand where its interests lie.

The U.S. stress on democratic principles and procedures.

The unsophistication of Americans about the outside world.

Cultural Patterns

The openness of male-female relations.

The emphasis on pleasure and sex.

The stress on frankness at the expense of appearances.

The greater concern for efficiency than for good relations.

The rigid concepts of time and space.

The critical conceptual and cultural divergences that separate the Middle Eastern from the Western world are so antithetical that they resist reconciliation, and a mere imparting of accurate knowledge through lectures and outside readings is unlikely to produce significant changes within those exposed to it. In recognition of this problem, human relations and cross-cultural training programs always include a practical component, designed to provide the trainees with an experience in culture shock survival under controlled conditions. Such an activity may consist of a simulation game, in which the learners interact with members of an "alien" society and, later on, examine the process they went through in terms of conflicts and alternative resolutions.

Although the survey respondents were fully aware of the difficulties encountered by their students in translating theoretical information into practice at the cognitive, affective, and psychomotor levels of behavior, none of them listed role playing activities as a means of actualizing for them the "worlds" of other societies. They did, however, offer several other recommendations to achieve this goal: exposure to international scholars, media presentations, sharing of personal experiences, and class discussions on aspects of life in a foreign land.

Although the suggested strategies may succeed in lessening the provincial outlook of individuals about foreign societies to some extent, nevertheless, it is doubtful that they would substantially reduce their innate prejudicial attitudes toward alien cultures, much less foster within them those skills of intercultural understanding that are essential to productive international relations. Under the circumstances, the products of such instruction could not, by any means, measure up to those rigorous standards of bicultural literacy that should be expected from bona fide Middle East specialists: the ability to analyze and interpret world events from a dual perspective; and to assist in the formulation of U.S. policies through the accurate prediction of Middle Eastern motives, expectations, actions, and reactions and, in so doing, to correct the flaw of Eurocentric bias noted by Dahlberg in existing theories of international relations.[18]

In retrospect, it seems clear that the results of the Rutgers survey do not only confirm those of previous studies cited in the present chapter, namely that the American people are generally lacking in international knowhow, particularly with respect to the Middle East; they also identify one major source of the problem—the inadequacy of Middle East studies in higher education. Quantitatively, graduate and undergraduate programs and courses currently in place are not sufficient in number to ensure an appreciable dissemination of objective information to educate Americans. And, qualitatively, the nature of those courses of study is such that, despite unmistakable signs of dissatisfaction with the status quo on the part of faculty members and a receptiveness to explore alternative options, university programs must still be rated as primarily traditional and restricted to factual content unlikely to generate the nucleus of U.S. Middle Eastern culture "mediators" so desperately needed today in a world threatened by recurrent international crises.

MIDDLE EAST EDUCATION VERSUS GLOBAL EDUCATION

Although Middle East education is growing slowly, global education has grown rapidly of late.[19] Many educational leaders feel that there is no other curriculum alternative in a twelve-hour world. Positive trends in the teaching of regional and international understandings are beginning to emerge and are being included in the American school curriculum at all levels of instruction. A number of educators and others are taking initiatives to counteract "international illiteracy" and "cultural diversity ignorance" long prevalent in our schools and society. They are calling for a more tolerant, inclusive, and realistic vision of American identity and non-Anglo-Saxon cultures than now exists. One important example of such initiatives is a report, "One Nation, Many Peoples: A Declaration of Cultural Independence," which was submitted to the New York state education commissioner in June 1991.[20]

The report, according to an editorial in the *New York Times,* "offers a thoughtful approach to social studies, emphasizing analysis rather than rote learning."[21] It repudiates the prevalent emphasis on Americanization and assimilation of non-Anglo-Saxon cultures; it equally rejects parcelling American history into incompatible histories of diverse ethnic groups. Rather, it attempts to give equal weight to the *pluribus* and *unum.* Thus, in a "key sentence," the report states that "Social studies should seek to make clear the common concerns, achievements and aspirations that are the source of national unity, but also the distinctive historical roles, traditions and contributions of the different peoples who together have struggled to create the United States."[22] The report underscores the "right to cultural diversity" and urges the reflection of "cultural interdependence" in the classroom. Teachers, it maintains, must learn to "struggle with contradictions" and students must be taught to develop concepts rather than master large and ever-increasing amounts of information. The report also provides guidelines for amending the teaching of history and social studies in the state's public schools for giving greater recognition to the role of nonwhite cultures in American society. It also sets to correct a variety of terms wrongly prevalent in books on world history and geography such as *Middle East* or *Far East*. It criticizes many history texts long used in the public schools as insensitive to minority cultures and recommends new approaches. In particular,

> Columbus would not be proclaimed as the discoverer of America, but as a voyager to an already settled land. Schoolchildren would then debate among themselves his significance in the continent's history.
>
> Thanksgiving would not be described simply as a joyous holiday. It would be presented as a day that some cultural groups have come to see as a cause for celebration but that other groups believe should be a day of mourning. Schoolchildren would be encouraged to discuss why this is so.
>
> There would be no slaves in the antebellum South. Instead, there would be "enslaved persons," a distinction the panel described as critical to helping schoolchildren understand that slavery was a condition into which people were forced, not a chosen role like "gardener, cook or carpenter."
>
> Its most controversial specifics call[s] for replacing such terms as Oriental with Asian, Middle East with Southwest Asia and North Africa, [Far East with East Asia], slaves with enslaved persons and minorities with "part of the world's majorities."[23]

The report also calls for teaching students to see "race as a cultural phenomenon, not a physical description," eliminating the use of white male examples of achievement and updating the obsolete maps in U.S. schools. Most important, in a section that, according to *New York Times,* has already "generated considerable discussion," the report asserts that the existing instruction of the European colonialization of Africa, Latin America, and Asia, among other parts of the world, "inadequately addresses the great loss of lives and the eradication of many varieties of traditional culture and knowledge." Authors of this chapter may invite attention to a similar tendency in the American media and official establishment who have emphasized the heroic victory over Iraq in the Persian Gulf War, while downplaying the great loss of Iraqi lives and colossal material and environmental damage inflicted on the region.

Although the New York report may become a turning point in multicultural studies in the United States and perhaps the world over, there has already been a steady increase in the number of area and cultural education projects being offered in social studies programs. Mandatory courses in world history and world cultures are being added to statewide high school curriculums across the nation.[24] New Jersey for example has recently required high schools to teach a third year of social studies, either World History or Global Cultures, to satisfy the need to broaden the education of students for life in the intercultural and interdependent twenty-first century. Also, at the college level, thematic courses in regional issues have been expanded in some instances. Well-supported specialized-curriculum centers for the advancement of learning about specific countries and regions have been established at a number of colleges and universities throughout the land. Most encouraging was the recognition of the need to focus national attention on geographic learning, which led to a resolution passed by both houses of Congress and signed into law by President Ronald Reagan in 1987, setting aside November 15 to 21, as Geography Awareness Week. The government action was in response to the concern that America's young people lacked basic understanding about the world around them.

Indeed, in a place map test administered in 1988 to 11,000 people in nine nations, American and Soviet citizens revealed an astonishing lack of awareness of the world around them. In the survey of their geographic knowledge, the National Geographic Society found that younger people in the Soviet Union, between ages 18 and 24, did significantly better than their American counterparts. Young Americans scored in last place for geographical knowledge among the ten nations in which the test was given. In their ability to correctly locate sixteen places on a world map (one was the Persian Gulf) American adults ranked sixth among the ten nations where the test was given, with 8.6 correct.[25] In examining attitudes on what subjects people considered important to be well educated, knowledge of geography was rated absolutely necessary by 52 percent of Russians, compared with 37 percent of Americans. Knowledge of history was rated necessary by 72 percent of Russians, compared with only 36 percent of Americans.[26]

The highly respected National Geographic Society has embarked upon a major educational campaign to upgrade geographic teaching and the furtherance of global studies in U.S. schools.[27] That organization is undertaking the funding and sponsorship of summer institutes at universities for the purpose of enhancing the teaching of geography education in the United States. Similarly important educational projects have been sponsored and aired by public TV (Public Broadcasting Service). Many private foundations and educational institutions throughout the United States have also shown an increasing interest in geographic education and awareness programs.

Universities throughout the United States are also sponsoring summer institutes, many of which focus on global education, area studies, and social science disciplines. Princeton University, for example, supported by the National Endowment for the Humanities, presented a 1988 campus summer institute for elementary and high school teachers of social studies entitled, "The Islamic Historical Experience and Its Legacy in the Contemporary Near East." Rutgers, the State University of New Jersey, held a similar summer institute in the summer of 1990, supported by a grant from the New Jersey State Department of Higher Education. University of California at Berkeley has been a leader in cross-cultural education programs in recent years. Other major universities such as Chicago, Harvard, and Columbia have also sponsored continuing education on the Middle East. The recent increase in university-conducted workshops and conferences focusing on international education, and timely regional issues, have also contributed much to the knowledge of world affairs for participants attending such meetings.

Despite the relatively recent trend in providing a wide scope of curricula offerings for global studies in the nation's schools and colleges, American students and citizens are considerably less informed about the world than their counterparts in other advanced industrial nations. Unfortunately, vested interests on the part of a substantial number of faculties in school districts throughout the nation still tend to retain existing concentrations on Western civilization progress in their curriculum offerings. Teachers are inclined to teach what they know best and therefore the introduction of courses or extensive units on the Middle East, despite the acknowledgment of the region's growing economic and strategic importance, appear to lag in establishing content priorities. In addition, the present curriculum provides a full, if not demanding, complement of courses within the prescribed time for instruction. This necessitates making critical decisions about what to relinquish in the program, what to maintain, and what to add.

And, unfortunately, the region where the dearth of knowledge and misperceptions appear to be the most pronounced is coincidentally recognized as the world's most volatile flash point—the Middle East.[28] It is this region, more than any other, that requires much greater attention in our schools and colleges and where curriculum implications loom large. Where colleges and universities have heretofore established area studies departments, it is most regrettable that Middle East course offerings still tend to lag in amount and diversity at most institutions of secondary and higher education.

Yet, restructuring the existing Middle East curricula and introducing new Middle East studies programs are now easier than ever before despite many odds. One important facilitating factor is the increasing supply of teaching materials. In particular, in the 1980s an ample supply of instructional resources dealing with the Middle East became available for school use. The Educational Film Locator of the Consortium of University Film Centers listed 115 films with subjects or titles about the Middle East.[29] Moreover many videos and film strips have been produced focusing on Middle East topics. The three largest map companies in the United States have manufactured up-to-date 44" × 32" spring roller physical or physical-political wall maps of this very important area of the world. Each company also offers 8½" × 14" desk activity maps of the region.

High school world culture textbooks now generally allocate an equal coverage of Middle East topics with other regions. *Global Insights,* the nation's leading textbook on peoples and cultures, provides six comprehensive chapters on the Middle East. The treatment covers the environment and people, the mosaic of peoples, the way of life, religion and the state, conflicts, and the Middle East today.[30] The *Enchantment of the World* set of sixty-three books about cultures of the world, written for the middle school readers, is considered America's most popular series of books in its category. Six of the titles are about Middle Eastern nations.[31]

Thus, it can be established that a reasonable supply of curriculum materials relating to the Middle East is currently available for school adoption. Regrettably, however, the underlying dilemma for those educators who realize how significant and meaningful the study of the Middle East would be for their students lies in the limitation of time. At the school level, legislatively mandated studies often preclude preempting required courses of long standing. Existing programs that are more familiar to teachers more often than not take precedence over the introduction of new courses or subjects, as vital as they may be. Educational changes, especially in regard to curriculum matters develop slowly. No matter what the urgency, the status quo tends to remain a bedrock force.

Global education and world culture courses are indeed beginning to take on greater emphasis in the social studies curriculum of U.S. schools. This is often manifested by the deemphasis of Western civilization-centered studies. The evolutionary pace for this essential revision must be accelerated. Present-day ignorance and misconceptions held by the young Americans about the Middle East in particular need to be remedied and focused on, and facts constructively taught. Events that will take place there in the years ahead, along with the history and geography of the region, may play a tremendous role in shaping their personal lives, as well as that of all citizens of the world in the twenty-first century.

RECOMMENDATIONS FOR ENRICHING MIDDLE EAST EDUCATION

On the basis of the findings derived from the Rutgers survey and other studies, we support the approach offered by the New York report and offer the following additional recommendations as guidelines for upgrading, revising, and constructing a Middle East curriculum. This should lead to the development of an enriched and diversified Middle East program, designed to meet the needs of the United States on the eve of a new century. It must be noted that the following recommendations are made for both secondary and higher education; each level, however, has its own particular requirements, and educators designing Middle East curricula should consider the specificities of each case and level of education:

1. An immediate expansion of programs and courses, paralleled by a systematic recruitment of students here and abroad.

2. The inclusion of "immersion" experiences: study abroad for undergraduate students, and exchange internships for graduate students at Middle East universities of comparable status and reputation.

3. A methodical review of existing courses of study to encompass such diversified offerings as Cultural Anthropology, Language–Area Study, Cross-Cultural Communication, and at least one Middle Eastern language taught in its appropriate cultural context.

4. A partnership between Schools of Education and Middle East programs to reach the public schools through a systematic enlightenment of their teachers about international relations in general and the Middle East in particular.

5. A diversification of instructional strategies, to provide students with experiential activities as well as theoretical knowledge about Middle East policies and international relations. Of timely value in this endeavor would be an updated version of a simulation game designed by Travis in 1975 to "teach students about the Middle East Conflict."[32] Equally useful would be an interactive pedagogy proposed by Hooshang Amirahmadi and the Bafá Bafá game, a role-playing activity involving students in interlingual-intercultural interactions.[33]

6. An understanding of the physical geography of the region and how it affects the geopolitical situation as well as life-styles of the people and their daily living.

7. An identification and characterization of the various ethnic groups that populate the area and their intergroup or international relationships.

8. Understanding the role of the family and social customs and how changes are altering traditional ways, especially amongst the young.

9. Knowledge of the three principal religions of the Middle East and their importance in shaping events there, past and present.

10. Study of the history of colonialism, nationalism, religious factionalism, and territorial disputes that have resulted in years of conflict and strife.

11. A description of contemporary issues in the Middle East today and the efforts of the people there, along with outside forces, to address problems relating to security, autonomy, sovereignty, and land disputes.

12. An appreciation of how the Middle East has played an important role in world civilization throughout much of history and how the region's past has shaped the present.

13. An awareness of the Middle East and its significance to world peace in the immediate future.

14. A knowledge of the factors that have led to the conditions contributing to the millions of dispossessed and alienated peoples in the area.

15. A knowledge of disparities in the region between the "have" nations and the "have not" nations, as well as the wide differences in resources and distribution of wealth amongst the inhabitants of the region.

16. Understanding of the need to hire contract labor from abroad to perform work in countries that are underpopulated, underdeveloped, or where native residents are disinclined to perform certain laborious tasks.

17. An appreciation of the cultural disparities, nationalism, ancient animosities, and territorial rivalries between factions in the area.

18. The need to stress the merit of peoples and nations settling disputes through direct dialogue, communication, and compromises rather than through acts of violence, terrorism, and war.

19. The realization that there is a common thread of universality among all peoples and that diversity and shared responsibility are positive elements in fostering constructive international relations.

A number of general and interdisciplinary strands also need to be woven into the fabric of the Middle East curriculum. They include these recommendations, emphases, and the following forewarning. It is imperative that course content take into account the cultural bias portrayed in the media and reflected by many U.S. citizens against those having Arab or Islamic backgrounds. The stereotypic information about the peoples and cultures of the Middle East needs to be undone. More valid and positive perceptions need to be taught. And, teachers need to be more prudent and selective in their textbook adoptions and reading lists, making sure that there are no glaring omissions in the fair treatment of Middle East issues. They also need to be certain that problems and controversial issues about the region show opposing viewpoints, objectivity, and evenhandedness. The information presented should not be based on false assumptions. Moreover, it is essential that a much wider array of courses concerned with the Middle East, both survey and in-depth, be afforded the students for their general studies requirements.

Curriculum emphasis on Middle East studies needs to include much greater utilization of maps that lead to valid geographic understandings. Even the physical dimensions of the term *Middle East* is often unclear. Geographers, foreign policy makers, media people, students, and many others have been consistently confused by the vague interpretations of its boundaries. The relationship of site and situation to geopolitics must be explored as well.

The Middle East may connote one set of parameters for religious or culture patterns of settlement, another for economic aspects, and a third criterion set by political division. The map of the Middle East provides enriching opportunities for the study of the area's etymology, which can often assist in comprehending historical origins. And a thorough examination of a physical-political map of the Middle East may also aid in explaining underlying causes for events of the past, as well as reasons for current conflicts based on the theory of "geographic determinism." The instructor must be alert and critically selective when resorting to published graphics and maps of the Middle East. Some may show a distorted projection or indicate subjective or questionable data collected to support a vested interest or special viewpoint, thus misrepresenting validity.

The Middle East curriculum needs to clarify the concept that the physical resources of the region that are so greatly coveted by foreign nations, especially oil and minerals, are not necessarily the resources most valued by the people of the region. Water actually exceeds oil in terms of local importance because its scarcity restricts the growth of Middle East economies. Both agricultural and industrial pursuits depend on its availability, and the inhabitants most often rely on it for survival. This phenomena has usually been overlooked as an important factor in teaching about political unrest in the region. Competition over water rights—which may often result in life-or-death struggles—has been a continuing factor in the area's instability since biblical times.

Teachers should underscore how a succession of powerful foreign forces have craved Middle East resources for centuries. The former USSR's quest for warm water ports to her south, Britain and France's interest in controlling the trade of the eastern Mediterranean, and the existing goal of the United States to maintain access to Persian Gulf oil have frequently clashed with regional and national interests. Middle East countries have often been helpless to prevent their past dominance, exploitation and invasions.

The curriculum essentials of the Middle East need to focus on the common people of the region and their internal and domestic concerns and events, such as injustices, power struggles, population pressures, and other pertinent, perennial aspects of life there. Examples of realistic cases and situations may be highlighted by inviting materials, speakers, and other knowledgeable resource persons to the classroom to share their experiences with students. By using short stories, videotapes of news reports, primary source documentary films, and translations from newspaper and periodical articles a more visual, realistic and current picture of events in the Middle East can be achieved.

Information about Middle East religions and customs must be taught from a neutral stance, and differences must be coupled with emphasis on similarities to the students' own religious heritages.

There should never be subtle or overt indoctrination. The teacher must be certain that religious vocabulary and theological teachings are accurately translated, or even deliberately omitted, to avoid misinterpretations and misconceptions. Teachers and students must also be careful not to equate traditional Moslem, Christian, and Judaic religious beliefs and values with the militant practices of some Middle East groups. It must be emphasized that most inhabitants of the region do not advocate lawlessness, martyrdom, hostage taking, terrorism, *jihad,* the establishment of clandestine brigades, or fundamentalism.

Both micro and macro approaches to the Middle East need to include topical coverage about its economic importance, yesterday and today. As a focal center of three continents its significance to African, Asian, and European trade should not be minimized. Its raw materials and resources are strategic worldwide. Global positions on foreign policy, diplomacy, geopolitical strategies, international relations, and most important, military planning must take the most recent economic statistics of the region into its analyses and projections. Accounts of gross national production figures, trade relationships, per capita incomes, living standards, technological advancements, and employment status are all indicators of the economic and political climates found in the region, often identifying which regimes may be stable or unstable—and to what degree there will be nationalization, socialism, capitalism, or even communist inroads manifesting themselves within the country. Many of the aforementioned factors are curriculum imperatives.

In teaching the Middle East one must stay abreast of all fast-moving political changes taking place. Zionism and communism have made their presence felt there in the twentieth century. So has religious fundamentalism and Arabism as personified by past and present aggressive would-be leaders attempting to dominate Middle Eastern nations through their political and military actions. Soviet and American rivalries with their selective arms sales, political pressures, and economic interests in supporting various states and factions in the region are as keen as ever. The vital interests of the Third World alignments must be treated as well. The issue of petroleum exports and acute socioeconomic disparities have been and remain a major factor in the stabilization and destabilization of the region. The perplexing problems of Lebanon, religious struggles, the quest for ethnic and cultural self-determination, the claims of the Kurds, the Iran-Iraq War, the Arab-Israeli confrontations, and various revolutionary threats deserve periodic reviews. Special attention needs to be directed toward the cause and effect of the Iraq-Kuwait Conflict of 1990 and the subsequent United States–led war against Iraq. The real possibility of a coup d'efat or a rapid change in a regime could be imminent almost anywhere in the region at any time.

The age-old history of colonialism, the independence movements, the past centuries of foreign imperialistic rule, religious warfare, expansionism, and the role of the United Nations in the region all need to be listed as topical curriculum guidelines worthy of inclusion in the syllabus. Curriculum implications need to go beyond the study of major problems, and issues. Subtopics such as cultural contributions of Islamic civilization, the kibbutz movement, education, Arabic language and literature, holy places, biographies, religious practices and customs, Muslim women, and village life are but a few of the many interesting subjects that may be treated in depth during a Middle East course. They may be investigated and learned through special lectures, films, assigned readings, research studies, case studies, and the use of an array of oral history procedures with people having direct experience or expertise in the area.

In sum, to achieve a more emphatic understanding of the Middle East it is imperative that the curriculum of the area include the following seven teaching components. Students should (1) understand the basic political, physical and economic geography of the region; (2) become familiar with the correct meaning, pronunciation and spelling of Middle East terms, places, and names; (3) understand the general, if not specific, time chronology of the sequence of Middle East events during past and recent historical periods; (4) study and have an appreciation of the Middle East's predominant religions (Judaism, Eastern Christianity, and Islam) and their roles in shaping modern institutions there and elsewhere; (5) endeavor to be objective and maintain a balanced nonjudgmental, critical attitude about the many emotional and controversial issues in the region; (6) dismiss media-generated stereotypes and exaggerated hypes and misconceptions that are often invalid or negative about Middle East people and their customs and characteristics; and (7) be aware of the Middle East's major importance in world affairs and geopolitical relationships.

There needs to be much more critical thinking and problem solving about Middle Eastern issues: the traditions, political behaviors, conflicts, ideologies, economies, tensions, and foreign policy. Understanding would best be served if the curriculum writers and teachers were to put more instructional attention on the underlying causes and effects that go to shape regional matters there. And major inquiries directed toward the "why" rather than the "what" need to be specified within the course guide.

The Middle East curriculum should certainly allow enough pliability and latitude for the instructors and students to introduce for class consideration and evaluation any serious and well thought-out proposal, theory, or hypothesis, no matter how provocative or unique it may appear. The Middle East region is much too strategic and explosive to discount or disregard any possible solution to the seemingly insurmountable age-old problems existing there.

Finally, at the high school level, one possible way for Middle East education to make incursion into the tightly insulated, if not saturated, social studies programs is for the teacher to construct mini-seminar units based on Middle Eastern themes. They can readily evolve around a timely current event or contemporary affair. Here the very effective present to past principle of teaching can be utilized.

These suggestions are not simply the product of interdisciplinary speculations based on data collection, analysis, and interpretation; they also represent a workable plan of action now being enacted at the Middle Eastern Studies Program at Rutgers University. Its implementation has included a variety of activities, such as conferences and seminars on the Middle East, the involvement of Rutgers University professors in widely different subject fields to design and field test instructional modules on aspects of the Middle East as integral components of selected course syllabi, and the introduction of new courses in the target area. Faculty and student responses to these innovations have been, so far, most favorable, as have been the assessments of outside specialists brought in to evaluate program activities and products.

As matters stand now in the real world outside the sheltered confines of academe, the global involvement of countries in the search for a solution to Middle East crises has clearly placed university programs relevant to this area on the cutting edge of international education. It is, therefore, imperative that institutions of higher education in the United States initiate the revisions tentatively identified by their respective faculties to develop the needed goal of skilled specialists in that field. Simultaneously, a redirection of scholarly attention is needed away from the compartmentalized, classical approach to research of yesteryear, toward a collaborative, interdisciplinary exploration of worldwide issues that threaten peace and human survival. It is only through such innovations that the quality of academic knowledge imparted on the Middle East will achieve the ideal envisioned by Banks—the creation of a society, endowed with a multinational perspective on world affairs, whose leaders understand the intricacies of "foreign" minds and have the vision to formulate policies ultimately beneficial to all humankind.[34]

NOTES

1. Ali Mazrui, *Cultural Forces in World Politics* (London: James Currey, 1990).

2. S. Szalay *et al.*, "U.S.-Arabic Communication Lexicon of Cultural Meanings," *Monograph*. (Washington, D.C.: Institute of Comparative Social and Cultural Studies, 1978).

3. William A. Dorman and Mansour Farhang, *The U.S. Press and Iran: Foreign Policy and Journalism of Deference* (Berkeley: University of California Press, 1987).

4. Elahe Mir-Djalali, "The Failure of Language to Communicate," *International Journal of Intercultural Relations* 4 (1980): 307–28.

5. Tsan-Kuo Chang *et al.*, "Determinants of International News Coverage in the U.S. Media," *Communication Research* 14, no. 4 (August 1987): 396–414.

6. Noam Chomsky, "Middle East Terrorism and the American Ideological System," *Race and Class* 28, no. 1 (1986): 13.

7. Herman Kahn, *The Emerging Japanese Superstate, Challenge and Response* (Englewood Cliffs, N.J.: Prentice Hall, 1971).

8. Masami Atarashi, "Culture as an Explanation or an Excuse," presentation at the Symposium on U.S.-Japan Relations in the 1990s, East-West Center, University of Hawaii, 1989.

9. Orin D. Parker et al., "Cultural Clues to Middle Eastern Students," in Joyce Merrill Valdes, ed., *Culture Bound* (Cambridge, Mass.: Cambridge University Press, 1987).

10. John P. Fieg and John G. Blasi, *There Is a Difference* (Washington, D.C.: Meridian House International, 1975).

11. Edward Hall, *The Silent Language* (New York: Doubleday and Co., 1959).

12. Robert B. Woyach, "Enriching International Studies in the Schools: New Directions for ISA," *International Studies Notes* 9, no. 2 (Summer 1982): 18–22.

13. Derek Bok, "Annual Report," *Harvard Graduate School of Education Alumni Bulletin* 34, no. 3 (Summer 1990), pp. 2–5.

14. James A. Banks, "Ethnic Studies as a Process of Curriculum Reform," *Social Education* 40, no. 2 (February 1976): 76–80.

15. Washington Platt, *National Character in Action: Intelligence Factors in Foreign Relations* (New Brunswick, N.J.: Rutgers University Press, 1961).

16. Urie Bronfenbrenner, "The Mirror Image in Soviet-American Relations: A Psychological Report," *Journal of Social Issues* 17, no. 1 (1961): 46–50.

17. Glen Fisher, "The Crosscultural Dimension in International Negotiations," paper presented at a Training Session of the U.S. Foreign Service Institute, Department of State, Washington, D.C. (1980), pp. 1–46.

18. K. A. Dahlberg, "The Technological Ethic and the Spirit of International Relations," *The International Studies Quarterly* 17, no. 1: 55–88.

19. Ad Hoc Committee on Global Education: "Global Education: In Bounds or Out?" *Social Education* 51, no. 4 (April–May 1987).

20. For a summary of the report and debate on its pros and cons, see *New York Times* (June 21, 1991), pp. A1 and B4.

21. "More Pluribus, More Unum," *New York Times* (June 23, 1991), p. 14.

22. Ibid.

23. *New York Times* (June 21, 1991).

24. Willard M. Kniep, "Global Education: The Road Ahead," *Social Education* 50, no. 6 (October 1986).

25. Lloyd H. Elliott, "President Grosvenor Announces the National Geographic Society Education Foundation," *National Geographic* 173, no. 3 (March 1988).

26. "Two Superpowers Failing Geography," *New York Times* (November 9, 1989).

27. *New York Times* (November 9, 1989).

28. William J. Griswold, "Middle East," *Social Education* 50, no. 5 (September 1986).

29. *Educational Film Locator of the Consortium of University Film Centers,* (New York: R. R. Bowker Company, 1980).

30. James Neil Houtula *et al., Global Insights* (Columbus, Ohio: Merrill Publishing Company, 1987).

31. *Children's Press Catalog* (Chicago: Children's Press, 1990–1991).

32. Tom Travis, "The Use of Simulation to Teach About Middle East Conflict," *International Studies Notes* 1, no. 2 (Summer 1975): 21–23.

33. Hooshang Amirahmadi, "Universalism in Planning Education: Toward an Interactive Pedagogy," *Ekistics* 55, nos. 328, 329, 330 (1988); and Garry R. Shirts, *Bafá Bafá* (Del Mar, Calif.: Simile II, 1977).

34. Banks, "Ethnic Studies."

PART 7

Conclusions

CHAPTER 13

Global Restructuring, the Persian Gulf War, and the U.S. Quest for World Leadership

Hooshang Amirahmadi

INTRODUCTION

In August 2, 1990, Iraq invaded and then annexed the tiny country of Kuwait, citing its historic claim over that territory as its prime reason. The United States reacted almost immediately by sending a 200,000-strong "defensive" force to the region to create a "Desert Shield" against possible Iraqi invasion of Saudi Arabia. President George Bush also put together an immense, though largely Western, coalition against Iraq in the United Nations and on site in the Saudi desert. The United States subsequently increased its forces to over 500,000 and declared their mission as basically "offensive." Meanwhile, twelve UN Security Council resolutions were passed against Iraq in less than a few months, an event unprecedented in the agency's forty-six-year history. The resolutions imposed a variety of demands and conditions on Iraq, including total and unconditional withdrawal from Kuwait, economic sanctions, military blockade, and reparation for the damage done to Kuwait. A final resolution before the war authorized the use of "all necessary means" against Iraq if it did not withdraw from Kuwait by January 15, 1991.[1] Iraq did not comply by the deadline and the United States—led multinational forces began their devastating air campaign against Iraq on January 16, less than six months after Iraq had invaded Kuwait. On February 28, less than forty-two days after the air war had begun and only 100 hours into the ground war, President Bush declared it all over with Kuwait liberated, the 1 million-man Iraqi army cut down to size, and its weapons of mass destruction eliminated.[2]

The United States—led "Desert Storm" has caused the near catastrophic destruction of Iraq and Kuwait and brought colossal damage to the regional ecosystem. It has also ushered in a new period in the already turbulent politics of the Middle East. Although the war's long-term and global implications remain largely unpredictable, it is generally understood that "the Middle East will never be the same again." This well-placed prediction is shared by both advocates of the status quo and those who wish to see democratic changes as a result of this first major post-Cold War confrontation. Beyond the Middle East, the United States is the one force that will be the most affected by the crisis. This is so not only because the United States has had the most critical role in the war, but also because the crisis took place at a *transitional moment* in world politics, when the Cold War era was being left behind while the shape of a substitute remained largely indeterminate.

In this chapter, I shall argue that in waging the war against Iraq, the United States was motivated by a complex set of factors, but most fundamentally by a desire to influence the shape of the emerging world order in its favor. The war was also to end the rising criticism against the Bush administration for lacking a clear vision of a new American paradigm in world leadership and for taking an allegedly anti-Israeli stand in the Arab-Israeli Conflict. Thus, the central concern of this chapter is to indicate the prospect for the U.S. quest for world leadership in the wake of the Persian Gulf War (PGW) and the ongoing global restructuring process. I shall argue that unless the domestic situation in the United States changes toward a more dynamic and all-embracing socioeconomic development, the United States may not be able to sustain its newfound world hegemonic role. Domestic politics can also impose restraints on U.S. leadership in the 1990s. Other major constraints emanate from forces seemingly external to the United States, including the emergent multipolar world, diminishing utility and acceptability of offensive force, and the lack of a new paradigm of social change and leadership. The military victory in the PGW and the near-collapse of the Soviet empire will do little to change the situation in U.S. favor.

This chapter is organized into five parts. In the first part, I focus on major U.S. motivations for its swift and decisive military intervention in the crisis. The U.S. quest for world leadership emerges as the primary reason among a web of other important objectives and interests. The second part gives a balance sheet of U.S. achievements and failures in the wake of the PGW. In the third part, I focus on the forces that may constrain the U.S. quest for world leadership in the 1990s and beyond, which include the emergence of a multipolar world and the diminishing utility of offensive (military) force. In part four, I concentrate on the reactions of the superpowers to the ongoing global changes. Finally, the arguments are concluded and a few policy recommendations are advanced.

U.S. MOTIVATIONS FOR THE PERSIAN GULF WAR

In this part, I focus on the major U.S. motivations for the swift and decisive military intervention in the Kuwaiti crisis. The U.S. quest for world leadership emerges as the primary reason among a web of other important objectives and interests. I contend that this quest for a new "pax Americana" is indicative of a shift in policy, but not a complete break from the past. The war was also to end the rising criticism against the Bush administration for not developing a clear-cut, new American paradigm of world leadership and for supposedly assuming an anti-Israeli stand in the Arab-Israeli Conflict. Next, the United States had increasingly become concerned with the changing balance of power in the Middle East. Iraq was considered, somewhat exaggeratedly, a new threat to the security of the American friends in the region, Israel in particular. In addition, there were other old as well as new concerns: oil, petro-capital, and the future of the Western alliance. These and other concerns were reflected in a series of announcements made by American officials throughout the crisis, before and after the war.

To begin with, President Bush originally cited four reasons for his swift and decisive response: reversal of the aggression, security of Saudi Arabia and the Persian Gulf states, restoration of the al-Sabah rule, and safety of Americans in the area.[3] Later, he added the oil factor, "the American way of life," Saddam Hussein's danger to Israel and the world peace (citing his weapons of mass destruction and missiles that could deliver them), and finally, the creation of a "new world order." Similar reasons were also echoed by other high-ranking American officials including Secretary of State James Baker. In a speech delivered before the Los Angeles World Affairs Council on October 29, 1990, he argued that Hussein's aggression "challenges world peace," "is a regional challenge," and "challenges the global economy" that depends on "secure access to the energy resources of the Persian Gulf"; namely, oil.[4] In other speeches and interviews, Mr. Baker asserted that the Gulf War was for the American "jobs," "pocketbook," and "standard of living."[5]

After the victory, Bush outlined his vision of a new order for the Middle East in the following four objectives: first, "to create shared security arrangements in the region," which means "American participation in joint exercises involving both air and ground forces," and "maintaining a capable U.S. naval presence in the region"; second, "to control the proliferation of weapons of mass destruction and the missiles used to deliver them"; third, "to create new opportunities for peace and stability in the Middle East" by ending the Arab-Israeli Conflict and solving the Palestinian problem, which in Bush's view "must be grounded in United Nations Security Council Resolutions 242 and 338 and the principle of territory for peace"; and fourth, to "foster economic development for the sake of peace and progress" and "economic freedom and prosperity for all people of the region."[6] Note that the two most pressing problems of the region, extreme inter- and intranational wealth and income inequality and the lack of political democracy, are not included in President's agenda for the troubled region.

President Bush also indicated that the PGW's impact will go well beyond shaping the new order in the Middle East. "Our success in the Gulf," he told Americans, "will shape not only the new world order we seek but our mission here at home." He defined the *new world order* as "a world order in which the principles of justice and fair play protect the weak against the strong; a world where the United Nations freed from the Cold War stalemate is poised to fulfill the historic vision of its founders; a world in which freedom and respect for human rights find a home among all nations. The Gulf war put this new world to its first test. My fellow Americans, we passed that test." President Bush then made a reference to his agenda "to prepare for the next American Century."[7]

How do these objectives and the "new vision" differ from the traditional U.S. interests in the region and vision of the world order? To arrive at a more informed answer, we must take a historical perspective of U.S. Middle East policy. Traditionally, the policy has been based on four pillars: (1) containment of alleged Soviet expansionism; (2) assurance of the flow of inexpensive oil to the West; (3) protection of the security of Israel; and (4) preservation of the status quo by supporting conservative and anticommunist regimes. The guiding policy principle was, however, the "Soviet threat" to the well-being of the capitalist world and to the U.S. national security. In the wake of the Iranian Revolution in 1979 and the Soviet military intervention in Afghanistan, President Jimmy Carter declared the Middle East a region of "vital interest" to the United States. This doctrine continues to guide U.S. policy in the Middle East, but the ingredients of the vital interest are changing.

Specifically, in the post-Cold War period, while the Soviet threat has disappeared, U.S. Middle East policy has sharpened its focus on oil and countering unfriendly regional powers. This is also seen as a test of a new American paradigm of world leadership in the post-Cold War period when the other superpower has temporarily left the scene. We are also witnessing a gradual return to what was once called the *Nixon Doctrine,* as indicated by talks about the formation of a new regional security system, in which U.S. friends in the Middle East will have the leading role with peripheral U.S. participation. "The Carter Doctrine" called for direct U.S. military response to external threat (that is, the Soviet threat and to a lesser extent revolutionary Iran's threat to its wealthy Arab neighbors in the Persian Gulf) to the Middle East and was in essence based on the concept of a "balance of power." The Nixon Doctrine, on the other hand, called for reliance on regional powers (subimperialists) such as the late Shah of Iran for policing the Persian Gulf, a doctrine based on hegemonic designs.

The "containment" strategy began to change following Mikhail Gorbachev's *glasnost* and *perestroika* policies, the collapse of the so-called socialist regimes in Eastern Europe, and disintegration of the Warsaw Pact. The United States no longer adheres to the Cold-War idea that the Soviet Union poses a threat to Iran, Middle East oil, or any country in the area friendly to the United States—an idea dropped by the Bush administration in early 1990.[8] Even before that date, President Bush had indicated that "the United States now has its goal much more than simply containing Soviet expansionism. We seek the integration of the Soviet Union into the community of nations."[9] The unprecedented cooperation between the United States and the USSR during the Kuwaiti crisis, the war against Iraq, and in the postwar period served only to reinforce American policy makers' view that the Soviet Union was no longer a threat to the Middle East.

In his speech at the Forty-Fifth Session of the UN General Assembly on October 9, 1990, President Bush characterized the containment strategy as an idea of the past and hinted toward a more cautiously conceived, accommodative approach to the U.S.-Soviet relations. This new approach became gradually solidified in the course of the Kuwaiti crisis and a few summit meetings between Bush and Gorbachev. According to a *New York Times* editorial, after the July 1991 summit in Moscow, the two "superpowers" will become "allies."[10] The U.S. policy makers are hardly mistaken in charting such a bold new direction. Clearly, changes in Soviet international thought are strategic, based on profound ideological rather than tactical revisions emanating from the nation's deep economic and political crisis.

The West's vulnerability to the flow of inexpensive oil was originally related to the Soviet threat, and therefore, it had developed a military and strategic dimension. However, as the Cold-War ideology faded, the United States discovered a new threat to its regional interests: unfriendly regional powers such as Iraq and Iran, which are said to possess the potential to take control of OPEC oil production and pricing away from pro-American Saudi Arabia and its Persian Gulf allies, or create instability in the status quo favorable to American interests. For the United States, the seriousness of this threat is underscored by the fact that the Persian Gulf oil reserves will last longer than other world reserves and production cost is the least expensive. This dependency on oil supplies from the Persian Gulf must also be viewed in relation to the predicted increase in demand for oil in the West and the world as a whole.[11] Meanwhile, the ailing American economy has become even more sensitive to higher oil prices and other unexpected external shocks under the prevailing conditions of a chronic fiscal deficit, trade imbalance, savings and loan crisis, and a huge public debt.[12] Thus, it is no wonder that the U.S. "vital interest" in the Middle East has increasingly become defined in terms of assuring the uninterrupted flow of inexpensive oil made possible by preserving the dominant role of Saudi Arabia within OPEC. The Bush administration's overreaction to the Kuwaiti crisis is partly explained on the basis of this concern.[13]

Yet, the threat to the flow of inexpensive oil is exaggerated. For example, even before the PGW destroyed Iraq, that country's economy was in ruin because of the Iran-Iraq War and could hardly afford to use the "oil weapon" against the West, its main customer. On the contrary, Iraq needed (and desperately needs) to sell oil at an increasing volume to maintain its huge and dependent army, import food, and reconstruct its war-devastated economy. This is also true of other countries in the Middle East, particularly those more or less hostile to the United States. These nations compete to export more oil and OPEC's main problem over the last decade has been to regulate overproduction. Indeed only the pro-Western Persian Gulf states may survive without exporting oil for a while because they have huge cash reserves. Besides, even if Iraq wanted to withhold its oil supplies, the impact on the oil market would still be marginal. As Doug Bandow has shown, "even if Saddam Hussein conquered the gulf and hung onto his empire into the next century, he would never have the sort of control over oil that the widely cited 50 percent figure implies."[14] Note also that, since August 1990, oil from Iraq and Kuwait has stopped flowing into the West. Yet the effect on world oil supplies and prices has been minimal, except for short-term fluctuations in response to speculative trading.

The experience in the 1980s also indicates that OPEC oil prices are not determined primarily by monopoly pricing but by market forces, the demand side in particular. These prices have become increasingly sensitive to transformations in the structure and level of demand in the West and Japan. Thus, the oil glut caused by Saudi and Iraqi overproduction in 1979–80 could not prevent a major price hike whereas a lesser glut in 1985–86, caused by

Saudis and Kuwaitis, depressed the price of OPEC oil significantly in 1986. Contrary to the widespread belief, OPEC in the 1980s has largely been a price taker rather than a price maker. Additionally, no single state in the Middle East, including Iraq and Saudi Arabia, has the capability to influence the oil market in the near future.

To effectively use oil as a weapon, no fewer than three or even four major OPEC producers must be able to coordinate their actions and succeed in intimidating others. The economic and political realities in the Middle East will not permit this to happen. The July (1990) OPEC meeting was able to raise the price not just because of Iraq's threat to use force against Kuwait, but also because most OPEC members, including Saudi Arabia and Iran, were disturbed by the sharp decline in oil prices in the preceding months and wanted "to see higher oil prices in the next few years."[15] It had declined to as low as $13 a barrel while OPEC's benchmark price was $18 a barrel. The sharp drop was also a source of concern for the Bush administration and the U.S. oil companies, which remained happy with the official OPEC price at the time.[16] In the post-PGW period, oil prices have risen to around where they were before the crisis (close to OPEC's prices) and the United States has made no effort to use its new-found power vis-à-vis OPEC to lower its prices.

We must also be reminded that anytime in the past several decades when Western forces intervened in the Middle East to assure a steady flow of inexpensive oil from the region, the result has been just the reverse: less oil has flown out at exorbitant prices. The so-called tankers war in 1988 in the Persian Gulf and the Kuwaiti crisis are two most recent examples. Incidently, the United States (which depends on the Middle East for less than 10 percent of its energy) remains far less vulnerable to an interruption in oil flow from the region than do other members of the OECD. Western Europe and Japan, for example, import more than 50 percent of their oil from the region. The United States also has the option of developing its own domestic oil production (an option western Europe and Japan lack) and encourage conservation as in the late 1970s. That is perhaps a more prudent energy policy than policing the Middle East oil or fighting on the side of the undemocratic oil-rich monarchs, sheikhs, and emirs in the Persian Gulf area.

From the preceding paragraphs it may be concluded that, although the United States remains very concerned about the Persian Gulf oil, the source of that concern is only partially related to its own economy. Moreover, the United States is only marginally concerned about a sharp rise in OPEC oil prices, use of oil as a political weapon by any member of OPEC, or a sudden drop in world oil supplies. The real source of the Bush administration's concern about oil and "the American way of life" should thus be located elsewhere. In particular, U.S. control over oil supplies in the 1990s and beyond will also enable it to control the world economy and directly or indirectly control the economies of two powerful competitors, Japan and Germany. From this perspective, oil has become a new medium in the U.S. quest for world leadership and consequently more vital to the United States than anytime in the past.

The nature of the Israeli dilemma for U.S. Middle East policy is also changing. While the security issue remains a source of concern, policy makers are rightly shifting attention to mitigating tension between the Arabs and the Israelis in the hope of finding an acceptable peace formula. Already in May 1989, Secretary Baker in a speech to the American-Israeli Public Affairs Committee (the Israel lobby) had called on Israel to "lay aside once and for all the unrealistic vision of a Greater Israel."[17] While the Kuwaiti crisis was in progress, President Bush stressed the need for a solution to the Palestinian question in his address to the Forty-Fifth Session of the UN General Assembly in October 9, 1990. The United States also voted with the UN Security Council twice during the same month to condemn Israel for its mistreatment of the Palestinians and the lack of cooperation with the United Nations.[18] Although the Bush administration was anxious to see that the Arab-Israeli Conflict did not become a cause for probable disintegration of the alliance against Iraq, it was also motivated by concern for the Palestinian problem.

The fact that the U.S. opposition to link the Kuwaiti and Palestinian questions was not an opposition to a settlement of the Palestinian question became evident in the post-PGW period when the new U.S. approach to the Arab-Israeli Conflict became even more visible. As noted previously, President Bush's four-point vision for the post-PGW Midale East included an important policy statement about the Palestinian question and the Arab-Israeli Conflict. He emphasized that the solution "must be grounded in United Nations Security Council Resolutions 242 and 338 and the principle of territory for peace." Days after the PGW, Secretary Baker began his "shuttle diplomacy" in the region, focusing on confidence-building measures and organization of a regional peace conference. The new diplomacy has already succeeded in making the conflicting parties participate in a largely ceremonial regional peace conference in October 1991.

There are several reasons for this change in policy. From the American and Israeli perspective, the PGW has enhanced Israeli security by destroying the Iraqi army. Israelis are, generally speaking, very pleased with President Bush for the war, the free Patriot Missile protection, and increased financial and military assistance in the aftermath of the war. Even before the PGW was over, the Israelis "present[ed] the United States with a bill: $13 billion." [19] At least another of Israel's potentially powerful enemies, Syria, is now in the U.S. camp and may also be considered as neutralized. President Hafez al Assad's concessions and acceptance of the U.S. compromise plan for a regional peace conference must be viewed from this perspective.[20] Other Arab states in the alliance against Iraq have made similar concessions and demanded that the U.S. reward them by solving the Arab-Israeli Conflict and the Palestinian problem. The United States could not afford to ignore their request because it well reflects their vulnerability to the growing domestic grass-roots pressure and Islamic radicalism.

Mounting international pressure on the United States was also evident during the Kuwaiti crisis when the Security Council was passing resolution after resolution against Iraq. The issue of the "double standard" had already become part of the criticism against the new UN-U.S. political discourse. It is also the first time in the Arab-Israeli Conflict that the United States finds itself in the middle of it. Any future cross-fire will have to go through the United States, a situation that has become a new source of concern in Washington. The Bush administration also realizes that with the Soviet Union effectively withdrawing support from its client Arab states and with the Arab states in total disarray no credible threat exists to Israel's security, now and in the foreseeable future. Indeed, Israel's security is being challenged by no other force but the Palestinians in the West Bank and Gaza, hardly a "high tech" military force. The *intifada* (uprising) there has shaken the foundations of Israeli politics and continue to undermine the state's legitimacy at home and abroad.[21]

Moreover, if a "new order" is to emerge in the Middle East under the U.S. leadership, then the Arab-Israeli Conflict and the Palestinian problem have to be resolved. The United States cannot consider itself a new world leader and yet patronize the small state of Israel, whose "strategic" value has come into question in the wake of the PGW; Egypt may indeed have already replaced that "asset" for American diplomacy in the region.[22] The increased strategic value of oil also makes it imperative for the United States to forge an even stronger alliance with the Persian Gulf states. Finally, the sharpening global economic competition so vital for securing world leadership has made Americans even more attentive to closer friendship and relations with Arab nations. From this perspective, a solution to the Arab-Israeli Conflict and the Palestinian problem also becomes a necessary component of the U.S. quest for world leadership.

One area of U.S. Middle East policy that awaits significant change is American protection for conservative and dictatorial regimes who hide their largely undemocratic practices behind their so-called pro-American policy. It is no wonder that protecting the Saudi regime and restoring the al-Sabah family rule in Kuwait were among the four-point objectives which President Bush announced when he dispatched American troops to the Saudi desert. Ironically, almost all Arab states that took sides with the democratic United States are undemocratic and abusive of human rights. They include Saudi Arabia, the Persian Gulf emirates, Morocco, Egypt, and Syria. In sharp contrast, most Arab states which sympathized with the undemocratic Iraqi regime have been experiencing democratic changes in the recent years. They include Jordan, Tunisia, Yemen, and Algeria. The House of Saud, the Emirate of Kuwait, and the United Arab Emirates are "feudal monarchies", according to a *New York Times* editorial.[23] The Kingdom of Saudi Arabia lacks a constitution and does not permit women to drive. Nor is Kuwait a democratic state. There, a fragile parliamentary process was brought to a complete halt in 1986 when the present Emir al-Sabah closed the parliament. The emir's undemocratic practices in the postwar Kuwait have become a source of embarrassment for the Bush administration who helped restore his throne. "Liberated in Kuwait" said *New York Times,* is "arrogance."[24]

Unfortunately these undemocratic regimes remain a vital component of the new American diplomacy toward oil, Arab-Israeli relations, arm sales, and the U.S. quest for world leadership in a highly uncertain post-Cold War era. This is despite the fact that communism will not be a serious threat in the foreseeable future and the rapidly changing world will make it impossible for the reform resisters and undemocratic forces to survive. Unless resolved, the contradiction between the need for preserving these regimes and their dislocation in a new world order will eventually run U.S. Middle East policy into an explosive deadlock. Which way and how soon the United States will resolve the contradiction remains largely unpredictable. As past experiences indicate, the status quo will be preserved until resistance to a change becomes untenable or it develops into a real fetter to the U.S. quest for world leadership.

Although the United States has modified some of its traditional concerns in the Middle East, it is adding new ones to the list as the world enters a new era in international relations. Most significantly, "the Soviet threat" is being replaced with threats from marginalized groups and unfriendly regional powers who tend to destabilize the emerging post-Cold War order by attempting to alter the status quo. Secretary Baker's point that Iraq represented a threat to world peace emanated from this new perspective on emerging regional powers. In his testimony before the House Foreign Affairs Committee, Mr. Baker said: "We are entering an era in which ethnic and sectarian identities could easily breed new violence and new conflicts. It is an era in which new hostilities and threats could erupt as misguided leaders are tempted to assert regional dominance before the ground rules of a new order can be accepted."[25] Although some previously less significant developing countries are growing stronger, the United States exaggerates their danger to the American interests, among other reasons, with the purpose of maintaining a sense of crisis to legitimize the continuation of the ideology of the national security state. A sense of external threat can also legitimize the maintenance of the high defense budget on which the prosperity of the U.S. military-industrial complexes depend.

Iraq is a case in point.[26] To begin with, the myth the United States created about the Iraqi military might prove to be just that: a myth.[27] The Iraqi "million-man" army which was propagated as "the fourth largest in the world" was defeated in less than forty-two days and could not sustain the ground war for more than a mere 100 hours! Iraq would have also been defeated in its war against Iran if it had not received support from the United States, the Soviet Union, France, England, Saudi Arabia, Egypt, and Kuwait, among other countries. These countries, the United States in particular, helped build and maintain the Iraqi war machinery and its weapons of mass destruction.[28] Even with such support, out of eight years of war between the two countries, no less than five years were fought inside Iraqi territory and Iran had taken at least three major Iraqi cities and ports.

Saddam Hussein's unprincipled use of the Westerners in Iraq and Kuwait as "foreign guests" or "human shields" to ward off possible American air attacks on Iraq's strategic installations should have served to underscore his extreme vulnerability to a major confrontation with the United States. The "Hitler of the new age" also did not dare to use even a drop of his chemical agents against the United States–led forces and accepted all terms and conditions that the United States–led UN Security Council imposed on Iraq for a cease-fire. The Iraqi missile attacks on Israel were also a desperate attempt to involve that country in the hope of extending its losing war to the whole of the Arab world and perhaps beyond. The "madman of Baghdad" also proved to be an intelligent survivor who could convince his enemies that he was a better choice for postwar Iraq than either the Kurdish or the Shi'ite rebels.[29]

Incidently, President Hussein's real power originated from his initial popularity among a sizeable segment of the disenchanted, poverty-stricken, and humiliated Arab masses. Yet, they were as useless to the pan-Arabist Saddam Hussein as they were to the Pan-Arabist Gamal Abdul Nasser in 1967, for they are divided into twenty-one pieces throughout a disunited Arab world mostly dominated by dictators. Hussein was not known to most Arab masses as a champion of the have-nots. On the contrary, as shown on CBS "60 Minutes" on August 11, 1991, Saddam Hussein is among the wealthiest of world leaders; he has stolen billions from the Iraqi treasury (oil revenue) and deposited them into his own bank accounts around the world. Besides, most politically active members of these Arab people belonged to Islamic movements in the region and knew that Saddam Hussein was a secular leader with little devotion to Islam as an ideology of the modern state. Saddam Hussein's hypocritic call for a "holy war" and a proposal (August 12, 1990) to withdraw from Kuwait in return for an Israeli withdrawal from the occupied territories indicated only how desperately he needed the Arab masses for his survival in the crisis.

Iraq's threat to Israel was also exaggerated. As demonstrated by the war, Iraqi air power was no match for that of the Israelis, and Iraq's chemical weapons were at the least matched by those of Israel. This inequality of forces is further exacerbated by the fact that Israel is already a nuclear power, indeed the only nuclear power in the region whereas Iraq would not have reached that stage for some years to come. It is also important to note that Iraq has, in the past, only tangentially been drawn into a war with Israel, with whom it shares no border. Thus, an effective Iraqi ground war against Israel was also an impossibility since Iraqi forces had first to cross into Syria, Jordan, or Saudi Arabia. None of these options could be considered serious under the prevailing prewar conditions in the region. Even if President Hussein had a Hitler mentality, he hardly had the means to back it up.

Saddam Hussein made a tactical mistake by challenging Israel. The "butcher of Baghdad" thought he may have a chance to replace Israel as a "strategic asset" for the United States and also become the master of the Arab world. For the United States, however, the choice between Iraq and Israel was an easy one. Even before Iraq invaded Kuwait, the American media had waged a crusade against Saddam Hussein, reminding their readers and the administration of Iraq's danger to Israeli security. Congress was also busy drafting bills to ban trade with Iraq and U.S. secret agents were busy uncovering illegal shipments of sensitive technologies to that country.[30] Meanwhile, the Israel lobby was waging a propaganda campaign against President Bush's alleged anti-Israeli stand on issues ranging from peace and aid to settlement of the Russian Jews in the occupied territories.[31]

The Kuwaiti Crisis, thus, came at an opportune moment for the Bush administration. Followers of the conspiracy theory have even argued that the administration tricked Iraq into invading

Kuwait. They give as evidence the public statements coming out of Washington during the two weeks prior to the Iraqi invasion of Kuwait and from April C. Glaspie, the U.S. ambassador in Baghdad. They particularly focus on the July 25, 1990, meeting between President Hussein and the ambassador. According to the *New York Times,* the Washington message to Baghdad was that: "the United States was concerned about Iraq's military buildup on its borders with Kuwait, but did not intend to take sides in what it perceived as a no-win border dispute between Arab neighbors."[32] Whether the conspiracy theorists are right or wrong does not change the fact that when the crisis occurred, the Bush administration used it as a god-given opportunity to reassert American military might. It is not surprising that the administration argued against waiting for the sanctions to work and feared a possible early Iraqi pullout from Kuwait, which could have become a "nightmare" for the administration, according to the *New York Times.*[33] "The officials [were also] concerned," wrote Thomas Friedman of the *New York Times,* "that the natural instinct of Saudi Arabia and its neighbors to bargain with Iraq could weaken efforts to force a withdrawal through a combination of a worldwide oil boycott against Baghdad and an American military buildup in the Persian Gulf."[34]

From Washington's perspective, Iraq had to be destroyed and subordinated to Israel because a dominant Iraq would be contrary to the U.S. policy shift on the Arab-Israeli Conflict: it would have made both the Arabs and the Israelis less flexible in the peace process. But the "Hitler" had to survive for the time being so that a sense of continuous threat could be maintained. Otherwise the world could not be easily characterized, as President Bush did several times during the crisis, as "a dangerous and unstable place" and the national security state would lose its underlying logic in the post-Cold War era.[35] "The Vietnam war syndrome" also had to vanish and be replaced with a new patriotic spirit of victory and strength. The war also set a new example of how the U.S. might fight against a developing nation if it were to misbehave: it would not be like the Vietnam war, but like the one against Iraq. This intention was alluded to in President Bush's 1991 State of the Union address: "We will succeed in the gulf. And when we do, the world community will have sent an enduring warning to any dictator or despot, present or future, who contemplates outlaw aggression."[36]

The United States also exaggerated Iraqi stamina as a balance-altering force and purposefully overreacted to the crisis to make the world see the PGW as a test of a new American resolve for global hegemony and rally the world behind its leadership—a trick that actually worked. President Bush also demonstrated to an increasingly rebellious Western Europe that it still needed the United States in the post-Cold War era to police the world against hostile regional powers.[37] The U.S. reaction to the crisis was also meant to show the newly united Germany and Japan, its two powerful economic competitors, that it is still Washington, not Tokyo or Bonn, that can "draw a line in the sand."[38] Both of these countries have recently been asking for a bigger leadership role in the world than they have been given since their defeat in World War II.[39] Meanwhile, the Bush administration's argument for the modernization of NATO would gain, as it did, increased credibility.[40] He also used the crisis to build support for reversing defense budget cuts. In a speech to the Veterans of Foreign Wars a few weeks after Iraq invaded Kuwait, President Bush pleaded to them: "help me convince the Congress, given recent events, to take another look to adequately fund our defense budget."[41] The administration also used the crisis to deploy part of the U.S. European forces in the Middle East.[42] The move would bring American forces closer to the Soviet Union where, according to the administration, the situation remains uncertain to say the least.

The crisis also provided the United States with a golden opportunity to turn the Saudi desert, Kuwait, and Iraq into a testing field for its new military technology; various American administrations had long sought military bases in the region and wanted to make the Saudis loudly acknowledge their friendship with and dependency on the United States. Finally, the crisis helped the Bush administration to put a temporary stop to the rising criticism against his administration's inability to cope with the changing international environment and domestic problems.[43] The essence of that disappointment is aptly summarized by Flora Lewis: "The Bush Administration is being criticized for passivity and lack of 'the vision thing.' The real failure now isn't in not commanding the world but in not giving a clear sense of our new relations with it and why they matter."[44]

In sum, the crisis in the Persian Gulf generated by Iraqi President Saddam Hussein's gamble on Kuwait provided the United States a "window of opportunity" to establish its leadership, or in the words of one critical analyst, to establish "strategic bridgeheads, secure the Gulf, and ensure that it retains a virtual monopoly on global violence."[45] American troop deployment in the region under the rubric of Operation Desert Shield, and their use against Iraq in Operation Desert Storm, will test the principles of the emerging Bush Doctrine. This doctrine envisions a post-Cold War global arrangement dominated by the United States, with Western Europe, Japan, and the Soviet Union acting as junior partners. As stated more bluntly by Michael Vlahos, director of the U.S. State Department's Center for the Study of Foreign Affairs, "If we [the United States] marched right into Baghdad, brought Saddam Hussein back in a cage and paraded him down Pennsylvania Avenue, the world would take notice. We would have great freedom of action in the world for the next 10 to 20 years, . . . People would truly respect us, and if we said that we didn't like what they did, they'd sit up and take notice."[46] Mr. Vlahos's wish was not fully realized but the "victory parade" in New York City and Washington, D.C., sent a similar message to the world on T-shirts for sale: "Don't mess with US."

U.S. ACHIEVEMENTS AND FAILURES

This section offers a balance sheet of U.S. achievements and failures in the wake of the PGW, indicating various constraints on U.S. Middle East policy for creating a new order in the region, as outlined in President Bush's post-PGW four-point plan. Also discussed are implications for the U.S. quest for world leadership. To begin, the military victory has achieved several of President Bush's prewar objectives; namely, the "liberation" of Kuwait, restoration of the al-Sabah family autocracy there, security of the House of al-Saud, and destruction of Iraq's military capabilities (actual and potential) for some time to come. Most significantly, "Iraq no longer serves as the Arab deterrent to a nuclear-armed Israel."[47] All these achievements are to serve the status quo in favor of the United States and to establish firmer American control over Middle East oil and political structures. The victory has also improved the U.S. chance for mediating a settlement of the Arab-Israeli Conflict and thus altering the Palestinian plight.

However, the victory was not a "clean win" as General Colin Powell, chairman of the Joint Chiefs of Staff, termed it.[48] In reality, Americans are not safe in the long run because anti-Americanism will surely increase in the region both at the practical and intellectual levels. Moreover, the larger question of security in the region remains unsettled as national interests of various regional players clash over the form and content of the new system. Yet, rapidly finalizing a new regional security arrangement is a matter of high significance for President Bush's new world order, which he defined in his 1991 State of the Union address as a world of "peace and security, freedom, and the rule of law." Indeed, the war has not as yet achieved any of these objectives in the Middle East. Possible political instability in Iraq continues to disturb even Saddam Hussein's enemies, Arab-Iranian tension could intensify over a security system for the Persian Gulf, despots continue to rule, and the tension between the Palestinians and Israelis has increased in the aftermath of the war. Indeed, they killed more of each other during the crisis than during any similar time frame in the past. Moreover, potential for political instability remains high in most so-called pro-American states in the region as dictators and ancient family autocracies are losing much of whatever legitimacy they commanded for ruling their respective nations. Meanwhile, American sales of military hardware to these countries has increased substantially following the PGW, adding more fuel to an already explosive situation.[49] This action of the Bush administration is contrary to the president's stated objective of reducing weapon sales to the Middle East.

Next to these problems remain a whole set of issues that existed before the crisis or have been created because of the war. Among the new problems, human loss, economic damage, moralistic issues, political instability, and environmental damage have to be emphasized. The human toll on the Iraqi side is estimated at tens of thousands. According to the Defense Intelligence Agency of the U.S. Defense Department, the Iraqi toll includes about 100,000 killed and another 300,000 injured. The figures do not include civilian casualties. Commenting on these figures, the *New York Times* wrote that: "By applying the D.I.A.'s error factor of 50 percent, today's estimate suggests that Iraqi casualties and desertions could have been as low as 275,000 and as high as 775,000."[50] But on the allies' side, the human loss is not so great, though not negligible, with American and European losses estimated at about 400 and "over a hundred," respectively, and those of the Arab forces in "several thousands." To these figures we must also add the millions of civilians in Iraq and Kuwait who died, were disabled or maimed, lost their homes and jobs, and became refugees. Over 2 million Iraqi Kurds fled to refugee camps on the Iranian and Turkish borders, with some 400 to 1,000 dying every day. According to the *New York Times,* the death rate later "stabilized at about 500 a day."[51] Representatives of international relief organizations estimated that some 5 million people from thirty countries were displaced; and as a State Department refugee official put it, the PGW created "A world on the move."[52] A UN report put the number of Iraqis who became homeless at 72,000.[53]

Environmental damage to the region is simply arch. The Gulf oil spill is the largest in history, estimated at 450 million gallons of crude oil. That is, it was a spill forty times the size of the Exxon *Valdez* spill in Alaska, stretched over an area 100 miles long and 40 miles wide in the eastern Saudi coastline, 15 inches thick in some areas. The ecological calamity has already included thousands of wild-life exterminated and many fishing industries and fishermen's lives destroyed. Its cleanup will require from five to ten years of hard and complicated work, from $1 billion to $5 billion in investments and expenditures, and close, continuous international cooperation.[54] It is also reported that most of the area is covered by heavy smoke from burning oil wells and on rainy days, according to local observers in southern Iran, "black rain" pours on the people and their life environment. The fires from the burning oil wells have "sent soot as far as the Himalayas."[55] Commenting on the conflicting reports of the National Science Foundation team and the Friends of the Earth on the environmental impact of the PGW, the *New York Times* concluded that "the two reports were, in effect, a declaration by environmentalists that the situation is half way to catastrophe."[56] According to one estimate, as reported in the *New York Times,* "50,000 people in the Kuwait region will have their lives shortened in some way in the next several years because of the smoke."[57]

The economic costs of the war have been simply enormous. Billions of dollars, needed at home and in the Third World, were wasted in the Saudi desert and elsewhere in the Middle East. At the end, the total cost of the war to all sides could amount to something close to half a trillion dollars. To the world community as a whole, it was immaterial where the money came from or who lost it.[58] The U.S. appeal for financial help from Japan, Germany, Saudi Arabia, Kuwait, among other nations, was both counterproductive and humiliating. It is the first time that Americans were seen as "mercenaries" overseas, policing the Western and Japanese interests in return for money.[59] Billions of dollars were also paid to Egypt, Turkey, Jordan, and many Eastern European countries that lost substantial trade with Iraq by going along with the UN sanctions.[60] These economic loses will harm the Eastern European democratic changes and Middle Eastern economies, with far reaching consequences for political stability in these parts of the world.

The economic loss on the Iraqi side could amount to some $150 billion, with the nation's industrial, military, and physical infrastructures in almost complete ruin. According to a UN report: "The recent conflict has wrought near-apocalyptic results upon the economic infrastructure of what had been, until January 1991, a rather highly urbanized and mechanized society. Now, most means of modern life support have been destroyed or rendered tenuous. Iraq has, for some time to come, been relegated to a pre-industrial age, but with all the disabilities of post-industrial dependency on an intensive use of energy and technology."[61] In a subsequent article based on "a series of interviews with administration analysts," the *New York Times* reported that the Bush administration's internal findings "parallel" those reported by the UN special mission, and that the CIA "estimates a national repair bill in Iraq of up to $30 billion."[62] The article also spoke of a "catastrophic health crisis" in the summer of 1991 and quoted a Harvard University report which said that "the collapse of electrical generating capacity has been a crucial factor in this public health catastrophe."[63]

The economic cost is equally high on the allied side. Kuwait is largely destroyed, with some 740–750 of its oil wells on fire (290 had been capped by August 1991), costing at least $100 million a day.[64] "Kuwait is burning almost as many gallons of oil each day as the United States consumes in gasoline."[65] The damage to its economy and physical infrastructures is put at about $50 billion. The total costs of the military campaign to the U.S. taxpayers is put at about $61 billion, $54 billion of which is covered by the wealthy Arab allies, Japan, and Germany. Note, however, that not all such payments have been in American dollars; $6 billion is in kind, and a portion of the cash contributions from Japan and Germany is paid in their respective currencies, ultimately against their exports to the United States at a future time. The United States also hopes to recover the remaining $7 billion estimated costs from a war-induced economic growth at home, the postwar reconstruction in Kuwait, and sales of new military hardware to the wealthy Persian Gulf Arab states. In the end, the United States may well end up making a small "profit" from the war.[66] However, the costs and benefits will be unevenly distributed across various income groups, with a minority at the upper end of the social hierarchy accruing most of the benefits while those at the bottom end will pay for a lion's share of the costs. Also it was mostly the children of this same group who were sent to the Saudi desert to fight.[67]

On the political side, the cost has ostensibly been negligible for most top political participants: all the precrisis leaders remain in power and streets did not fall into the hands of the Arab masses as some had predicted. Changes in the popularity of different leaders and groups can also be considered temporary and indeed insignificant, given the magnitude of the events that have taken place. However, looking deeper into the political scene, we see losses to all sides. Saddam Hussein is no longer an effective force in the region for some time to come, despite his success in putting down the Shi'ite and Kurdish uprisings. The war was particularly devastating to these last two groups who were encouraged by the allies to take up arms against the central government in Baghdad and were then left alone to be crushed by Saddam Hussein's Republican Guards. The U.S. pretext for not supporting the Iraqi Kurds and Shi'ite population was that it did not wish to see the Lebanization of Iraq; in reality, however, the Bush administration, along with the Saudis, preferred President Hussein's heavy-handed approach over a possible democratization of Iraq.[68]

The Arab world has also been divided into antagonistic camps: the poorer Arab states are mostly on the opposite side of the rich Arabs with far-reaching implications for intra-Arab distribution of Arab funds and cooperation for economic development and regional integration. After the Kuwaitis and Iraqis, the Palestinians are at third place in terms of the magnitude of losses that they have incurred from the war. Israelis have also sustained damage: they were humiliated by SCUD missiles, their value as a "strategic asset" for the United States is now questionable, and they may find it difficult to resist the U.S. peace formula that underscores territory for peace. With these costs set aside, however, Israelis benefitted from the war that destroyed Iraq's potential military threat to their future security. Moreover, tension among the nations as well as anti-Western feeling in the region still runs high in the post-PGW period, but remains subdued for the time being.

There are also the issues of morality and justice. Saddam Hussein is a cruel dictator with no respect for the sanctity of life or human rights. The atrocities of his men in Kuwait, and before that in Iran and Iraq, are deplorable and should be emphasized in all ethical and legal debates about the crisis. Yet, the allies have been no less brutal in their destruction of Iraq. The amount of bombing on Baghdad alone is said to equal six times the bombing poured on Hiroshima during World War II, and the number of sorties flown on Iraqi cities are several times larger than the total sorties flown by all forces during World War II. Never before in recent history has a nation been subjected to such a brutal and disproportionate response, regardless of the magnitude of its crime, including Nazi Germany. The National Council of Churches, a major voice of mainline Christians representing over 40 million Americans, passed a resolution criticizing the Bush administration for "reckless rhetoric" and "imprudent behavior" and warned him against a war in the Middle East. The National Conference of Catholic Bishops also argued that the U.S. military involvement in the Persian Gulf could well fail the traditional Catholic "just war" standard. In sharp contrast, the Council of Jewish Federations supported President Bush's war policy.[69]

Among the old problems, I wish to include the Palestinian question, the regional security issue and traditional interstate rivalries, the lack of democracy in the region, and extreme inequality in wealth and income distribution among the states and social classes in the Middle East. The crisis exposed these and other problems as never before. The link between the Kuwaiti crisis and the Palestinian problem and the issue of double standards became sources of significant agony for the allies during the crisis. Significant border problems remain as sources of international disputes and potential wars in the region. The American public was also exposed to the reality of life in Kuwait and Saudi Arabia, where not laws but whims of the emir and the king rule. It is safe to assert that the Middle East is practically the only world region where the current global democratic movement has not produced tangible changes. Many in the world have also come to know that not all Arabs own oil wells as stereotypes suggest and that more than two-thirds of them live a life of absolute destitution whereas a very tiny minority has accumulated legendary wealth, held in the Western banks, investment portfolios, and luxury palaces.

Kuwait holds over $120 billion in foreign investments, almost all in the West. Last February, one Saudi prince, Waleed bin Talal, bought some $590 million worth of Citicorp shares as reported by the *New York Times,* making him "the largest single shareholder in Citicorp."[70] The man who lost $1 billion in one of the biggest banking collapses in the West was not an American, European, or Japanese; he was Sheikh Zayed bin Sultan al-Nahyan of Abu Dhabi. He owned, according to *The Sunday Times* of London, 77 percent of the assets of the Bank of Credit and Commerce International, the so-called "cocaine bank."[71] Meanwhile, many Arabs are unable to feed their children in Yemen, Egypt, and the Sudan, to name only a few examples. It is no wonder that the Arab masses hardly manifested any love for the rich Kuwaitis even though many objected to Iraq's invasion and annexation. Disparity among these states is also widening, resulting in increased interstate tension. While the poorer Arab nations have received only meager assistance (but a lot of humiliation) from the wealthy oil exporting Persian Gulf states, the oil wealth has been corrupted by the ruling groups and then deposited and invested in the West at a rapidly increasing pace and scale in recent years.

It was with some of these old and new problems in mind that President Bush outlined his four-point vision for the postwar Middle East and Secretary of State James Baker began his shuttle diplomacy in the region on February 27 to look for ways to create a "new order" there as a prelude to a new American paradigm of world leadership. The administration is particularly right in emphasizing a resolution to the Arab-Israeli Conflict and the Palestinian problem, the creation of a new regional security system, and economic development in the region. If there is to be a new order in the Middle East, these problems have to be resolved. However, the issues of political democracy and economic justice should also be addressed. One cannot build a new structure using the same old elements and form.

What, then, does it take for the United States to create a new order in the region? Above all, it takes a change of perspective and a real commitment to creating such an order according to a "balance of interests" concept. Is the United States ready for such a bold approach? My response is largely on the negative side, although significant shifts are occurring in U.S. Middle East policy in the post-Cold War era. One major exception is a new U.S. commitment to end the Arab-Israeli dispute and solve the Palestinian problem. The old policy of preserving the emirs, sheikhs, and kings will not change. Restoring the al-Sabah family rule and preserving the House of Saud were among President Bush's declared four-point objective for sending troops to the region. The United States will not put pressure on the Saudi and Kuwaiti despots to open up their closed feudal societies and allow for democracy and role of law there. As President Bush candidly said in a statement reported by the *New York Times,* the PGW was not fought for creating democracy in the region, Kuwait in particular. The lack of enthusiasm on the part of the United States, for democratic changes in the region, will no doubt weaken reformist forces; grass-roots pressure, however, is making it difficult for reform resisters to adhere to their autocratic practices.

The question of wealth distribution will also remain unaddressable. First of all, some of the poorer states were on the Iraqi side (Yemen, Jordan, the Sudan), rendering them unlikely to receive enumeration for there unfriendly behavior toward the Persian Gulf Arab states; second, these wealthy states, including Kuwait and

Saudi Arabia, have pledged billions of dollars in financial help to the United States and other allies to pay for the war expenses; third, Saudi Arabia is already in the market to borrow money to pay for its debt, whereas Kuwait faces tremendous money expenditures to rebuild its destroyed economy and infrastructures; and last, the oil revenue of Saudi Arabia will decline in the near future as Iraq and Kuwait begin producing again. Not only will the United States not press for any major change in the wealth status quo in the region; it will make sure that its share is paid first. Note that the Bush administration faces tremendous budgetary problems at home. It is also certain that most of whatever benefit that the postwar reconstruction generates will go to the Western countries in the alliance, the United States in particular. The remainder will flow to the wealthier segments of Arab nations, further exacerbating social inequalities.

One important area in which the Bush administration is interested and wishes to act as a "catalyst" is the Palestinian problem. Secretary Baker's shuttle diplomacy has led to a significant narrowing of the gap between Arabs and Israelis on the peace question. Concessions from the Arab states and a "conditional" yes from Israel to a largely muted American plan produced a regional peace conference in October 1991.[72] The Soviet Union, the initiator of the conference idea, is its cosponsor. It is hoped that the conference will result in bilateral and multilateral talks among the Israelis and the various Arab states leading to a more comprehensive peace among them. There are several reasons for this U.S. policy shift. In a nutshell, overwhelming changes have occurred in the regional balance of power in favor of Israel. Pressure from international public opinion has been mounting since the issue of the double standard became a word of mouth during the Kuwaiti crisis. The United States finds its new position in the middle of the belligerents precarious at best in the post-PGW Middle East environment. The Bush administration also seems convinced that the Israelis will benefit more from a two-state solution to the conflict based on the principle of territory for peace. The Iraqi SCUDS must have also convinced the Israelis that more territory does not mean a more peaceful environment. The future political stability of the Arab states who supported the United States in the PGW also depends, to a large extent, on a solution to the Palestinian problem.

These and other favorable conditions could be frustrated if the Bush administration tries to use old tactics against the Palestine Liberation Organization. There is a temptation to ignore the PLO because it has supported Iraq. Some argued that the United States should capitalize on the new earned popularity of King Hussein of Jordan and ask him to represent the Palestinians. Others have gone even further to argue that the Palestinians be incorporated into a larger Jordan that will include the West Bank. The representation issue for the regional conference was solved by creating a delegation of "prominent Palestinians" from the West Bank. The problem is that none of these schemes will work at the end, unless the PLO is brought into the process more directly. The Bush administration will be missing a great opportunity if it tries to bypass the PLO, which remains the sole representative of the Palestinian people. What then I am saying is that in essence, the Palestinian question is back again to square one with regard to the PLO question, but new opportunities have developed that are making a solution more accessible.

President Bush has also spoken about establishing a new security system in the Persian Gulf. The original outline of the system was given by Secretary Baker in December 1990 and rectified in February 1991.[73] It amounted to this: the Gulf Cooperation Council was to be joined together with Iran and possibly Iraq into a security framework. Baker said Iran should play a "major role" in such an arrangement. U.S. forces would also remain in the area but their number will be sharply reduced from the wartime level but significantly increased compared to the prewar period. The United States would also maintain military bases and an inventory of military hardware in almost all GCC states, including Kuwait and Saudi Arabia. Even the forward headquarters of the U.S. Central Command is planned for establishment in Bahrain.[74] This will be the first time that the United States will operate bases in the Persian Gulf states.

The exact U.S. involvement was spelled out by President Bush himself. He disclosed that his administration wanted "to create shared security arrangements in the region" that would include "American participation in joint exercises involving both air and ground forces" and "maintaining a capable U.S. naval presence in the region."[75] Later on, the administration also arranged with the allies to maintain a small contingent in Turkey to "protect" the Kurds from Saddam's atrocities. There is no provision for cooperation with the Soviets within the proposed American "shared security" framework. The president also did not disclose membership in the collective. Indeed, the proposed system seeks total domination by the United States of a region that was previously shared by the United States and the USSR. I suppose that this exclusiveness defines the newness in President Bush's "new order" in the Middle East.

Could this be a realistic approach to collective security in the region? If past experiences are any indication, the answer is negative. Iran still does not have diplomatic relations with the United States and Egypt. This will become an obstacle for its participation in the security collective. Yet, without Iran's active participation in such a system, security may not be achieved in the region. A similar problem exists concerning Iraq, the second largest Persian Gulf state after Iran. Syria and Egypt are mostly irrelevant to the Persian Gulf security as they are too far away from it and do not have a historical legitimacy for involvement there. This leaves the GCC states the only participants in the United States–led security system for the region. However, these states are too weak to make reliable partners. The most powerful of them, Saudi Arabia, had to request U.S. assistance for its defense even before the Iraqi army appeared on its borders. Moreover, the Soviets (or the Russians) and the U.S.-European allies would challenge the U.S. quest for a hegemonic dominance in the Middle East.

Finally, let us focus on the economic side of the new U.S. plan for the Middle East. Can President Bush's call for economic development and prosperity for the region materialize? The prospect, at best, is nil. First, there are few financial resources for the purpose because many billions of dollars have fled the region during the crisis and most will not return.[76] Second, existing financial resources in the region are unevenly divided among states, with the more needy ones possessing the least. Third, some of the poorest states supported Iraq and will not be favored by the allies, including the Arab billionaires, for economic assistance. Finally, wealthy states such as Kuwait and Saudi Arabia are themselves in economic ruin and distress. Kuwait has to spend some $100 billion in the next ten years for economic reconstruction, environmental clean up, and military purchases while it will not be pumping much oil for the next few years. The country is also under heavy obligation to reimburse the allies for a part of their military expenses during the crisis. Kuwait has also promised to lend money to a good number of countries for their help during the crisis. These include the Soviet Union, Egypt, Turkey, Syria, and many more. Saudi Arabia is equally distressed financially. The kingdom has been running an $8 to $10 billion budget deficit for the past few years. In addition, it has also contributed some $48 billion to the U.S. military operation and pledged billions to a variety of nations including the Soviet Union, Egypt, Turkey, and Syria. The kingdom will also buy billions of dollars worth of military hardware and spend many millions more for postwar reconstruction and environmental clean up.

The postwar reconstruction will not generate any lasting economic prosperity in the region. Reconstruction activities are planned in stages, the first of which will be devoted to emergency clean up followed by patch-up jobs and restoration of some basic necessities. Only then will real developmental reconstruction begin. The stage approach will be more manageable and realistic because Kuwait faces a severe labor shortage; but it will also prevent an economic boom from emerging in the immediate future. Besides, most contracts will be awarded to the industrialized nations, with businesses in the region receiving the less lucrative subcontracting jobs. Days after the cease-fire, the fight over the largest share in Kuwait's postwar reconstruction began among the Western members of the anti-Iraqi alliance. The U.S. government established a Reconstruction Center in the Commerce Department to help American businesses sign contracts with the Kuwaitis and the Saudis and the U.S. Army Corp of Engineers monopolized most of the emergency clean-up activities in Kuwait. Reportedly, some 70 percent of the 200 or so contracts (worth more than $800 million) that the Kuwaitis signed in the first three weeks following the war were awarded to American firms. The Army Corps of Engineers, Caterpillar, Raytheon, AT&T, Bechtel Group, Flour and Parsons Corporations, GM, Ford, and Chrysler have all bagged major contracts, wrote the *New York Times*. The rest of the Fortune 500 were, the newspaper wrote, also in line.[77]

The regional impact of Kuwait's reconstruction will be particularly limited if the Kuwaiti government was to actually implement the new emigration and industrial policies announced after the war. Accordingly, Kuwait will adopt a selective and restrictive emigration policy and follow a capital-intensive industrial development approach that will require far fewer foreign workers than would otherwise be the case. Note that the largest contribution of Kuwait to the Middle East was the low-skilled jobs that it provided to over 1.5 million workers from all over the region. This new Kuwaiti policy will thus have far reaching consequences for working people in the region, Palestinians, Yemenis, and Iraqis in particular.

In conclusion, the military victory has, at best, produced a mixed result for the United States and the region. It has generated new opportunities for change and tremendous constraints on top of existing ones. To facilitate opportunities and mitigate constraints, a new approach is needed: one that is as bold in its outlook and practice as "Operation Desert Storm." Otherwise, much time and energy will be lost with no concrete gains for either the United States or the other players in the region. However, is the United States as competent in the economic, political, and diplomatic arenas as it has been in the Persian Gulf War? The future could be as unpromising as the past has proved, given the new confidence in militaristic approach.

American policy makers could come to the dangerous conclusion that the world has become unipolar and amenable to the U.S. hegemonic leadership. Referring to the United States–led coalition against Iraq, President Bush said in his 1991 State of the Union address that "Among the nations of the world, only the United States of America has had both the moral standing, and the means to back it up. We are the only nation on this earth that could assemble the forces of peace."[78] Every nation has the right to demand world leadership. What is questionable is the means used to achieve it. The Japanese and the Germans have gained world leadership through economic growth and competition since World War II. However, the U.S. comparative advantage lies within its military strength. Therefore, it is safe and reasonable to assume that the United States may attempt to impose its leadership on the world by military means if necessary. In that case, the world will be, to use President Bush's phrase, "a dangerous and unstable place."

GLOBAL RESTRUCTURING AND THE U.S. QUEST FOR WORLD LEADERSHIP

This section will focus on two specific aspects of the new global condition that may constrain the U.S. quest for world leadership in the 1990s and beyond. They are the emerging *multipolarity* in the world system and the consequent *diminishing utility of offensive force*. I shall also discuss the superpowers' reactions and the implications of these changes for a new foreign policy perspective for the United States. In particular, I wish to underscore the irrelevancy of a foreign policy based on the assumptions of a *unipolar* world and the use of *offensive* force for sustaining world leadership. These assumptions form the foundation of a new interventionist thought in certain sectors of American foreign policy establishment. The military victory in the PGW and the near-collapse of the Soviet empire have reinforced these assumptions and the new belief that has followed.

Emerging Multipolar World

World War II was a turning point in human history, which has led to the emergence of the *nation-state* as the key player in domestic and world politics. The collapse of the colonial order was the prime cause of this development. Among the emergent nation-states, the United States and the USSR became *hegemonic*, each with its respective sphere of influence. A *hegemon* is defined as an actor that has both the ambition and the power to organize and lead a system of nation-states and control the external and internal behavior of the system's members in the direction of its expanded reproduction and common objectives. This control is never total or absolute as even the weakest nation-states tend to enjoy certain degree of *relative autonomy*.

In the late 1960s, after the Soviet Union achieved nuclear parity with the United States, the planet was for all practical purposes, divided into two antagonistic world systems of capitalism and socialism, under the hegemonic control of the United States and the USSR, respectively. A new *bipolar* world was born. This division notwithstanding, the key players remained nation-states within the two systems. Because they were more or less autonomous and pursued differing *national interests,* instability and *structural anarchy* remained major characteristics of international politics between the two systems and within them. Therefore, it is not surprising that the search for causes of wars and conflicts, and for conditions of peace, security, and cooperation between the two systems and among nation-states were the central problems and processes in postwar international politics.

The two hegemons, or superpowers, however, found another way to bring the intrasystem instability under control: system *integration.* In the absence of any significant nongovernmental actors, this task was focused on nation-states. Both economic and extra-economic forces were applied. In particular, rapid and sustained economic growth and relative economic strength were among major factors that enabled the superpowers to maintain a powerful military force and use it to impose hegemonic leadership on their respective systems for the purpose of system integration. Meanwhile, the process was facilitated by the formation of various multilateral and bilateral organizations.[79] In the "capitalist camp" they included the International Bank for Reconstruction and Development (the World Bank), International Monetary Funds (IMF), General Agreements on Tariff and Trade (GATT), European Economic Community (EEC), Organization for Economic Cooperation and Development (OECD), North Atlantic Treaty Organization (NATO), Organization of American States (OAS), Australian-New Zealand-United States Treaty (ANZUST), and International Energy Agency (IEA). The "socialist camp", on the other hand, formed the Council for Mutual Economic Cooperation (COMECON), the Warsaw Pact, and International Meeting of Communist and Workers Parties (IMCWP).

Integration within each system was also facilitated by the advancements in transport, telecommunication, and information technologies. Integration of the capitalist camp took place at the levels of the state and the private sector, assisted by multinational corporations, progressive trade liberalization, removal of barriers to capital and money transfers, globalization of production sites, achievement of convertible currencies, formation of free trade zones and custom unions, various regional integration schemes, and the culture that international firms have used to propagate their business throughout the world.[80] Although market forces played a significant role, government policies were catalysts in capitalist integration. The main instrument of the socialist integration, on the other hand, was a "planned socialist division of labor" among the various states. Hardly any integrative schemes were developed at the level of private citizens or nongovernmental organizations. Market forces rendered negligible service to this process and interstate planning and policies played the leading role.[81]

The Cold War ideology and the wars in a number of Third World countries, in Vietnam and Korea in particular, also played a significant role in unifying parts within each system, reducing intrasystem instability while securing the division between the two poles. The hegemons also developed certain interests for maintaining the division. For example, the military-industrial interests in the United States used the "Soviet threat" to legitimize a growing defense budget, and the bureaucrats of the Communist Party of the USSR used the Cold War to maintain their dominance over Soviet society and Eastern Europe. The East-West division was also maintained and reproduced by a paradigmatic partition within the field of development, between the capitalist model and the socialist path. The two camps hardly learned from each other or acknowledged the rival's contributions. Instead, they were defined in mutually exclusive terms. Thus, instead of mutual understanding and cooperation, the two camps developed dogmatic and extremist perspectives about each other.

To be sure, many countries, including the People's Republic of China and India, remained outside the two camps and a good number of them formed various economic and political alliances such as the Nonaligned Movement, Organization of Petroleum Exporting Countries (OPEC), Association of South Asian Nations (ASAN), Organization of African Unity (OAU), the Arab League, and the Islamic Conference Organization (ICO). Regional integration and common market schemes were also attempted, largely unsuccessfully, in Latin America, the Middle East, Africa, and Asia. The world outside the two poles, however, played only a peripheral role in the postwar international political economy and their demand (since the early 1970s) for a new international economic order (NIEO) has not been successful.[82] Theoretically, the

United Nations was the only international organization that stood above these divisions. Practically, however, the agency proved largely incapable of functioning effectively in a divided world ruled by the superpowers and torn by conflicts and antagonistic relations. The United States and its allies (Britain and France) are on record for using their veto power more frequently than the Soviet Union and China.[83] Such vetoes were used to block the passage of almost all possible resolutions that may not directly or indirectly have benefitted the capitalist world.

This divided picture of the world began to change in the early 1970s when an asymmetrically *interdependent* one-world system began to emerge.[84] *Interdependency* is defined in terms of interlocking, common interests and issues among nation-states; that is, interests and issues that extend beyond national borders, recognize no political geography, and are universally applicable to the human race. Examples of these are AIDS, global warming, human rights, and peace in a nuclear age. Let us also consider the following: U.S. dependency on European markets, on Japanese banks, and on the Soviet and Chinese cooperation to fight Iraq; Europe's and Japan's dependency on U.S. market and military protection and on Middle East oil; or China's and the USSR's dependency on assistance from the West for technology and economic development. In the same way, the global spread of production and resources and the consequent multisourcing and multimarketing strategies of most transnational corporations have resulted in interdependencies among firms from various countries and between them and the nation-states where they buy resources and sell their goods.

Even the Third World's dependency on the developed countries is no more unidirectional than it was in the past. For example, the world's monetary system is very much threatened by the instability caused by the Third World debt problem. A debtor Third World with little means to pay for its international trade is of the least use for economic development in the industrialized countries. Therefore, it is of little wonder that the West has become interested in debt relief for the Third World.[85] Further complicating this picture of interdependency is a gradual rise in power of what is called *nongovernmental organizations* (NGOs). These forces are in direct competition with nation-states and operate both locally and transnationally. The result is the insertion of another layer of players in world and domestic politics, creating what James Rosenau has termed a *bifurcated* world system, composed of two "state-centric" and "multicentric" systems that have lives of their own but interact with each other as well.[86]

Ironically, the very *world-integrating forces* that had consolidated the two-world system became the causes of its transformation into an integrated one-world system, at least economically for the time being. Globalization of economic and political relations and the rapid growth of telecommunication, information, and transportation technology has brought nation-states and their citizens ever closer to each other. Meanwhile, the spread of international trade, global finance, and multinational corporations has further helped to break the boundaries between the two world systems. The universalization of demand for human rights, democracy, social justice, and environmental safety soon followed. Finally, the demise of the very Cold War ideology became a source of new world integration, so well symbolized by the collapse of the Berlin Wall in 1989 and subsequent German reunification.

The primary force that has melted the ice between the East and the West was President Mikhail Gorbachev of the Soviet Union. Even his direct rival, President Bush, had to praise him for "instituting reforms that changed the world" and for "his uncommon vision and courage in replacing [the] old orthodoxy."[87] Gorbachev's *glasnost* and *perestroika* opened the door to a revolution in world politics that continues to transform international relations toward a safer, less dogmatic, and more pluralistic world. His courageous concession to the United States made the historic INF and START treaties possible, and his gallant redefinition of socialism has brought the market back to where it once operated: streets of the old East Bloc. A new kind of outlook in economic development is also gaining ground, promoting a hybrid "third way" in which contributions of market and planning mechanisms, private and public sectors, domestic resources and foreign investment and trade, global interdependence of interests, and international cooperation are acknowledged.[88] Moreover, although individualism is on the rise, concern for the social and cultural aspects of life is receiving added attention in the emerging development paradigm.

All these changes have brought capitalism and socialism closer, melting them into each other.

However, the world-integrating forces have generated their counterparts; namely, the *world-disintegrating forces,* which are undermining the emerging world unity, leading to the creation of a multipolar world system. These forces include, above all, the *relative* economic decline and crises in the hegemonic nations of the United States and the USSR and a corresponding growth in the productive and competitive powers of Japan, the EEC (particularly Germany), and the newly industrializing countries (NICs). No less responsible for the emerging world discord were the rising level of world education and mass awareness, growing ethnic and gender consciousness, widening cultural and religious diversities, and the mounting populist and nationalist resistance movements in the Third World. At the same time, the nuclear parity between the two postwar superpowers has led to increasing brevity among the less-powerful nations and thus to further chaos in the world order in which the weaker nations were, more or less, forcibly incorporated. Last, as the two postwar blocs have weakened and lost their internal coherence, we are witnessing the emergence of what I like to call *pan-continentalism* and *neonationalism,* both of which feed into the rising neomercantilism and regionalism in international trade and capital flows.

As Paul Kennedy has demonstrated, no nation can lead the world or even remain a great power without a solid economic strength.[89] The problem is further complicated because economic strength in international system, just like military strength, is measured in *relative* terms; and without economic strength, military strength cannot be sustained for any significant period of time. Yet relative strength is not an immutable state; on the contrary, it is an ever-changing phenomenon rooted in the laws of change and uneven economic growth rates across nations. Thus, great powers may become weaker (fall) or grew stronger (rise) relative to each other as time passes. The rate of this uneven development may be retarded or accelerated but it cannot be stopped or reversed by normal economic means because the factors that contribute to it remain largely outside the sphere of influence of any given great power. For example, the new pattern of uneven development in the capitalist world has resulted from the growing globalization of the world political economy, a transformation that could not be controlled by the superpowers or their new rivals. In the past, the great powers resorted to wars in response to secular shifts in balance of power among them. In the present age, however, nuclear weapons have become a fetter to a global war, making that solution impossible. Thus, although economic strength is the only feasible means to great power status, its sustenance has become increasingly difficult as the world political economy changes unevenly.

The U.S. gross domestic product (GDP) has declined from about half of the world gross product in 1950 to less than a quarter of it in 1989. Compared to OECD's total, its GDP fell from 51 percent in 1965 to 37 percent in 1987. The United States also has lagged behind in per capita growth rate when compared to the EEC, Japan, and the Third World as a whole. The country also puts a smaller percentage of its gross national product (GNP) into investment (16 percent in 1987) than does Japan, Germany, or the OECD as a whole (30, 20, and 21 percent, respectively).[90] Japan has also led the United States in new stock sales since the stock market crash in October 1987. For example, in the first eight months of 1989, "Japanese corporations raised more than $110 billion, compared with $20 billion by American companies."[91] Americans also save and invest less and consume more when compared to their rivals in OECD. The result has been a decline in productivity and a gradual transformation of the economy from one based on manufacturing to one dominated by services and low-paying jobs.[92] Among a small group of dynamic manufacturing industries still remaining in the 1980s, the military-industrial complex was in a distinctive lead because of President Reagan's huge defense spending. Even the service sector is losing its dynamism as was indicated by the sector's job loss in 1990–1991 for the first time in decades. Meanwhile, the U.S. economy could not pull itself out of a recession that began in 1988–1989.

The U.S. direct foreign investment and share of total world exports have declined substantially and the country has become a debtor nation. The U.S. nonfinancial debt stood at about $9.5 trillion or 180 percent of the nation's GNP in 1989, of which about $3 trillion was the government's share. The huge private debt is taking its toll: "The number of Americans declaring personal bankruptcy has grown by 152 percent in six years, from 285,000 in 1984 to 718,000 last year [1990], and the trend shows no sign of abating immediately."[93] The estimated interests on the government debt alone in 1989 was $200 billion. This is a figure close to two-thirds of the defense budget or 15 percent of all government spending. By 1993, the government debt is estimated to hit $4 trillion.[94] A part of this debt is owned by foreign nationals and was incurred to finance a growing budget deficit that grew to a historic peak during the Reagan years when the defense budget sky-rocketed. In 1991 it is $279 billion and will rise to $362 billion in 1992.[95] The U.S.'s twin deficits (budget and trade) have, in recent years, been major sources of worry for both its allies and competitors. In particular, the country's deficit spending strategy has led to increased interest rate and the consequent inflow of capital from overseas including the Third World.[96] The foreign ownership of the debt has also increased the specter of a "hard landing" for the economy at some future point. Meanwhile, foreign purchases of American concerns continue to climb, with British, French, and Japanese in the lead.[97] The United States is also suffering from an overglobalization of its large and major firms. They are no longer controllable by Washington or useful for foreign policy purposes.

Transformation of the economy from a welfare into a warfare system under the Reagan administration was partly responsible for this debt explosion.[98] Although the economy was stabilized at a moderate rate of growth, inflation, and employment in the 1980s, military spending increased to the historic peacetime peak of $300 billion in 1990. Attempts to reduce the size of the government and its nonmilitary expenditures largely failed. On the contrary, the state became even bigger under Reagan, who carried the banner of "the least government the best government" with him to the White House. Policies of the conservative governments under Presidents Reagan and Bush have also led to significant inequalities and social problems: taxation became less progressive, income inequality widened, social programs were reduced, the educational standard declined, the cost of health care became prohibitive, infant mortality increased, the number of homeless people swelled, drugs became a national problem, the crime rate soared, and pollution became a major source of public concern. For example, "from 1979 to 1987 the standard of living for the poorest fifth of the population fell by 9 percent. At the same time, the living standard of the top fifth rose 19 percent."[99]

As a consequence of Reaganomics, violence has also increased substantially. A study at the National Center for Health Statistics indicated that the United States is by far the homicide capital of the industrialized nations. For example, "4,223 American men from 15 to 24 years old were killed in 1987, a rate of 21.9 per 100,000 . . . the rate for black men in that age group was 85.6 per 100,000, an increase of 40 percent since a low in 1984. In contrast, the rates in other countries for men in the same age group ranged from a high of 5 per 100,000 in Scotland, to a low of 0.3 per 100,000 in Austria."[100] Another study finds that "young men in Harlem are less likely to reach age 40 than are young men in Bangladesh, one of the poorest and most overcrowded of all nations."[101]

At the same time, tremendous corruption has ravaged savings and loan associations, major banks, stock markets, and public offices.[102] The cost of the S & L bailout to the American taxpayers is estimated at no less than $300 billion in the next thirty years, a rather conservative estimate.[103] Even more pervasive and dangerous is political corruption. In a report on "The Trouble with Politics," *New York Times* wrote that "The pursuit of money is a central part of officeholders' lives, and the rules are written to make it almost impossible for politicians to avoid either the appearance or reality of conflict of interest." The report then goes on to say that "The average senator who was elected in 1988 spent $3.7 million on his or her campaign, a 22 percent rise from only two years before. The winning candidates for House seats spent, on average, $393,000, an increase of more than 10 percent over 1986."[104] The problem, however, does not end here. The system has also created "a new superstructure of politics that makes ideas harder to discuss and exalts public opinion over leadership."[105] One major consequence of these changes have been a reduced public confidence in the nation's political process with far-reaching implication for American democracy: in the last presidential election in 1988 "about half the eligible voters stayed home."[106] The American public is at the same time beset by what Paul Krugman, an MIT economist, calls "diminished expectations."[107]

Similarly, the Soviet Union has also been weakened since the

1970s, and could indeed soon disintegrate, both politically and economically. Ethnic conflicts and political chaos that followed the *glasnost* (openness) in the mid-1980s have crippled the central government's ability to affect an orderly transition to a wholly new society based on the so-called market or democratic socialism. Even in the absence of such conflicts and chaos, the Soviet Union would still have to struggle with the ideological crisis that it is facing at present. The economy particularly has been in bad shape since 1989 when the pace of changes became increasingly less manageable. Tragically, the economy refuses to improve despite various structural and other adjustment programs that have been or are being implemented. In the meantime, a more drastic *perestroika* (restructuring) strategy has become harder to implement under the condition of political chaos and lack of consensus among the various domestic players in the Soviet game over a theory of transition to a new system. It is by now obvious that the country has lost its position of leadership in the socialist-oriented Third World and Eastern Europe, and its trade with these latter countries has all but totally collapsed.

A low level of economic growth and labor productivity along with allocative imbalances and structural distortions continue to remain among the major economic problems of the Soviet Union. Added to these are a highly centralized bureaucracy that refuses to delegate management authority to those below the power bloc, a comprehensive planning system that finds itself unable to program an extremely complex economy and yet hesitates to make the market a full partner, and a property relation that only partly corresponds to greedy human nature. On top of all these is a level of military spending and commitment that has become impossible to sustain at the present level of economic growth. These and other problems have also sharpened political struggles at the ethnic and republic levels for democracy and decentralization. Meanwhile, the economy is being opened to new ideas and foreign economic players, making a more complex and confusing situation even less manageable.

In sharp contrast to the decline of the United States and the USSR, particularly in relative economic terms, Japan, the EEC, China, NICs, and a few other countries have been growing in their productive and competitive abilities, both in absolute and relative terms. These emerging economic powers, without being able to replace the United States or the USSR as the world leaders, at least for the time being (particularly for lack of adequate military power), have contributed to the superpowers' gradual demise. This is particularly true in the case of the United States whose decline is more relative than absolute, which is the case with the Soviet Union. Ironically, diffusion and relocation of major American transnational firms have been partly responsible for the growing strength of the U.S. competitors. The NICs are, for example, a product of (among other factors) a new international division of labor (NIDL) that began to develop in the 1970s following the increased direct foreign investment by the American (and Japanese) multinational corporations. The NIDL is based on global industrial production as opposed to the old system, which was based primarily on industrial production in the West.[108] In the meantime, the United States lost its leading edge in scientific and technological inventions and innovations, particularly to Japan and West Germany, but also to many other nations.[109]

Japan and Germany, both "losers" of World War II, are at present the major sources of world's technological advancements and economic surpluses, far ahead of the "winners" of that war.[110] Many of the leading banks in the world are now Japanese, as are such consumer industries as automobiles, computers, televisions, and VCRs. In 1990, for example, only one U.S. bank ranked among the top twenty in the world compared to eleven of Japan, of which six were at the very top.[111] That country also leads the world in electronics, transportation, and communication technology, production management, and manufacturing processes. Japan has also become the number one donor nation with a foreign aid package of over $10 billion for the Third World in 1989, some $1 billion more than the foreign aid granted by the United States in 1988.[112] The nation has also taken a leading role in the Third World debt crisis to such an extent that the American officials "jokingly refer to the 'Brady plan" as the "Bra-Zawa' plan."[113] Japan has also declared its readiness "to shoulder more of the cost of America's international commitments, as long as it receives more decision-making power in return."[114] These moves will undoubtedly increase Japan's influence in the world and in the United

Nations, among other multilateral organizations. In Spring 1990, Japan was also acknowledged as being second to the United States in the IMF power structure, having already secured the second-ranking status in the World Bank. In the meantime, Japan's defense budget, already the sixth largest in the world, is rapidly increasing. It is expected that the expanding Japanese military-industrial complex will soon replace the U.S. military presence in Asia.[115] The specter of a Japanese military build-up and its rapprochement with China is already creating tension within the OECD, adding new complications to the existing trade tension within the so-called group of seven. Meanwhile, the growing tension between the United States and Japan over economic matters is turning into the major global contradiction of the 1990s.

Germany is rightly considered "the locomotive of Europe." Its reunification has further increased the nation's economic and political potential to a significant degree, adding to its already momentous technological progress, production capacities and global market expansion. Along with the rest of EEC nations, Germany is now looking forward to the huge market that the Europe of 1992 promises and to an economic union with the Eastern European nations and perhaps the Soviet Union, where it is putting much of its attention and foreign investment resources these days.[116] Under the economic leadership of Germany, a wholly new European Bank for Reconstruction and Development has been formed to assist in the speedy transformation of the East and its integration into the reemerging European capitalist world economy (the original system existed from 1500 to the World War I in 1914). The European bank "is the first of the major international lending institutions in which the United States does not have the power to block important decisions."[117] Germany has also been taking an increasingly more independent approach vis-à-vis the United States in dealing with the Soviet Union and in NATO.[118] Now that Germans are again united, the United States can expect further assertiveness on their part.

Significant for the emerging world discord were also a rising level of mass education and political awareness, flourishing ethnic and gender consciousness, widening cultural and religious diversities, growing desire for revival of native cultures, and mounting populist and nationalist resistance to underdevelopment, inequality, and dictatorship. These trends reflect the growing importance of grass-roots politics, informal institutions, and nongovernmental organizations (NGOs) as new competitors for the nation-state and interstate formal organizations at domestic and international levels. Along with such nongovernmental internationalizing agents such as multinational corporations and a global flow of cultures, information, politics, and economics, these new tendencies have also led to a growing tension between centralizing tendencies of "authority-bound" formal structures and decentralizing demands of "authority-free" informal subgroups.[119]

The *Third World reassertion* in the Cold War period and its wavering balance-altering allegiance to this or that superpower also helped to increase tension at the world level and create a multipolar system. Therefore, it is no wonder that, during the Cold War, all bloody hot wars were fought in the Third World with direct or indirect involvement of the two rival superpowers. In the post–Cold War period and as the bipolar world melts down, the Third World has become, both a potential friend and a dangerous enemy for developed countries. The dwindling influence of the two superpowers has increasingly emboldened previously less significant regional powers. Meanwhile, as the East-West tension has declined, the North-South conflict has become more direct. The Third World is also searching for friendship and assistance in the many poles that are emerging. Consider Saudi Arabia's new warm relations with the Soviet Union, Ethiopia's new cordiality with the United States, China's growing interaction with Japan, and Iran's expanding ties with the EEC and the Soviet Union. Indeed, in a historic reversal, most Third World countries now advocate a development strategy that emphasizes foreign assistance and investment despite their bitter experience with the ballooning debt problem ($1.3 trillion in 1989), trade imbalance, and capital flight (some $20 billion in 1990, mostly lost to the United States).[120] At the same time, the Third World is trying to redefine its new priorities on the basis of more reliance on local resources and a "third way" development strategy that will supposedly combine the best of capitalism and socialism, a model also attempted in the post-Cold War Eastern Europe. However, this new approach must be viewed in the context of Third World dependency on the capitalist world market for economic growth in the medium-term.

The *nuclear parity* between the United States and the USSR is another important factor in the emergence of the multipolar world. Although this development has made any major confrontation between the two superpowers almost impossible in the foreseeable future, it has emboldened smaller power centers around the world (particularly those with economic strength). Added to this trend is a new pressure on the superpowers to contain their arms race at a time that mass destructive weapons are being proliferated at a frightening speed.[121] Meanwhile, the Warsaw Pact has disappeared and NATO will not last for long even at the present feeble level. Moreover, as the two postwar blocs have lost their internal coherence, member nations are attempting to create their own security forces. In particular, Japan is expanding its defensive capability at a rapid rate, and the European nations are forming a new Europe-wide security order. China is already a major military force, and its potential to develop into a world superpower, particularly in case of a possible alliance with Japan, should not be underestimated. The military strength of many Third World nations has also increased substantially in recent years and in such critical areas as nuclear and chemical weapons testing, production, or use. Iraq was one example; others include Brazil and India, to name only the two most significant cases. Thus, whereas the two superpowers have achieved a stable parity and are forced to contain their absurd arms race, other nations are taking advantage of the situation by producing chaos or strengthening their relative military power.

Meanwhile, a *neomercantilist* tendency is undermining the emerging world unity, within the Western alliance in particular.[122] Neomercantilism is basically reflected in a growing selective protectionism in world trade, rising jingoism in international diplomacy, and *increasing* (rather than decreasing) government involvement in both domestic and global political economies.[123] It is different from the old Western mercantilism, which used brute force in the form of colonialism and military interventions to further its trade interests. Neomercantilism is based on an emerging *neonationalism,* which is in turn based on a new definition of the *nation-state.* In sharp contrast to the old conception of nation-state as a politically independent territory to which one related with intense belongingness, loyalty, and patriotism, the new concept focuses on the shared destiny and management of that politically independent entity. Thus, issues such as democracy and participation have become integral parts of a definition of a nation-state and neonationalism.

Neonationalism is also developing along the lines of ethnic, religious, and continental interests focused on the economic well-being and cultural distinctiveness of the respective community. Thus, pan-Arabism, pan-Islamism, pan-Africanism, pan-Europeanism, pan-Americanism, and pan-Asianism are on the rise again. Of these interests, *pan-continentalism* is becoming a dominant feature of the emerging neonationalism and of international political economy. An indication of this trend is the rise in regional trading groups, largely demarcated along the existing continental lines. Thus, the three most notable trading blocs are being formed in North America, Europe, and Asia/Pacific Rim. This is partly because the new one-world system is also polarized along continental and regional lines. Significantly, the European nations are actively promoting pan-Europeanism, based on Eurocentrism, at the expense of the prevailing pan-Westernism that includes North America. Ideas such as the Europe of 1992, a European United Nations (the Paris Charter), Conference on Security and Cooperation in Europe, or a "common European home," to use Gorbachev's favored phrase, are reflections of this new trend.[124] Similarly, Asian and African politicians and intellectuals have increasingly become conscious of their continental interests and views. "The next century is the Asia Century" or "Africa will rise again" is commonly heard nowadays in the Asian and African intellectual circles.

Thus, simultaneously with the breaking of the old boundaries between the two poles of power and the emergence of new players on world scene, we are witnessing a progressive division of the "global village" into a multipolar world system in which many small and large economic, political, and cultural clusters are expected to engage in competition and cooperation. This conception of multipolarity refutes unipolarity (the United States) and is based on certain assumptions that need further clarification. The world is still *bipolar* when military strength is considered (the United States and the USSR); it is *tripolar* when economic strength is used as a criterion (the United States, Japan, and EEC); and it is *multipolar* when cultural and political-economic differences are emphasized.[125] Yet, the bipolarity and tripolarity conditions may be considered *transitional* as the world moves beyond the Cold War era. Moreover, these conditions reduce international players to major nation-states, as realist and neorealist models do, ignoring many smaller, more dynamic nation-states and numerous subgroups and NGOs (ethnic, racial, cultural, and gender organizations; transnational firms; multilateral and bilateral agencies; etc.) that have become active and effective at local and global levels. When all these players and the transitory nature of the present stage are considered, then "multipolar" becomes a better adjective for defining the emerging world system than rival characterizations.

Diminishing Utility of Offensive Force

The Cold War international relations were regulated largely on the basis of the assumption that offensive force, military or otherwise, may be used to achieve foreign policy objectives. Whereas this might have been an acceptable assumption for the pre-1970s world, it does not apply to the present global reality. Specifically, I argue that the *utility* or usefulness of *offensive* (i.e., military) force in gaining societal hegemony in the current world environment is *diminishing* to a significant degree. Offensive forces has also become increasingly unacceptable thereby leading to a more determined resistance to it, which results making it less effective in gaining intended objectives. Societal hegemony may be defined as the ability to control foreign and domestic policies of nation-states within the world system in accordance with the hegemon's needs and purposes. A hegemon may be a nation-state or a dictator. Offensive force, on the other hand, refers to any violent capacity used to introduce, postpone, or reverse a change in or impose domination and control (partial or complete) over something in spite of its will or the will of the larger community to which it is a loyal and useful member. This is distinguished from *defensive* force, which is used to resist such a change or domination and control. An offensive force that intends to reverse an original offense is a defense. What makes a force offensive is not its application but the intention behind its use. Note that offensive and defensive forces may still be used to destroy an enemy or impose temporary conditions. They may also change place in the course of a struggle; thus, an offensive force can take the form of a defensive force and vice versa. It is therefore needless to say that force continues to retain its destructive power; the destroyer, however, cannot hope to advance its cause.

Examples of the failed application of offensive force in recent international history include the American wars against Vietnam and Nicaragua, the Soviet intervention in Afghanistan, Iraqi war against Iran and its annexation of Kuwait, Israeli invasion of Lebanon in 1982, South Africa's war against the resistance movement in Namibia and the African National Congress, and the civil wars in Angola, Ethiopia, Nicaragua, Liberia, and El Salvador, to name only a few but important cases. Although these episodes have inflicted tremendous damage on the defending parties, they have not been able to achieve their real aim; namely, to impose their desired changes in or domination over the conflicting parties. It is notable that what President Reagan and his Contra forces could not achieve in Nicaragua was achieved by an election: the ouster of Sandinista from power, at least for the time being. It is equally notable that the Afghan Mujahedins should succeed in forcing the Soviet army out of their country but fail to overthrow the ostensibly unpopular Najibullah regime afterward?

Ostensibly, the examples of the Falklands (Malvinas) war between the British and Argentineans, the U.S. invasions of Grenada and Panama, and the United States–led war against Iraq do not fit in the thesis I have advanced here. However, they were either insignificant in world politics—the Grenada and Panama invasions—or were defensive as in the case of Falklands (Malvinas) and Iraq. Recall that British soldiers were not fighting to take the island from the Argentines. On the contrary, they went to war to retake it from the Argentineans who had used offensive force to regain possession of their own island, which was under the British domination. The United States–led war against Iraq was also "defensive" in that it was fought against an invader, a would-be hegemon, an offensive force; its aims were clearly defensive in nature although the Bush administration used the occasion to flex its muscles and leave a demonstration effect. Other examples of defensive use of force in recent times include the national resistance movements in El Salvador, Ethiopia, South Africa, the West Bank and Gaza, Liberia, and Chad.

We have also witnessed the collapse of dictators (although some have reemerged in other forms) in many parts of the world including Iran, Nicaragua, Paraguay, Chile, Brazil, South Korea, Pakistan, the Philippines, Haiti, Spain, Portugal, and Romania, to name the most significant cases of the last decade or so. Demand and political pressure for democratization and decentralization of the state-people relationship is also growing throughout the world. In the Soviet Union and Eastern Europe, the Communist and Workers' Parties have lost their grip over these societies, and such changes could soon shake China, Cuba, and other socialist countries. In South Africa, Nelson Mandela was freed after about twenty-eight years in the prisons of the apartheid regime that has also been forced to eliminate its legal foundation, recognizing the African National Congress and negotiating with it for a "new" South Africa. Finally, the Palestinians' *intifadah* (uprising) in the West Bank and Gaza against Israeli occupation has created wide cracks in Israeli politics and national unity; its impact has created the strongest urgency yet for a solution to the Palestinian question.

This impotency of offensive force in my opinion reflects the new global condition brought about by the profound structural changes outlined previously. Specifically, the *world-integrating* forces have brought nation-states ever closer to each other in an integrated and interdependent world system, making them sensitive to each other's behavior, policies, and needs. At the same time, the *world-disintegrating* forces have created a multipolar world system with many smaller poles of power, nation-states, and NGOs, reducing the power of the main hegemons and thus creating a crisis of leadership. Thus, the global community is caught between two diametrically opposing tendencies of integration and disintegration, generating significant tension and instability in the world order.

Under this condition, international balance of power and political stability has become a complex matter and extremely sensitive to any major change, particularly to those brought about by the use of offensive, *balance-altering*, forces. This sensitivity was well demonstrated by the unprecedented global unity against Iraq. Given the enormity and complexity of international infrastructures and the nuclear parity between the old hegemons, only forces that are truly enormous in their destructive or countervailing power could be considered balance altering. Note also that under the bipolar system, a simple balance of power was largely achieved by means of a force-parity formula between the two hegemons. In the multipolar system, on the other hand, an overall balance of power has to be negotiated among *all* poles of powers in the system.[126]

Reaction from the Superpowers

How have the superpowers reacted or adjusted their foreign and domestic policies with respect to these changes? In a nutshell, the USSR is far ahead of the United States in conforming to the ongoing global restructuring and the Soviet domestic reality. The Soviet policy makers seem to have a fairly well-articulated understanding of their nation's problems and capabilities, relative international standing, the multipolar world, and implications of all these for defense, use of force, and importance of economic growth. Their problem is an ideological one, related to a lack of a theory of practice and indecision regarding how best to manage the declining conditions at home and changing circumstances abroad. For all these and other reasons, the present Soviet leadership has also *discarded the nation's ambition* for a superpower status in world politics. However, Russian nationalism is on the rise, a factor that could revive the 19th century regional politics known as the Eastern Question.

Significantly, Gorbachev, *Time* magazine's "Man of the Decade," the winner of the Nobel Peace Prize, and perhaps a traitor to Socialists, was first among world leaders who detected the ongoing global restructuring and reformulated Soviet domestic and foreign policies accordingly in an astonishingly short time. Without his *glasnost, perestroika,* and "new thinking" in foreign policy, the world would still be frozen in the Cold War era.[127] As was clearly outlined in Gorbachev's historic speech at the United Nations in December 1988, Soviet foreign policy had ceased to view the world in bipolar terms, divided into antagonistic camps of socialism and capitalism, a view that formed the cornerstone of its foreign policy for most of the Cold War period. Instead, it actively promoted a view of the world that corresponded to the multipolar conception and as an essentially unified and interdependent system of nation-states in which the "interests of humanity," to use Gorbachev's term, took precedence over class or national interests.

Accordingly, the Soviet foreign policy has called for a "balancing" of such interests across the globe by means of negotiation and UN mediation. It also insisted that there will be no winner in a nuclear war and that security has to be based on political rather than military instruments. Arms control and settlement of regional conflicts should receive particular attention. Gorbachev also introduced "the principle of defensive (or reasonable) sufficiency and defensive (or non-offensive) defense in order to bring the political effects and the economic costs of defense policy under control."[128] Thus, the new Soviet military strategy focuses on prevention of war and the ability to retaliate in case of an attack. Gorbachev has already promised in the United Nations that the Soviet Union will not strike first, a commitment that the United States refuses to make.

Further, Gorbachev insisted that socialism and capitalism cannot develop in isolation because they are parts of one and the same human civilization. This view is radically different from the pre-Gorbachev coexistence policy that was based on the assumption that the correlation of forces in the world was moving in favor of socialism.[129] Indeed, Gorbachev's "new thinking" even gives a high priority to peace over socialism if a conflict was to emerge between the two systems. Holloway summarizes this Gorbachev's perspective clearly: "In an interdependent world it is cooperation in defense of universal values, not the conflict between capitalism and socialism, that is at the heart of international relations."[130]

The genuineness of the new policy is reflected in a number of policy practices: (1) the decision to cut the Soviet army by almost about a million men; (2) dismantling of the Warsaw Pact and COMECON; (3) signing the INF and START treaties with the United States, both of which were made possible only because of tremendous Soviet concessions; and (4) promotion of radical democratic changes in Eastern Europe and the Soviet Union, where political pluralism is replacing Stalinism and market mechanisms are being promoted to complement state planning and create economic pluralism or free-market socialism.[131] The world nervously watches and Soviet society trembles under various contradictions and conflicts as Gorbachev puts his views to practice. His main challenge in the post-August 1991 coup is how to resolve the problem of rising neonationalism and keep the USSR together, without relying on the repressive measures used by Stalin but through accommodation as in the West. Whether he will succeed in preserving the USSR and finishing the plan he originally envisioned remains in doubt; one thing is certain, however: after Gorbachev, the world and the Soviet Union will be radically different from what they were before he took office in 1985.

In sharp contrast, the United States policy makers seem baffled and uncertain about the nature and teleology of the ongoing global restructuring process and detached from the nation's enormous domestic problems. They are equally unprepared to deal with the implications of global changes and local declines for the United States relative international standing and foreign policy. For the lack of a better vision, many of them consider global changes in terms of a transition from socialism to capitalism and a defeat of the Soviet Union in the Cold War struggle. Francis Fukuyama speaks for many in the Bush administration when he conceptualizes the changes in the East as reflecting the end of history and the ultimate victory of liberal democracy over communism in the historic battle of ideas.[132] Just like many policy makers, he fails to recognize or acknowledge the enormous negative consequences of that struggle for the U.S. domestic and international conditions and implications that could follow in the foreseeable future. To give one example, the New York Times called the military-industrial environmental contamination "almost unimaginable." The clean-up project is estimated to cost "$400 billion, making it four times as costly as the Mercury, Gemini, and Apollo space programs combined and a $100 billion more than the building of the interstate highway system."[133]

Despite their perception of the USSR as declining and irrelevant to world politics, in words of one analyst, playing "second banana" on the world stage, American policy makers continue to react too over cautiously to the emerging global trends and Soviet initiatives in international relations.[134] Worse yet, they only followed the Soviet lead whenever they responded to such initiatives, without almost any significant original contribution of their own to the processes that are creating a new world order. Indeed, as Dimitri Simes wrote, "Mr. Gorbachev leaves American diplomacy with no choice but to adjust to the new international environment or to be constantly outmaneuvered by Moscow."[135] The United States has also used the Soviet demand for change as an opportunity to extract significant concessions from Gorbachev. It has further used the vacuum created by the Soviet withdrawal from the Third World to intervene in their domestic affairs and impose wars as in Grenada, Panama, and Iraq.

There is as yet hardly any consensus on U.S. domestic and foreign policy at the threshold of the new world. In particular and just like in the past, the current debate is dominated by the Hamiltonian "interventionists" and the Jeffersonian "isolationists."[136] Note that this division does not follow the conservative-liberal divide, as interventionist and isolationists could come from either of the two tendencies.[137] The emerging global order, argue the interventionist policy makers and their "organic intellectuals," is unipolar and ripe for a new American paradigm of world leadership. Under this condition, U.S. foreign policy should adopt a unilateral approach to promoting global peace and economic well-being toward a new "pax Americana."[138] They fail on at least two counts: to acknowledge the constraining impact of domestic problems on such leadership, a problem Paul Kennedy has called *imperial overstretch;* and to take account of the fact that even during its "golden age" in the early Cold War period, the United States could not manage even its part of the world effectively and remained entangled in a good number of cases in the Third World, the Middle East in particular. It is not astonishing that they became disappointed with President Bush's multilateral approach to the Kuwaiti crisis and his unwillingness to finish the job by going all the way to Baghdad; as the *New York Times* wrote, they had "hoped the war would give rise to a Pax Americana."[139]

If the limits to American power yesterday were real, it is more so today when domestic conditions are rapidly deteriorating as international conditions pose greater challenge. The fact that the rival superpower, the Soviet Union, has declined and the war in the Persian Gulf has been won hardly changes the situation in the United States' favor. The isolationists, from the Right, the Left, and the center, focus on these and other problems.[140] In particular, Flora Lewis states:

> At the extremes, the right is saying the world is too bad a place, with too many hostile conspirators, for the U.S. to be involved. The left says the U.S. is too bad, too arrogant, too flawed to presume to lead. Both are moving toward a new isolationism,

laced with resentment at economic challenges from former clients.

The more moderate ask what the U.S. is doing locked into alliances and supporting a huge military establishment if there is no longer a serious Soviet threat . . .

There is concern about deterioration within American society, the foreign debt, the decaying infrastructure, the huge gap between the comfortable and the interclass.[141] The isolationists call for drastic changes in domestic and international policies and for an "America First" policy. They argue that unless the domestic situation is improved, a successful foreign policy could not be sustained for any significant period of time. Expansion abroad in the absence of domestic economic revitalization and growth could lead to what Paul Kennedy has termed *imperial overstretch*. Their primary demand is thus for a shift of government attention and public resources from abroad and the military sector towards domestic problems and the economy. They also call for more spending in such critical areas as education, infrastructures, public welfare, and the environment.

The interventionist strategy was revived under the Reagan presidency, which began with extreme hostility toward the Soviet Union, socialist countries, and nonconforming Third World nations. The president initially used to refer to the Soviet Union as an "evil empire". The Reagan *quasi*-doctrine postulated a new world order in which "nondemocratic" (meaning socialist and radical Third World) governments were considered "illegitimate." His prescription for such governments was simple but horrifying: "Against such illegitimate governments, and particularly against Marxist-Leninist governments, there is a right of intervention."[142] The United States was also said to have "moral responsibility" to aid pro-Western insurgencies against them. The "inspiration of the Reagan Doctrine [was] offensive," wrote Robert Tucker. "Its intent [was] to show that communist revolutions [were] indeed reversible, thereby exposing a crucial myth."[143]

President Reagan was hardly successful and his major project to overthrow the Sandinistas in Nicaragua failed miserably; ironically, they were ultimately driven out of power not by the Contras or the "Freedom Fighters" as the president used to call them, but through a democratic electoral process. Nor were the changes in

Eastern Europe and the Soviet Union a result of the Reagan Doctrine; rather they are best characterized as Gorbachev's revolutions! President Reagan also visited the Soviet Union, accepted accommodation with it, changed his view of the country from an "evil empire" to a "peace-loving nation," and signed an important INF treaty with Gorbachev.[144] Despite these normalizing steps, he continued to remain a prisoner of the obsolete Cold War rhetoric and policies.

The "more gradualist and less visionary" Bush administration has initially followed a similar policy of slowly reducing tension with the Soviet Union in certain foreign policy areas while remaining loyal to the outdated approaches to foreign policy in other areas.[145] The U.S. invasion of Panama occurred when the Soviet Union was watching Nicholas Ceaucescu's fall in Romania. Just like President Reagan, President Bush also believes in "American moral responsibility" and its right to intervene, by force if necessary, whenever and wherever a member of the international system violates its set rules, functions, and procedures. More unacceptable yet, the president has claimed that the United States is the *only* country with such moral responsibility because it is the *only* country on the earth that has the means to back it up.[146]

With the Soviet withdrawal from world politics in recent years and because of other significant global changes, the Bush administration was expected to undertake a major reevaluation of its strategy in the Middle East and its foreign policy in general. As was demonstrated in the course of the Kuwaiti crisis and after, such an effort has not yet been made although certain shifts are detectable. Days after the Iraqi invasion, President Bush set a nonnegotiable agenda for Iraq and kept his option open for the use of force. Besides, as realization of some of the items in President Bush's demands for the resolution of the crisis could not be possible in the course of a normal diplomatic effort, the need for the use of force was already built into his agenda. As the *New York Times* wrote, "Mr. Bush was determined to go on the offensive from the start, against the military . . . the President only affected a posture of due deliberation."[147] The United States also used the United Nations and American military might to intimidate Saddam Hussein rather than encourage him to negotiate. This is not to say that Saddam Hussein would have negotiated in good faith, but to indicate the failure of the Bush administration to make a serious attempt in that direction.

The Bush administration is yet to produce a coherent policy for the post-Cold War period. As William Quandt explained to Andrew Rosenthal of the *New York Times,* "we [Americans] didn't have a grand design going in and we don't have a grand design coming out."[148] When and whether a coherent policy will be formulated remains to be seen. As Michael Mandelbaum has aptly summarized:

> The post-Cold War international agenda is beginning to take shape. It is not likely to be dominated by military confrontations between great nuclear powers, or even by crises like the one in the Persian Gulf. Instead, economic issues will dominate, particularly as formerly communist Europe and countries in other regions move toward market institutions and practices. For these challenges President Bush's style of leadership seems less appropriate. The attributes he lacks—the capacity to define clearly American interests abroad and the policies necessary to pursue them, a mastery of the intricacies of economic affairs, and a determination to redress the chronic imbalances of the American economy—may well be the qualities required for effective leadership in the post-Cold War era.[149]

Yet, and as David Boren, Democrat of Oklahoma, wrote, "Unless we are prepared to develop and implement a new American strategy in international politics, we could well see our own influence decline in parallel with the Soviet Union's."[150]

CONCLUSIONS AND POLICY RECOMMENDATIONS

This final part concludes the arguments made previously and advances a few policy recommendations. In sum, I have argued that the United States is motivated by a new paradigm of world leadership in the post-Cold War era. The war in the Persian Gulf was partly, if not predominantly, fought to underscore this new orientation in U.S. foreign policy. The perspective finds its advocates in "interventionists" throughout the American foreign policy establishment. However, the United States faces tremendous odds for the full realization of this dream. Even with the victory in the Persian Gulf and Soviet cooperation and decline, the United States has ended up with many seemingly unmanageable problems in the Middle East, not the least of which is the very defeated Saddam Hussein who continues to remain in power and unfriendly to his neighbors.

The ongoing global restructuring process places additional new obstacles on the U.S. drive for a hegemonic role in world politics. In particular, the global community is moving away from a *bipolar* toward a *multipolar* world system, caught between two diametrically opposing tendencies of integration and disintegration. Whereas the *world-integrating* forces have brought nation-states ever closer to each other, making them more interdependent than ever before, *world-disintegrating* forces have created many smaller poles of power, reducing the power of the main hegemons and thus creating a crisis of leadership. Consequently, a global multicentric balance of power is coming into existence and world political stability is becoming increasingly more sensitive to any *balance-altering* offensive force as was indicated by the world's decisive response to Iraq's annexation of Kuwait in August 1990.

The new situation has led to several important changes in world politics and insinuates significant implications for world peace and development. First of all, the *utility of offensive force* has diminished and, under this condition, an undesirable status quo, wherever it may exist, cannot be sustained. Dictators would also have to change their strategies as they did in the 1980s. Nor could civil or international wars be considered means for gaining dominance over the others as in the past. Thus, it can be expected that the current competition among nations to build offensive forces will be replaced by technological competition for building means for *show of force* and deterrence.

Because the military cost of force projection and deterrence is significantly lower than the military cost of building an offensive force apparatus or waging wars, less money will and should go into the military and warfare in the future. Indeed, the idea of "disarmament for development" will gain increasing global acceptability and, as international tension and militarism decrease, the "peace dividend" will grow in size in many parts of the world. Whereas military (offensive) force is diminishing in terms of its acceptability and effectiveness, *economic force* has become the most popular means of influence and domination. Japan and Germany have grown into powerful international forces almost solely by means of their economic strength. On the contrary, the United States and the Soviet Union have been increasingly weakened in international politics despite their growing military might. If it is understood that economics is emerging as a field of force, then economic development could become a part of the national defence strategy. This would, in turn, lead to a shift of more resources to nonmilitary sectors. In the meantime, increasing global awareness about environment and resource exhaustibility is expected to cause a change of policy from spending more of such resources on intensive, as oppose to extensive, projects.

Equally growing is the utility of *defensive force,* which is used to resist offensive force or domination and neutralize their impact. This particular trend implies that a more democratic and interdependent (domestically and internationally) course of development is becoming possible for smaller, less powerful countries. It also implies that the Third World will enjoy an increased negotiating power vis-à-vis the developed world in the coming years. The interdependency of the world, however, makes it impossible for the Third World to use that power negatively, as it needs to also pursue a policy of integration to realize the full potential of the world-integrating forces. This trend toward a growing utility of defensive force is assisted by the increasing utility of multilateral *negotiation* and the growing effectiveness of the United Nations in resolving many stalemated international and national conflicts over the past several years.

Indeed, the more military force becomes useless in resolving international disputes and national discord, the more nations have reverted to negotiations through such mediating forces as the United Nations. Examples of "negotiated settlements" include some twenty-two conflicts throughout the world since 1988. The most notable ones are the Iran-Iraq War, the Angola-South Africa-Cuba war over Namibia, and the U.S.-USSR-Afghanistan-Pakistan war or hostility over the Afghan question. Most these disputes have been supervised or mediated by the United Nations, which has been activated in recent years as never before, reaching a new peak during the Kuwaiti Crisis. The agency is also being supported by almost all member states, a rather unprecedented phenomenon. Even the United States, its main antagonist in the Cold War period, has been gradually moving in the direction of strengthening the agency. After years of refusing to pay its share of the UN budget, the United States paid its debt of about a billion dollars in 1990.[151] It must be noted, however, that the United States is now attempting to use the United Nations to legitimize its "go-it-alone tendency" in international politics as was demonstrated during the Kuwaiti crisis.[152]

Negotiated transitions are also promoting political democracy in many parts of the world. Examples include the countries of Eastern Europe, Spain, Portugal, Brazil, Chile, South Korea, Pakistan, the Philippines, Burma, Algeria, and Nicaragua. As a result, more people have been brought into the national political administration and development process, partly satisfying the current thirst for participation and decentralization. In short, a new political culture seems to be emerging in the world. Whatever the nature of the emerging ideologies, it is almost certain that the Cold War ideological rigidity concerning the public, private, and cooperative sectors is waning, and the idea of a *pluralistic economy* along with emerging *political pluralism* is gaining increasing acceptability. The various sectors, rather than being considered in antagonistic terms, will be viewed in terms of their intense cooperation. The present gap between planning and market forces will also be bridged in the new approach.

To be sure, the old trends continue and the new trends have yet to become material forces to significantly reshape our planet. Yet, even at their emerging stage, the new trends have had noticeable positive impacts on intersocietal relationships at international and national levels. Democracy is spreading with an unprecedented speed across the globe and there has already emerged a growing sense of optimism for world peace and development and for a more sensible and flexible world order. To appreciate the new age, one need only take note of the tremendous changes that have occurred in the East-West relations in the last few years. The Kuwaiti Crisis was an aberration, something that can happen again, but only if another attempt is made to change the status quo.

If these trends are of any serious indications, then having *ambition* alone cannot guarantee the United States a leadership position in the world; rather it needs to develop a new paradigm of social change and leadership in line with the emerging political culture.

That paradigm should take account of both domestic problems and global issues and abandon the old myths and modes of operations in favor of new realities and alternative perspectives. A paradigm that assumes that liberal democracy is the only surviving alternative, offensive force can be used effectively, the world is unipolar (i.e., the United States is the only superpower), and the status quo could be maintained or altered in favor of a "pax Americana" is simply irrelevant to the present multipolar world where a wide range of possibilities and constraints are emerging. The real challenge for American intellectuals and policy makers, the "isolationists" in particular, in the coming years is to theorize and put to practice this new paradigm.

Concerning the Middle East, a more prudent policy should encourage a better understanding of the region, utilize the United Nations more fully, and emphasize negotiation principles. U.S. interests are best served by promoting peace, democracy, and reform in the Middle East. Instead of relying on an Al-Saud or an Al-Sabah family for protection of its interests, the United States should build a lasting alliance with the aspiring middle-class intelligentsia and help it transform the region along more democratic lines. This is a more credible policy than reverting to the obsolete Nixon Doctrine or questing for world leadership in abstract terms. The Kuwaiti Crisis also indicated that a better approach to countering a balance-altering offensive force is the collective will and conscience of the world, the United Nations, rather than separate action by individual states. The United States should make every attempt to strengthen the UN role in mediating international and regional conflicts. It should at the same time avoid turning the UN into a "United Nations of America" as some Third World countries have charged. The United States must also apply the same standards to all outstanding Middle East conflicts. Application of a double standard will not be acceptable to the international community in the newly emerging world.

American interests would also be served best if the U.S. improves its image in the Middle East and the image of the Middle East in the United States. It is unfortunate that the Middle East, one of the oldest in world civilization, home of the three major world religions, and an ethnically rich community, should be seen in terms of the worst possible stereotypes: in terms of its oil wealth, geopolitical importance to the West, internal conflicts, and above all, terrorism. The number of Westerners who think all Middle Easterners are Arabs, all Arabs are Muslim, and all Muslims are terrorists is by no means insignificant. Only by changing this image can Americans assist in resolving the region's ever-increasing and potentially explosive demographic, social, economic, and political problems.

Improving the Middle East's image in the United States will demand increased cross-cultural understanding and a more realistic and better treatment of Middle Eastern content education in the U.S. high schools and colleges. Such an education should advocate internationalization of the curriculum as well as incorporation of national-specific perceptions and experiences. As Professor Ali Mazrui has shown, a more *cultural* approach to courses on world politics is particularly critical for a genuine international education.[153] The primary aim of such an education should be to promote negotiation and cross-cultural communication to foster better global relations and understanding. But it should also promote the new understanding that the use of offensive force will not be plausible in the emerging world community. Such an education should, wrote David Boren, chairman of the Senate Select Committee on Intelligence, "raise the international sensitivity of the next generation and built strong ties with nations that we had neglected because of our past focus on large bloc and superpower relationships."[154] A major condition for such a learning process involves a pedagogy that combines into a common format what is shared between nations and what divides them and increases international consciousness through contrasts, comparisons, and mutual influence.[155] The American policy makers, media, and the intellectual community have a special responsibility to make this happen. Disappearing ideas usually tend to give rise to restorationist ideologies in the same why that declining empires tend to resist change. Can the United States prove an exception to the rule?

NOTES

1. See *New York Times* (November 30, 1990), p. A10; (October 14, 1990), p. A10; (October 9, 1990), p. A12; (September 17, 1990), p. A11; and (August 26, 1990), p. A15.

2. *New York Times* (March 7, 1991), p. A8.

3. *New York Times* (December 1, 1990).

4. James Baker, "Why America Is in the Gulf," *Dispatch* 1, no. 10 (November 5, 1990). This is a publication of the U.S. Department of State.

5. *New York Times* (November 14, 1990), p. A14.

6. *New York Times* (March 7, 1991), p. A8.

7. *New York Times* (March 7, 1991), p. A8.

8. *New York Times* (February 7, 1990), p. A13.

9. *New York Times* (May 13, 1989), p. A6.

10. *New York Times* (July 28), 1991, p. A14 (editorial).

11. *New York Times* (February 24, 1990), p. A1.

12. *Business Week* (August 20, 1990); *New York Times* (January 4, 1989), p. A21; (February 16, 1989), p. D1; and (September 30, 1990), p. A1.

13. An editorial in the *New York Times* wrote that "Before the war, the administration had vacillated between reassuring and provoking Saddam Hussein. Having unwisely doubted an invasion, the President and people closest to him reacted angrily once it occurred" (May 5, 1991).

14. Doug Bandow, "The Myth of Iraq's Oil Stranglehold," *New York Times* (September 17, 1990), p. A23.

15. *New York Times* (July 25, 1990), p. A8; see also (July 26, 1990), p. A1; (July 18, 1990), p. D1; (June 28, 1990), p. D1; and (June 5, 1989), p. D2.

16. In 1986, when OPEC oil prices sharply declined, George Bush, then vice-president, went to Saudi Arabia to plead for a halt on the Saudi overproduction. "Mr. Bush told the Saudis that their overproduction, by driving down the price, was jeopardizing the American oil industry, in turn undermining the nation's economic strength and security" *New York Times* (August 18, 1990), p. A1.

17. *New York Times* (October 21, 1990), p. 1 (sec. 4); see also (December 15, 1988), p. A1, and (May 23, 1989), p. A1.

18. *New York Times* (October 25, 1990), p. A1, and (December 18, 1990), p. A1.

19. Joel Brinkley, "Israel Asks U.S. for Extra $13 Billion," *New York Times* (January 23, 1991), p. A7.

20. *New York Times* (July 19, 1991), p. A1; (July 17, 1991), p. A6; and (July 21, 1991), p. E2.

21. Harold H. Saunders, "For Israel, the Danger Is Within," *New York Times* (December 7, 1990) (op. ed.).

22. William B. Quandt, "Egypt: Now a Strategic Asset," *New York Times* (August 30, 1990), p. A23.

23. "Autocracy and Democracy in the Sand", *New York Times* (August 13, 1990), p. A14 (editorial).

24. *New York Times* (May 21, 1991), p. A20 (editorial). See also Andrew Whitley, "The Dirty War in Kuwait," *New York Times* (April 2, 1991).

25. *New York Times* (September 5, 1990), p. A14.

26. *New York Times* (September 23, 1990), p. 1E.

27. See also Efraim Karsh, "Myths About Hussein and Iraq," *New York Times* (August 13, 1990), p. A15.

28. David A. Korn, "Iraq's Criminal Credit Line," *New York Times* (October 26, 1989), p. A27; and Michael Wines, "U.S. Aid Helped Hussein's Climb; Now, Critics Say, the Bill Is Due," *New York Times* (August 13, 1990), p. A1.

29. See Flora Lewis, "Cut the Saudis Down to Size," *New York Times* (July 19, 1991), p. A27. See also *New York Times* (March 27, 1991), p. A1; (April 7, 1991), p. 1 (sec. 4); and A. M. Rosenthal, "Why the Betrayal?" *New York Times* (April 2, 1991), p. A19.

30. See *Newsweek* (April 23, 1990), p. 45, and (April 9, 1990), p. 26; *Time*, (April 9, 1990), p. 44, and (April 16, 1990), p. 30; *New York Times Magazine* (December 8, 1989), p. D1, (March 30, 1990), (April 3, 1990) (editorial), (April 30, 1990), p. A1; (August 31, 1990), p. A1, and (July 29, 1990), p. E1.

31. *New York Times* (March 15, 1990), p. A22 (editorial), (August 17, 1989), p. A1, (February 24, 1990), p. A4, Thomas A. Dine, "Bush's Assault on Israel," *New York Times* (March 15, 1990), p. A23, and William Safire, "Bush Versus Israel" *New York Times* (March 26, 1990) (op. ed.).

32. *New York Times* (September 23, 1990), p. A1. See also (March 21, 1991), p. A15; (March 23, 1991), p. A22 (editorial); and (July 31, 1991). For the text of the July 25, 1990, meeting between Hussein and Glaspie, see *New York Times* (September 23, 1990), p. A19.

33. *New York Times* (December 19, 1990), p. A16.

34. *New York Times* (August 5, 1990), p. 12; see also (February 20, 1991), p. A27.

35. *New York Times* (November 22, 1990), p. A20.

36. George Bush, "State of the Union 1991," *Vital Speeches of the Day* 62, no. 9 (February 15, 1991): 261.

37. *New York Times* (December 26, 1990), p. A10; (May 28, 1991); and (January 25, 1991), p. A11.

38. *New York Times* (August 20, 1990), p. A6.

39. *New York Times* (May 1, 1989), p. A11; (March 7, 1989), p. A1; and (April 28, 1989), p. A1.

40. *New York Times* (April 19, 1989), p. A8; (June 8, 1990); and (December 20, 1990), p. A14.

41. *New York Times* (August 21, 1990), p. A12.

42. *New York Times* (November 18, 1990).

43. See William G. Hyland, "Bush's Foreign Policy: Pragmatism or Indecision?" *New York Times* (April 26, 1989), p. A27; Michael Mandelbaum, "The Bush Foreign Policy," *Foreign Affairs* 70, no. 1 (1991): 6.

44. Flora Lewis, "On or Off the World? *New York Times* (February 20, 1990), p. A21.

45. Martin Walker, "The U.S. and the Persian Gulf Crisis," *World Policy Journal* 7, no. 4 (Fall 1990): 796.

46. Quoted in *Insight* (December 24, 1990–January 7, 1991), p. 14.

47. *New York Times* (July 28, 1991), p. 12.

48. *New York Times* (March 31, 1991), p. 1 (sec. 4).

49. Flora Lewis, "Here We Go Again Arming the Middle East," *New York Times* (March 21, 1991), p. A23; see also *New York Times*, (September 19, 1990), p. A5, and (August 11, 1991), p. 9.

50. Patrick E. Tyler, "Iraq's War Toll Estimated by U.S.," in *New York Times* (June 5, 1991), p. A5.

51. *New York Times* (April 25, 1991), p. A12; (April 5, 1991), p. A8; and (May 1, 1991), p. A24.

52. *New York Times* (June 16, 1991), p. 3.

53. *Annex: Report of the Secretary-General on Humanitarian Needs in Kuwait and Iraq in the Immediate Post-Crisis Environment by a Mission to the Area Led by Mr. Martti Ahtisaari, Under-Secretary-General for Administration and Management, Dated 20 March 1991.*

54. *New York Times* (February 21, 1991), p. A12; see also *New York Times* (February 9, 1991), p. A7; and *Village Voice* (July 30, 1991), p. 17.

55. *New York Times* (April 22, 1991), p. A10.

56. *New York Times* (July 7, 1991), p. 4.

57. *New York Times* (August 14, 1991), p. A7.

58. *New York Times* (October 8, 1990) (editorial), (December 10, 1990), p. A1, and (February 22, 1991), p. A8.

59. Noam Chomsky, "The New World Order," Open Magazine Pamphlet Series (1991), p. 24.

60. *New York Times* (November 6, 1990), p. A14, and (April 10, 1990), p. D1.

61. *Annex: Report of the Secretary-General*, p. 5.

62. Patrick E. Tyler, "U.S. Officials Believe Iraq Will Take Years to Rebuild," *New York Times* (June 3, 1991), pp. A1, A8.

63. See also *New York Times* (June 24, 1991), p. A1.

64. *New York Times* (July 7, 1991), p. A4.

65. *New York Times* (April 22, 1991), p. A10.

66. *New York Times* (August 16, 1991), pp. A1, A12, and D2.

67. See the Democratic response to the 1991 State of the Union address by Senator George Mitchell, printed in *Vital Speeches of the Day* no. 9 (February 1991), p. 263. See also *New York Times* (November 26, 1990) and *The Persian Gulf War, Iraq Under Fire, DATACENTER* (February 1991), p. 22.

68. Flora Lewis, "Cut the Saudis down to Size," *New York Times* (July 19, 1991), p. A27.

69. *New York Times* (October 12, 1990), p. A1, and (November 16, 1990), p. A13.

70. See *New York Times* (February 22, 1991), p. D5.

71. "The Arab Sheikh Who Lost a Billion in the Cocaine Bank," *The [London] Sunday Times* (July 7, 1991), pp. 1, 20.

72. *New York Times* (August 2, 1991), p. A1.

73. *New York Times* (February 7, 1991), p. A1, 17.

74. *New York Times* (March 25, 1991), p. A9.

75. *New York Times* (March 7, 1991), p. A8.

76. *New York Times* (August 27, 1990), p. D1.

77. *New York Times* (February 28, 1991), p. A11, and (February 27, 1991), p. A22.

78. George Bush, "State of the Union 1991," p. 261.

79. Theodore Geiger, *The Future of the International System: The United States and the World Political Economy* (Boston: Unwin Hyman, 1988); Noam Chomsky, *Towards a New Cold War: Essays on the Current Crisis and How We Got There* (New York: Pantheon Books, 1982); and Robert O. Keohane, ed., *Neorealism and Its Critics* (New York: Columbia University Press, 1986).

80. Robert Gilpin, *The Political Economy of International Relations* (Princeton, N.J.: Princeton University Press, 1987); Stephen Gill and David Law, *The Global Political Economy: Perspectives, Problems and Policies* (Baltimore: Johns Hopkins University Press, 1988); Hague Radice, ed., *International Firms and Modern Imperialism* (Baltimore: Penguin Books, 1975); Immanuel Wallerstein, "Patterns and Perspectives of the Capitalist World-Economy," *Comparative Marxism*, no. 9 (1984): 59–70; and Rhys Jenkins, *Transnational Corporations and Uneven Development* (New York: Methuen, 1988).

81. *Socialist Integration* (Moscow: Progress Publishers, 1974).

82. Edwin P. Reuben, ed., *The Challenge of the New International Economic Order* (Boulder, Colo.: Westview Press, 1981).

83.   Chomsky, *The New World Order.*

84.   Stuart Corbridge, "The Asymmetry of Interdependence," *Comparative International Development,* (Spring 1988): 3–29; Louis Emmerij, ed., *One World or Several?* (Paris: OECD, 1989); and Michael Stewart, *The Age of Interdependence; Economic Policy in a Shrinking World* (Boston: MIT Press, 1984).

85.   WIDER, *Debt Reduction,* Study Group Series no. 3 (Helsinki: World Institute for Development Economics Research of the United Nations University, 1989).

86.   James N. Rosenau, *Turbulence in World Politics: A Theory of Change and Continuity* (Princeton, N.J.: Princeton University Press, 1990).

87.   *New York Times* (July 31, 1991), p. A1.

88.   O. Blanchard *et al., World Imbalances: WIDER World Economy Group 1989 Report* (Helsinki: World Institute for Development Economics Research of the United Nations University, 1989); Mikhail Gorbachev, *Perestroika* (London: Fontana, 1987); Janos Kornai, *The Road to a Free Economy, Shifting from a Socialist System: The Case of Hungary* (New York: W. W. Norton and Company, 1990); and John Naisbitt and Patricia Aburdene, *Megatrends 2000: Ten New Directions for the 1990s* (New York: William Morrow and Company, 1990).

89.   Paul Kennedy, *The Rise and Fall of the Great Powers* (New York: Vintage Books, 1989), pp. 536–40.

90.   Max W. Corden, "American Decline and the End of Hegemony," *SAIS Review* 10, no. 2 (Summer–Fall, 1990): 13–26; and Michael H. Hunt, "American Decline and the Great Debate: A Historical Perspective," *SAIS Review* 10, no. 2 (Summer–Fall, 1990): 27–40.

91.   *New York Times* (October 27, 1989), p. A1.

92.   Stephen Cohen and John Zysman, *Manufacturing Matters: The Myths of the Post Industrial Economy* (New York: Basic Books, 1987).

93.   *New York Times* (August 11, 1991), p. E5.

94.   *New York Times* (November 24, 1989) (editorial).

95.   *New York Times* (August 16, 1991), p. A1.

96.   Blanchard *et al., World Imbalances.*

97.   *New York Times* (July 17, 1990), p. D2.

98.   Manuel Castells, "High Technology, Economic Restructuring, and the Urban-Regional Process in the United States," M. Castells, ed., *High Technology, Space and Society* (Beverly Hills, Calif.: Sage, 1985).

99.   *New York Times* (July 16, 1989), p. A1.

100.   *New York Times* (June 27, 1990).

101.   Tom Wicker, "Violence and Hypocrisy," *New York Times* (July 9, 1990), p. A17.

102.   Henry Kaufman, "Wall Street Heads for Darker Days," *New York Times* (February 23, 1990), p. A31 (on Drexel Burnham's collapse); *New York Times* (August 13, 1989), p. 1 (sec. 4) (on "H.U.D. Mess"); and (August 16, 1991), p. A1 (Salomon Brothers' illegal bidding in the government securities).

103.   Anthony Lewis, "The Cost of Reagan," *New York Times* (September 7, 1989), p. A27; see also *New York Times* (July 31, 1990), p. A1, and (March 13, 1990), p. D1.

104.   *New York Times* (March 20, 1990), p. A1.

105.   *New York Times* (March 18, 1990), p. A1.

106.   "Showdown for Democracy in the House," *New York Times* (February 6, 1990), p. A28 (editorial).

107.   Paul Krugman, *The Age of Diminished Expectations* (Cambridge, Mass.: MIT Press, 1990).

108.   R. B. Cohen, "The New International Division of Labor, Multinational Corporations and Urban Hierarchy," in Michael Dear and Allen Scott, eds., *Urbanization and Planning in Capitalist Society* (New York: Methuen, 1981).

109.   *World Press Review* (October 1986): 17–19; and *New York Times* (January 9, 1989), p. A16.

110.   WIDER, *Mobilizing International Surpluses for World Development: A WIDER Plan for a Japanese Initiative,* (Helsinki: World Institute for Development Economics Research of the United Nations University 1987); and *Supplement: A Collection of Comments from the International Press,* Study Group Series no. 2. See also *New York Times* (January 19, 1989), p. D26.

111.   *New York Times* (July 21, 1991).

112.   *New York Times* (January 20, 1989), p. A4.

113.   *Bra* refers to Nicholas F. Brady, the U.S. Treasury Secretary and *Zawa* to his former Japanese counterpart, Kiichi Miyazawa. See *New York Times* (April 17, 1989), p. A1.

114.   *New York Times* (March 7, 1989), p. A1.

115.   Dov S. Zakheim, "Japan's Emerging Military-Industrial Machine," *New York Times* (June 27, 1990), p. A23.

116.   *New York Times* (April 3, 1990).

117.   *New York Times* (August 4, 1990), p. L32.

118.   *New York Times* (April 28, 1989), p. A1.

119.   Rosenau, *Turbulence in World Politics.*

120.   Blanchard *et al., World Imbalances.*

121.   Leonard S. Spector, *Nuclear Proliferation Today* (New York: Vintage Books, 1984).

122.   *New York Times* (December 27, 1988), (December 8, 1990), and (July 25, 1989).

123.   Geiger, *The Future of the International System.*

124.   *New York Times* (November 22, 1990), p. A1, (November 19, 1990), p. A6, and (June 28, 1989), p. A1.

125.   Chomsky, *The New World Order.*

126.   Heldley Bull, *The Anarchical Society: A Study of Order in World Politics* (New York: Columbia University Press, 1977).

127.   Gorbachev, *Perestroika;* Mikhail Gorbachev, "The October Revolution and Today's World," *Soviet Life* (January 1987); and Francis Fukuyama, *Gorbachev and the New Soviet Agenda in the Third World* (Santa Monica, Calif.: Rand, 1989).

128.   David Holloway, "Gorbachev's New Thinking," *Foreign Affairs* 68, no. 1 (1988–1989); 73.

129.   Ibid., pp. 66–81; Hooshang Amirahmadi, "The Non-Capitalist Way of Development," *Review of Radical Political Economics* 19, no. 1 (Spring 1987): 22–46; and Yedgeniy Primakov, "A New Philosophy of Foreign Policy," *The Current Digests of the Soviet Press* (June 1988).

130.   Holloway, "Gorbachev's New Thinking."

131.   Naisbitt and Aburdene, *Megatrends 2000.*

132.   Francis Fukuyama, "Are We at the End of History?" *Fortune* (January 15, 1990), pp. 75–78.

133.   *New York Times* (August 5, 1991), p. A1.

134.   *New York Times* (July 30, 1991), p. A7, (August 4, 1991), p. 1 (sec. 4), (March 7, 1990), p. A13, (March 13, 1990), p. A15, and (August 12, 1991), p. A14 (editorial): "The Senate found a strange way to celebrate the recent signing of a landmark treaty [START] with the Soviet Union to cut nuclear arms. Within days it voted to deploy anti-missile defenses that could now spur the Soviets to reverse course and build additional arms."

135.   Dimitri K. Simes, "If the Cold War Is over, Then What?" *New York Times* (December 27, 1988).

136.   Michael H. Hunt, "American Decline and the Great Debate: A Historical Perspective," *SAIS Review* 10, no. 2 (Summer–Fall 1990): 27–40.

137.   Randall Rothenberg, "The Battle of the Columnists: Telling Leaders How to Think," *New York Times,* (September 23, 1990), p. E4.

138.   Charles Krauthammer, "The Unipolar Moment," *Foreign Affairs* 70, no. 1 (1991); 23–33; Richard Spielman, "The Emerging Unipo-

lar World," *New York Times* (August 21, 1990), p. A27; and Joshua Muravchik, "At Last, Pax Americana," *New York Times* (January 24, 1991), p. A23.

139. *New York Times* (August 2, 1991), p. A26 (editorial).

140. Leslie H. Gelb, "Look Homeward," *New York Times* (April 29, 1991) (op. ed.); and William G. Hyland, "Downgrade Foreign Policy," *New York Times* (May 20, 1991), p. A15 (op. ed.).

141. Lewis, "On or Off the World?" p. A21.

142. Robert W. Tucker, "Reagan's Foreign Policy," *Foreign Affairs* 68, no. 1 (1988): 1–27.

143. Ibid.

144. Herbert Bix, "The INF Treaty," *Monthly Review* 40, no. 2 (1988): 1–17.

145. Soul Landau, "Imperialism, Bush-Style," *New York Times* (December 22, 1989), p. A39; and Walter Lafeber, "From Roosevelt, to Wilson, to Bush," *New York Times* (December 27, 1989), p. A23.

146. George Bush, "State of the Union 1991."

147. "Lunging for War?" *New York Times* (May 5, 1991) (editorial).

148. *New York Times* (March 24, 1991) (op. ed.).

149. Mandelbaum, "The Bush Foreign Policy."

150. David Boren, "New Decade, New World, New Strategy," *New York Times* (January 2, 1990), p. A19.

151. *New York Times* (July 28, 1988), p. A30, (April 8, 1990), (September 13, 1990), p. A10, and (September 24, 1990), p. A18 (editorial).

152. R. K. Ramazani, *Future Security in the Persian Gulf: America's Role,* Policy Review No. 2, (Washington, D.C.: Middle East Insight, 1991), pp. 9–10.

153. Ali Mazrui, *Cultural Forces in World Politics* (London: James Currey, 1990).

154. David Boren, "New Decade, New World, New Strategy," p. A19.

155. Hooshang Amirahmadi, "From Diversity to Universalism in Planning Education: Toward an Interactive Pedagogy," *Ekistics* 55 (1988): 69–76.

BIBLIOGRAPHY

Hooshang Amirahmadi

The following selected list of sources on the Middle East is organized into two basic categories: published books on the Middle East and related issues, and published articles in journals, periodicals, etc. In addition, a list of recent *New York Times* articles on Middle East–related matters is included, organized by subject. In preparing the bibliography, Hooshang Amirahmadi was assisted by Edward Ramsamy and Kavitha Ramachandran.

BOOKS

Abdulghani, J. M. *Iraq and Iran: The Years of the Crisis*. Baltimore: Johns Hopkins University Press, 1984.

Abrahamian, Ervand. *Iran: Between Two Revolutions*. Princeton, N.J.: Princeton University Press, 1982.

Acharya, A. "US Strategy in the Persian Gulf: the Rapid Deployment Force as an Instrument of Policy." Ph.D. Thesis. Australia: Murdoch University, 1986.

Afkhami, Gholam. *The Iranian Revolution: Thanatos on a National Scale*. Washington, D.C.: The Middle East Institute, 1985.

Ahrari, Mohammed E. *OPEC: The Failing Giant*. Lexington: University of Kentucky Press, 1984.

Akhavi, Shahrough. *Religion and Politics in Contemporary Iran: Clergy-State Relations in the Pahlavi Period*. Albany: State University of New York Press, 1980.

Al-Sadr, Ayatollah Baqer. *Islam and Schools of Economics*. New York: Islamic Seminary, 1982.

Algar, Hamid. *The Roots of the Islamic Revolution*. London: Open Press, 1983.

Alla, M. Ata. *The Arab Struggle for Economic Independence*. Moscow: Progress Publishers, 1974.

Allison, Graham. *Essence of Decision*. Boston: Little, Brown, and Co., 1971.

Alnasrawi, Abbas. *OPEC in a Changing World Economy*. Baltimore: Johns Hopkins University Press, 1985.

Amirahmadi, Hooshang. *Revolution and Economic Transition: The Iranian Experience*. Albany: State University New York Press, 1990.

Amirahmadi, Hooshang, and Entessar, Nader. *Iran and the Arab World*. London and New York: St. Martin's Press and Macmillan Press, 1992.

Amirahmadi, Hooshang, and Parvin, Manoucher, eds. *Post-Revolutionary Iran*. Boulder, Colo.: Westview Press, 1988.

Amirahmadi, Hooshang, and Entessar, Nader. *Reconstruction and Regional Diplomacy in the Persian Gulf*. London: Routledge, 1992.

Annex: Report of the Secretary-General on the Humanitarian Needs in Kuwait and Iraq in the Immediate Post-Crisis Environment by a Mission to the Area Led by Mr. Martti Ahtisaari, Under-Secretary-General for Administration and Management, dated 20 March 1991. New York: United Nations, 1991.

Arjomand, Said Amir. *The Turban for the Crown: The Islamic Revolution in Iran*. New York: Oxford University Press, 1988.

Aronoff, M. J. *Israeli Visions and Divisions: Cultural Change and Political Conflict*. New Brunswick, N.J.: Transaction, 1989.

Asad, T., and Owen, R., eds. *The Middle East*. New York: MR Press, 1983.

Badeau, John S. *The American Approach to the Arab World*. New York: Harper and Row, 1968.

Bakhash, Shaul. *The Reign of the Ayatollahs: Iran and the Islamic Revolution*. New York: Basic Books, 1984.

Balta, Paul. *Iran-Irak: Une guerre de 5000 ans*. Paris: Editions Anthropos, 1987.

Beit-Hallami, Benjamin. *The Israeli Connection: Who Israel Arms and Why*. New York: Pantheon, 1987.

Ben Meir, Yehuda. *National Security Decision Making: The Israeli Case*. Boulder, Colo.: Westview Press, 1986.

Bill, James. *The Eagle and the Lion: The Tragedy of American-Iranian Relations*. New Haven, Conn.: Yale University Press, 1988.

Bina, Cyrus. *The Economics of the Oil Crisis.* New York: St. Martin's Press, 1985.

Bradsher, Henry S. *Afghanistan and the Soviet Union.* Durham, N.C.: Duke University Press Policy Studies, 1983.

Braudel, Fernand. *The Mediterranean and the Mediterranean World in the Age of Philip II,* vol. 1. New York: Harper and Row, 1972.

Brookings Middle East Study Group. *Toward Peace in the Middle East: Report of a Study Group.* Washington, D.C.: Brookings Institution, 1975.

Brookings Study Group on Arab-Israeli Peace, *Toward Arab-Israeli Peace: Report of a Study Group.* Washington, D.C.: Brookings Institution, 1988.

Brown, L. Carl. *International Politics and the Middle East: Old Rules, Dangerous Game.* Princeton, N.J.: Princeton University Press, 1984.

Brzezinski, Zbigniew. *Power and Principle: Memoirs of the National Security Adviser, 1977–1981.* New York: Farrar Straus and Giroux, 1983.

Bulliet, R. W. *The Camel and the Wheel,* Cambridge, Mass.: Harvard University Press, 1975.

Campbell, John C. *Defense of the Middle East: Problems of American Politics.* New York: Harper, 1958.

Carter, Jimmy. *Keeping the Faith: Memoirs of a President.* New York: Bantam Press, 1982.

Chafets, Ze'ev. *A Double Vision: How the Press Distorts America's View of the Middle East.* New York: William Morrow and Co., 1985.

Chalian, G., ed. *People Without a Country: The Kurds and Kurdestan.* London: Zed Press, 1980.

Chomsky, Noam. *Toward a New Cold War: Essays on the Current Crisis and How We Got There.* New York: Pantheon Books, 1982.

———. *The Fateful Triangle: The United States, Israel, and the Palestinians.* Boston: South End Press, 1983.

Christopher, Warren, *et al. American Hostages in Iran: The Conduct of a Crisis.* New Haven, Conn.: Yale University Press, 1984.

Chubin, Shahram, and Sepehr, Zabih. *The Foreign Relations of Iran: A Developing State in a Zone of Great Power Conflict.* Berkeley: The University of California Press, 1974.

Chubin, Shahram & Tripp, Charles. *Iran and Iraq at War.* London: I. B. Tauris & Co., 1988.

Cockburn, Leslie. *Out of Control: The Story of the Reagan Administration's Secret War in Nicaragua, the Illegal Arms Pipeline, and the Contra Drug Connection.* New York: Atlantic Monthly Press, 1987.

Cohen, Bernard C. *The Press and Foreign Policy.* Princeton, N.J.: Princeton University Press, 1963.

Cohen, Michael J. *Truman and Israel.* Berkeley: University of California Press, 1990.

Cohen, William S., and Mitchell, George J. *Men of Zeal: A Candid Inside Story of the Iran-Contra Hearings.* New York: Viking Penguin, 1988.

Cooper, C. A., and Alexander, S. S. *Economic Development and Population Growth in the Middle East.* New York: American Elsevier Press, 1972.

Copeland, Miles. *The Game of Nations.* London: Weidenfield and Nicolson, 1969.

Cottam, Richard W. *Iran and the United States: A Cold War Case Study.* Pittsburgh: University of Pittsburgh Press, 1988.

Cremeans, Charles. *The Arabs and the World.* New York: Praeger, 1963.

Curtiss, Richard. *Steal the PACS: How the Israeli-American Lobby Took Control of US–Middle East Policy.* Washington, D.C.: American Educational Trust, 1990.

Dallek, Robert. *The American Style of Foreign Policy: Cultural Politics and World Affairs.* New York: Alfred A. Knopf, 1982.

Dawisha, Adeed, ed. *Islam in Foreign Policy.* Cambridge: Cambridge University Press, 1983.

Dawisha, Adeed, and Dawisha, Karen, eds. *The Soviet Union in the Middle East.* New York: St. Martin's Press, 1982.

Dayan, Moshe. *Diary of the Sinai Campaign.* Jerusalem: Steinatzky Agency Ltd., 1966.

Dorman, William A., Manoff, Robert Karl, and Weeks, Jennifer. *American Press Coverage of US-Soviet Relations, the Soviet Union, Nuclear Weapons, Arms Control, and National Security: A Bibliography.* New York: Center for War, Peace, and the News Media, New York University, 1988.

Dorman, William A., and Farhang, Mansour. *The US Press and Iran: Foreign Policy and the Journalism of Deference.* Berkeley: University of California Press, 1987.

Duignan, Peter, and Gann, L. H. *The Middle East and North Africa: The Challenge to Western Security.* Stanford, Calif.: Hoover Institution Press, 1981.

El Azhary, M. S., ed. *Iran-Iraq War: An Historical, Economic and Political Analysis.* New York: St. Martin's Press, 1984.

Enayat, Hamid. *Modern Islamic Political Thought.* Austin: University of Texas Press, 1982.

Epstein, J. *Strategy and Force Planning: The Case of the Persian Gulf.* Washington, D.C.: Brookings Institution, 1987.

Esposito, John L. *Islam and Development: Religion and Sociopolitical Change.* Syracuse, N.Y.: Syracuse University Press, 1980.

Evance, Lawrence. *United States Policy and the Partition of Turkey, 1914–1924.* Baltimore: Johns Hopkins University Press, 1965.

Fadil, Mahmoud Abdel. *The Political Economy of Nasserism.* Cambridge: Cambridge University Press, 1980.

Farah, Elyas. *Evolution of Arab Revolutionary Ideology.* Madrid: Arab Baath Socialist Party, 1978.

Fesharaki, Feriedun. *Revolution and Energy Policy in Iran.* London: Economist Intelligent Unit, 1982.

Fesharaki, Fereidun, and Isaak, David. *OPEC, the Gulf, and the World Petroleum Market: A Study in Government Policy and Downstream Operations.* Boulder, Colo.: Westview Press, 1983.

Fieg, John P., and Blasi, John G. *There Is a Difference.* Washington, D.C.: Meridian House International, 1975.

Fischer, Michael M. J. *Iran: From Religious Dispute to Revolution.* Cambridge, Mass.: Harvard University Press, 1980.

Flapan, Simha. *The Birth of Israel.* New York: Pantheon, 1987.

Fromkin, David. *A Peace to End All Peace: The Fall of the Ottoman Empire and the Creation of the Modern Middle East.* New York: Avon Books, 1989.

Gamlen, E. "US Military Intervention in the Iran-Iraq War 1987–8," Peace Research Report No. 21, School of Peace Studies. University of Bradford, 1989.

Gellner, Ernest. *Saints of the Atlas.* Chicago: Chicago University Press, 1969.

George, Alexander, and Smoke, Richard. *Deterrence in American Foreign Policy: Theory and Practice.* New York: Columbia University Press, 1974.

Gurtov, Melvin. *The United States Against the Third World: Anti-Nationalism and Intervention.* New York: Praeger, 1974.

Haffa, R. *The Half War: Planning US Rapid Deployment Forces to Meet a Limited Contingency, 1960–83.* Boulder, Colo.: Westview, 1984.

Halliday, Fred. *Arabia Without Sultans.* London: Penguin Books, 1974.

Handel, Michael I. *Israel's Political-Military Doctrine.* Cambridge, Mass.: Center For International Affairs, Harvard University, 1973.

Harrison, Selig. *The Widening Gulf: Asian Nationalism and American Policy.* New York: Free Press, 1978.

Heller, Mark. *A Palestinian State: The Implications for Israel.* Cambridge, Mass.: Harvard University Press, 1983.

Hersh, Seymour M. *The Samson Option: Israel's Nuclear Arsenal and American Foreign Policy.* N.Y.: Random House, 1991.

Hiro, Dilip. *Inside the Middle East*. New York: McGraw-Hill; London: Routledge and Kegan Paul, 1982.

_____. *Iran Under the Ayatollahs,* rev. ed. London and New York: Routledge and Kegan Paul, 1987.

Hudson, M. *Arab Politics: The Search for Legitimacy.* New Haven, Conn.: Yale University Press, 1977.

_____. ed. *Alternative Approaches to the Arab-Israeli Conflict.* Washington, D.C.: Georgetown University Center for Contemporary Arab Studies, 1984.

_____. ed. *The Palestinians: New Directions.* Washington, D.C.: Georgetown University Center for Contemporary Arab Studies, 1990.

Hudson, M., and Acharya, A. *US Military Strategy in the Gulf: Origins and Evolution Under the Carter and Reagan Administrations.* London: Routledge, 1989.

Hunter, S. *Iran and the World: Continuity in a Revolutionary Decade.* Bloomington: Indiana University Press, 1990.

Hussain, Asaf. *Islamic Iran.* New York: St. Martin's Press, 1985.

Ismael, Tareq Y. *Iraq and Iran: Roots of Conflict.* Syracuse, N.Y.: Syracuse University Press, 1982.

Jamail, Milton, and Gutierrez, Margo. *It's No Secret: Israel's Military Involvement in Central America.* Belmont, Calif.: AAUAG Press, 1986.

Joffe, George, and McLachlan, Keith. *Iran and Iraq: The Next Five Years,* London: The Economist Publications, 1987.

Jordan, Hamilton. *Crisis: The Last Year of the Carter Presidency.* New York: G. P. Putnam's Sons, 1982.

Katouzian, Homa. *Political Economy of Modern Iran, 1926–1979.* New York: New York University Press, 1981.

Keddie, Nikki. *Roots of Revolution.* New Haven, Conn.: Yale University Press, 1981.

Kennedy, Paul. *The Rise and Fall of the Great Powers.* New York: Vintage Books, 1989.

Kerr, Malcolm H. *Elusive Peace in the Middle East.* Albany: State University of New York Press, 1975.

Khaddauri, Majid. *The Gulf War: The Origins and Implications of the Iran-Iraq Conflict.* New York: Oxford University Press, 1988.

Khalidi, Rashid. *Under Seige.* New York: Columbia University Press, 1985.

Khomeini, Imam (Ayatollah Rouholla). *Islam and Revolution: Writings and Declarations,* trans. and annotated Hamid Algar. London: KPI, 1985.

Khouri, Fred J. *The Arab-Israeli Dilemma,* 3d ed. Syracuse, N.Y.: Syracuse University Press, 1985.

Kissinger, Henry. *White House Years*. Boston: Little, Brown and Company, 1979.

Kuniholm, Bruce. *The Origins of the Cold War in the Near East: Great Power Conflict and Diplomacy in Iran, Turkey and Greece*. Princeton, N.J.: Princeton University Press, 1980.

Kupchan, C. A. *The Persian Gulf and the West: The Dilemmas of Security*. New York: Allen and Unwin, 1987.

Ledeen, Michael A. *Perilous Statecraft: An Insider's Account of the Iran-Contra Affair*. New York: Charles Scribner's Sons, 1988.

Lewis, Bernard. *The Middle East and the West*. New York: Harper Torchbooks, 1960.

Lissak, M., ed. *Israeli Society and Its Defense Establishment: The Social and Political Impact of a Protracted Violent Conflict*. London: Frank Cass, 1984.

Looney, Robert E. *Economic Origins of the Iranian Revolution*. New York: Pergamon Press, 1982.

Louis, W. R., and Owen, R., eds., *Suez 1956: The Crisis and Its Consequences*. Oxford: Clarendon Press, 1989.

Marshall, Jonathan, Scott, Peter Dale, and Hunter, Jane. *The Iran-Contra Connection: Secret Teams and Covert Operations in the Reagan Era*. Boston: South End Press, 1987.

Mazrui, Ali. *Cultural Forces in World Politics*. London: James Currey, 1990.

Milani, Mohsen. *The Making of Iran's Islamic Revolution: From Monarchy to Islamic Republic*. Boulder, Colo.: Westview Press, 1988.

Motahhari, Morteza. *Fundamental of Islamic Thought*, trans. R. Campbell. Berkeley, Calif.: Mizan Press, 1982.

Munson, Henry. *Islam and Revolution in the Middle East*. New Haven: Yale University Press, forthcoming.

Neff, Donald. *Warriors at Suez: Eisenhower Takes America Into The Middle East*. New York: Linden Press and Simon & Schuster, 1981.

Palumbo, Michael. *The Palestinian Catastrophe: The 1948 Expulsion of a People from their Homeland*. London: Quartet Books, 1987.

Peri, Yoram. *Between Battles and Ballots: Israeli Military in Politics*. Cambridge: Cambridge University Press, 1983.

Peri, Yoram, and Neubach, Amnon. *The Military-Industrial Complex in Israel: A Pilot Study*, Tel Aviv: International Center for Peace in the Middle East, 1985.

Platt, Washington. *National Character in Action: Intelligence Factors in Foreign Relations*. New Brunswick, N.J.: Rutgers University Press, 1961.

Polk, William R. *The United States and the Arab World,* 3d ed. Cambridge, Mass.: Harvard University Press, 1975.

Quandt, William B. *Decade of Decisions: American Policy Toward the Arab-Israeli Conflict, 1967–1976.* Berkeley: University of California Press, 1977.

Quandt, William B. *Camp David: Peacemaking and Politics.* Washington, D.C.: Brookings Institution, 1986.

Quandt, William B., Lesch, Ann M., and Jabber, Fuad. *The Politics of Palestinian Nationalism.* Berkeley: University of California Press, 1972.

Rajaee, Farhang. *Islamic Values and World View: Khomeini on Man, the State and International Politics.* Lanham, Md.: University Press of America, 1983.

Ramazani, R. K. *Iran's Foreign Policy: A Study of Foreign Policy of a Modernizing Nation.* Charlottesville: University of Virginia Press, 1973.

Ramazani, R. K. *Revolutionary Iran: Challenge and Response.* Baltimore: Johns Hopkins University Press, 1986.

Rodinson, Maxime. *Islam and Capitalism,* trans. Brian Pearce. Austin: University of Texas Press, 1978.

Rubenberg, Cheryl. *Israel and the American National Interest.* Urbana: University of Illinois Press, 1986.

Rubinstein, Alvin Z. *Red Star on the Nile: The Soviet Egyptian Relationship Since the June War.* Princeton, N.J.: Princeton University Press, 1977.

Ryan, Paul B. *The Iranian Rescue Mission: Why It Failed.* Annapolis, Md.: Naval Institute Press, 1985.

Safran, Nadav. *Israel: The Embattled Ally.* Cambridge, Mass.: Harvard University Press, 1981.

Said, Edward. *Orientalism.* New York: Vintage Book, 1979.

_____. *Covering Islam: How the Media and the Experts Determine How We See the Rest of the World.* New York: Pantheon Books, 1981.

Schelling, Thomas. *Arms and Influence.* New Haven, Conn.: Yale University Press, 1966.

Schiff, Ze'ev, and Ya'ari, Ehud. *Israel's Lebanon War.* New York: Simon and Schuster, 1984.

Seale, Patrick. *The Struggle for Syria.* London: Oxford University Press, 1965.

Segev, Samuel. *The Iranian Triangle: The Untold Story of Israel's Role in the Iran Contra Affair.* New York: Free Press, 1988.

Seymour, Ian. *OPEC, Instrument of Change.* London: Macmillan Press, 1980.

Shaffer, Ed. *The United States and Control of World Oil.* New York: St. Martin's Press, 1983.

Shahak, Israel. *Israel's Global Role: Weapons For Repression.* Belmont, Calif.: AAUAG Press, 1982.

Sick, Gary. *October Surprise: America's Hostages in Iran and the Election of Ronald Reagan.* N.Y.: Times Books, 1991.

Sick, Gary. *All Fall Down: America's Tragic Encounter with Iran.* New York: Random House, 1985.

Spiegel, Steven L. *The Other Arab-Israeli Conflict.* Chicago: University of Chicago Press, 1985.

Stowasser, B. F., ed. *The Islamic Impulse.* London: Croom Helm, 1987.

Suleiman, Michael. *The Arabs in the Mind of America,* Brattleboro: Amana Books, 1988.

Sullivan, William A. *Mission to Iran.* New York: W. W. Norton, 1981.

Tareq, Y. Ismael. *Iraq and Iran: Roots of Conflict.* Syracuse, N.Y.: Syracuse University Press, 1982.

Terzian, Pierre. *OPEC: The Inside Story.* London: Zed Books, 1985.

Tillman, Seth P. *The United States in the Middle East: Interests and Obstacles.* Bloomington: Indiana University Press, 1982.

Tivnan, Edward. *The Lobby: Jewish Political Power and American Foreign Policy.* New York: Simon and Schuster, 1987.

Valdes, J. M., ed. *Culture Bound.* Cambridge: Cambridge University Press, 1987.

Urquhart, Brian, and Sick, Gary, eds. *The United Nations and the Iran-Iraq War.* New York: Ford Foundation Conference Report, August 1987.

Woodward, Robert. *Veil: The Secret Wars of the CIA 1981–1987.* New York: Simon and Schuster, 1987.

Young, Ronald J. *Missed Opportunities for Peace: US Middle East Policy 1981–1986.* Philadelphia: American Friends Service Committee, 1987.

ARTICLES

Abel, Elie. "Who Weakened the Case For Israel?" *New York Times Book Review* (November 4, 1984).

Ajami, Fuad. "Egypt Retreats From Economic Nationalism," in Khalek, G. Abdel, and Tignor, R., eds. *The Political Economy of Income Distribution in Egypt.* New York: Holmes and Meier, 1982.

Akhavi, Shahrough. "Elite Functionalism in the Islamic Republic of Iran." *Middle East Journal* (Spring 1987): 194–201.

Al-Bustany, Basil. "Development Strategy: Iraq and the War Effort: Dynamics of Challenge." In M. S. El Azhary, ed., *Iran-Iraq War: An Historical, Economic and Political Analysis.* New York: St. Martin's Press, 1984.

Alnasrawi, Abbas. "Economic Consequences of the Iran-Iraq War." *Third World Quarterly* 8, no. 3 (July 1986): 869–94.

Amirahmadi, Hooshang. "A Theory of Ethnic Collective Movements and Its Application to Iran." *Ethnic and Racial Studies* 10, no. 4 (October 1987): 363–91.

_____. "War Damage and Reconstruction in the Islamic Republic of Iran." In Hooshang Amirahmadi and Manoucher Parvin, eds., *Post-Revolutionary Iran,* pp. 126–49. Boulder, Colo.: Westview Press, 1988.

_____. "The State and Territorial Social Justice in Post Revolutionary Iran." *International Journal of Urban and Regional Research* 13, no. 1 (March 1989): 92–120.

_____. "Economic Reconstruction of Iran: Costing the War Damage." *Third World Quarterly* 12, no. 1 (January 1990): 26–47.

Aruri, Naseer. "The United States and Palestine: Reagan's Legacy to Bush." *Journal of Palestine Studies* 18, no. 3 (Spring 1989): 3–21.

_____. "The Timed Passivity of Bush and Baker." *Middle East International* [London] No. 363 (November 17, 1989): 16–17.

_____. "The Battle over Jerusalem in Washington." *The Return* 2 nos. 8 and 9, (April–May 1990): 29–33.

Ashraf, Ahmad, and Banuazizi, Ali. "The State, Classes and Modes of Mobilization in the Iranian Revolution." *State, Culture and Society* 1, no. 3 (Spring 1985): 3–40.

"Autocracy and Democracy in the Sand," Editorial. *New York Times* (August 13, 1990), p. A14.

Baker, James. "Why America Is in the Gulf?" *Dispatch* 1, no. 10 (November 5, 1990).

Bandow, Doug. "The Myth of Iraq's Oil Stranglehold." *New York Times* (September 17, 1990), p. A23.

Belkaoui, Janice Monti. "Images of Arabs and Israelis in the Prestige Press." *Journalism Quarterly* 55 (Winter 1978).

Bina, Cyrus. "Internationalization of the Oil Industry: Simple Oil Shocks or Structural Crisis?" *Review* 11, no. 3 (Summer 1988): 329–70.

Bix, Herbert. "The INF Treaty." *Monthly Review* 40, no. 2 (1988): 1–17.

Bonine, Michael. "MESA and Middle East Studies: An International Perspective from North America." *MESA Bulletin* 20, no. 2 (December 1986): 155–70.

Boren, David. "New Decade, New World, New Strategy." *New York Times* (January 2, 1990), p. A19.

Brinkley, Joel. "Israel Asks US for Extra $13 Billion." *New York Times* (January 23, 1991), p. A7.

Brongenbrenner, Urie. "The Mirror Image in Soviet-American Relations: A Psychological Report." *Journal of Social Issues* 17, no. 1 (1961): 46–50.

Buheiry, Marwan. "The Saunders Document." *Journal of Palestine Studies,* No. 29 (Autumn 1978).

Bush, George. "State of the Union 1991." *Vital Speeches of the Day* 62, no. 9 (February 15, 1991): 261.

Campbell, John C. "The Soviet Union in the Middle East." *The Middle East Journal* 32, no. 1 (Winter 1978).

Chang, Tsan-Kuo, *et al.* "Determinants of International News Coverage in the US Media." *Communication Research* 14, no. 4 (August 1987): 396–414.

Chomsky, Noam. "Middle East Terrorism and the American Ideological System." *Race and Class* 28, no. 1 (1986): 13.

———. "The New World Order." *Open Market Pamphlet Series* (1991): 24.

Corden, Max W. "American Decline and the End of Hegemony." *SAIS Review* 10, no. 2 (Summer–Fall 1990): 13–26.

Cordesman, Anthony H. "Arms to Iran: The Impact of US and Other Arms Sales on the Iran-Iraq War." *American-Arab Affairs,* no. 20 (Spring 1987): 20–21.

Curtiss, R. "A Changing Image: American Perceptions of the Arab-Israeli Dispute." *American Education Trust* (1982).

DeBoer, C. "The Polls: The Attitudes Toward the Arab-Israeli Conflict." *Public Opinion Quarterly* 47, no. 121 (1983): 31.

Dine, Thomas A. "Bush's Assault on Israel." *New York Times* (March 15, 1990), p. A23.

Dorman, William A., and Farhang, Mansour. "The US Press and Lebanon." *SAIS Review* (Winter–Spring 1983).

Entessar, Nader. "Superpowers and Persian Gulf Security: The Iranian Perspective." *Third World Quarterly* 10, no. 4 (October 1988): 1427–51.

Farhang, Mansour. "The Iran-Iraq War: The Feud, the Tragedy, the Spoils." *World Policy Journal* (Fall 1985): 659–80.

Friedman, Robert I. "Selling Israel to America: The Hasbara Project Targets the US Media." *Mother Jones* (February–March 1987), pp. 21–26.

Griswold, William J. "Middle East." *Social Education* 50, no. 5 (September 1986).

Hunt, Michael H. "American Decline and the Great Debate: A Historical Perspective." *SAIS Review* 10, no. 2 (Summer–Fall 1990): 27–40.

Hunter, Jane. "Israeli Arms Sales to Iran." *The Washington Report on Middle East Affairs* (November 1986): 2.

Hurewitz, J. C. "The Middle East: A Year Turmoil." *Foreign Affairs* 59 (1981): 540–77.

Hyland, William G. "Bush's Foreign Policy: Pragmatism or Indecision?" *New York Times* (April 26, 1989), p. A27.

Karsh, Efraim, and King, Ralph. "The Gulf War at the Crossroads. *The World Today* 42, no. 10, (October 1986): 168.

Kerr, Malcolm. "Coming to Terms with Nasser." *International Affairs* (January 1967): 73–76.

_____. "Nixon's Policy Prospects." *Journal of Palestine Studies* (Spring 1973): 25.

Lewis, Anthony. "The Cost of Reagan." *New York Times* (September 7, 1989), p. A27.

Lewis, Flora. "On or Off the World?" *New York Times* (February 20, 1990), p. A21.

_____. "Here We Go Again Arming the Middle East." *New York Times* (September 19, 1990), p. A5.

_____. "Cut the Saudis Down to Size." *New York Times* (July 19, 1991), p. A27.

Marshall, Jonathan. "Saudi Arabia and the Reagan Doctrine." *Middle East Report*, no. 155 (November–December 1988): 12–16.

Moghadam, Val. "Women, Work, and Ideology in the Islamic Republic." *International Journal of Middle East Studies* 20, no. 2 (May 1988): 221–43.

Newsome, David. "Hope or Delusion." *Christian Science Monitor* (December 27, 1983).

O'Brien, Richard, "Oil Markets and the Developing Countries." *Third World Quarterly* 8, no. 4 (October 1986).

Quandt, William B. "Egypt: Now a Strategic Asset." *New York Times* (August 30, 1990), p. A23.

Quint, Michael. "Price War Fears Send Oil Tumbling." *New York Times* (October 6, 1988), pp. D1, D16.

Rubenberg, Cheryl A. "US policy Toward Nicaragua and Iran and the Iran-Contra Affair: Reflections on the Continuity of American Foreign Policy." *Third World Quarterly* 10, no. 4 (October 1988): 1467–1504.

————. "US Policy Toward the Palestinians: A Twenty Year Assessment." *Arab Studies Quarterly,* 10, No. 1 (1988).

Said, Edward. "Irangate: A Many-Sided Crisis." *Journal of Palestine Studies* 16, no. 4 (Summer 1987): 64.

Saunders, Harold H. "For Israel, the Danger Is Within." *New York Times* (December 7, 1990).

Sick, Gary. "Iran's Quest For Superpower Status. *Foreign Affairs* 65, no. 4 (Spring 1987): 705–6.

————. "Trial by Error: Reflections on the Iran-Iraq War." *Middle East Journal,* vol 43, no. 2 (Spring 1989).

Sisco, Joseph, J. "Middle East: Progress or Lost Opportunity?" *Foreign Affairs* 61, no. 3 (1982).

Slade, Shelley. "The Image of the Arab in America: Analysis of a Poll on American Attitudes." *The Middle East Journal* (1981).

Stork, Joe. "Israel as a Strategic Asset." *MERIP Reports,* no. 105 (May 1982).

Stork, Joe, and Paul, James. "The War in Lebanon." *MERIP Reports,* nos. 108–109 (September–October 1982).

Suleiman, M. "National Stereotypes as Weapons in the Arab-Israeli Conflict." *Journal of Palestine Studies* 3 (Spring 1974).

Trice, R. "The American Elite Press and the Arab-Israeli Conflict." *Middle East Journal* 33, (1979).

Tucker, Robert W. "Reagan's Foreign Policy." *Foreign Affairs* 68, no. 1 (1988): 1–27.

Tyler, Patrick E. "US Officials Believe Iraq Will Take Years to Rebuild." *New York Times* (June 3, 1991), p. A1.

————. "Iraq's War Toll Estimated by US." *New York Times* (June 5, 1991), p. A5.

Walker, Martin. "The US and the Persian Gulf Crisis." *World Policy Journal* 7, no. 4 (Fall 1990): 796.

Whitley, Andrew. "The Dirty War in Kuwait" (op. ed.). *New York Times* (May 21, 1991), p. A21.

Wilson, Evan. "The Palestine Papers, 1943–1947." *Journal of Palestine Studies* 2, no. 4 (Summer 1973).

Wines, Michael. "US Aid Helped Hussein's Climb—Now Critics Say, the Bill Is Due." *New York Times* (August 13, 1990), p. A1.

RECENT NEW YORK TIMES ARTICLES

The following list of recent *New York Times* articles focus on a variety of subjects relating to the Middle East and United States foreign policy.

The New World Order and U.S. Relations with the UN,
the Soviet Union, Japan, EEC (NATO), and Others

"As US Warms to UN, It Finds Unpaid Debts Embarrassing." *New York Times* (September 13, 1990).

"Rising Slowly to Gorbachev's Challenge." *New York Times* (December 9, 1988).

"After Years in the Shadow of the US, Soviets Take the Mideast Initiative." *New York Times* (February 20, 1989).

"Transcript of Bush's Remarks on Transforming Soviet-American Relations." *New York Times* (May 13, 1989).

"US to Tell Allies It Will Aid Soviets by Using Experts." *New York Times* (July 9, 1990).

"US and the Soviets as Allies? It's the First Time Since 1945." *New York Times* (August 8, 1990).

"Baker Outlines Plan for Allied Aid to Soviet Union." *New York Times* (June 19, 1991).

"A Better Neighbor Policy." *New York Times* (July 9, 1990).

"US Plans to Be 'Midwife' to a New Rule in Ethiopia." *New York Times* (May 26, 1991).

"Japan, Growing Bolder, Tries to Nudge Burma." *New York Times* (August 18, 1988).

"The Ant and the Grasshopper." *New York Times* (January 9, 1989).

"Japan's Trade Surplus Hits a Record in December." *New York Times* (January 19, 1989).

"Japan to Be No. 1 Giver of Foreign Aid." *New York Times* (January 20, 1989).

"Japan Ready to Share Burden, But Also the Power, with US." *New York Times* (March 7, 1989).

"Japan Takes a Leading Role in Third World Debt Crisis." *New York Times* (April 17, 1989).

"Tokyo, Unsure of US Intentions, Talks of Developing Its Own Arms." *New York Times* (June 28, 1989).

"More Power for Japan's Protectionists." *New York Times* (July 25, 1989).

"Japan Far Ahead of US in Raising Corporate Capital." *New York Times* (October 27, 1989).

"Japanese Economy Surges at 9.3 percent Rate as Exports Rise." *New York Times* (December 7, 1989).

"Japan's Emerging Military-Industrial Machine." *New York Times* (June 27, 1990).

"Purchases by Japanese of US Concerns Climb." *New York Times* (July 17, 1990).

"For Japan's Military, Some Second Thoughts About Where the Enemy Is." *New York Times* (July 29, 1990).

"NATO Looks to Newer, Fewer Arms." *New York Times* (April 1989).

"The Bush Administration Faces the Issue, Is NATO Becoming Obsolete?" *New York Times* (April 19, 1989).

"NATO Decides to Tango." *New York Times* (May 31, 1989).

"Excerpts from Joint Communique by Leaders at NATO Summit Meeting." *New York Times* (May 31, 1989).

"A New Phase Begins in Europe's Unification." *New York Times* (July 2, 1989).

"Redefining Europe." *New York Times* (November 11, 1989).

"Now, NATO Is in Search of a New Self." *New York Times* (June 8, 1990).

"A 'Last Resort' for NATO." *New York Times* (July 5, 1990).

"NATO at a Glance." *New York Times* (July 7, 1990).

"Text of the Declaration After the NATO Talks." *New York Times* (July 7, 1990).

"Now a New Europe." *New York Times* (July 21, 1990).

"Designing the New Europe: Plenty to Argue About." *New York Times* (November 19, 1990).

"Excerpts from the Charter of Paris for a New Europe as Signed Yesterday." *New York Times* (November 22, 1990).

"34 Lands Proclaim a United Europe in Paris Charter." *New York Times* (November 22, 1990).

"West Europeans Formally Initiate Closer Federation." *New York Times* (December 16, 1990).

"The New Europe." *New York Times* (December 26, 1990).

"Amid the Gulf Crisis and the Cold War End, Questions on U.S. and NATO Roles." *New York Times* (December 26, 1990).

"US and France Are at Odds over a NATO Army." *New York Times* (May 28, 1991).

"If the Cold War Is over, Then What?" *New York Times* (December 27, 1988).

"The New Old World." *New York Times* (August 19, 1989).

"Imperialism, Bush Style." *New York Times* (December 22, 1989).

"As Two Worlds Warm, A Post-Postwar Order Awaits." *New York Times* (December 24, 1989).

"From Roosevelt, to Wilson, to Bush." *New York Times* (December 27, 1989).

"New Decade, New World, New Strategy." *New York Times* (January 2, 1990).

"On or Off the World." *New York Times* (February 20, 1990).

"After the Cold War." *New York Times* (July 10, 1990).

"A New Kind of Crisis." *New York Times* (August 9, 1990).

"No, the US Isn't in Decline." *New York Times* (October 3, 1990).

"Policing the World." *New York Times* (October 17, 1990).

"The Emerging Unipolar World." *New York Times* (August 21, 1990).

"As Gulf Crisis Solidifies the World Order, Cuba Feels Left Out." (September 29, 1990).

"The New World Order." *New York Times* (October 23, 1990).

"At Last, Pax Americana." *New York Times* (January 24, 1991).

"The New World Order Checklist," *New York Times* (February 19, 1991).

"What Kind of Order?" *New York Times* (June 8, 1991).

"Along the East-West Fault Line, Signs of Stress as Ideology Erodes," *New York Times* (February 26, 1989).

"Ending Where It Began," *New York Times* (February 27, 1989).

"Excerpts from Czech Chief's Address to Congress," *New York Times* (February 22, 1990).

"For Eastern Europe, Security Means More Than Tanks and Guns," *New York Times* (June 23, 1991).

"Excerpts from Gorbachev Speech Before 28th Communist Party Congress," *New York Times* (July 3, 1990).

"Reading Tea Leaves of Soviet Fate: US Experts Look Ahead," *New York Times* (December 22, 1990).

"A 'Gorbachev Doctrine' Takes Shape," *New York Times* (January 16, 1991).

"Gorbachev's Address," *New York Times* (December 8, 1988).

"Excerpts from Speech by Gorbachev in France," *New York Times* (July 7, 1989).

"Before Our Eyes, the Bloc Splinters," *New York Times* (August 25, 1989).

"Gorbachev, in Finland, Disavows Any Right of Regional Intervention," *New York Times* (October 26, 1989).

"Gorbachev, in Oslo, Links World Peace to Perestroika," *New York Times* (June 6, 1991).

"A Guide to Some of the Scariest Things on Earth," *New York Times* (December 25, 1988).

"How to Fight Global Warming," *New York Times* (February 7, 1990).

"Too Cool on Global Warming," *New York Times* (February 8, 1990).

"Europeans Begin to Calculate the Price of Pollution," *New York Times* (December 9, 1990).

"Euphoria Gives Way to Fractured Feelings of Gloom," *New York Times* (December 23, 1990).

"Cold War II Has Begun," *New York Times* (February 14, 1991).

"Avoiding New World Disorder," *New York Times* (February 25, 1991).

"A Revived UN Needs US Cash," *New York Times* (July 22, 1988).

"Bush, the UN and Too Many People," *New York Times* (September 22, 1989).

"US May Cut Dues to UN Over Arab Resolution," *New York Times* (November 26, 1989).

"US Threatens to Halt UN Payments," *New York Times* (November 28, 1989).

"Bush Would Pay off UN Debt over Five Years," *New York Times* (February 3, 1990).

"Congress Holds up Part of UN Dues," *New York Times* (April 8, 1990).

"The United Nations Comes of Age, Causing Some Anxiety," *New York Times* (August 5, 1990).

"UN as Well, Is Entering the Post-Cold-War Era," *New York Times* (September 24, 1990).

"Getting Serious About the UN," *New York Times* (September 24, 1990).

"Transcript of President's Address to UN General Assembly," *New York Times* (October 2, 1990).

"Bush Rebuffs Gorbachev's Move For Swifter Cuts in Nuclear Arms," *New York Times* (July 7, 1989).

"We've Forgotten About the Bomb," *New York Times* (November 4, 1989).

The United States and Middle East Politics

"Iran Says Talks with US Are Postponed Indefinitely," *New York Times* (December 15, 1990).

"Text of Resolution on the Palestinians," *New York Times* (December 12, 1990).

"A Tragic Convergence," *New York Times* (January 11, 1991).

"PLO Militant Reportedly Leaves Syria for Iraq," *New York Times* (September 13, 1990).

"US Urges Talks on Missiles in Mideast," *New York Times* (December 27, 1988).

"US to Sell Saudis $20 Billion in Arms; Weapons Deal Is Largest in History," *New York Times* (September 15, 1990).

"US Explores New Strategies to Limit Weapons of Mass Destruction," *New York Times* (September 30, 1990).

"$13 Billion Weapons Sale to Saudis Will Be Delayed," *New York Times* (January 5, 1991).

"US Aims in Gulf Are Questioned," *New York Times* (February 24, 1991).

"Disarming the Gulf," *New York Times* (March 2, 1991).

"Here We Go Again—Arming the Mideast," *New York Times* (March 21, 1991).

"Bizarre Priorities on Arms," *New York Times* (March 21, 1991).

"US Says Iraqis' Uranium Is Still Enough for One Bomb," *New York Times* (May 1, 1991).

"Bush Unveils Plan for Arms Control in the Middle East," *New York Times* (May 30, 1991).

"Cheney Says US Plans New Arms Sale to the Mideast," *New York Times* (June 5, 1991).

"On Mideast, US Isn't Pausing for Transition," *New York Times* (January 1, 1989).

"Bush's Foreign Policy: Pragmatism or Indecision?" *New York Times* (April 26, 1989).

"The Mideast, as Seen by James Baker," *New York Times* (October 15, 1989).

"Only Washington Can Break Mideast Stalemate," *New York Times* (June 15, 1990).

"Ill Equipped for the Crisis of the 1990s," *New York Times* (August 7, 1990).

"Old Habits Ensnare the Middle East Again," *New York Times* (April 21, 1991).

"Baker Seeks Peace Talks in Two Stages," *New York Times* (April 22, 1991).

"Baker Tours the Mideast on a Shuttle That Leaves No Tracks," *New York Times* (April 23, 1991).

"Mideast Peace: Grasp This Chance," *New York Times* (April 25, 1991).

"US Is Said to Offer to Back Israel with Veto in UN," *New York Times* (June 19, 1991).

"Rethinking Foreign Aid," *New York Times* (April 9, 1990).

"Gulf Special Aid: $13 Billion," *New York Times* (November 6, 1990).

"Egypt Presses US over Peace Plans," *New York Times* (May 17, 1989).

"Islamic Fundamentalism Is Winning Votes," *New York Times* (July 1, 1990).

"US Wants Saudi Torture Suit Settled," *New York Times* (April 23, 1991).

"Syria Seen as Isolated by Iran Support and Lebanon Setbacks," *New York Times* (September 26, 1988).

"Syrians Let Egypt Go to Arab Summit," *New York Times* (May 15, 1989).

"The Deadly Syrian Gamble: Lebanon Is the Stake," *New York Times* (August 17, 1989).

"Syrian Leader Visits Cairo, Mending Ties," *New York Times* (July 15, 1990).

"Israel Accedes to US Rights Monitoring," *New York Times* (June 26, 1988).

"US Agrees to Talks with PLO, Saying Arafat Accepts Israel and Renounces Terrorism," *New York Times* (December 15, 1988).

"Baker's Decision-Making Process an Early Test from the PLO," *New York Times,* (February 2, 1989).

"Israel-US Talks May Pave Way for Peace Plan," *New York Times* (March 11, 1989).

"Baker, in a Middle East Blueprint, Asks Israel to Reach out to Arabs," *New York Times* (May 23, 1989).

"Behind US-Israeli-Facade, Tension on Hostages," *New York Times* (August 17, 1989).

"Bush and Baker Press the Israeli to End Deadlock on Peace Plan," *New York Times* (February 23, 1990).

"Baker Press Israel to Open Peace Talks," *New York Times* (February 24, 1990).

"Bush's Assault on Israel," *New York Times* (March 15, 1990).

"The Right Bush Push on Israel" (Editorial), *New York Times* (March 15, 1990).

"Bush Versus Israel," *New York Times* (March 26, 1990).

"Baker Seeks to Avoid Breaking off PLO Talks," *New York Times* (June 9, 1990).

"Baker Rebukes Israel on Peace Terms," *New York Times* (June 14, 1990).

"Americans' Support for Israel: Solid, But Not the Rock It Was," *New York Times* (July 9, 1990).

"Israel's Friends and Enemy" (Editorial), *New York Times* (October 18, 1990).

"Arab League Rebuffs PLO; Won't Condemn US," *New York Times* (October 19, 1990).

"A New Anti-Israel Move at the UN Is Vexing US," *New York Times* (October 20, 1990).

"Special Relationship Reaches Its Limits," *New York Times* (October 21, 1990).

"US Joins in Second Vote at UN to Criticize Israel over 21 Slain," *New York Times* (October 25, 1990).

"US Backs UN Bid Criticizing Israel," *New York Times* (December 18, 1990).

"Needed: Middle East Peace Talks," *New York Times* (January 2, 1991).

"Israel Asks US for Extra $13 Billion," *New York Times* (January 23, 1991).

"Impact of Missiles: Israel and US Attend to Each Other Better," *New York Times* (January 27, 1991).

"US Approves $400 Million in Guarantees for Israeli Housing," *New York Times* (February 21, 1991).

"Arafat Meets Formally with European Community," *New York Times* (January 28, 1989).

"PLO and Israel to Get Ideas from Bush on Easing Mideast Tension," *New York Times* (March 21, 1989).

"No Peace from Mr. Shamir," *New York Times* (April 4, 1989).

"Arafat, Yielding, Now Backs Palestinian-Israeli Dialogue," *New York Times* (February 24, 1990).

"Again, Palestinians Suffer," *New York Times* (March 6, 1990).

OPEC and the Oil Factor in Middle East Politics

"Meet OPEC's New Friend, US," *New York Times* (January 4, 1989).

"Energy Prices Move Higher as OPEC Pact Is Expected," *New York Times* (May 25, 1989).

"Saudis and Kuwait at Odds on Oil Output," *New York Times* (June 5, 1989).

"OPEC in Strong Position at Meeting," *New York Times* (March 16, 1990).

"Iraq Seeks Bigger Role in OPEC," *New York Times* (June 28, 1990).

"Threat Issued by Iraqis on Oil Overproduction," *New York Times* (July 18, 1990).

"OPEC Meets Today; Talks Are Clouded by Iraq's Threat to Kuwait," *New York Times* (July 25, 1990).

"Iraq Said to Prevail in Oil Dispute with Kuwait and Arab Emirates," *New York Times* (July 26, 1990).

"OPEC in Agreement to Raise Oil Price by Cutting Output," *New York Times* (July 28, 1990).

"OPEC Comes Under the Sway of Iraq," *New York Times* (July 29, 1990).

"Saudis Raise Oil Supply, Even Without OPEC," *New York Times* (August 19, 1990).

"Attempt to Set OPEC Meeting Fails," *New York Times* (August 23, 1990).

"OPEC Members Close to Raising Output Ceiling," *New York Times* (August 28, 1990).

"Delay Sought in Meeting of OPEC," *New York Times* (August 29, 1990).

"Increased Oil Production Is Authorized by OPEC," *New York Times* (August 30, 1990).

"Big Oilfield Is at the Heart of Iraq-Kuwait Dispute," *New York Times* (September 3, 1990).

"Oil Exports by Saudis Rise Sharply, Making up Loss from Embargo," *New York Times* (November 4, 1990).

"OPEC Planning to Restore Oil Quotas After Crisis Ends," *New York Times* (December 13, 1990).

"Oil Imports in January Topped Output in US," *New York Times* (February 16, 1989).

"Oil Prices Seen Rising by 50 percent in Next Five Years," *New York Times* (February 24, 1990).

"Oil Crisis Like 1973's? It's Not Necessarily So," *New York Times* (August 13, 1990).

"Energy Policy Trade-Off," *New York Times* (August 18, 1990).

"Oil Prices Rise Above $31 a Barrel," *New York Times* (August 23, 1990).

"The Real Cost of Mideast Oil," *New York Times* (September 4, 1990).

"Gulf Crisis Activates Loan Plans," *New York Times* (September 17, 1990).

"Oil Drops to $25.35 a Barrel, Lowest Price Since August 3," *New York Times* (December 13, 1990).

"Shell Oil Shareholders Awarded $110 Million, *New York Times* (December 13, 1990).

"Saudi Prince to Become Citicorp's Top Stockholder," *New York Times* (February 22, 1991).

The Persian Gulf War: Origins and Consequences

"Bush Jumped the Gun in the Gulf," *New York Times* (August 18, 1990).

"Arafat Stresses Linkage in Settling Gulf Crisis," *New York Times* (November 26, 1990).

"Sure Losers: the Palestinians," *New York Times* (January 27, 1991).

"Israel Fears That Peace in the Persian Gulf Will Unleash a Bitter Foe," *New York Times* (July 24, 1988).

"Iraqis Announce Test of a Rocket," *New York Times* (December 8, 1989).

"Iraq Said to Build Launchers for Its 400-Mile Missiles," *New York Times* (March 30, 1990).

"Iraq's Murderous Threats," *New York Times* (April 3, 1990).

"Iraq Chief, Boasting of Poison Gas, Warns of Disaster If Israelis Strike," *New York Times* (April 30, 1990).

"US Ready to Give Israel New Arms as Signal to Iraq, *New York Times* (August 31, 1990).

"Top Israelis Warn of Deep Worry over Diplomatic Accord in Gulf," *New York Times* (December 4, 1990).

"Israel Warns Against a Gulf Retreat," *New York Times* (December 6, 1990).

"Israel and Iraq, Unlinked," *New York Times* (December 19, 1990).

"Experts Tally the Cost of Rebuilding Kuwait," *New York Times* (September 17, 1990).

"The Staggering Costs of a Mideast War," *New York Times* (September 27, 1990).

"Who Will Pay for the Gulf Crisis," *New York Times* (October 8, 1990).

"Cost Estimate over $10 Billion for US Gulf Force," *New York Times* (December 10, 1990).

"Why War Is Irrelevant," *New York Times* (January 9, 1991).

"Oil Company Ecologist Fears Slick Will Leave a 'Dead Gulf'," *New York Times* (February 9, 1991).

"The Gulf Oil Spill Cleanup Flounders in Bureaucracy," *New York Times* (February 21, 1991).

"Gulf War May Cost $77 Billion in Fiscal 1991, US Data Show," *New York Times* (February 22, 1991).

"War Damage," *New York Times* (February 25, 1991).

"Excerpts from UN Report on Need for Humanitarian Assistance in Iraq," *New York Times* (March 23, 1991).

"UN Survey Says Iraq Suffered Vast Damage," *New York Times* (March 23, 1991).

"The Dirty War in Kuwait," *New York Times* (April 2, 1991).

"Iran Says One Million Iraqi Kurds Are on Its Border and May Be Admitted," *New York Times* (April 5, 1991).

"Iraq Is Left to the Mercy of Saddam Hussein," *New York Times* (April 7, 1991).

"US and Europe Agree on Safe Haven for Kurds," *New York Times* (April 12, 1991).

"Private Relief Agencies Find Big Obstacles to Aiding Kurds," *New York Times* (April 12, 1991).

"Slow Progress Frustrates All Involved as Oil Wells Burn at $1000 a Second," *New York Times* (April 22, 1991).

"UN Uncertain of Death Rate at Kurds' Camps," *New York Times* (April 25, 1991).

"US May Send More to Kurds in Iran," *New York Times* (April 30, 1991).

"Gulf War II," *New York Times* (May 1, 1992).

"US Officials Believe Iraq Will Take Years to Rebuild," *New York Times* (June 3, 1991).

"Iraq's War Toll Estimated by US," *New York Times* (June 5, 1991).

"Displaced in the Gulf War: 5 Million Refugees," *New York Times* (June 16, 1991).

"Shoulder to Shoulder with the Soviets Against Iraq," *New York Times* (September 10, 1990).

"US and Soviets Say More UN Action Is Needed to Oust the Iraqis," *New York Times* (November 21, 1990).

"For Some, a US Victory Would Be the Third World's Loss, *New York Times* (January 27, 1991).

"Japan Offering Billions to Arabs to Help Offset Gulf Crisis Losses," *New York Times* (August 23, 1990).

"Japan Counts the Costs of Gulf Action—or Inaction," *New York Times* (January 27, 1991).

"Pope, in Christmas Message, Warns on Gulf War," *New York Times* (December 26, 1990).

"Gorbachev Cheers Iranian in Moscow," *New York Times* (June 21, 1989).

"Soviets Issue Their First Criticism of American Presence in the Gulf," *New York Times* (August 31, 1990).

"Soviets Suggest Conference Combining Issues of Mideast," *New York Times* (September 5, 1990).

"Bush and Gorbachev Say Iraqis Must Obey UN and Quit Kuwait," *New York Times* (September 10, 1990).

"Top Soviet General Tells US Not to Attack in the Gulf," *New York Times* (October 3, 1990).

"Soviet Envoy, in US, Voices Worry at Conduct of War," *New York Times* (January 27, 1991).

"Excerpts from Statement by Gorbachev on the Gulf," *New York Times* (February 10, 1991).

"Reflecting a Cooling by Kremlin, Press Grows Critical of Iraq War," *New York Times* (February 15, 1991).

"Moscow Welcomes Baghdad's Offer," *New York Times* (February 16, 1991).

"Moscow's Statement on the Iraqis' Response," *New York Times* (February 22, 1991).

"For Bush, Half a Loaf?" *New York Times* (February 20, 1991).

"US Gives Gorbachev a Detailed Response to Kremlin Proposal," *New York Times* (February 20, 1991).

"Transcript of White House Statement and News Conference on Soviet Plan," *New York Times* (February 22, 1991).

"Moscow Sends Revised Plan to Baghdad," *New York Times* (February 23, 1991).

"Transcript of Comments on Soviet Peace Proposal," *New York Times* (February 23, 1991).

"Statement by Iraqi Revolutionary Council," *New York Times* (February 23, 1991).

"Soviet, at UN, Sides with Allies on Setting Terms For Cease-Fire," *New York Times* (February 27, 1991).

"Excerpts from Gorbachev's Speech," *New York Times* (June 6, 1991).

"US Is Seeking to Forestall any Arab Deal for Kuwait," *New York Times* (August 5, 1990).

"A President Puts Himself on the Spot," *New York Times* (August 6, 1990).

"The Uses of Force," *New York Times* (August 7, 1990).

"A US Strategy for the Gulf Crisis," *New York Times* (August 7, 1990).

"Strategy: Embargo," *New York Times* (August 9, 1990).

"Excerpts from Bush's News Conference on the Iraqi Invasion of Kuwait," *New York Times* (August 9, 1990).

"First American Deployment to Gulf Is 'Tip of Wedge,' the Pentagon Says," *New York Times* (August 9, 1990).

"US May Send Saudis a Force of 50,000, Iraqis Respond by 'Annexing Kuwait'," *New York Times* (August 9, 1990).

"Reading Saddam's Mind," *New York Times* (August 10, 1990).

"Once More, the US Misreads the Arab World," *New York Times* (August 10, 1990).

"Bush Threatens a Blockade of Jordan Port Aiding Iraq," *New York Times* (August 15, 1990).

"Bush Says Iraqi Aggression Threatens 'Our Way of Life'," *New York Times* (August 16, 1990).

"Bush Tells Iraqis Leaders Put Them on Brink of War," *New York Times* (September 17, 1990).

"Excerpts from Bush's Remarks on His Order to Enlarge US Gulf Force," *New York Times* (November 9, 1990).

"Text of Report by Iraq Accepting US Plan," *New York Times* (January 5, 1991).

"Text of Letter from Bush to Hussein," *New York Times* (January 13, 1991).

"Why the Betrayal?" *New York Times* (April 2, 1991).

"The Minimum for Gulf Peace," *New York Times* (August 29, 1990).

"Baker Foresees a Long Stay for US Troops in Mideast; Urges a Regional Alliance," *New York Times* (September 5, 1990).

"US Officials Begin Tour to Seek Financial Backing for Gulf Force," *New York Times* (September 5, 1990).

"America Broadens Its Mideast Involvement," *New York Times* (September 9, 1990).

"A Peace Strategy for the Persian Gulf," *New York Times* (December 26, 1990).

"Needed Middle East Peace Talks," *New York Times* (January 2, 1991).

"Games over Dates," *New York Times* (January 4, 1991).

"Don't Take Hussein's Bait," *New York Times* (February 7, 1991).

"Political Cost of Victory Questioned," *New York Times* (December 6, 1990).

"Limited War, Maximum Advantage," *New York Times* (February 4, 1991).

"Many Cooks for the Middle East Pot," *New York Times* (February 10, 1991).

"For Lasting Peace: Tougher Terms," *New York Times* (February 20, 1991).

"What's the Real Goal?" *New York Times* (February 20, 1991).

"Aides Discuss Pressing for Hussein's Removal," *New York Times* (February 25, 1991).

"After the War, the Saudis Prepare for a New Role Among the Arabs," *New York Times* (March 2, 1991).

"Powell Says US Will Stay in Iraq for Some Months," *New York Times* (March 23, 1991).

"What the US Wants to Happen in Iraq Remains Unclear," *New York Times* (March 24, 1991).

"US and Bahrain Near Pact on Permanent Military Base," *New York Times* (March 25, 1991).

"Schwarzkopf Says Truce Enabled Iraqis to Escape," *New York Times* (March 27, 1991).

"US Offers a Plan for Mideast Talks," *New York Times* (March 28, 1991).

"Liberated in Kuwait: Arrogance," *New York Times* (May 21, 1991).

"Worried Turks Prefer Iraq to Remain Whole," *New York Times* (March 6, 1991).

"How Can the US Stand Idly By?" *New York Times* (April 2, 1991).

"Iraqi Kurds Reject Autonomy Accord as Allied Plan Stirs Some Confidence," *New York Times* (June 30, 1991).

"UN Expected to Approve Iraq and Kuwait Trade Ban," *New York Times* (August 6, 1990).

"Security Council, 13 to 0, Votes to Block Trade with Baghdad; Facing Boycott, Iraq Slows Oil," *New York Times* (August 7, 1990).

"UN Council Declares Void Iraqi Annexation of Kuwait," *New York Times* (August 10, 1990).

"Soviets and UN Differ on UN's Progress in Talks on Use of Force," *New York Times* (August 24, 1990).

"Text of Resolution by UN Security Council," *New York Times* (August 26, 1990).

"US Insists Individual Nations Can't Break Blockade of Iraq," *New York Times* (September 8, 1990).

"Text of the Resolution Condemning Action by Iraq," *New York Times* (September 17, 1990).

"Iraq, at UN, Accuses US of 'Western Imperialism'," *New York Times* (October 6, 1990).

"Text of Resolution Adopted by UN Council," *New York Times* (October 14, 1990).

"Delegates Make an Appeal for a UN Role in Mideast," *New York Times* (October 14, 1990).

"UN Sponsorship of a War in the Gulf Is No Simple Matter," *New York Times* (October 28, 1990).

"Text of the UN Security Council," *New York Times* (October 30, 1990).

"Aides Urge UN Chief to Offer Iraq Mideast Talks If It Quits Kuwait," *New York Times* (January 12, 1991).

"Text of Statement by UN Chief in Appeal to Iraq," *New York Times* (January 16, 1991).

"Last Minute Debating; Then Final Plea to Iraq," *New York Times* (January 16, 1991).

"New Peace Plan at UN," *New York Times* (February 15, 1991).

"US and Britain Assert UN Power," *New York Times* (February 22, 1991).

"UN Security Council Drafts Plan to Scrap Most Deadly Iraqi Arms," *New York Times* (March 27, 1991).

"Excerpts From Letter to UN: Iraqis 'Accept This Resolution'," *New York Times* (April 8, 1991).

"Egypt's Reward: Forgiven Debt," *New York Times* (April 10, 1991).

"US Delegation to Press Iraq on Reparations in Stark Case," *New York Times* (March 22, 1989).

"Iraq's Criminal Credit Line," *New York Times* (October 26, 1989).

"Congress Backs Curbs Against Iraq," *New York Times* (July 28, 1990).

"Must the US Give Brazil and Iraq the Bomb," *New York Times* (July 29, 1990).

"US Aid Helped Hussein's Climb; Now, Critics Say, the Bill Is Due," *New York Times* (August 13, 1990).

"US Gave Iraq Little Reason Not to Mount Kuwait Assault," *New York Times* (September 23, 1990).

"Six Held in Britain in Scheme to end Atom Gear to Iraq," *New York Times* (March 29, 1990).

"Germany and Japan Draw Harsh Attacks on Gulf Crisis Costs," *New York Times* (September 13, 1990).

"Germany Pledges $1.87 Billion to Aid Gulf Effort," *New York Times* (September 16, 1990).

"Western Europe Urges Air Embargo Against Iraq," *New York Times* (September 19, 1990).

"Mitterand at UN Links Pullout by Iraqis to Solutions in Mideast," *New York Times* (September 25, 1990).

"Hussein Seeks a 'Debate' with France," *New York Times* (October 1, 1990).

"Bush in Germany, Finds Kohl Cool to Gulf Policy, Stressing Talks Instead," *New York Times* (November 19, 1990).

"Embolden Hussein's Opponents," *New York Times* (November 24, 1990).

"Europe's Statement Urging a Total Pullout," *New York Times* (January 5, 1991).

"French Maneuvering: Taking the Lead for Europe," *New York Times* (January 6, 1991).

"The French Vow to Explore a New Solution," *New York Times* (January 8, 1991).

"France Will Pursue Peace Till 16th, Mitterand Says," *New York Times* (January 10, 1991).

"France and Three Arab States Issue an Appeal to Hussein," *New York Times* (January 15, 1991).

"Paris Says Its Last-Ditch Peace Effort Has Failed," *New York Times* (January 16, 1991).

"Anti-War Protest is Staged in Bonn," *New York Times* (January 27, 1991).

"Arabs Put off Talks as Iraqis Consolidate," *New York Times* (August 5, 1990).

"Arabs' Summit Meeting off; Iraqi Units in Kuwait Dig in; Europe Bars Baghdad's Oil," *New York Times* (August 5, 1990).

"Arab States Vote to Send Troops to Join Americans in Defense of Saudi Arabia," *New York Times* (August 11, 1990).

"Jordan Denounces US for 'Explosive' Tactics," *New York Times* (August 14, 1990).

"Hussein's Support: Deeper Than We Think?" *New York Times* (August 28, 1990).

"Egypt: Now a Strategic Asset," *New York Times* (August 30, 1990).

"Saudi Minister Says US Force Is Only Defensive," *New York Times* (September 2, 1990).

"US to Sell Saudis 385 of Best Tanks," *New York Times* (September 8, 1990).

"The Saudis, the GI's and the Common Cause: Allies, But at Arm's Length," *New York Times* (October 3, 1990).

"Islamic Influence Weighed Differently Since Crisis," *New York Times* (October 4, 1990).

"For Saudis, Little War Preparation But Much Placing of Blame," *New York Times* (October 5, 1990).

"The Arab Nightmare," *New York Times* (October 9, 1990).

"A Time of Confusion Draws the Arab World into a Troubled Search of Its Own Soul," *New York Times* (October 14, 1990).

"King Hussein on Kuwait and Dashed Hope," *New York Times* (October 16, 1990).

"Jordanian Economy Devastated by Effects of the Gulf Crisis," *New York Times* (October 21, 1990).

"Saudi Curbs on Yemeni Workers Sets off a Migration," *New York Times* (October 22, 1990).

"Saudi Prince Hints at Deal with Iraq for Kuwaiti Port," *New York Times* (October 23, 1990).

"Yemen's Chief Assails Saudis on Gulf Crisis," *New York Times* (October 26, 1990).

"Keep to Hard Line, Saudi King Orders," *New York Times* (October 27, 1990).

"Arab Countries in the Middle: Leverage with the Adversaries Is Growing," *New York Times* (November 28, 1990).

"Gulf Summit Talks End on a Mixed Note," *New York Times* (December 26, 1990).

"Mubarak Cites Mandate of UN and Arab League," *New York Times* (January 25, 1991).

"US Is Approaching Syria and Iran on Anti-Iraq Effort," *New York Times* (August 9, 1990).

"Arab Troops Join Saudi Force; Bush Says He Hopes the Iraqis 'Do Something' About Hussein," *New York Times* (August 12, 1990).

"More Syrian Anti-Iraq Aid Reported," *New York Times* (September 14, 1990).

"Assad Assures Baker of Support in Gulf," *New York Times* (September 15, 1990).

"Iran Joins Syria Opposing Invasion," *New York Times* (September 26, 1990).

"Syrian Chief Risks Anger at Home over Policies," *New York Times* (October 11, 1990).

"Assad and Bush," *New York Times* (November 27, 1990).

"Mubarak Urges Alliance with Syrians and Saudis," *New York Times* (December 5, 1990).

"Assad Urges 'Brother' to Quit Kuwait," *New York Times* (January 13, 1991).

"Iraqi Dissidents in Syria Reflecting Damascus' Complex Policy on War," *New York Times* (February 17, 1991).

"Iraq Walks out of Talks with Kuwait," *New York Times* (August 2, 1990).

"Hussein Must Be Stopped and Sanctions Can Do the Trick," *New York Times* (August 3, 1990).

"Robin Hood or Nasser? For Baghdad, It's Poor vs. Rich, and Hate of Enemy," *New York Times* (August 9, 1990).

"Myths About Hussein and Iraq," *New York Times* (September 13, 1990).

"Proposals by Iraqi President: Excerpts from His Address," *New York Times* (August 13, 1990).

"Hussein's Next Move, US Remains at a Loss," *New York Times* (August 15, 1990).

"Throughout the Middle East, Iraq's Challenge Redraws the Political Lines," *New York Times* (September 3, 1990).

"Iraq's Propaganda May Seem Crude, But It's Effective," *New York Times* (September 16, 1990).

"The Myth of Iraq's Oil Stranglehold," *New York Times* (September 17, 1990).

"Excerpts from Iraqi Document on Meeting with US Envoy," *New York Times* (September 13, 1990).

"Excerpts from Statement by Iraqi President Warning of the Effects of War," *New York Times* (September 24, 1990).

"Iraqis Are Hinting at a Compromise; US Rejects Terms," *New York Times* (October 17, 1990).

"Iraq Asserts It 'Will Never Succumb'," *New York Times* (November 28, 1990).

"Excerpts from the Interview with President Hussein," *New York Times* (December 3, 1990).

"Iraq Says It Is Still Seeking 'Deep Dialogue' with US," *New York Times* (December 16, 1990).

"Iraq Summons Muslims for Conference on Jan. 9," *New York Times* (December 31, 1990).

"Excerpts from Saddam Hussein's Comments on the Gulf War," *New York Times* (January 31, 1991).

"Iraq's Shift in Position: Not Enough for the US," *New York Times* (February 24, 1991).

"As Baghdad Calls for Peace, Bomb Blasts Shake the City," *New York Times* (February 28, 1991).

"This Aggression Will Not Stand," *New York Times* (March 1, 1991).

"Iran Is Motivated to Offer Iraq Aid," *New York Times* (September 7, 1990).

"Iraq and Iranians Restore Links," *New York Times* (September 11, 1990).

"Resist US in Gulf, Top Iranian Cleric Urges All Muslims," *New York Times* (September 13, 1990).

"Iran's Dangerous Game," *New York Times* (September 14, 1990).

"Iran and Iraq Agree on a Half-Mile Border Zone," *New York Times* (January 9, 1991).

"Iran Said to Play Both Sides in Gulf," *New York Times* (January 31, 1991).

"Iraq's Warplanes Continue to Seek Safe Haven in Iran," *New York Times* (January 28, 1991).

"Rafsanjani Offers Himself as Gulf War Mediator," *New York Times* (February 5, 1991).

"Tehran Says Its Peace Plan Drew Positive Iraqi Response," *New York Times* (February 29, 1991).

"Iran Says Iraq Is Ready for Unconditional Pullout," *New York Times* (February 20, 1991).

U.S. DOMESTIC PROBLEMS AND DEBATE
ON FOREIGN POLICY

"Peace Dividend: $50,000 per Prisoner," *New York Times* (February 26, 1990).

"The Peace Dividend, Unredeemed," *New York Times* (November 17, 1990).

"Is the Peace Dividend Being Engulfed?" *New York Times* (September 19, 1990).

"Peace Dividend Casualty in the Gulf," *New York Times* (August 30, 1990).

"Forces in Society, and Reaganism, Helped Dig Deeper Hole for Poor," *New York Times* (July 16, 1989).

"The Cost of Reagan," *New York Times* (September 7, 1989).

"$2,885,181,319,134.72—and Counting," *New York Times* (November 24, 1989).

"The Homeless Are Dying in the Subway," *New York Times* (February 17, 1990).

"US Is by Far the Homicide Capital of the World," *New York Times* (June 27, 1990).

"Violence and Hypocrisy," *New York Times* (July 9, 1990).

"The S & L Horror Show: Act II," *New York Times* (July 24, 1990).

"Savings Regulator Seeks $100 Billion For Bailout in 1991," *New York Times* (July 31, 1990).

"Cutting Budget Gap Now Discounted," *New York Times* (August 7, 1990).

"We Can Afford to Fight Iraq," *New York Times* (August 21, 1990).

"Deceit, Danger, and the Deficit," *New York Times* (October 5, 1990).

"For a Sober Balance," *New York Times* (December 11, 1990).

"Conservativism: The Agony of Victory," *New York Times* (October 27, 1989).

"Stop Hussein with Force If Necessary," *New York Times* (August 5, 1990).

"Many Prominent Americans Support the President's Action in the Gulf," *New York Times* (August 13, 1990).

"Excerpts from Baker Testimony on US and Gulf, *New York Times* (September 5, 1990).

"Opponents to US Move Have Poverty in Common," *New York Times* (September 8, 1990).

"Poll Finds Strong Support for Bush's Goals, But Reluctance to Start a War," *New York Times* (October 1, 1990).

"Patience in the Persian Gulf, Not War," *New York Times* (October 7, 1990).

"Church Leaders Voice Doubts on US Gulf Policy," *New York Times* (October 12, 1990).

"Senators Urge Bush to Ask Congress on Iraq Move," *New York Times* (October 18, 1990).

"Thousands March in Sixteen Cities to Protest US Intervention in Gulf," *New York Times* (October 21, 1990).

"Council of Churches Condemns US Policy in Gulf," *New York Times,* (November 16, 1990).

"Americans More Wary of Gulf Policy, Poll Finds," *New York Times* (November 20, 1990).

"Some in the Military Are Now Resisting Combat," (November 26, 1990).

"Two Ex-Military Chiefs Urge Bush to Delay Gulf War," *New York Times* (November 29, 1990).

"A Weak Case for War in the Gulf," *New York Times* (December 2, 1990).

"Ex-Defense Secretaries Advise Patience in Gulf," *New York Times* (December 4, 1990).

"Consent of Congress," *New York Times* (December 6, 1990).

"Will There Be War?" *New York Times* (December 10, 1990).

"Gulf Analogy: Munich or Vietnam?" *New York Times* (December 10, 1990).

"The Argument for War," *New York Times* (December 14, 1990).

"Excerpts of Resolutions Debated by Congress," *New York Times* (January 13, 1991).

"Liberal in Search of Values Run into Discord over War," *New York Times* (January 27, 1991).

"Powell Was Right," *New York Times* (May 3, 1991).

"New Isolationism, Same Old Mistake," *New York Times* (August 28, 1990).

INDEX